Accounting for Financial Instruments

Accounting for Financial Instruments

Cormac Butler

WILEY

A John Wiley and Sons, Ltd, Publication

Other Wiley Editorial Offices

John Wiley & Sons Inc., 111 River Street, Hoboken, NJ 07030, USA

Jossey-Bass, 989 Market Street, San Francisco, CA 94103-1741, USA

Wiley-VCH Verlag GmbH, Boschstr. 12, D-69469 Weinheim, Germany

John Wiley & Sons Australia Ltd, 42 McDougall Street, Milton, Queensland 4064, Australia

John Wiley & Sons (Asia) Pte Ltd, 2 Clementi Loop #02-01, Jin Xing Distripark, Singapore 129809

John Wiley & Sons Canada Ltd, 6045 Freemont Blvd, Mississauga, Ontario, L5R 4J3 Canada

Wiley also publishes its books in a variety of electronic formats. Some content that appears in print may not be
available in electronic books.

Library of Congress Cataloging-in-Publication Data

A catalogue record for this book is available from the Library of Congress

HF
5681
.F54
B88
2009

British Library Cataloguing in Publication Data

A catalogue record for this book is available from the British Library

ISBN 978-0-470-69980-5(H/B)

Typeset in 10/12pt Times by Integra Software Services Pvt. Ltd, Pondicherry, India
Printed and bound in Great Britain by CPI Antony Rowe, Chippenham, Wiltshire

To Anna

Contents

Preface   **xi**

1   Introduction   **1**
   1.1   Introduction   1
   1.2   Scope of the book   4
   1.3   Background   6
   1.4   Concerns over the misuse of financial instruments   8
   1.5   Complexity   10
   1.6   Revenue recognition   11
   1.7   Inappropriate reward incentives   11
   1.8   Protection for shareholders   15
   1.9   Measuring the 'traders' dilemma'   16

2   Accounting Foundations   **21**
   2.1   Introduction   21
   2.2   IASB improvements   22
   2.3   The framework   23
   2.4   Fair value or cost   24
   2.5   Artificial volatility   26
   2.6   Cost model   28
   2.7   Cherry-picking   28
   2.8   Subjective valuations   29
   2.9   Proactive vs. reactive   29
   2.10 Goodwill   29
   2.11 Market value accounting   30
   2.12 IFRS and its contribution to banking crises   31
   2.13 IFRS post-Enron   32
   2.14 Conclusion   41

3   Corporate Governance   **43**
  3.1   Introduction   43
  3.2   Corporate governance   44
  3.3   Small vs. large shareholdings   45
  3.4   Traders' dilemma   46
  3.5   Moral hazard   47
  3.6   Credit rating agencies I   48
  3.7   Shareholder democracy   49
  3.8   Structured products   50
  3.9   Revenue recognition   53
  3.10   Non-consolidation   54
  3.11   Credit rating agencies II   57
  3.12   Accounting standards and lobbying   59
  3.13   Investment entities   60
  3.14   Conclusion   61
         Appendix: Constant proportion debt obligations   62

4   Hedge Accounting   **65**
  4.1   Introduction   65
  4.2   Accounting for forward contracts   66
  4.3   Accounting pre-IAS 39   67
  4.4   Artificial volatility   68
  4.5   Hedge accounting rules   69
  4.6   Example: Forward rate agreement   74
  4.7   Conclusion   76

5   Illustrative Examples: Hedge Accounting   **77**
  5.1   Introduction   77
  5.2   Illustration: Fair value hedge   78
  5.3   Credit spreads   83
  5.4   Cash flow interest rate swaps   91
  5.5   Time value vs. change in interest rates   94
  5.6   Long method fair value hedge   97
  5.7   Foreign exchange hedge   100
         Appendix: Documentation   114

6   Accounting for Structured Products (Market Risk)   **117**
  6.1   Introduction   117
  6.2   Risk adjusted return on capital   118
  6.3   Bifurcation rules   120
  6.4   The reward for risk   121
  6.5   Protection for shareholders   121
  6.6   Illustration: The structured products problem   122
  6.7   The accounting treatment under embedded derivative rules   126
  6.8   Past mistakes   127
  6.9   Conclusion   128

Appendix 6.1: Overview of embedded derivative rules in international
accounting reporting standards 129
Appendix 6.2: Introduction to derivatives 129

7 Accounting for Credit Risk **139**
7.1   Introduction 139
7.2   Loan approvals 142
7.3   Credit spreads 144
7.4   Accounting standards 146
7.5   Credit rating agencies 147
7.6   Credit derivatives 148
7.7   Accounting for loans 151
7.8   Changes in the accounting standards 153
7.9   Accounting rules on credit derivatives and financial
       guarantees 156
7.10   Structured credit products: an extra layer of complexity 156

8 Accounting for Structured Products (Credit Risk) **159**
8.1   Introduction 159
8.2   Securitisation overview 160
8.3   Regulatory arbitrage 162
8.4   Prepayment risk synthetic securitisations 162
8.5   Accounting for credit risk 164
8.6   Accountants, regulators and credit agencies 165
8.7   Complexity 168
8.8   Disclosure 169
8.9   Credit Suisse fiasco 169
8.10   Monoline insurance companies 171
8.11   Accounting implications 172
8.12   First to default 173
8.13   SFAS 157 valuations 174
8.14   Conclusion 174

9 Off-Balance Sheet Accounting **177**
9.1   Introduction 177
9.2   Off-balance sheet manipulation 178
9.3   Case studies: off-balance sheet 180
9.4   Accounting implications 185

10 Reconciliation **199**
10.1   Introduction 199
10.2   Middle office 201
10.3   Initial and variation margin 204
10.4   Example: Illustration of reconciliation 208
10.5   Conclusion 216

11 Moving Towards Mark-to-Market Accounting   **217**
    11.1 Introduction   217
    11.2 Liquidity and fair value   217
    11.3 Banking vs. trading book   219
    11.4 VaR   223
    11.5 Basel 2   230
    11.6 Accounting for VaR and IFRS 7   235
    11.7 Conclusion   241

12 Accounting for Insurance   **243**
    12.1 Introduction   243
    12.2 Significance of insurance risk   244
    12.3 IFRS vs. embedded value reporting   248
    12.4 Finite insurance and unbundling   250
    12.5 Other aspects of IFRS 4   252
    12.6 Phase two embedded value   253
          Appendix: The collapse of AIG   255

13 Conclusion   **259**

Glossary   **265**

Index   **267**

Preface

The former Chairman of the American Federal Reserve, Alan Greenspan, once believed that lending institutions were doing a good job of protecting their shareholders. Following the credit crunch experience he admitted to being in a 'state of shocked disbelief'. Perhaps this 'shocked disbelief' could now extend to investors and regulators (and indeed accountants themselves) who once believed that the accounting standards for financial instruments were robust, reliable and capable of self-correction. A central theme of this book is to identify if the already overburdened accounting standards are capable of evolving to capture the complexities of financial instruments.

There is no shortage of books on how to account for financial instruments. The style of these books varies, some paraphrase the paragraphs in the standards while others go into more detail with practical examples. However, not all of the practical examples, even those produced by the standard setters themselves, follow a transparent logic – they are therefore difficult to understand, let alone implement. Furthermore, the complexity and variety of financial instruments also means that not every situation is covered by the pages of guidance issued by the standard setters. This book firstly attempts to address these issues, and the concepts of the main derivative accounting standards are examined in detail; the development and logic behind the rules are then considered and followed up with practical examples.

Even before the credit crunch emerged, practitioners uncovered major shortcomings with the accounting standards on financial instruments. In Europe, for instance, the former French President Jacque Chiraq complained to the European Union about the practical difficulties that French and other banks faced and joined others who wanted standards like the controversial IAS 39 to be substantially amended or in some cases withdrawn. The problem at issue is that IAS 39 has developed a lot of pedantic and restrictive rules (known as hedge accounting) which are at considerable variance with what is happening in practice. The result is that many banks might legitimately hedge the interest and foreign exchange exposure using derivatives only to find that the auditor, interpreting the accounting rules too literally, assumes that the same bank is speculating with these 'hedging' derivatives. The published accounts could therefore be misleading. The book examines this area in detail, focusing on how traders and treasurers use derivatives to reduce risk and how accountants view the same transactions. The differences in approach are compared.

Many practitioners might have accepted that although the accounting standards had some technical flaws they were able pretty much to do the job intended. Perhaps this is true in the non-financial world, but clearly the experience of the credit crunch will have changed that perception for entities operating in financial centres like Wall Street and London. Banks, for instance, were forced to recognise huge losses, causing people to question a banking model which in the space of a few months paid record-breaking remuneration packages while at the same time seeking record-breaking state bail-outs and decimating shareholder value. Many bankers will, of course, claim that they were simply victims of an unforeseen but substantial change in circumstances or a 'market dislocation'. Normal credit and economic cycles will, of course, explain part of the huge losses but their sheer size points to a serious defect in the banking model, the regulatory system and the accounting regime. An auditor attempting to audit the financial institutions concerned, without fully understanding the flaws of the banking model, will of course find the process stressful and worrying. This book makes an attempt to look at the weaknesses of the banking model and the accounting implications.

What has encouraged responsible bankers to invest in toxic financial derivatives or 'weapons of mass destruction' as Warren Buffet once called them? Has the answer to do with the fact that they are investing other people's money and not their own? The remuneration of many banking executives encourages high risk and high leverage, yet these same banking executives of course are very anxious to hide from the shareholder and regulator what they are doing. Structured financial instruments (particularly the credit variety) often allow entities to take on huge leverage and to recognise artificial profits up-front simply because the accounting standards themselves have not caught up with the complexities of these products. Clearly, there is pressure on the accounting standard setters to keep the status quo by allowing 'off-balance sheet' opportunities. The book examines corporate governance and its impact on the 'off-balance sheet' debate.

There is worrying evidence that because financial entities have found ways to pass on risks, they are reluctant to learn from past mistakes. This appears to be the case in the sub-prime credit sector, where banks originated questionable loans and simply didn't bother to assess the borrower's ability to repay, instead confining themselves to ticking a few boxes for compliance purposes. Also, the willingness of banks to take on customers whose history they did not know flies in the face of sound banking practice. By passing on the risk to the taxpayer and the shareholder, banking executives focused on the fees and rewards and ignored the risks. This is also true in other areas of the financial markets. The concept of 'rogue trader' raises its head so often that there is clear evidence bankers are not learning from past mistakes, perhaps again because once losses are discovered, it is fundamentally a shareholder problem – banking executives, on the whole, tend to escape scot-free save for the occasional token scapegoat.

The book is intended primarily for any accountant who is involved with the preparation of accounts that involve financial instruments. The book will also appeal to investors who want to evaluate the risk profile of entities using derivatives. Accounting jargon has been kept to a minimum so that non-accountants can see the issues. The book will also assist regulators who are directly involved with financial instruments.

My thanks to Jenny McCall, Sarah Lewis, Karen Weller and Kerry Batcock of John Wiley & Sons for their assistance and also to Richard Flavell and Juan Ramirez for their guidance.

Contacting the Author

Whilst I have taken every effort to reduce and eliminate errors, the huge volume of technical material makes the task very difficult. If you have comments on my interpretation of the standards or if you feel that the book could include additional material, suggestions and recommend-ations would be very welcome. Please feel free to contact me at Quanta Films (UK) telephone +44(0)1666 826366 or via my website at www.answerback.org. The publishers, John Wiley & Sons, have also set up a dedicated website where you can download the spreadsheets used in this book: www.wiley.com/go/butler_accounting. The spreadsheets will also be available from www.answerback.org.

1

Introduction

1.1 INTRODUCTION

One question on the mind of the general public following the global credit turmoil of 2007 and 2008 is why major banks can announce huge bonuses at a time when they are suffering considerable losses. The former Chief of the Fed Paul Volcker, who is attempting to improve the international accounting standards, said[1]

> [bankers' compensation packages] were most invidious of all ... the mantra of aligning incentives seems to be lost in the failure to impose symmetrical losses – or frequently any loss at all – when failures ensue

The problems with banker incentives are complex, but few could argue that those who received substantial bonuses at the end of 2006 and 2007 always acted in the interests of their shareholders. In the wider world, senior bankers created a very volatile and fragile financial system that was on the verge of breaking down, saved only by generous handouts from various central banks. An accountant might argue that bonuses, even if badly designed, are outside the scope of his responsibility, which is to calculate the profit or loss and reveal this in a consistent manner to the shareholder. However, this is a dangerous view. There is very clear evidence that banks, through off-balance sheet vehicles and mis-valuing of financial instruments, did not reveal all that the shareholder needed to know and therefore it is questionable as to whether they complied with the accounting standards framework. There is also evidence that inappropriately designed bonuses are putting pressure on the accounting profession to simultaneously comply with the accounting standards and mislead the shareholders as to what is going on. Unfortunately, though the accounting standard setters have devoted a lot of time and resources towards improving the accounting standards, there are still underlying problems that they must address as a matter of urgency. In particular, there are instances where financial institutions claim to be in compliance with accounting standards while simultaneously hiding assets and liabilities through off-balance sheet vehicles. There is also the worry that the accounting standards cannot cope with the increasing complexity of financial instruments, particularly when it comes to hedge accounting. Indeed, so strong was the objection to the hedge accounting rules for financial instruments that the International Accounting Standards Board (IASB) was forced by the European Union (EU) to revise International Accounting Standard IAS 39, *Financial Instruments: Recognition and Measurement*. In fact, the EU introduced 'carve outs' designed to make the accounting standards easier to adopt and more reliable. In effect, the EU told entities to ignore some of the rules that the IASB had devised. In addition, many practitioners argue that the standard setters are getting things badly wrong when it comes to specialist areas like insurance – where insurance companies feel that they have to publish two

---

[1] Chrystia Freeland, 'A towering disciplinarian', *Financial Times*, 12 April 2008.

sets of accounting results each year, one in compliance with the international accounting standards but totally misleading and another which ignores the accounting standards but paints a more realistic picture of underlying profitability.

Quite a lot of guidance is available on both the international accounting standards which are used in Europe, Asia and Africa and also the American standards. However, when it comes to financial instruments, many practising accountants argue that the accounting standards themselves are difficult to interpret and the simple examples provided by the various accounting standards boards and the accountancy firms do not get to the heart of accounting for complex financial instruments.

Contributors to the financial crises:

- **Bonuses**. People usually associate bonuses with rewards for increasing the profit of the entity. Few could argue with the idea that if employees are bringing in profits to a business they should be rewarded with a bonus. However, the bonus systems of many senior bankers are flawed, in that they encourage traders to make banking profits more volatile and riskier and not necessarily more profitable. Accountants and auditors often allow a situation where bankers can show high profits, and achieve high bonuses, while in reality they are simply transferring wealth to themselves at the expense of shareholders without revealing to the shareholder what is going on.
- **Poor risk measurement**. Financial institutions often boast that they have the latest risk management tools to measure market risk and credit risk and they emphasise that, being well regulated, their ability to take risk is limited. But, the mere fact that sophisticated banks buy complicated structured credit products that often they themselves don't understand suggests otherwise. This is simply a side-effect of the fact that many senior finance executives either don't measure risk or don't take seriously the risks that they measure. Also, the explosion of the credit derivative market and complex securitisation market suggests that banks are often anxious to buy products whose risk is difficult to measure.
- **Other people's money**. Investment trusts and institutional investors may have voting power over certain shares but they don't always have beneficial interest. In other words, those with voting power are investing other people's money and therefore don't suffer too much when shares fall in price. They are often tempted (though not all do) to exploit this through malpractices by voting in a manner which maximises their fees rather than the return to the shareholder. For instance, a corporate finance firm might put pressure on its pension arm to vote in incompetent directors if they feel it will help them to secure a corporate finance mandate.
- **Conflicts**. Auditors and credit rating agencies in theory work on behalf of the investor, but in reality their fees are paid by directors and traders who are motivated to conceal bad news and credit risk. Auditors and credit rating agencies are therefore often motivated to maximise fees by giving their assurances too liberally.
- **Ability to hide losses**. Entities often use different accounting treatments for the same type of economic asset. In some cases assets are shown on the balance sheet at market value, but in many cases the assets are taken 'off-balance sheet'. For instance, an entity that borrows say £10,000,000 to buy an asset that has fallen in value to £9,000,000 would be forced to show a loss of £1,000,000 if the asset and liability were brought on to the balance sheet. However, the entity might be tempted to hold the asset and liability in an off-balance sheet company and therefore conceal from the shareholder and regulator the true economic position.

- **Complexity**. Where there is complexity there is confusion and where there is confusion there is the ability to mislead. Auditors, credit rating agencies and regulators often don't have the resources to deal effectively with complex structured products. This in itself makes the products attractive to bonus-hungry traders who want to take on risk but simultaneously conceal risks and losses.
- **Lobbying pressure and poor accounting standards**. There is evidence that lobbyists on behalf of financial entities and corporates attempt to use their influence to leave the accounting standards as they are, even if they are weak. This lobbying pressure was certainly in evidence when the American Financial Accounting Standards Board (FASB) attempted to treat stock options as an expense in the Profit & Loss account.

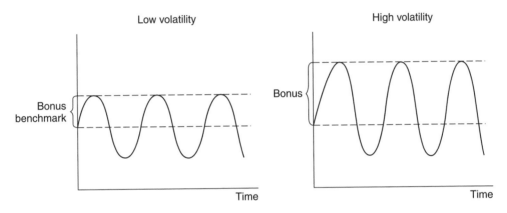

Figure 1.1   Bonuses

Case Study: Fannie Mae

The calculation of Earnings Per Share (EPS) is very much linked to how an entity interprets the accounting standard. In May 2006, the Office of Federal Housing Enterprise Oversight produced a report on accounting irregularities at Fannie Mae.[2] The report concluded that 'improper earnings management at Fannie Mae increased the annual bonuses and other compensation linked to EPS that senior management received'.

The worrying fact here is that senior executives may find that their bonuses are enhanced if they spend more time stretching the accounting standards rather than running the underlying business to suit the needs of the shareholder. In the case of Fannie Mae, the annual bonus was linked to EPS, which is in turn influenced by the accounting standards. Indeed, compensation for senior executives that was driven by or linked to EPS dwarfed basic salary and benefits. For CEO Franklin Raines, for example, two compensation components directly tied to meeting EPS goals accounted for more than $20 million for the six years from 1998 through 2003. Three-year EPS goals also played a crucial role in determining the size of the approximately $32 million awarded to Mr Raines during that six-year period under a long-term executive compensation programme. In total, over $52 million of Mr Raines' compensation of $90 million during the period was directly tied to achieving EPS targets.

There were two aspects of Fannie Mae which had an impact on the way that they interpreted the accounting standards. On the one hand, they clearly wanted to take risks and did take

---

[2] Report of the Special Examination of Fannie Mae, Office of Federal Housing Enterprise Oversight, May 2006.

Case Study: (Continued)

them – but they also wanted to give the impression that they were making substantial profits. On the other hand, they wanted to smooth out earnings so that they gave the impression of being a risk-averse financial entity whose earnings were predictable. According to the OFHSO report, 'The Enterprise achieved double-digit growth in earnings per common share (EPS) for 15 straight years and leveraged its extraordinary financial success into enormous political influence. That financial and political success gave rise to a corporate culture at Fannie Mae in which senior management promoted the Enterprise as one of the lowest-risk financial institutions in the world and as "best in class" in terms of risk management, financial reporting, internal control, and corporate governance'.

Clearly, there is strong evidence that the accounting standards were stretched to smooth out the earnings. In other words, Fannie Mae was taking on a lot more risk than they wanted their shareholders to know about. They achieved this by profit smoothing. In good years, they would take excess profits and make artificial provisions so that the profits came down to a level consistent with a risk-averse company. In bad years, with high losses, they would release the provisions. This tactic proved rewarding in terms of bonuses, since by keeping unnecessary provisions and later releasing them they could keep profits above target every year rather than just in some years.

Arthur Levitt, the former Chairman of the SEC, referred to this type of earnings management as '[a] gray area where the accounting is being perverted; where managers are cutting corners; and, where earnings reports reflect the desires of management rather than the underlying financial performance of the company'. Mr Levitt included 'cookie jar' reserves, the premature recognition of revenue, and the abuse of the concept of materiality among the five most common and popular forms of inappropriate earnings management.

1.2 SCOPE OF THE BOOK

1. Introduction
2. Accounting Foundations
3. Corporate Governance
4. Hedge Accounting
5. Illustrative Examples: Hedge Accounting
6. Accounting for Structured Products (Market Risk)
7. Accounting for Credit Risk
8. Accounting for Structured Products (Credit Risk)
9. Off-Balance Sheet Accounting
10. Reconciliation
11. Mark-to-Market Accounting
12. Accounting for Insurance
13. Conclusion

This book is designed to address the practical difficulties that accountants face when dealing with financial instruments. In Chapter 2 we look at the problems with accounting, in particular the confusing mixed model used in the accounting standards where some assets are shown at cost while others are shown at market value; some assets and liabilities are carried at a value which represents neither cost nor market value. Although this mixed-model approach has not proved to be a difficult problem in the past, the use of complex financial instruments puts a strain on an accounting system which relies on the mixed-model approach. Needless to say, the ambiguity created by the standard setters opens the door to a lot of misleading or creative accounting. One question on most people's minds is why the accounting standards cannot deal with the complexities of financial instruments. There is no simple answer to this, though poor corporate governance may perhaps explain why people with vested interests are slow to correct the problem. The main standard covering financial instruments in Europe, Africa and Asia – IAS 39, *Financial Instruments: Recognition and Measurement* – is examined in detail in Chapter 4 and Chapter 5 looks in more detail, using a number of examples, at how IAS 39 is implemented in practice.

Securitisation is an area that has preoccupied accountants for a number of years, particularly because different banks appear to be using different approaches to account for securitisations. It is also important from a litigation perspective, since many banks were accused of using securitisations as an excuse to keep certain non-performing assets off-balance sheet and therefore conceal losses that entities have made. The topic is broken down as follows. Chapter 6 focuses on the use of structured products that are exposed to market risk, i.e. inverse floaters and foreign exchange products. We focus on the complexity of these products and in particular why institutions such as banks are motivated from an accounting perspective to buy these instruments. The rules of embedded derivatives are examined in detail. However, the embedded derivative rules are quite complex and, more importantly, difficult to apply to certain credit products. In Chapter 7 we examine credit risk and how the accounting standards deal with it. Chapter 8 focuses on securitisation and other complex structured products, and Chapter 9 examines the confusing accounting rules in place to deal with securitisation. The difference between the American and European accounting standards in tackling the problems of off-balance sheet is also explored. It appears that the problems of accounting for financial instruments are not confined to complex credit structured products and off-balance sheet entities. Accountants and auditors are also having difficulty with simple derivatives. In early 2008, Société Générale became exposed to a 'rogue trader' scandal; critics raised questions on internal controls and, in particular, why one single trader had the ability to effectively borrow €50 billion and gamble it without his superiors finding out. Accountants and auditors here have an important role in detecting and preventing instances where rogue traders clock up huge liabilities and conceal them. Chapter 10 examines this area in detail.

Following complaints from various banks to the EU, the IASB were forced to revisit their rules for certain aspects of hedge accounting, particularly as it applies to banks with deposit accounts. The EU, motivated by the practical difficulties that banks were facing, informed the IASB that they themselves would modify IAS 39 by carving out two features of IAS 39 (one of the carve-out features known as the 'fair value option' is now resolved). The result is that there are two versions of IAS 39, the unamended version as produced by the IASB and the amended version as adjusted by the EU. The circumstances surrounding these carve-outs, and the proposed solution to the complex area of applying the hedge accounting rules to the banking book, are examined in detail in Chapter 11. The disclosure requirements of the new standard IFRS 7, *Financial Instruments: Disclosures* covers the risk disclosure requirements that financial institutions are required to reveal to shareholders, particularly how financial instruments affect the risk profile of entities. It is important of course that accountants understand the risks that financial instruments create and so risk measurement techniques like Value at Risk and the regulatory Basel 2 requirements are discussed. Chapter 11 also focuses on the arguments put forward by critics of the accounting standards – namely that showing all financial instruments at market value on the balance sheet may turn out to be against the interests of shareholders.

Chapter 12 deals with accounting for insurance, focusing on the problems of life assurance companies where certain insurance products are shown at cost on the balance sheet or even kept off-balance sheet while investment products, though having similar characteristics to some insurance products, are brought on to the balance sheet, causing confusion and misleading results.

1.3 BACKGROUND

Case Study: DB Zwirn Hedge Fund

There is a trend in the financial markets to move away from simple products to products that even hedge funds have difficulty valuing. Why are financial institutions, investment managers and hedge funds willing to take on the additional operational, credit and liquidity risk associated with these products? The answer may be the flawed incentive scheme that many financial institutions operate under. Auditors, credit rating agencies and regulators face huge difficulty measuring the risks associated with complex illiquid instruments. The result is that risk is not measured. Given that flawed incentive schemes reward those who take risks with their shareholders' money there is a tendency, as this case study reveals, to take on huge risks in products that cannot be measured.

In May 2008, the Securities and Exchange Commission (SEC) launched an investigation into DB Zwirn, focusing on how the $5 billion hedge fund valued its assets and calculated its profits and incentives. The SEC's concern stemmed from the fact that the managers of some hedge funds often award themselves a bonus based on 20% of the profits. A rosy valuation of some of the more illiquid assets leads of course to higher bonuses. Financial institutions differ from companies in that the latter must generally wait until an asset is sold and the cash received before they can recognise a profit. Hedge fund managers simply calculate the difference between the original purchase price and current market value to determine their profit and bonus. In the case of illiquid assets, hedge funds and financial institutions generally have to make assumptions. There is the obvious conflict of interest that financial institutions will choose assumptions that maximise their fees or bonus.

Needless to say, following the credit crunch banks were tempted to hide losses using optimistic estimated values of assets held by all kinds of financial institutions, in particular, investments in illiquid assets such as loans to private companies and other debt instruments. The SEC has asked DB Zwirn to provide extra information on these valuations. The hedge fund invested in corporate loans and other credits where the market was illiquid. In particular, they lent to smaller companies around the world for which there was no clear price.

Often, these loans appear at par value on the balance sheet because they are not traded. However, in many cases the loans may have lost considerable value, owing to the credit crises, yet those losses are not reflected on the balance sheet. Where the assets are not reflected at current fair value on the balance sheet, there is a risk that hedge funds will 'cherry-pick', i.e. sell loans that have made a profit but keep loss-making loans on the balance sheet at cost where it is easier to hide losses.

In May 2008, DB Zwirn was under pressure to return money to shareholders but had difficulty selling some of its loans – an indication that the loans were overpriced on its balance sheet. There is a risk that the hedge fund is using its own staff to decide on the value of some loans and also using outside 'independent' valuers to value them. However in practice, staff may not always give an unbiased result since they themselves may earn bonuses based on the valuation or at least be influenced by those that do earn bonuses. In the same way the 'independent' valuers may suffer from the same conflicts of interest that auditors and credit rating agencies face, i.e. they are being paid by the managers of the hedge fund who themselves are on bonus schemes. There is a risk therefore that the external valuers will simply 'rubber stamp' whatever valuations the hedge fund managers want.

Most accountants will agree that accounting for, and auditing of, financial instruments has become a lot more challenging and difficult than ever before. Not only must the accountant know how to value financial instruments, he must also be able to understand and disclose the ways in which they change the risk profile of an organisation and report in a manner which complies with the most difficult and controversial accounting standards ever written, IAS 39 and its American equivalent FAS 133. There is evidence that accounting for financial instruments is breaking down in practice. In 2007, for instance, many major banks such as Merrill Lynch, Citibank and UBS were forced to reveal substantial losses causing their share prices to suffer badly, which in turn led to chief executives resigning. What was worrying, however, from an accounting point of view was the extent to which banks and institutions were hiding losses. At one stage in 2007, many banks suffered share price declines as high as 50%. The investment world no longer trusted the annual reports published by these institutions. Indeed, in some cases, assurances by the banks themselves that they were not hiding losses were ignored by investors who continued to mark share prices downwards. Bear Stearns, for instance, reassured the world that it did not have a liquidity crisis but was eventually forced, within days, to seek assistance from the American government. Needless to say, some accountants will feel quite worried by the threat of litigation.

A few years ago, the legendary investor Warren Buffet described the main tools of financial engineering, derivatives, as 'weapons of mass destruction'. Why? What is wrong with innovation in the financial sector? Advocates of financial engineering argue that the entire community – from mortgage borrowers and companies, to investors – have benefited from innovation. Derivatives have allowed both funds and companies to manage their risk profile in an optimal manner and it is because of derivatives that personal borrowers can lock into fixed rates, thus removing financial risks from their lives. But this benefit is confined to the proper use of derivatives and sensible financial engineering policies. In reality, derivatives are often used to 'create' profits and allow banks, along with other financial institutions, to award themselves very high bonuses at the expense of the shareholders and, sometimes, tax-payers. What many investors and accountants don't fully appreciate is that poorly designed bonus systems encourage financial institutions to take on huge risks and, by clever use of the accounting standards, to hide those risks from the shareholders. In short, the complexity of financial instruments allows financial institutions to conceal from their shareholders, as well as regulators, what is really going on. Warren Buffet's words of wisdom certainly proved to be correct in 2007.

Consider credit derivatives. These derivatives are similar to insurance products in that the party who wishes to avoid the risk of a credit loss pays a premium to the party willing to take on the risk. Banks and investors are heavy users of financial instruments that transfer credit risk from one party to another. In return for a premium, a bank can insure itself against customers defaulting by entering into a credit default swap with a counterparty. By removing excess risk and uncertainty, banks can do what they do best – that is, originate loans with customers and raise money from deposit holders. Banks of course are regulated by various governments, through the so-called Basel rules. They must also abide by very complex accounting standards and in America, regulation designed after the fall of Enron and World-Com, Sarbanes-Oxley. It is reasonable to say, however, that if banks can transfer their risks to other counterparties and simplify their procedures, compliance with the various regulatory requirements is a lot easier. So, based on this argument, are credit derivatives a positive influence? The answer of course is that they are. However, if credit-based financial instruments allow banks to hide losses, then they are clearly a force for destruction. Unfortunately, there is evidence, as discussed below, that the accounting standards are either not implemented correctly or not designed correctly to deal with credit derivatives, with the result that the words 'off-balance sheet losses' continue to cloud the reputation and integrity of the accounting profession.

Some argue that if risk is transferred around many financial institutions and not concentrated on one, then the financial markets can absorb shocks. One important contribution credit derivatives make to the financial world is that they transfer risk from regulated institutions to non-regulated entities. Hedge funds and pension funds, for instance, are not regulated in the same way as banks. In fact, hedge funds are really not regulated at all, though there is a growing army of people who say they should be. For a long period of time, pension funds were only lightly regulated, but this is changing. In the UK, for instance, a pension regulator was recently appointed to deal with insufficiently funded pensions. In broad terms, nevertheless, the regulatory and accounting requirements for hedge funds are a lot less than for banks. Banks take deposits from, and hold current accounts on behalf of, customers. These customers do not place money with their banks because they want to speculate on stock markets and bond prices, etc. They put the money on deposit for transactionary purposes. The consequences of a large retail bank collapse would be devastating, hence the need for the Basel rules. For hedge funds, however, investors understand that they are taking risks and achieving higher rewards. Therefore, there is no need for the bureaucratic requirements of Basel and the accounting treatment, as we shall see, is a lot more straightforward. For this reason alone, credit derivatives make an important positive contribution. Risk is transferred away from regulated institutions to entities that can accommodate risk better. But this is not the only advantage.

Apart from the regulatory advantage, hedge funds need to diversify their exposures. Hedge funds invest in a broad range of assets. It is important to do so because it allows for diversification, and therefore reduces the risk of concentration, i.e. putting too many eggs in one basket. It is easy, for instance, for a hedge fund to gain exposure to equities, foreign exchange, interest rates and commodities but, in the absence of credit derivatives, gaining exposure to the credit market is quite restricted. Unlike banks, hedge funds do not have a high street presence and therefore find it difficult to initiate loans. So, if the manager of a hedge fund believes that the yield on loans is too high, he can gain exposure by insuring bank loans through credit derivatives and make money if the premium received exceeds any bad debt losses experienced. Credit derivatives are just one way of gaining this exposure. Bonds and securitisation (to be discussed later) are another means, but by far the most efficient method is through credit derivatives.

1.4 CONCERNS OVER THE MISUSE OF FINANCIAL INSTRUMENTS

When the President of the European Central Bank, Jean-Claude Trichet, addressed the International Swaps Dealers Association (ISDA) in April 2007, he spoke of concern about the credit derivatives market. He warned that the markets may have become 'excessively complacent'. If there was excessive complacency in the derivatives market, the consequences would be unimaginable given the size of the market. In 2006, for instance, the total outstanding volume of credit derivative contracts doubled to $34,500 billion. Unlike ordinary derivatives, credit derivatives are difficult to both monitor and process. Occasionally, credit derivatives are difficult to price, despite their high volume. For instance, sometimes those who buy credit derivatives (i.e. pay a premium and buy protection) are not 100% sure if the default language on the loan documentation is similar to the default language on the credit derivative documentation. This is because loan documentation is not always standardised, whereas credit derivative documentation is more or less standardised. The consequence of this is that banks may find they have paid a premium for a type of insurance protection only to find that when the loan defaults the credit derivative counterparty finds a clever lawyer who can wangle his way out of compensating the bank for the loss. There are other complications. Often, there is a high leverage factor between the amount of loans issued and the amount of credit protection in the markets on those loans. For instance, a company might have £10 million bonds in issue but there may be £70 million of outstanding credit derivatives on that bond. Why? Because not everyone who buys credit protection does so for hedging purposes. A hedge fund might have purchased, say, £8 million of the bonds but subsequently taken the view that the company is going to get into difficulty. Solution, buy £8 million worth of credit protection through a credit derivative and buy additional protection of, say, £12 million so that the hedge fund can profit from the company's expected demise. If the company did get into difficulty, a lot of complications could arise. Although the bond would fall in value, the fall might not be as great as one predicted because those who bought credit protection without owning the bond (speculators who want to benefit from the crash) would have to buy and deliver the bond to the credit derivative counterparty in order to receive compensation through the credit derivative. A further complicating factor is the conflict of interest the hedge fund has by owning the bond and having even more credit protection. A hedge fund might, in such circumstances, use any voting power contained in the bond to prevent a restructuring or loan negotiation since, although the value of the bond would fall, the value of the credit derivative would increase substantially, as would the overall profit of the hedge fund. This conflict of interest is partly the reason why regulators are insisting on more rules and better transparency from the hedge fund industry. An accountant could reasonably argue that all these problems are something that the trader and regulators have to worry about but not the accountant. This, however, is not entirely true. As we shall see later in this book, if an instrument is difficult to value then the International Financial Reporting Standards (IFRS), and their equivalent in the USA, will have difficulty in dealing with them. An asset or liability that is not shown on the balance sheet at the correct market value is known as 'off-balance sheet'. In such cases a creative accountant will find it easier to hide losses but can also enhance profits (by cashing in the credit derivative before maturity). Therefore, if a trader is offered the opportunity to buy a credit derivative, he might reason as follows: 'If I make a profit I can cash it in and my bonus goes up. If I make a loss the accountants will most probably record it incorrectly (due to its complex off-balance sheet nature) and therefore I can hide losses indefinitely, so my bonus won't suffer.' This line of argument is perhaps an oversimplification, but the important point to remember is that if a credit instrument is complex and cannot be valued, there are huge operational difficulties and opportunities to engage in creative accounting. Also, if the bonus system of the trader is incorrectly devised (as they often are), the temptation to exploit complex credit derivatives is very high.

So, should the accounting profession be worried about the increased use of complexity in the financial instruments market? The answer is a resounding yes. Many investment trusts, corporates, banks and hedge funds have found themselves in severe difficulty because they have purchased complex illiquid assets that they subsequently could not sell. Insurance companies were at one stage notorious for getting themselves involved in complex derivative arrangements which they could neither understand nor handle. Indeed, it was the purchase of an insurance company and the inability of its new owner Warren Buffet to close out the loss-making risky derivative contracts that led to the famous description of derivatives as 'weapons of mass destruction'. As long as entities are using these products, accountants and auditors will have difficulty in complying with the demanding international accounting standards.

In 2006, ABN Amro launched a credit derivative known as the Constant Proportion Debt Obligation (CPDO). From a marketing perspective, the product was easy to sell. It paid a handsome return. Investors could receive Libor + 2%. The extra 2% was compensation for the risks undertaken (i.e. the risk that a basket of loans would suffer a bad debt experience). What made the product unusual was that a rating agency gave the product a triple-A rating, indicating to the investor that they were taking on very little credit risk. The result – an opportunity to invest in a product that was virtually risk-free yet paid a high return. The superficial conclusion is that the investor is getting a high return for nothing. In reality, the investor bore a lot more risk than the triple-A rating indicated. The product was quite complex. In essence, the investor was guaranteed a fixed return of Libor + 2%. However, if the pool of loans had a bad debt experience, the issuer would simply make up the loss by widening the number of loans being protected. The additional fees from selling protection on the new loans would pay for the loss on the existing loans. Cynics of this product claim that it is more dangerous than entering into a casino and playing doubles or quits until you recover your initial losses. Did the people buying these products understand what they were buying? More importantly, given that the accountant must show these products at their market value on the balance sheet, are they doing it correctly? Is there a conflict of interest within the rating agency system that the regulators have stopped? Can the accountant deal with the off-balance sheet opportunities presented to creative accountants and traders who are bonus-hungry? In theory, there is nothing to worry about. The regulators, credit rating agencies and accountants have their reputations to protect. The reality is more worrying. Many of the aforementioned parties do not have the resources or experience to deal with complex financial instruments and often, those that do allow their fees and potential bonus payments to guide their decisions. Are they worried about ending up in court if the scheme blows over? Yes, they are, but they will often use the fact that the complexity of financial instruments and the even more demanding accounting standards make life very difficult for regulators, accountants and rating agencies. It is this complexity that protects wrongdoers. Very few prosecutors will be able to unravel the complexities of financial instruments or the accounting standards to make a compelling 'beyond doubt' prosecution case for the lay jury to understand.

1.5 COMPLEXITY

There are two important attributes that an accountant should understand about complexity. Firstly, banks can often use complexity to disguise the amount of fees that they earn. Simple products like bonds and shares earn only a very basic commission. It is quite easy for an investor to see how much a bank lays on in charges and the investor can quite easily obtain a competitive quote amongst banks or brokers. Complex structured products, including certain types of credit derivatives, however, are more difficult to compare and so the investor does not know how much he is paying in fees and of course the bank is under no obligation to disclose this. Seasoned travellers will know that if a hotel is going to charge exorbitant prices for telephone calls or the mini-bar they are unlikely to advertise the price they charge. The hotel guest must wait until he checks out before the cost is revealed and then he is not in a position to do anything about it. Some banks operate on the same principle – except the amounts are substantially larger and an investor may have to wait years down the line before he realises he has paid too much. Again, the accountant must concern himself with these issues since, under IAS 39, most fees charged on structured products must be identified and released to the Profit & Loss account immediately. In practice, accountants may not be adequately equipped with the skills to do this, and the issuing bank is unlikely to assist. The last thing they want to do is reveal how much they have charged in fees. The risk that accountants may account for structured products and credit derivatives incorrectly is therefore quite high.

1.6   REVENUE RECOGNITION

A second feature of structured products is the reward-now/risk-later phenomenon. Consider a bond issued in 2007 which pays a high coupon but exposes the investor to a huge amount of leveraged risk. Say a bond is issued for $10,000,000 where the coupon is Libor+3% but the investor may lose his principal if one of eight loans defaults in two years' time. Assume that the risk of default on each of these loans is 1%. The structurer is in effect offering insurance on eight loans and therefore receives approximately 8% in fees for insuring the loans. He passes only 3% to the investor and retains the remaining 5% as 'fees'. The leverage factor in this simple example is 8, which means that there is a high probability that the investor will lose his principal. However, if the risk is not communicated to the investor, he focuses on the 3% above Libor and of course the bank selling the product earns 5% so everyone is happy. Given the investors' naivety and poor ability to measure risk, the issuing bank might be tempted to increase the leverage further and earn more fees. For instance, if he increased the leverage to 10, then fees would jump from 5% to 7%. Therefore, the important lesson to bear in mind is that the structured product arrangers are, through the fee mechanism, encouraged to pass on a considerable amount of risk to the investor. The 'ideal' investor is someone who doesn't fully understand the risks involved and is also spending other people's money. The 'other people' rely on the accountant to expose the fees under IAS 39 and the risks under IFRS 7, but it is fair to say that accountants often don't fully understand the risks and therefore account for these products incorrectly.

1.7   INAPPROPRIATE REWARD INCENTIVES

One of the major driving factors behind the weak accounting standards is an inappropriate reward incentive. Clearly, it is desirable to have a bonus system that rewards risk, but problems do arise when banking executives keep the rewards themselves and pass on the risk either to their customers or to their shareholders. The incentive is to take on huge amounts of risk and to conceal what they are doing. Regulators are, of course, there to stop this and the accounting standards are there, in part, to disclose the risks that the shareholder is exposed to. However, as was revealed over 2007 and 2008, banking executives continue to take huge risks, retain fat bonuses and exploit the accounting standards to conceal their losses and hide their risks. The problem, known as the 'traders' dilemma', is not just confined to traders and banking directors, it is evident also in the investment fund industry. An example of how it applies in the fund industry is given below.

Example: Fund industry

Consider a fund manager who raises $10,000,000 from shareholders and manages the fund on their behalf. In return, he is compensated with 2% of assets under management and 20% of any profits. Table 1.1 shows the return on the asset class that the fund manager has invested in, together with the fees that he earns.

Table 1.1   Unleveraged portfolio

| Funds raised from shareholders | $10,000,000 |
| Borrowings | $0 |

| Funds under management | $10,000,000 |

| Funds under management fee | 2% |
| Performance fee | 20% |

Year	Fund performance	Profit/loss of fund	Performance fee	Funds under management fee	Total to manager
1	10%	$1,000,000	$200,000	$200,000	$400,000
2	8%	$800,000	$160,000	$200,000	$360,000
3	9%	$900,000	$180,000	$200,000	$380,000
4	−15%	−$1,500,000	$0	$200,000	$200,000
5	12%	$1,200,000	$240,000	$200,000	$440,000
6	13%	$1,300,000	$260,000	$200,000	$460,000
7	−10%	−$1,000,000	$0	$200,000	$200,000
8	5%	$500,000	$100,000	$200,000	$300,000
9	−8%	−$800,000	$0	$200,000	$200,000
10	−12%	-$1,200,000	$0	$200,000	$200,000
Average return	1%			Average return	$314,000
				Total return	$3,140,000

The overall return for each of the first 10 years is shown in the second column. The average return over the 10 years, a mere 1%, is not great. In the first year, the fund manager becomes entitled to 20% of the fund's return, i.e. $200,000, and an additional $200,000 being 2% of the assets under management. The overall return over the 10 years is $314,000, which isn't terribly disappointing given that the return on the portfolio was on average 1% a year and the manager took on no risk (apart from reputation risk).

Now consider the fees that the fund manager makes if he decides to 'gear up' the portfolio, i.e. borrow an additional $10 million on top of the $10 million originally raised from the shareholders. We assume in Table 1.2 that the fund manager borrows money at an interest rate of 5%.

The overall return on the asset class in percentage terms is the same as before, with the average return per year being 1%. This time the profit in the first year is 10% of the funds under management, i.e. $2 million, less $500,000 in interest charged on the loan (5% of $10,000,000), giving a total profit of $1,500,000. The fund manager becomes entitled to 20%

Table 1.2   Geared portfolio

Funds raised from shareholders	$10,000,000			
Borrowings	$10,000,000	Interest charge	5%	
Funds under management	$20,000,000			
Funds under management fee	2%			
Performance fee	20%			

Year	Fund performance	Profit/loss of fund	Performance fee	Funds under management fee	Total to manager
1	10%	$1,500,000	$300,000	$400,000	$700,000
2	8%	$1,100,000	$220,000	$400,000	$620,000
3	9%	$1,300,000	$260,000	$400,000	$660,000
4	−15%	−$3,500,000	$0	$400,000	$400,000
5	12%	$1,900,000	$380,000	$400,000	$780,000
6	13%	$2,100,000	$420,000	$400,000	$820,000
7	−10%	−$2,500,000	$0	$400,000	$400,000
8	5%	$500,000	$100,000	$400,000	$500,000
9	−8%	−$2,100,000	$0	$400,000	$400,000
10	−12%	−$2,900,000	$0	$400,000	$400,000
	1%	−$2,600,000		Average return	$568,000
				Total return	$5,680,000

of this figure as well as 2% of the assets under management of $20 million. The total return for year 1 is therefore $700,000. The average return is now $568,000, a considerable increase on the previous case where the fund manager did not borrow. The benefits of gearing to the fund manager should therefore be obvious. The increase in the fund manager's bonus does not arise because he has performed better. It arises because the fund manager has put the shareholders' funds at greater risk. What is interesting about the second fund is that because of the interest payments, the fund has actually made a loss for the investor of −$2,600,000 over the 10 years, yet the fund manager still manages to extract a performance fee. The loss to the shareholder climbs to −$8,280,000 when fees to the manager are taken into account. It becomes clear from the example that the fund manager has an incentive to gear up the portfolio as much as possible. If it is possible to hide this fact from the shareholder, the fund manager will clearly benefit.

Very often, the fund manager's ability to borrow money is restricted. However, fund managers can overcome this restriction by using derivatives instead of borrowing money. In Table 1.3 we illustrate how a fund manager uses a combination of derivatives and loans to leverage up the portfolio. As before, the fund manager is able to simultaneously make losses over the 10-year period and extract not only a management fee but also a performance fee.

Derivatives broadly come in two forms, linear and non-linear. Linear derivatives are where the trader agrees to buy an asset in the future. In Table 1.3, the fund manager has borrowed an extra $10,000,000 and has used linear derivatives to increase the exposure by a further $60,000,000. Although the funds under management fee remains at 2% of $20,000,000, the performance fee is based on the total exposure, i.e. $80,000,000. In the first year, for instance,

Table 1.3   Geared portfolio with derivatives

Funds raised from shareholders	$10,000,000				
Borrowings	$10,000,000	Interest charge	5%		
Funds under management	$20,000,000				
Additional exposure from derivatives	$60,000,000	Implied interest	5%		
	$80,000,000				
Funds under management fee	2%				
Performance fee	20%				

Year	Fund performance	Profit/loss of fund	Performance fee	Funds under management fee	Total to manager
1	10%	$4,500,000	$900,000	$400,000	$1,300,000
2	8%	$2,900,000	$580,000	$400,000	$980,000
3	9%	$3,700,000	$740,000	$400,000	$1,140,000
4	−15%	−$15,500,000	$0	$400,000	$400,000
5	12%	$6,100,000	$1,220,000	$400,000	$1,620,000
6	13%	$6,900,000	$1,380,000	$400,000	$1,780,000
7	−10%	−$11,500,000	$0	$400,000	$400,000
8	5%	$500,000	$100,000	$400,000	$500,000
9	−8%	−$9,900,000	$0	$400,000	$400,000
10	−12%	−$13,100,000	$0	$400,000	$400,000
Average return	1%	−$25,400,000		Average return	$892,000
				Total return	$8,920,000

the performance fee is effectively 20% of $4,500,000 and the profit of $4,500,000 is calculated as follows: $80,000,000×10% less interest at 5% of total effective borrowings $70,000,000. As before, the return to the shareholder is negative yet the fund manager receives a substantial fee along with a performance benefit. The problem, often referred to as the 'traders' dilemma', is not confined to investment fund managers. Anyone in a bank who is on a bonus scheme is tempted to put the shareholders' funds at greater risk as long as he can walk away from losses. Indeed, the 'traders' dilemma' may explain why banks were more than willing to make sub-prime loans to credit-risky individuals – in the knowledge that if property prices rose the bankers would get an enhanced bonus and if property prices fell (as they did in America throughout 2007) they could walk away from the losses, though after receiving a substantial compensation. Treasurers of corporates are also in the same predicament. In the past, they could use derivatives to leverage up the assets of the corporate and generate huge losses. Derivatives also gave these corporates the opportunity to hide losses when they occurred. As always, these treasurers could jump ship along with huge bonuses well in advance of the entity having to report losses to shareholders. At the start of 2007, the financial press reported on the huge bonuses that City executives had received. In London alone, the bonuses were estimated at STG 8.8 billion. One could conclude that they received these bonuses because of the substantial benefit that they provided for their customers. However, given that four months later the financial institutions awarding these bonuses were announcing substantial losses, one could conclude that some of the bonuses arose because the recipients were rewarded for exposing their employers, the banks, to huge risks. The argument for linking bonuses to losses is perhaps unfair, but few will deny that unless the bonus calculating procedure is sophisticated enough to measure and disclose risks, the banking crises of 2007 may resurface again and again, though in other forms, in the future – perhaps with more lethal consequences. The shareholders often cannot do anything about this and therefore have to rely on the regulators to remove the temptation for some City traders to reap huge bonuses while destroying shareholder value simultaneously. Shareholders will also have to rely on accountants to disclose the risks and losses in a timely fashion. It is obviously a good idea if the shareholder realises the risks when he makes the investment, rather than having to wait until huge losses amass before the risks are properly disclosed. Also, a shareholder would rather hear of losses when they occur and not have the bad news deferred. The accounting standards therefore have an important role in protecting shareholders from the 'traders' dilemma'. To some extent they have done so by forcing entities to calculate the loss to shareholders by awarding share option schemes – prior to IFRS 2 it was possible to hide losses. However, they have not coped sufficiently with the prospect that employees on share incentive schemes are tempted to make these incentives more valuable by making the shares more volatile (as discussed above). This represents, of course, a hidden loss to the shareholder.

1.8   PROTECTION FOR SHAREHOLDERS

One can clearly see the attraction of using leveraged financial instruments. What have the accountants and regulators done to protect the investor from such losses? From a regulatory perspective there are a number of rules. Basel 2, for instance, indirectly protects shareholders by forcing banks to measure and disclose the risks that they are taking on. This is known as the Pillar 3 requirement. The benefit for the regulators is that if shareholders see that banks are taking on too much risk they will abandon the shares, causing problems for the bonuses of the bank's directors. Of course, the primary role of the Basel committee is to prevent banks from going bankrupt. By forcing banks to disclose the risks they undertake, the committee ends up protecting shareholders.

As far as the accounting standards are concerned, it would be very obvious from any annual report if a fund manager or company decided to gear up its portfolio through borrowings. Under IAS 32.11(a), for instance, the term 'liability' is defined as an obligation to deliver cash in the future. Virtually all loans would meet this definition. The use of derivatives is, of course, covered under IAS 39. Although IAS 39 was an unwelcome innovation for many accountants, on the grounds that it is difficult to implement, it did constrain treasurers, traders and bank directors from taking on too much risk and hiding losses. IFRS 7, the disclosure standard for financial instruments, achieves the same purpose because entities are required to disclose how financial instruments alter the risk profile of the entity.

1.9   MEASURING THE 'TRADERS' DILEMMA'

The above example should reveal that when there is 'optionality' in the bonus structure, i.e. the ability to walk away from losses, there is an incentive for managers/traders to take on more risk. However, the use of optionality in bonuses means that there is also a huge transfer of wealth from the shareholder/investor to the fund manager or trader. In certain bonus systems, i.e. share incentive schemes, the transfer of wealth from shareholder to employee is recorded as an expense through the Profit & Loss account. IFRS 2 (*Share Based Payments*), for instance, now requires directors (of corporates as well as banks) to estimate the value of the transfer, i.e. the loss to the shareholder, and treat this as an expense to the Profit & Loss account. However, there are certain other types of bonuses where optionality is present but not captured under IFRS 2. Hedge fund bonuses, for instance, are as dangerous and perhaps even more costly than share incentive schemes but there is no requirement to disclose the transfer of wealth or to disclose the incentive to increase the risks that the investor/shareholder faces.

What is even more surprising, however, is that the regulators, whose responsibility is effectively to prevent banks from taking on too much risk, ignore, in their calculations, bonus schemes that encourage traders and bank directors to take on too much risk. One could argue that the technology to measure this risk is not available, but that is not so. The Black–Scholes model, used by option traders to price call and put options, can easily be adjusted to identify and measure the perverse incentive of many bonus schemes operating within financial institutions.

Table 1.4 illustrates how the Black–Scholes model prices a call option. A trader has the right but not the obligation to buy a share for 98, its current market price, in approximately two-and-a-half months (0.2 of one year). Obviously, if during this period the share price rises, the trader will buy it at the agreed exercise price of 98. If the share price falls he can walk away from the transaction without incurring a loss.

Table 1.4   Black–Scholes model

Asset price (S)	98	98	98	98
Strike price (X)	98	98	98	98
Time to maturity (T)	0.2	0.2	0.2	0.2
Risk-free rate (r)	10%	10%	10%	10%
Volatility (σ)	**20%**	**30%**	**40%**	**50%**
Value				
d1 numerator	0.02400	0.02900	0.03600	0.04500
d1 denominator	0.08944	0.13416	0.17889	0.22361
d1	0.26833	0.21615	0.20125	0.20125
Delta	0.60578	0.58557	0.57975	0.57975
N(d2)	0.57099	0.53267	0.50892	0.49108
Exponential	0.98020	0.98020	0.98020	0.98020
Call	£4.52	£6.22	£7.93	£9.64

What the table reveals is that the value of the option increases as the underlying volatility increases. When the volatility is 20% the value of the option is only £4.52. When the volatility is 50% the value climbs to £9.64. However, the conclusion should be obvious, if a bonus scheme allows a trader to participate in the gains but walk away from the losses, it encourages the trader or bank director to make the portfolio more volatile. Clearly, the regulators should penalise banks if they implement incentive schemes that encourage this type of risk. The figures of £4.62 and £9.64 represent the loss of wealth from the shareholder to the trader/fund manager. If the bonus scheme comes under IFRS 2 (*Share Based Payments*) then the cost of the option is correctly recognised as an expense in the Profit & Loss since it is, in effect, a loss to the shareholder. As mentioned, many bonus schemes have 'optionality' but are not captured by IFRS 2 and so the shareholder is losing out in two ways. He is clearly losing the value of the option, but perhaps more importantly in today's environment, the bonus scheme encourages management to take a lot more risk with the shareholder's money.

In the case of Northern Rock, one could argue that the bonus scheme of its directors may have contributed to the problem. If the directors are allowed to participate in profits but walk away from losses there is a very clear incentive to take on as much leverage as possible. Leverage, of course, increases volatility and volatility increases the value of bonuses. It could possibly explain why banks are so willing to take on huge risks at the expense of their shareholders. Also, financial institutions may be tempted to use complex structured products to achieve this leverage, perhaps knowing that the regulators cannot measure the risk of complex products and the accountant cannot deal with it properly under the accounting standards.

Case Study: Freddie Mac accounting manipulation

In a court case against the former Chief Executive of Freddie Mac, Leland Brendsel, Warren Buffet revealed that he had considerable worries about how Freddie Mac was run.[3] Brendsel was accused of accounting manipulation and running Freddie Mac in a reckless manner. Buffet outlined two areas of concern. Firstly, he was worried about the investments that Freddie Mac was making. In many cases the risks were excessive and sometimes speculated in areas that had nothing to do with the underlying business. The second concern was the extent to which Freddie Mac was manipulating earnings in order to conceal the risks and losses that they were making with some of these investments.

There is little doubt that bonuses contributed to the problem. According to *Mortgage News Daily*,[4] bonuses were at the centre of the motivation for accounting manipulation, not only in Freddie Mac but also its sister company, Fannie Mae. In 2006 *Mortgage News Daily* observed:

'Last month the Office of Federal Housing Enterprise Oversight (OFHEO), the division of the Department of Housing and Urban Development charged with regulating Fannie Mae and its sister organization Freddie Mac, issued a scathing report on Fannie's financial manipulations, stating outright that some of the motivation was to protect those executive bonuses.'

Both companies were brought down by the 2007/2008 credit crises, and are now in existence only because of subsidies that the US government has given (by way of guarantees). As mentioned elsewhere in this book, poorly devised bonus schemes encourage risk-taking and put pressure on directors to manipulate the accounting standards in order to conceal these risks and losses.

Off-balance sheet

According to the OFHEO,[5] Freddie Mac wanted to portray a 'Steady Freddie' image, i.e. that its earnings were not volatile but instead fairly steady, growing at a constant rate per annum. Obviously, if a bonus system rewards excessive profitability then the temptation is to take on as much

---

[3] David S. Hilzenrath, 'Buffet testifies that he saw early signs of Freddie Mac's woes', *Washington Post*, 31 October 2007, p. D03.

[4] http://www.mortgagenewsdaily.com/6152006_Fannie_Mae_Bonuses.asp

[5] OFHEO Freddie Mac Report 2003.

Case Study: (Continued)

risk as possible and then use accounting manipulation to smooth out earnings. That means in good years hiding profits and in bad years releasing those profits. The two creative accounting methods often used to achieve this are 'off-balance sheet' tactics, i.e. not reflecting assets at their true value on the balance sheet, and the creation of fictitious provisions (referred to by Arthur Levitt – formerly Head of the SEC – as 'cookie jar' reserve accounting). The ability of entities to engage in this form of creative accounting is now largely curtailed by IAS 37.

Freddie Mac and FAS 133, Accounting for Financial Instruments and Hedging

There is little doubt that the emergence of FAS 133 in 2001 caused problems for Freddie Mac. Certain financial instruments which were kept off the balance sheet prior to 2001 started to appear on the balance sheet since FAS 133 requires that entities show all derivatives on their balance sheet at market value. Also, there is evidence that Freddie Mac was using these derivatives for speculative purposes and therefore could not avail itself of the hedge accounting rules that allow entities to delay recognition of the profit or loss on derivatives. The result was that Freddie Mac had to reveal the extent to which it was speculating and was unable to maintain the pretence that its earnings were steady and non-volatile.

Needless to say, Freddie Mac objected to FAS 133, arguing that it was too complex and cumbersome and decided to 'transact around FAS 133 since it did not fully reflect the economic fundamentals of the company's business'. There is little doubt that some of these criticisms were true, but opponents of FAS 133 and its European equivalent IAS 39 fall into two camps, those who find it difficult to implement because of its sheer complexity and those who do not want to give up the advantages of manipulating their bonuses through off-balance sheet accounting. The OFHEO report suggests that many Freddie Mac employees in the accounting side did not know how to implement FAS 133 correctly, and also that Freddie Mac went to extraordinary lengths to continue to keep items off the balance sheet despite the FAS 133 requirements.

Classification

One of the first tasks that Freddie Mac had to deal with, on implementing FAS 133, was to smooth out the profits. Freddie Mac had used derivatives and these had made a substantial amount of money (possibly from speculating). By smoothing these profits, i.e. recognising small profits over a period of years rather than all at once, Freddie Mac would be able to disguise the volatility of its earnings. The way that Freddie Mac chose to do this was by reclassifying assets in the 'Held to Maturity' portfolio to the 'Trading' portfolio. As stated earlier in this book, there is always a risk that assets shown at cost on the balance sheet contain unrecognised losses. Freddie Mac therefore effectively decided to recognise these losses to coincide with the recognition of the derivative gains, hence the Profit & Loss account appeared smoother. In essence, Freddie Mac exploited the cherry-picking opportunities inherent in the accounting standards. There is some justification for Freddie Mac's activities. One technical weakness of FAS 133 is that it is clumsy and therefore produces unintended artificial volatility in the Profit & Loss account. However, the OFHEO were of the opinion that Freddie Mac's motivation was to manipulate bonuses and to conceal volatility.

Another technique that Freddie Mac used to conceal volatility was to classify assets from 'Trading' to 'Available for Sale'. Trading assets are shown on the balance sheet at market value with any changes in market value going through the Profit & Loss account. Although the assets are shown on the balance sheet at fair value, the change in value does not go through the Profit & Loss account and so although the assets appear on the balance sheet, the advantages of 'off-balance sheet' are maintained. The 'Available for Sale' category allows entities to conceal any gain or loss on a financial instrument into 'Equity Reserve' – the result being that an entity could suffer huge losses on certain complex products (like securitisations) and conceal their losses. Also, by sidestepping the

Profit & Loss account the real volatility of the entity is concealed. Freddie Mac's interpretation of the accounting standards was, however, flawed. It is not possible to transfer assets from the 'Trading' portfolio to the 'Available for Sale' portfolio and from the 'Held to Maturity' portfolio to the 'Trading' portfolio in the manner that Freddie Mac did. Freddie Mac appeared to claim that it sold the assets and then bought other assets and so there was not a change of classification, but the sale of one asset and the purchase of another. However, FAS 125, *Accounting for Transfer of Assets and Extinguishment of Liabilities* makes clear when an asset is sold and Freddie Mac did not meet the requirements. Therefore, the transfer between the portfolios was inappropriate. IFRS has similar provisions to the American accounting standards. Under IAS 18, *Revenue Recognition* control must pass and beneficial (or economic interest) must pass before a true sale can take place. This did not happen with Freddie Mac, so the accounting treatment was inappropriate.

Swaptions

Freddie Mac's treatment of Swaptions in its annual report is revealing and illustrates why financial institutions across the world prefer complex financial instruments that are difficult to value, possibly loss-making even when purchased and contain huge operational risks, all to the detriment of the shareholder and (in Freddie Mac's case) to the detriment of the US taxpayer as well. The preference for complex products arises because they are illiquid, difficult to value and therefore traders can invent valuation techniques and assumptions that maximise their bonuses.

An employee within Freddie Mac was able to convince the accountants and auditors that certain swaps were illiquid and therefore needed a special mathematical model for their valuation. Often, however, these mathematical models require certain variables such as volatility estimates to value the derivatives. Different data providers often provide different estimates on the same variables, allowing Freddie Mac and others to choose the most 'suitable' variable. It appears that Freddie Mac changed the inputs to suit its circumstances and achieve its results. In short, it decided what the profit level should be and then worked out what valuation was necessary to achieve those profits. It then picked the assumptions that achieved these valuations. It is always dangerous for external auditors to allow their clients to change their valuation techniques for this reason, even if the client convinces the auditor that the revised valuation methodology is more sophisticated and more correct.

As the OFHEO report observed:

'It is equally clear that the [revised] valuation policy was implemented with the advice and concurrence of Arthur Anderson. Interviews indicate that the [revised] approach was presented to Arthur Andersen at a December 20, 2000 SFAS 133 transition meeting, and that Arthur Andersen indicated that it could "sign-off" on such a model provided it had intellectual merit.'

The valuation requirements for financial instruments with quoted prices are set out in SFAS 107, which states that quoted prices must be used where available. 'Accordingly, only in those circumstances where there are not quoted prices for the financial instruments is management permitted to rely on its best estimate of fair value.' Freddie Mac never concluded that market volatility quotes or dealer quotes were unavailable, only that the quotes did not reflect a price at which Freddie Mac believed it would be able to transact. This is not a permitted conclusion under SFAS.

2
Accounting Foundations

2.1 INTRODUCTION

A fundamental problem with the accounting standards is that not all assets and liabilities are shown on the balance sheet at market value. The result is that for certain categories of assets or liabilities, the change in market value is ignored, i.e. the asset is carried at cost and any increase or decrease in the value of the asset is ignored both on the balance sheet and on the Profit & Loss account. Inevitably this causes problems.

Illustration

An entity borrows £10 million at 5% and uses it to finance the purchase of a bond, again for £10 million, which has a coupon of 5.25%. The entity intends to sell the bond before maturity and is therefore forced to classify the bond as trading and show it on the balance sheet at market value. The loan, however, must be shown at cost. Within days of buying the bond, Libor moves from 5% to 6%. This causes the market value of both the bond and the loan to fall in value together by roughly the same amount, resulting in only a slight change to the Profit & Loss account. However, the obscure accounting rules force the entity to record the change in value of the bond only on the balance sheet and not the loan. The result is that the entity is forced to record a significant accounting loss when in reality it has not made a loss.

These unnecessarily complicated accounting rules often force entities to show losses or profits in their annual report which are 'artificial' in nature. Creative accountants can take advantage of these rules to show an artificial profit if they wish. The accounting standard setters have responded with hundreds and hundreds of pedantic rules to prevent this from happening. The result is a set of very complex accounting rules which are not always effective, since they fail to close all the loopholes.

These loopholes have allowed entities to keep certain items 'off-balance sheet'. Indeed, there is a possibility that for this reason the accounting standards themselves contributed to the 2007/2008 credit crunch in allowing financial institutions to conceal risks and losses. Since the collapse of Enron in 2001, various accounting standard setters around the world have changed the standards in an attempt to avoid the abuses that Enron and other companies entered into. There is no doubt, as we shall see later in this chapter, that they have made improvements that have prevented abuses. However, a potential problem is that they have devised too many rules, some of which are conflicting, giving accountants, particularly creative accountants, too much choice. This chapter focuses on the 'mixed model' foundations of accounting. By 'mixed model' we mean that different measurement rules apply to different assets. Some of the measurement rules as outlined above force entities to show assets and liabilities at market value and others at cost.

The accounting standards, for generations, have followed this 'mixed model' approach. This compromising accounting model creates confusion and puts the standards on a very weak foundation, creating uncertainty. The comments by the Bank of Ireland recently reveal the problem that the standard setters have regarding consistency:

> Bank of Ireland treats its SIVs [Structured Investment Vehicles] as loans and advances to customers and so the charge hits our loan loss charge directly. This contributes about 3 basis points of our expected loan loss charge for the year and this treatment is different from any other institutions who treat their SIVs as available for sale assets and take the movements on them through reserves.[1]

The suggestion here is that other institutions may be hiding losses or at least delaying recognition of losses from the shareholder as the 'available for sale' accounting treatment often allows entities to hide losses. Trying to adopt accounting standards to capture sophisticated financial instruments becomes difficult as hundreds of rules are needed to deal with the complexity – otherwise misleading situations could arise. Often, however, too many rules and too much choice can also lead to misleading reports. Profit and loss figures, for instance, could be subject to huge gyrations, not because the underlying entity is risky but because the mixed model approach creates 'artificial volatility' which we examine later. We discuss below why this may be the case, but more importantly, why it is confusing and why it is necessary to develop hundreds of pedantic rules, particularly hedge accounting rules to overcome these weaknesses.

2.2   IASB IMPROVEMENTS

We first look at recent changes that entities have had to adopt as a result of their conversion to the International Financial Reporting Standards. The improvements that IASB have made to the accounting standards are summarised below.

IFRS 2 *Share Based Payments*: Entities must reveal the cost of bonuses, particularly with optionality (i.e. call options) as an expense in the Profit & Loss account. The rule, however, is confined only to share-based payments.

IFRS 3/IAS 27 *Consolidation*: Entities are now required to consolidate other companies if there is evidence that they control such companies. As a result, consolidated entities cannot create intercompany profits, i.e. where an entity sells an overpriced asset to a company it controls. Neither can the entity hide losses or loss-making assets through a subsidiary. Enron-style abuses are therefore curtailed.

IAS 39 *Effective Interest Rates*: Financial institutions were often tempted to make risky loans and recognise revenue prematurely by taking a large 'administration' fee up-front to the Profit & Loss account. The accounting rules now state that the profit on a loan must be spread evenly throughout the life of the loan, therefore forcing banks to recognise revenue in line with risk.

---

[1] Bank of Ireland Group, Interim Management Statement, 15 February 2008.

(Continued)

IAS 39 *Hedge Accounting*: This is a very controversial area for reasons we will see below. However, the hedge accounting rules are designed to ensure that if a financial institution uses derivatives for hedging purposes, it can keep any profit or loss on the derivative out of the Profit & Loss account for a temporary period. If the same derivative is used for speculative purposes, the entity must recognise the profit or loss straight away and so losses on certain financial instruments are more difficult to hide.

IAS 39 *Beneficial Interest*: If an entity is exposed to an asset's value going up or down, it is generally prevented from taking that asset off the balance sheet. For instance, an entity cannot simultaneously sell a loan and guarantee that the loan will not default. This method was used by some entities to record profits prematurely and to hide losses as they were able to take poorly performing loans off the balance sheet.

IAS 18 *Revenue Recognition*: Following various forms of accounting abuse in the dot.com era, when internet companies, attempting to raise capital, inflated their profits (and profit forecasts), both the American accounting standard setters and their IAS equivalents introduced rules which prevent entities from recognising revenue until there is no doubt that the profit is earned. In America, the SEC devised a document called SAB 101 to remind accountants not to recognise profits based on estimated sales revenue. Instead, the entity has to wait until the service is performed or goods supplied.

IAS 37 *Provisions*: These rules are designed to avoid 'cookie jar' reserve accounting where entities try to hide the volatility of their Profit & Loss account by hiding excess profits in good years and releasing them in bad years. This practice has often been used to conceal from the shareholder risks that an entity is taking.

IFRS 7 *Disclosures*: Entities are now required to disclose how their risk profile changes as a result of using financial instruments.

These rules are discussed in more detail later in this chapter. Clearly, these rules are necessary given the scandals of Enron, WorldCom, Xerox, Dynergy, etc. What is happening, however, is that to implement the above principles there are thousands of rules, some of which conflict with each other and others which create anomalies requiring more rules to fix. The accounting standards are now so complex that it takes a very long time to amend them to suit the needs of specialist areas like insurance.

2.3   THE FRAMEWORK

The first task of the standard setters is to identify whether assets and liabilities be shown on the balance sheet at current market value or shown at cost. The question is one that has vexed accounting standard setters for generations. What is happening, however, is that we are moving more and more towards market value accounting; the reason being that entities like Enron were able to create artificial profits by not showing assets and liabilities at true market value on the balance sheet and were therefore able to hide losses. However, showing assets and liabilities on the balance sheet at market value introduces a new set of problems. In particular, some assets are difficult to value because of their subjective nature, the 'goodwill' of an entity being a good example. Certainly, some financial instruments fall into this category.

Commenting on the need for regulation for investment banks, Tony Jackson of the *Financial Times* said:

> Part of the answer to the question [regarding the need for regulation] lies with asset-backed securities. Most of those went on to the bank's books at more than they were worth, so at least some of the writedowns will prove permanent.[2]

Obviously, with bonuses on people's minds directors and traders may choose a value that maximises profits. Nevertheless, there is also the risk, particularly with financial institutions, that a 'spiral recession' could occur. For instance, if all financial entities reduced the value of their financial instruments linked to the sub-prime lending sector they would have to show losses, which would in turn constrain their ability to lend, causing more problems for borrowers and therefore forcing banks to lower the value of their financial instruments even further, starting a vicious circle. Many experts believe that this phenomenon contributed to the credit crises of 2007/2008. The standard setters have tried to deal with these problems by showing only some assets at market value and showing others at cost. This mixed model approach, however, is a compromise solution and one that leads to a great deal of confusion. The problem is even more compounded when the standard setters try to deal with the complex area of derivatives and financial instruments. Indeed, the compromise model may explain why the International Financial Reporting Standards committee took so long to come up with a suitable accounting standard not only for financial instruments, but also for insurance.

2.4   FAIR VALUE OR COST

The box below illustrates how the accounting standards, particularly IAS 39, treat various assets on the balance sheet and through the Profit & Loss account.

Held to Maturity assets	These are shown on the balance sheet at cost – as opposed to market value. The yield on these assets goes through the Profit & Loss account.
Loans & Receivables	Generally, this group of assets (and liabilities) is treated in the same way as Held to Maturity assets. They are shown at cost on the balance sheet with the yield (i.e. the interest income payments go through the Profit & Loss account).
Trading assets	This group of assets is generally held for the short term and is often used for speculation. The group also includes assets bought and sold to satisfy client/investor needs (i.e. market-making activities). Unlike the first two groups, these assets are shown at market value on the balance sheet and any change in market value goes through the Profit & Loss account.
Available for Sale	These are non-derivative assets, unhelpfully defined in the accounting standards (IAS 39.9) as any assets that are not Loans & Receivables, Held to Maturity or Trading. This loose definition means that different entities treat the same asset in different ways. They are shown at market value on the balance sheet and any change in the market value goes through the Equity Reserve account, as opposed to the Profit & Loss account, until the asset is sold, when it goes through the Profit & Loss account.

---

[2] Tony Jackson, 'Regulation? Plus ça change for investment banks', *Financial Times*, 7 April 2008.

The illustration below shows how a simple transaction is accounted for under the various methods discussed above (see Table 2.1 for a summary).

An entrepreneur sets up a company and invests, through ordinary shares, €1,000,000. The entity borrows an additional €2,000,000 and invests the entire proceeds in an asset worth €3,000,000. At the end of the year, the asset increases in value by 20% to €3,600,000. To a

Table 2.1   Various accounting treatments

Held to Maturity Accounting	
Assets	
Tangible Assets	£3,000,000
Liabilities	
Loans	−£2,000,000
	£1,000,000
Shareholders' Funds	
Ordinary Shares	£1,000,000
Equity Reserve	
Profit & Loss	
	£1,000,000
Trading	
Assets	
Tangible Assets	£3,600,000
Liabilities	
Loans	−£2,000,000
	£1,600,000
Shareholders' Funds	
Ordinary Shares	£1,000,000
Equity Reserve	
Profit & Loss	£600,000
	£1,600,000
Available for Sale	
Assets	
Tangible Assets	£3,600,000
Liabilities	
Loans	−£2,000,000
	£1,600,000
Shareholders' Funds	
Ordinary Shares	£1,000,000
Equity Reserve	£600,000
Profit & Loss	
	£1,600,000

non-accountant, the question as to whether the company has made a profit is easy to answer – it has. However, deciding whether the company should report the profit under current accounting standards is, as we shall see, quite difficult to answer.

If the company uses a cost model, the asset will be recorded in the balance sheet at €3,000,000 at the end of the year, the market value is ignored. Therefore, the company will not show a profit. However, if the company is allowed to use the market value model, then the asset will be shown in the year-end balance sheet at the current market value, which is €3,600,000. The company is therefore allowed to record a profit of €600,000. Whether the company is allowed to use the cost model or market value model depends on a number of factors, and often auditors have difficulty deciding whether the cost model or the market value model is appropriate. As a general guideline, however, if the entity buys the asset with the intention of selling it in the short term, the asset is generally classified as trading and is shown on the balance sheet at market value and therefore, the entity is required to show a profit even though it has not sold the asset. On the other hand, if the entity intends to hold the asset for a very long time (i.e. to maturity), it may be permitted to show the asset at cost. An example is 'Held to Maturity' bonds.

To confuse matters further, the accounting standards permit what is known as the 'Available For Sale' category. This category is not very clear. It states that an entity must record the asset on the balance sheet at current market value but must record any profit or loss through a special account known as the Equity Reserve account. Only when the asset is sold, is the entity allowed to recognise a profit through its Profit & Loss account.

Even for the simplest of transactions, the accounting standards can confuse experienced accountants, along with investors. It is no surprise, therefore, that when it comes to more complex transactions involving financial instruments, the problems get out of hand.

2.5 ARTIFICIAL VOLATILITY

Despite these changes, the IASB along with its American counterparts must deal with the problems of 'artificial volatility'. Artificial volatility arises principally because some assets are carried on the balance sheet at market value while matching liabilities must be carried at cost. Therefore, when the asset changes in value, the difference must go through the Profit & Loss account but when the liability changes in value, the difference is effectively ignored. The result is that as the asset changes value the accounting Profit & Loss also changes value when in reality the asset may offset the liability. For instance, if an entity borrows money on a fixed rate basis to buy a bond which has a fixed coupon then, if interest rates change, any change in the asset is offset by a change in the liability. However, in some cases, the entity may not be allowed to recognise the change in the liability but forced to recognise the change in the asset, and so the accounting Profit & Loss appears more volatile than it actually is. The 'mixed model' approach therefore creates undesirable volatility – known as artificial volatility.

Table 2.2 reveals how derivatives – used to hedge an interest rate exposure – create an artificial volatility problem. In essence, the standards require certain items to be shown at market value (or fair value), while they may be financed by liabilities which the entity must show at cost.

A bank issues a fixed mortgage to a customer. As with all fixed rate financial instruments the market value fluctuates according to changes in interest rates. During year 2, for instance,

Table 2.2   Hedging interest rate margin

Fair Values	Year 1	Year 2	Year 3	Year 4	Year 5
FV fixed loans to customers	£100	£140	£90	£80	£150
Derivative	£–	−£40	£10	£20	−£50
Liabilities floating loans	−£100	−£100	−£100	−£100	−£100
Shareholders' funds	£–	£–	£–	£–	£–

interest rates fell causing the value of the fixed loan to increase. In year 3 interest rates rose, etc. The bank finances the fixed loans by using the inter-bank market and therefore has loans whose interest fluctuates as interest rates change (in other words a floating loan). Clearly, there is the risk that if interest rates go up, the interest paid out may exceed the fixed interest received (i.e. negative interest margin). The bank therefore decides to hedge the interest rate risk by converting the floating loan into a fixed loan. It does this by entering into a swap where it pays fixed and receives floating with a counterparty (usually separate from the bank that provided the loan). Therefore, when interest rates fall, the bank will pay out more than it receives and so the swap will acquire a negative market value but in year 3, when interest rates rise, the swap acquires a positive value. In this simplified example, the swap is a perfect hedge and so no ineffectiveness arises. In other words, as interest rates change, the value of the fixed mortgage changes but so too does the value of the swap, which, acting as a hedge, goes in the opposite direction. As with all perfect hedges, there is a 100% negative correlation.

Unfortunately, owing to problems with the accounting standards, the bank may be required to show the fixed mortgage and loan at book value while the derivative must be shown at market value. The result is that the accounting standards create artificial volatility and, in the absence of detailed and complex rules on hedge accounting, the difference must go through the Profit & Loss account as shown in Table 2.3.

Table 2.3   Artificial volatility

Balance Sheet	Year 1	Year 2	Year 3	Year 4	Year 5
Fixed loans to customers	£100	£100	£100	£100	£100
Derivative	£–	−£40	£10	£20	−£50
Liabilities floating loans	−£100	−£100	−£100	−£100	−£100
Shareholders' funds	£–	−£40	£10	£20	−£50
Shareholders' Funds Ordinary Shares Profit & Loss	£–	−£40	£10	£20	−£50
	£–	−£40	£10	£20	−£50

The volatility in this case is described as artificial as it does not reflect reality.

Hedge accounting rules (to be discussed in Chapter 4) allow a bank to avoid this artificial volatility but the hedging rules are confusing, complex, bureaucratic and often difficult to implement in practice. The EU recognised the problems with hedge accounting and therefore devised special accounting rules which would allow certain entities to ignore parts of the accounting standard, causing more confusion because there are now two versions of IAS 39 in issue, the IASB version and the EU version. The problem is still not resolved (it is discussed in more detail in Chapter 11).

2.6 COST MODEL

For the accounting standard setters, the cost model is a very attractive model, mainly because of its certainty. Auditors and accountants know exactly where they stand when the rules are black and white. There is little or no room for manoeuvrability and, therefore, if they come under outside pressure to inflate profits, by say overvaluing assets, the auditors can legitimately point out that they would be in clear breach of the accounting standards. The accounting profession therefore ends up applying the standards consistently across companies and their simplicity means that the risk of misinterpreting the standards is remote.

2.7 CHERRY-PICKING

However, over the years, creative accountants have discovered blatant loopholes in the cost model and have exploited these, often in response to pressure to inflate profits or turn real losses into accounting profits. The methodology is simple. Consider a case where a company buys five assets for €100 each. A year later, asset 1 has a value of €160 while assets 2, 3, 4 and 5 have a value of €20 each. The combined values of the assets are €240 but the purchase price for them collectively was €500 – therefore the company clearly made a loss of €260. However, by selling the first asset and receiving €160 and keeping the remaining four assets on the balance sheet at cost the company can show an accounting profit of €60 (see Table 2.4). The assets on the balance sheet show a combined value of €560 (cash €160 and assets carried at cost €400) whereas the combined purchase price was only €500. This process is known as cherry-picking, because the company can control its Profit & Loss by cashing in the most profitable asset.

Table 2.4   Economic loss vs. accounting profit

Asset	Cost	Current market value	Profit
1	£100	£160	£60
2	£100	£20	
3	£100	£20	
4	£100	£20	
5	£100	£20	
	£500	£240	
Economic loss		£260	

One might be tempted to conclude therefore that if everything is shown on the balance sheet at market value, the problems of cherry-picking are eliminated. That is true, but market value accounting brings about its own set of problems.

2.8   SUBJECTIVE VALUATIONS

If assets and liabilities are easy to value, market value (or mark-to-market) accounting has the potential to work. In the example above, when the company buys an asset and that asset goes up in value, so too does the Profit & Loss account and if the asset falls in value the entity is required to report a loss. Hedge funds, for instance, use this approach and therefore do not need to tie up resources employing hoards of accountants (unlike their banking counterparts where the accounting rules are quite different, being much more complex). The main problem, however, is that some assets are very difficult to value and so the Profit & Loss account could be very subjective. A huge operational risk facing a lot of banks and hedge funds, for instance, is that complex financial instruments are given too high a value on the balance sheet. The result is that profits are overinflated and traders end up receiving substantial bonuses when in reality they are destroying shareholder value by creating huge losses. The last thing that an operational risk manager wants is to pay traders huge bonuses to trade in complex financial instruments that are in reality difficult to understand, impossible to value and therefore create losses which the banks don't know about. In 2007, for instance, the City press focused on the huge bonuses traders received and months later wrote about the substantial losses that the banks paying the bonuses were making. This glaring inconsistency may explain why traders prefer complex financial instruments that are difficult to value as opposed to simple derivatives where the market value is easy to derive and therefore trades are easy to see through. Complexity can simultaneously hide losses and increase bonuses. These complex instruments are often purchased at inflated prices, causing further losses for the shareholder.

2.9   PROACTIVE VS. REACTIVE

Rather than being proactive, the standard setters tend to be reactive. Instead of designing accounting standards that are 'fit for purpose', i.e. fit for the complexities of today's financial industry, the standard setters have imposed an oversimplified model. They then wait until cracks appear and try to correct them by introducing additional rules. Every time a creative accounting scandal emerges, they come up with new rules. Often, the new rules are inconsistent with previous rules and therefore an additional set of rules is needed to overcome the inconsistencies. It follows therefore that when the accounting standard setters try to develop new accounting standards to deal with, say, financial instruments, insurance or petroleum accounting, they have to revise existing standards in order to eliminate or reduce anomalies. However, if there are too many rules already in place, the task of introducing new standards becomes Herculean. There is little doubt that for a number of years many entities exploited the off-balance sheet opportunities that financial instruments presented and today are exploiting the off-balance sheet opportunities that special purpose vehicles permit. The accounting standard setters have come up with more thorough (but also more complex) standards to deal with these issues, namely IAS 39, *Accounting for Financial Instruments* and IFRS 3/IAS 27, *Business Combinations*. Unfortunately, there is evidence, even today, that these new rules are not working properly.

2.10   GOODWILL

Other accounting abuses, apart from the above, have occurred over the last two decades. For instance, entities often acquired other companies at inflated prices. The losses were concealed from shareholders, buried in goodwill. Company A might pay €1000 for company B though the physical assets are only worth €200. The excess payment would be for the reputation or goodwill that the company has built up. As before, when company A acquires an asset or a business, it records the cost as €1000 represented in this case as physical assets €200 and goodwill €800. If, however, company A paid €3000 for company B the transaction would still be recorded at cost. Only this time the goodwill would be €2800 rather than €800. It follows that companies could acquire other companies at inflated prices and bury overpayments or losses in goodwill. This obviously encouraged a period when a lot of questionable takeovers took place at inflated prices, resulting in considerable damage to shareholder value. The shareholder was, of course, not even remotely aware of this value destruction. The standard setters attempted to resolve this by impairing goodwill, i.e. recording goodwill at the market value on the balance sheet, where the fair value falls below the cost that appears on the balance sheet.

However, it was the use of financial derivatives that signalled the end of pure cost accounting. A company, for instance, could take out two foreign currency forward contracts, one betting that the euro would go up in value against the dollar and a second one betting that the euro would depreciate against the dollar. Clearly, the combined economic impact to the company of taking out both contracts together would be zero, since one derivative is an exact mirror image of the other. However, creative accountants were able to 'manufacture' an accounting profit by cashing in the profit-making derivative and keeping quiet about the loss-making derivative, i.e. keeping it 'off-balance sheet'. The cost of a forward contract is normally zero, therefore, in the days prior to IAS 39, loss-making derivatives were shown at zero on the balance sheet even though they really are a liability. In the days prior to a special accounting standard on derivatives, this little trick was easy to perform. At the date of initial purchase, both derivatives would be recorded at cost on the balance sheet (zero). At the end of the accounting period, there was no requirement to show that the loss-making derivative, which was not cashed in, was in fact a liability. Therefore, by keeping loss-making derivatives 'off-balance sheet', a company could show an accounting profit, or more precisely, hide accounting losses.

2.11   MARKET VALUE ACCOUNTING

To avoid these accounting abuses, the accounting profession has moved very gradually towards what is known as mark-to-market accounting or mark-to-model accounting. Mark-to-market accounting simply means that if you can identify the current market price of an asset, show that value on the balance sheet and not the cost. Marking-to-model is a term generally used for financial instruments. If the market value of a financial instrument is not available, use a model (such as Black–Scholes) to value the financial instrument, and use the result as a proxy to the market value. It is unfortunate, though understandable, that the accounting profession does not use either the cost model in its entirety or the market value. Instead, they are compromising. They are using the cost model for some assets and liabilities and the market model for others. By compromising, and adopting a mixed model approach, the standard setters have created considerable confusion. The rules are very complex and it is this complexity that gives creative accountants the opportunity to mislead shareholders. The accounting profession has responded to creative accounting antics by devising more and more detailed rules. Sometimes, however, these rules are inconsistent, requiring even more rules. In a nutshell, the compromising model, which involves showing some assets at market value and others at cost, explains why the accounting standards are as awkward as they are today. It may also explain why certain accounting standards, such as accounting for financial instruments, have attracted such derision, not only from the accounting profession but also from banks and government ministers, particularly EU commissioners.

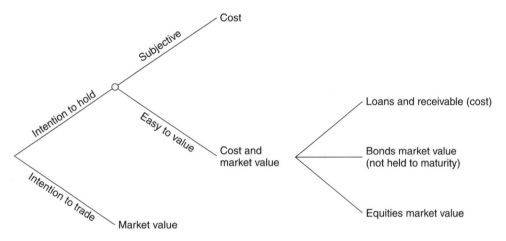

Figure 2.1   Treatment of assets and liabilities on the balance sheet

Figure 2.1 attempts to show which assets are shown at cost on the balance sheet and which assets are shown at market value. As a general guideline, if an entity buys an asset with the intention of using it in its business (i.e. cars, computers, equipment, etc.), these tend to be shown at cost on the balance sheet. Generally, entities do not buy these categories of assets with the intention of reselling immediately at a profit. Though, if they did, they would probably have to show them at market value. A second category of assets not shown at market value are those assets that entities tend to hold on to for a long period of time or until maturity. For instance, if an entity buys a 10-year bond that it intends to hold to maturity then it is the cash flow of the bond that is important and not the market value (except where the market value suggests a serious credit deterioration which will of course affect the cash flow). Generally, where assets are shown at cost as opposed to market value, the standards impose an impairment requirement. This means that if the market value falls below the cost of the asset, the entity must consider recognising the loss immediately. The same is not true of an asset going up in value. The concept is known as the 'prudence' concept. In other words, if an entity is expected to incur a loss, recognise the loss straight away but if there is an expected profit, wait until the asset is sold before the profit is recognised.

2.12 IFRS AND ITS CONTRIBUTION TO BANKING CRISES

The inconsistent rules, i.e. allowing some assets to be shown at cost and others at market value, mean that banks are accounting for the same transactions on an inconsistent basis. It is not difficult therefore to hide losses, even under the improved post-Enron regime. It hardly comes as a surprise that investors will want to hold a quasi-inquisition into what went wrong with the major investment banks that allowed very heavy losses to arise. All of these banks are heavily regulated to reduce the risks of default and they are all audited by major international accounting firms. So, why were they able to take huge risks with shareholders' money, why was this risk not disclosed to the shareholder and why are they forced to bring back onto the balance sheet structured investment vehicles that made huge losses? That there is a breakdown somewhere seems in no doubt. What is questionable is whether these investment banks complied with the accounting standards. If they did, then there are clearly some flaws with the accounting standards that shareholders would like to get to the bottom of. CTW Investment Group, a governance organisation which represents about $1.5 trillion in funds, intends to hold such an enquiry.[3] According to Michael Garland, CTW's Director of Value Strategies:

> Some of the meetings have re-enforced our skepticism, especially in relation to the balance sheets and accounts. We are mindful that directors are not responsible for managing risk but overseeing risk . . . we're questioning what management were doing to address that. So far they're all trying to make a case that this [the sub-prime write-downs] was an industry collapse.

The views of CTW are shared with the Association of British Insurers. Peter Montagnon, Director of Investment Affairs at the Association of British Insurers, thought that committees (probably including audit committees) had not understood the risks. Some investors have even called for audit of control and risk management systems. According to *Accountancy Age*, CTW has already met with the directors of major banks, including Morgan Stanley, Citigroup, Wachovia Bank and Merrill Lynch.

2.13   IFRS POST-ENRON

Introduction

What follows is a detailed analysis of how the International Financial Reporting Standards have revamped the accounting rules. Some financial institutions have only recently started to adopt IFRS. The major changes they have encountered are detailed below:

- Share-based payments (employee benefits)   IFRS 2
- Goodwill (business combinations)   IFRS 3
- Pension accounting (employee benefits)   IAS 19
- Consolidation   IAS 27
- Debt vs. equity classification   IAS 32
- Loan impairment   IAS 39
- Arrangement fees (effective interest rate)   IAS 39
- Hedge and derivative accounting   IAS 39
- Classification of financial instruments   IAS 39

---

[3] Penny Sukhraj, 'The risks in off-balance sheet vehicles', *Accountancy Age*, 6 March 2008.

Share-based payments (IFRS 2)

IFRS 2 (*Share Based Payments*) tackles the problem of employee and director share option schemes. This area was a cause for concern amongst corporate governance experts; share options allowed directors to conceal a lot of staff expenses. But, more importantly, executive share option schemes encouraged directors to put shareholders' funds at considerable risk. The more risky the entity, the more valuable the options were. IFRS 2 now states that employee share options must appear as an expense on the balance sheet at the date the option was granted. Also, full disclosure on the calculation method and assumptions is required. The expense does not have to hit the Profit & Loss account at once. If there is a condition that the employee remains with the entity for, say, three years before the option is granted, then the expense may be allocated over the three years.

Goodwill (IFRS 3)

Takeover activity was always something that concerned shareholders. Often, the acquirer of a company overpaid for companies that they acquired but the directors were not overly concerned since they could bury their losses in goodwill and therefore the shareholder would not know the extent of the overpayment. A further problem was merger accounting, which effectively allowed entities to record certain assets at book value even where the market value was well above book value. The difference was once again buried in goodwill. There are now special impairment rules which, if implemented correctly, force a company to reveal any losses they made by overpaying for their target companies. In addition, the standards do not allow merger accounting and this has contained some creative accounting tactics. In particular, companies cannot hide loans. Neither can they create artificial inter-company profits.

Pension accounting (IAS 19)

Many employers offer very generous pension terms to their employees, whereby the employer guarantees payments at certain levels until the employee dies. These guarantees of course come at a cost. Many of these costs were kept off the balance sheet, which meant that both the liability and the expense were hidden from the shareholder. A second problem was that the risks were also concealed from the shareholder. For instance, many employers invested in the stock market in order to meet future pension liabilities. Obviously, there is a risk that if the stock market underperforms or even goes negative, the entity and ultimately the shareholders will suffer. IAS 19 is quite a complicated accounting standard. It requires entities to show pension fund deficits as a liability on the balance sheet and, in certain cases, any change in the value of the deficit must go through the Profit & Loss account (though not all the changes must go through at once). The standard has proved controversial and, in many instances, has changed the way that entities manage their pension funds. For instance, many entities, as a result of the new accounting requirement, have used bonds instead of equities as an investment since bonds have – broadly speaking – similar risk profiles to pension liabilities and so risk is substantially reduced, but not eliminated. A major risk associated with pensions, which entities have difficulty in hedging, is longevity risk – i.e. the risk that ex-employees will live many years after they retire, thus increasing the payments that the entity must make and liabilities.

Consolidation (IAS 27)

Although the rules were tightened here, there are still instances where entities, particularly financial institutions, manage to avoid consolidation in certain circumstances. The term 'consolidation' refers to instances where one company controls another. The entity controlling the subsidiary must bring onto its balance sheet the assets and liabilities of the entity under control (the subsidiary). For instance, if company A takes over company B and company B's net assets have a market value of say £100m then, when company A produces its annual report, its consolidated balance sheet must include A's assets added to B's balance sheet. Company A therefore adds £100m to its own balance sheet. There are two important benefits of consolidation which increase clarity for the reader of accounts. Firstly, a company will find it more difficult to hide losses. Often, if A controls B, A might be tempted to force B into buying assets from A at above market value. Thus, A might force B to buy an asset worth £100 for £160. If A could avoid consolidation, A could show a profit but if A was forced to consolidate B's balance sheet, then A is effectively prevented from recognising inter-company profits. The result is that A's profits after consolidation would fall by £60 and the asset would be carried on the combined balance sheet at (probably) £100 and not £160. The second benefit of consolidation is that the consolidated balance sheet must reveal details of all borrowings both by the parent company and the subsidiary. Without consolidation, A could conceal borrowings it made in the name of company B.

Enron was of course guilty of this. They effectively exploited the rules of consolidation by controlling entities but didn't give the appearance of control. At the time, the relevant accounting standard in America (FAS 140) was a little weak in that it allowed entities like Enron to control other entities but keep them off the consolidated balance sheet. The result was that Enron could borrow substantial amounts of money and conceal the risk of high debt from the shareholder. Enron also sold questionable assets to entities which it controlled at inflated prices. The result was that Enron could record a profit, even though the profit was artificial in nature. Nevertheless, the accounting standards permitted (not willingly) complex structures where entities could control other companies without having to apply the consolidation rules.

Needless to say, the issue of 'off-balance sheet' and consolidation has preoccupied shareholders of large investment banks. There is a possibility that these banks should never have taken Structured Investment Vehicles off the balance sheet. By doing so, the investment banks were, of course, able to conceal losses and conceal the high risks of borrowing, not to mention the liquidity and operational risk of the complex structured financial instruments that they were investing in. Thus, they enjoyed the benefits of non-consolidation. What long-suffering shareholders of these banks need to determine is, who is at fault? Is it the banks because they failed to apply the accounting standards correctly or is it the accounting standards because the rules of consolidation are not tight enough to prevent entities from controlling special off-balance sheet entities and simultaneously enjoying the benefits of non-consolidation, i.e. hiding losses, fabricating profits and concealing risks. These arguments will be examined in more detail later in this book. Under IAS 27 more securitisations (and therefore more structured investment vehicles) should be consolidated, and therefore the perils of off-balance sheet activity will be reduced.

Debt vs. equity classification (IAS 32)

There is an important difference between equity and liability. If a bank is financed by equity, the investors are not allowed to withdraw their money, particularly in times of difficulty. The best they can hope for is that the shares are liquid and that they can sell them on the second-hand market. Lenders are of course different. Any money they put into a company is regarded as a liability and these liabilities usually contain a lot of covenants, which effectively allow them to withdraw their cash when the company is in trouble. The question of whether an entity should be financed by debt or equity is more of an issue for corporate financiers than accountants, since the accounting standards cannot dictate to a company how much of its funding should be in debt or in equity. As a general guideline, however, if the cash flows of an entity or project are difficult to predict or are very volatile, then equity finance is more appropriate. On the other hand, if the cash flows are predictable and relatively safe, loan financing may be more suitable.

It is nevertheless a feature of today's finance industry that gearing is kept as high as possible. The increase in leverage makes certain bonuses and employee share option schemes more valuable. So, what accountants need to watch out for are instances where certain financial instruments are treated as equity when in reality they have debt features. Needless to say, there is also a temptation to keep debt off the balance sheet. This may now be more difficult under IAS 32, which essentially looks at the economics of the financial instrument rather than the name. For example, prior to the changes in IFRS, it was common practice for financial institutions to hide their levels of gearing by treating perpetual instruments and preference shares as equity. Under IAS 32, redeemable preference shares and perpetual securities that have a contractual obligation to pay interest will be classified as debt, and of course the annual payments will be treated as interest and so deducted from interest income rather than treated as dividends.

Following the 2007 credit crunch there was considerable pressure on accountants to allow their entities to take huge risks and to hide the risks they were taking. Needless to say, the banks that benefited from the credit crunch were those that were well financed from customer deposits and did not rely too heavily on inter-bank borrowings. Many banks therefore used off-balance sheet structures to hide their gearing among other methods. Regulators, of course, should have picked up on this. Under the Basel rules, regulators must ensure that where banks are taking on huge risks they must be appropriately financed. However, one important difference between the Basel 1 rules and the improvements under Basel 2 is that Basel 1 virtually ignored risks that were off-balance sheet. Basel 2 doesn't, and therefore penalises banks that use Structured Investment Vehicles. However, at the time of writing, not all banks have applied the Basel 2 rules and so regulators are not able to do their job effectively. Accountants too may not, in all cases, have alerted shareholders to the considerable risks that these entities face. Writing for the *Financial Times*,[4] Anthony Bolton commented: 'In analysing my worst mistakes over the years, I have identified three recurring factors. They are: poor balance sheets, poor business models and poor managements. Of these three, by far the most common cause of grief has been the poor balance sheet.' This comment is certainly applicable to the financial sector today, where share prices in some investment banks have reached a 10-year low and others like Northern Rock have not only gone out of business but almost destabilised the financial system. Even if entities record their debt 'on-balance sheet' and even if they classify debt correctly, i.e. not as equity, there are still problems. In cases where debt levels are subject to seasonal fluctuations, the year-end figure (which is what the shareholder sees) may not represent the true level of debt. Ideally, entities should report average debt levels but they seldom do this.

---

[4] Anthony Bolton, The Anthony Bolton column, *Financial Times*, 1/2 March 2008.

Loan impairment (IAS 39)

In the past, banks along with other companies had what was known as a specific provision and a general provision for bad debts. Where banks identified a loan that was in difficulty or close to default, they would set aside a specific provision for bad debts. However, they also charged an additional amount known as a general provision which covered future potential bad debts not yet recognised. The problem for the accounting standard setters was that this general provision was subjective and banking directors were often tempted to set the level of general provision in a manner that maximised their bonuses. Suppose, for instance, directors of a bank were given bonuses if profits exceeded £1 billion and nothing otherwise. Also, suppose as a result of successful speculation that the bank produced profits of £1.3 billion. The bank's directors might be tempted to increase the general provision for bad debts by £290,000,000. This would bring profits down to £1,010,000,000 in the current year. If, next year, the profits of the bank declined, the directors could argue that the general provision was too high and release some of it. Therefore, for instance, if profits for the next year were only £900,000,000, the directors could release say £100,000,000 and secure a bonus in that year as well. Apart from bonuses, banks might want to give the impression that their Profit & Loss account is not volatile (and therefore not risky). General provisions were therefore used to smooth out the Profit & Loss account. The accounting standards have tightened this in two ways. Firstly, there are detailed rules in IAS 39 which make the calculation of the bad debts expense less of a subjective exercise and more of an objective exercise. A second standard, IAS 37 (*Provisions, Contingent Liabilities and Contingent Assets*), requires that an entity meet certain detailed conditions before putting in a provision against future losses.

The rules on impairment are often counter-intuitive to what a non-accountant would expect, and may indeed have contributed to the credit crises that the financial markets faced in late 2007/early 2008.

The problem is that banks are forced to underestimate losses they make on loans. For instance, if a borrower agrees a rate of Libor + 2% on a £1,000,000 loan for five years, but within a few months the credit quality of the borrower deteriorates so that it can only borrow at Libor + 8%, the bank has clearly made a loss on the loan of approximately 30% (the difference in the credit spread 6% × 5 years). The accounting standards generally do not permit recognition of the loss on the loan until the obligor defaults. This accounting rule increases the risk that a bank will underprice a loan because there is no obligation to recognise the loss to the shareholders.

Arrangement fees (IAS 39)

A possible motivation that encouraged banks to lend recklessly in the past was the ability to recognise up-front, profits that either should not have been recognised at all or should have been recognised over the life of the loan. An example illustrates the point in Table 2.5.

A corporate lending office is approached by a company that wants to borrow £10,000,000 for five years. The lending office estimates that there is a 4% chance that the company will go bankrupt, however they are anxious to improve short-term profitability and want the deal to go through regardless of the implications for the shareholder. By assisting the company in avoiding losses and concealing existing borrowings through off-balance sheet vehicles, the corporate lender is able to convince his credit committee that the loan has little or no risk and fixes the rate at approximately 7%. As soon as the loan is granted, the shareholder is facing a

Table 2.5 Loan details

Loan size	£10,000,000
Tenor (years)	5
Interest coupon	6 months
Fixed rate	7%
Libor	5%
Probability of default	4%
Daycount convention	a/365
Discount factor	0.708918814
Annuity factor	8.316605323
Repayment	£1,202,414

loss since the Libor rate is 5% and the probability of default is 4%. Therefore, the yield should be at least 9%. However, even if the auditor was suspicious of the deal he would be prevented, under both the old accounting standards and indeed under IFRS, from doing anything about it because the borrower has not defaulted.

Table 2.6 shows how the profit and loss is allocated. Under the 'cash flow' column, the principal that the borrower receives is shown at £10,000,000. The borrower agrees to make 10 repayments of £1,202,414, similar to a mortgage-style payment. The excess cash is £2,024,137. This is effectively the profit on the loan over the 10-year period and must be allocated to each of the 10 years. The method of doing this is to use the effective interest method. Under this method, the charge to the Profit & Loss account, expressed as a percentage of the opening balance, must be consistent from year to year. In this case, the effective interest rate is approximately 7%.

Table 2.7 shows that there is an economic loss to the shareholder by taking on this loan. Given that Libor rates are 5% and the credit spread should be approximately 4% (we assume in this simplified example that there is assumed to be no recovery if there is a default and so the credit spread reflects the probability of default), the true yield on the loan should be 5% + 4% = 9%. The loan therefore could be valued like a bond, i.e. discounting the future cash flows by the yield. As can be seen from the last column, the present value of the cash

Table 2.6 Allocation to Profit & Loss account

	Dates	Loan yield 7.00% Number of days	Opening balance	Profit & Loss	Cash flow	Closing balance
Period	01-Jan-08				£10,000,000	
1	30-Jun-08	181	£10,000,000	£347,339	−£1,202,414	£9,144,925
2	31-Dec-08	184	£9,144,925	£322,903	−£1,202,414	£8,265,415
3	30-Jun-09	181	£8,265,415	£287,090	−£1,202,414	£7,350,091
4	31-Dec-09	184	£7,350,091	£259,529	−£1,202,414	£6,407,206
5	30-Jun-10	181	£6,407,206	£222,547	−£1,202,414	£5,427,339
6	31-Dec-10	184	£5,427,339	£191,637	−£1,202,414	£4,416,563
7	30-Jun-11	181	£4,416,563	£153,404	−£1,202,414	£3,367,553
8	31-Dec-11	184	£3,367,553	£118,907	−£1,202,414	£2,284,047
9	30-Jun-12	182	£2,284,047	£79,772	−£1,202,414	£1,161,405
10	31-Dec-12	184	£1,161,405	£41,009	−£1,202,414	£0
				£2,024,137	−£2,024,137	

Table 2.7   Loan cash flow schedule

	Dates	Number of days	Yield Cash flow	9% Discount per period	Cumulative discount	
Period	01-Jan-08		£10,000,000			£10,000,000
1	30-Jun-08	181	−£1,202,414	0.9573	0.9573	−£1,151,042
2	31-Dec-08	184	−£1,202,414	0.9566	0.9157	−£1,101,086
3	30-Jun-09	181	−£1,202,414	0.9573	0.8766	−£1,054,044
4	31-Dec-09	184	−£1,202,414	0.9566	0.8386	−£1,008,298
5	30-Jun-10	181	−£1,202,414	0.9573	0.8027	−£965,220
6	31-Dec-10	184	−£1,202,414	0.9566	0.7679	−£923,329
7	30-Jun-11	181	−£1,202,414	0.9573	0.7351	−£883,881
8	31-Dec-11	184	−£1,202,414	0.9566	0.7032	−£845,520
9	30-Jun-12	182	−£1,202,414	0.9571	0.6730	−£809,205
10	31-Dec-12	184	−£1,202,414	0.9566	0.6438	−£774,085
			−£2,024,137			£484,289

inflows is less than the present value of the cash outflows. In effect this means that the bank has purchased a loan worth £9,515,711 (£10,000,000−£484,289). This represents the present value of the future cash flows on the loan. The auditor, however, is not expected to address this issue and may perhaps be prevented from doing so since this would involve impairing a loan that has not yet defaulted.

Although the IAS 39 standard has certain weaknesses, it has removed a problem area which allowed lenders to recognise profits prematurely and more importantly, to recognise profits on loans that were loss-making to begin with. Consider a case where the lender says to his customer, 'We will lend you £10,000,000 and accept 10 semi-annual payments of £1,202,414 per year, provided you accept the following term sheet' (Table 2.8).

Table 2.8   Revised term sheet

Loan size	£10,200,000
Fees to bank	£200,000
Yearly repayments	£1,202,414
Tenor	10

Obviously the loan size has increased from £10,000,000 to £10,200,000. The borrower, however, would not be unduly concerned since in pure cash flow terms he is receiving £10,000,000 and paying back £1,202,414 each year for the next 10 years. How the bank records the loan on its own books is really of no concern to the borrower, since the economics of the loan − i.e. the expected cash flows − stay the same. The benefit to the bank however is that, under the old accounting standards (pre IFRS), the bank could take an immediate profit of £200,000 up-front and then take a reduced yield in later years.

As Table 2.9 reveals, under pre-IFRS rules the bank was allowed to record a profit up-front of £200,000 on a loan which had an economic loss of £484,289. The effective interest for the remainder of the loan is 6.2255%. The final column shows the correct position. In essence, IFRS focuses on the cash flows and not on the legal form of the transaction. So, while the

IFRS standards have reduced the incentives for lending officers to make loss-making loans, they have not completely eliminated them.

Table 2.9   IFRS vs. pre-IFRS revenue recognition

	Dates	Loan yield Number of days	6.22% Opening balance	Pre-IFRS Profit & Loss	Cash flow	Closing balance	IFRS Profit & Loss
Period	01-Jan-08			£200,000	£10,000,000		£ –
1	30-Jun-08	181	£10,200,000	£314,707	−£1,202,414	£9,312,293	£347,339
2	31-Dec-08	184	£9,312,293	£292,080	−£1,202,414	£8,401,959	£322,903
3	30-Jun-09	181	£8,401,959	£259,231	−£1,202,414	£7,458,776	£287,090
4	31-Dec-09	184	£7,458,776	£233,944	−£1,202,414	£6,490,306	£259,529
5	30-Jun-10	181	£6,490,306	£200,249	−£1,202,414	£5,488,142	£222,547
6	31-Dec-10	184	£5,488,142	£172,135	−£1,202,414	£4,457,864	£191,637
7	30-Jun-11	181	£4,457,864	£137,541	−£1,202,414	£3,392,991	£153,404
8	31-Dec-11	184	£3,392,991	£106,421	−£1,202,414	£2,296,998	£118,907
9	30-Jun-12	182	£2,296,998	£71,262	−£1,202,414	£1,165,847	£79,772
10	31-Dec-12	184	£1,165,847	£36,567	−£1,202,414	£0	£41,009
				£2,024,137	−£2,024,137		£2,024,137

To recap, prior to the IFRS rules, fees on loans were recognised in the Profit & Loss account when receivable. Therefore a bank could, as shown, have originated a loan for £10,000,000 but put £10,200,000 on the documentation. Therefore, it was permitted to effectively show an asset for £10,200,000 on the balance sheet and a profit of £200,000 since it effectively bought the loan for £10,000,000. This poor accounting motivated lenders to take on loans regardless of the risks so that they could push up the Profit & Loss account, even on loss-making loans. IFRS does not permit this and is therefore a significant improvement.

Hedge and derivative accounting (IAS 39)

As Société Général discovered at the start of 2008, there are exposures to derivatives that, in terms of risk, set them apart from all other types of financial instruments. Derivatives are highly leveraged, meaning that their value changes significantly when there is a small change in say foreign exchange, interest rates, equity prices or commodity prices. In effect a trader can lose a lot more money than the cash he puts down. The exposure therefore is a lot greater than the cash paid up-front. With ordinary financial instruments, such as the purchase of bonds or shares, the trader cannot lose more than the purchase price. To deal with this, the accounting standards apply a special rule for derivatives that doesn't necessarily apply to other financial instruments. The rule is that the entity must calculate the market value or fair value of virtually all derivatives and show them as either assets or liabilities on the balance sheet. This process is known as 'marking to market'. Furthermore, any change in the value of the derivative must go through the Profit & Loss account, creating huge volatility. The only way that an entity using derivatives can avoid this excessive volatility is to apply hedge accounting. This type of accounting can be confusing and is certainly controversial. It allows an entity to temporarily put any profit or loss on a derivative through the Equity Reserve or adjust the underlying asset or liability (i.e. the asset or liability being hedged) by the change in the value of the derivative. The controversy surrounding hedge accounting stems from the fact that it is difficult to implement and can often lead to very confusing and misleading results. The IFRS have tried to address this issue by using what is known as the 'fair value option'. This gives banks more flexibility and allows them to virtually treat all financial instruments using a consistent accounting policy. The complexities of hedge accounting are dealt with later in this book.

Classification of assets (IAS 39)

Assets are normally classified as either Held to Maturity, Loans & Receivables, Trading or Available for Sale.

Held to Maturity assets are, as the name implies, assets that are bought with the intention of holding to maturity. Normally, if during the period of ownership, the asset's value goes up or down this is ignored since it will have no bearing on the cash flows. Therefore, a fixed coupon loan, for instance, would be recorded at cost on the balance sheet and its value would not be allowed to vary on the balance sheet even if market circumstances such as a change in interest rates altered the market value of the loan. This could mean that an asset is shown on the balance sheet at above market price; therefore, the entity has made losses which will not appear in its Profit & Loss account. The exception to this is if a credit event occurs, i.e. the borrower fails to pay when due – the asset must then be written down with the difference going through the Profit & Loss account.

Trading assets, on the other hand, are assets bought with the intention of selling before maturity. Unlike Held to Maturity assets, these assets must be shown on the balance sheet at market value and any change in the market value must go through the Profit & Loss account. An important practical difference between Trading assets and Held to Maturity assets from an accounting perspective is that it is much easier to account for Trading assets, which are hedged, than to account for Held to Maturity assets. This is because when Trading assets are hedged with derivatives, both the derivative and the underlying asset have a consistent accounting treatment, namely they are shown at market value and the difference goes through the Profit & Loss account. Obviously, if the hedge is working correctly, the gain on the derivative will offset the loss on the underlying and vice versa. Therefore, the Profit & Loss account will remain broadly unaffected if the derivative changes value. The same cannot be said for Held to Maturity assets. Therefore, if a bank converts a floating bond to a fixed bond by using an interest rate swap, that swap must be marked to market and the difference must go through the Profit & Loss account but the entity is not allowed to carry the underlying bond at market value. The result is artificial volatility in the Profit & Loss account which does not reflect economic reality.

A third category of financial instrument is Loans & Receivables. As mentioned earlier, financial institutions such as banks tend to break down their balance sheet between the 'banking book' and the 'trading book'. The banking book consists of traditional banking activities such as borrowing from one set of customers and lending to another. The trading book consists of proprietary trading and market-making activities. The term 'Loans & Receivables' refers to assets and liabilities in the banking book. Although most Loans & Receivables are shown at cost in the balance sheet, they have two important differences compared with Held to Maturity assets. Firstly, hedge accounting is permitted and secondly, it is possible to sell an asset before maturity without creating accounting complications. On the other hand, if an asset is classified as 'Held to Maturity' and is sold before maturity then the entire Held to Maturity portfolio must be reclassified and shown on the balance sheet at market value as opposed to cost. It is for this reason that many banks have a policy of not classifying anything as 'Held to Maturity'. Another difference is that the accounting standards permit hedge accounting on assets classified as Loans & Receivables but not on Held to Maturity assets.

2.14 CONCLUSION

An increase in the use of financial instruments over the last two decades has put considerable pressure on the accounting standards. The accounting model used for generations is flawed in that some assets are shown at cost on the balance sheet while others are shown at market value. Showing assets at cost has the advantage that the rules are simple and relatively easy to apply. The auditor simply needs to check the invoice to confirm the value. However, there are loopholes. Where assets are not shown at the correct value on the balance sheet it is easy for an entity, through cherry-picking opportunities, to hide losses and/or create an accounting profit. Needless to say, bonus-hungry executives have put pressure on accountants and auditors to stretch the accounting standards as much as possible. Rather than overhaul the accounting standards completely, the standard setters have instead taken a reactive approach – i.e. waited until a creative accounting event, such as Enron, exposed the weaknesses of the standards before coming up with rules to close the loopholes. Allowing entities to keep derivatives off-balance sheet, which was the case prior to IAS 39, certainly caused problems and abuses. However, it is questionable whether the solution (i.e. to bring some but not all assets on to the balance sheet) is working. Certainly, the changes brought about by IFRS has closed some loopholes, but the side-effect of this medicine is that it has created a huge amount of complexity, inconsistencies between the rules and therefore the need for layers of little rules to deal with the inconsistencies. The EU has objected to some of these rules and the accounting profession has responded with even more rules to alleviate some of the inconsistencies. The result is a confusing environment where financial institutions and some corporate entities are allowed to pick accounting policies which enable them to hide losses and risks. This lack of consistency does suggest that the accounting standards need a significant structural change, to overcome the off-balance sheet abuses. In reality, this is unlikely to take place. There is a huge lobby protecting the interests of traders/directors on huge bonuses who would prefer to allow sleeping dogs to lie. The next chapter focuses on the corporate governance problems that cause the standards to remain as weak as they are. In particular, we focus on the pressures facing the accounting profession resulting from the fact that those with voting power on ordinary shares may not be held accountable when they make decisions which are not to the benefit of the shareholders. As long as this conflict of interest exists, there will be pressure on accountants to conceal losses and hide what is truly going on. Progress towards improving the accounting standards is likely to remain affected until this problem is addressed.

3
Corporate Governance

3.1 INTRODUCTION

'When the music stops, in terms of liquidity, things will be complicated. But as long as the music is playing, you've got to get up and dance. We're still dancing.' This is the famous quote by Chuck Prince, former Chairman and Chief Executive of Citigroup, who was forced into retirement when Citigroup wrote off huge losses on structured financial instruments. He was commenting on the American sub-prime crisis. The quote, which was made just weeks before he retired, has generated quite a lot of column inches in the financial press. The comment possibly shows a disregard for shareholders. Citibank knowingly took huge risks with shareholders' money and earned generous fees for doing so. The problem is that many of these fees ended up as big bonuses for the directors, yet when things turned sour, it was the shareholder who suffered. One can see the pressures that the accounting profession faces in such an environment. There is the temptation to hide risks and so recognise revenue prematurely, contrary to IAS 18, and there is the temptation to hide risks from the shareholder, contrary to IFRS 7. One wonders if he would have taken the same sentiment if he risked his own private money rather than that of the shareholders of Citigroup. Perhaps he would have tried to anticipate the risks and concluded that even though the 'music is still playing' it has to stop at some point and it is better to bail out sooner and avoid huge losses rather than wait for the inevitable. Complex structured products, which Citibank uses, are a little like the game 'pass the parcel'. A financial institution buys them, puts them into a new more complicated structure and then sells them to another financial institution at a higher price, and they then do the same thing. At some stage, the parcel becomes very complicated, very expensive and very illiquid. Nevertheless, it is packaged in such a way that it produces a high yield, allowing banks to record an accounting profit. As soon as the music stops, someone is going to end up with a product he cannot sell, and if he has borrowed money to do so, he ends up in considerable trouble. The fact that he has kept this product 'off-balance sheet' will not help him. The lenders will want their money back and if the bank has no borrowing facilities problems will, of course, emerge. A question mark arises over why banks bother with these complex products. There are much easier ways to get credit exposure without resorting to such needless complexity. Yet, it is a feature of today's sophisticated banks that they are happy (or at least were happy) to spend shareholders' money on complex products that they didn't always understand. In the analysis of the credit crunch that regulators are likely to consider in the future, attention will be placed on who exactly is buying these products and if there is a correlation between investing in these difficult complex products and corporate governance. As long as corporate governance is poor, there is pressure on the accountant to paint a picture that the directors like, and this picture may be very different from economic reality. Complex structured products allow this flexibility.

3.2 CORPORATE GOVERNANCE

There are a few matters on corporate governance that both the accountant and the investor need to be aware of. Without this awareness, the accountant is tempted to accept whatever value is given for financial assets and liabilities, which may prove to be wrong. First of all, if a client cannot justify the use of a complex structured product that he has invested in, be suspicious. Often, they themselves don't know or understand what they are buying, in which case the investment bank selling the product is likely to extract huge fees and give the investor an asset that is overvalued. The accounting standards, as we shall see later, effectively require the accountant to break down structured products into their components and, where necessary, apply fair value or mark-to-market accounting. The process, covered in IAS 39, is known as bifurcation. If this is done correctly, the huge fees that the investor has paid for the structured product will appear as an up-front loss on his balance sheet. If the investor does understand the product, the motivation to buy the structured product may be accounting in nature, i.e. the need to hide losses, etc. An opportunity does exist to do so with certain structured products because of their very complex nature.

Rewarding directors and traders for failure is another red flag that the accountant needs to be concerned with. In short, if a director is rewarded for failure he can walk away from losses and so is tempted to take huge risks. The temptation then is to hide the risks and also hide the losses for as long as possible. IFRS 7 requires disclosures on risk and if an accountant does not understand the basics of risk management, then he is unlikely to pick up the salient features of risk within the entity that the shareholder should know about. Regulation, particularly in financial institutions, is necessary. Bear Stearns, for instance, was so big that the American taxpayer was forced to rescue it. Basel 2 rules are designed to ensure that banks don't fail (even though they did not necessarily apply to Bear Stearns). Accountants need to be aware of Basel 2 because if the regulators decide that a bank is subsidising a securitisation by taking responsibility for the risks, without receiving adequate compensation, then the accountant must consider doing likewise, i.e. bringing the asset on to the balance sheet. This is discussed in more detail later, in Chapter 8. Accountants of financial entities will find it easier to disclose information on risk (in accordance with IFRS 7) if they understand how Basel 2 measures risk. From a corporate governance perspective, the accountant should realise that many financial institutions are powerful enough to pay only lip service to risk management. As pointed out in earlier chapters, a banking executive interested in maximising his bonus will be tempted to take on as much risk as possible and conceal what he is doing. This is not altogether impossible. There are flaws in Basel 2, which essentially focuses on mathematical models to determine how much risk a bank is taking. Unfortunately, the model doesn't focus on the fact that a bank which gives incentives to directors to take risk is much riskier than a bank which forces directors to absorb personally some of the losses they create. Also, as the British regulators realised with Northern Rock, regulators often lack the resources or do not have enough clout to force a bank to reduce risk. The accounting standards are not always helpful in stopping this practice. It is important, therefore, not to ignore the moral hazard that arises when directors and traders can walk away from losses. Usually, losses represent a signal that there is something wrong which needs to be corrected. However, if losses and risks can be hidden, there is a temptation to keep going while the music is playing. One could argue, therefore, that the bonus system does not encourage self-correction in the financial world. It probably explains why accountants continue to be caught out by off-balance sheet problems, as highlighted by Terry Smith in *Accounting for Growth* (Century Business Press,

1992) almost 20 years ago. The incentive scheme may also explain why the accounting profession was slow to introduce rules requiring entities to show as an expense, share options granted to employees (now covered under IFRS 2).

3.3 SMALL VS. LARGE SHAREHOLDINGS

There is often an assumption amongst small shareholders that if large financial institutions co-own companies with them then all is well. The large financial institutions will have strong research teams, along with an abundance of expertise. In addition, they have the power, through their huge voting block, to do something about weak corporate governance, i.e. voting off directors or at least making them more accountable for their actions. However, what small shareholders may not necessarily realise is firstly that these financial institutions may have other relations with the companies apart from owning shares. The financial institution, for instance, may have a corporate finance arm which earns huge fees from takeovers and raising finance. Therefore, the financial institution may use their votes to maximise their fees and not necessarily to look after the interests of their shareholders. A second problem is that the financial institution may not have beneficial interest in the shares that they vote with. For instance, a client may ask a financial institution to construct a Contract for Difference (CFD) on a particular share. In essence, a CFD is where the client borrows money from the financial institution and uses it to buy an underlying share. The benefit to the client is that he can gain a lot of exposure without paying too much money up-front. The bank, however, also benefits. Apart from a fee, the bank buys the share to construct the CFD and then passes on the beneficial interest through the CFD to the client. The bank is therefore left with voting rights on a share that it has no beneficial interest in. If the share price subsequently goes up or down, it is the client who takes the risk (the beneficial interest) and not the bank. Therefore, the bank is left with voting rights and may use these to win a corporate finance, etc. In extreme cases, the bank may buy credit protection against the company defaulting and so use the voting power to force the company to become more risky. This pushes up the value of the credit protection and allows the bank to make a profit by voting in a manner which is destructive to shareholder value. Needless to say, these corporate governance problems put pressure on accountants. Some voters and some directors may feel that it is in their interest to act in a destructive manner, or at least in a manner where the shareholder does not benefit. The need, therefore, to cover up what is going on becomes paramount. Accountants and auditors have of course a duty to reveal losses and comment on the risk profile of the company. Few annual reports, however, will disclose the extent to which the above problems contribute to the risk profile of an entity. The ability to hide problems and to walk away from problems of their own making illustrates the slowness of the self-correcting mechanisms within not only the accounting profession but also the markets themselves. Indeed, many commentators, including George Soros, now believe that the markets cannot correct themselves and will therefore rely on regulators and the taxpayer for a lifeboat. The accounting standards, of course, are not completely responsible for this but one could argue that they do contribute in some small way.

Financial institutions such as Citibank and UBS have spent years building up expertise and experience on the management of credit. They are also aware of the consequences of complex structured products, namely that they are difficult to value, difficult to account for and easy to hide losses in. As regards the credit rating agencies, the financial institutions will have realised who pays the fees of such agencies and therefore the conflict of interest that exists.

Finally, they will know of the 'moral hazard' problem with securitisation, namely that if a bank is going to originate a loan and then sell it, the bank will not worry too much about the consequences of the loan and will therefore be more willing to lend to individuals who cannot afford to pay. Clearly, investing in complex securitisations is a risky business yet these banks did so and, in many cases, acted against the interests of their shareholders, creating huge losses. As stated in earlier chapters, the accounting standards, or at least a flexible and liberal interpretation of the accounting standards, allow traders to recognise profits prematurely and to hide losses. If directors are unwilling to change things, why don't shareholders? They, in theory, are the owners of the entity and therefore could sack directors if they encourage a bonus scheme that acts against their interests and they could of course dismiss auditors if they felt that the auditors were allowing directors and traders to conceal losses and create artificial profits. The problem could potentially boil down to a lack of voting power. The divorcing of beneficial interest from voting power means that those who vote are not always held accountable for the damage they inflict. Few corporate governance experts would deny that everything is working smoothly. There are certainly conflicts of interest that the regulators will be interested in identifying as they try to examine what extra regulation is necessary to prevent speculative banks remaining a threat to the financial system and a burden on the taxpayer when the markets experience volatility. In the meantime, while the problem exists, there will be pressure on auditors and accountants to prop up the current system by concealing what is going on. This somewhat gloomy analysis does suggest that the accounting standard setters have limited control over good corporate governance and will continue to face lobbying if they attempt to improve the accounting standards, particularly where these improvements lead to a reduction of high but inappropriate bonuses.

When Stan O'Neal retired from Merrill Lynch following the disclosure of $7.9bn of losses, an editorial in the *Financial Times* pointed out that a cushion for his humiliating retirement was a payoff of $160 million.[1] The editorial also pointed out that this reward for failure would cover the current salaries of the seven-member Federal Reserve Board for 160 years. The grim calculation reveals how the financial community allocates a lot more resources and power to banking directors and traders and very little to the regulators, middle office and back office. An argument, of course, in favour of the huge pay disparity is that the regulators have a comfortable job for life while bank chief executives are being rewarded not only for their expertise but also for the risks that they undertake. Perhaps, but the risk they undertake is borne not by themselves but by the shareholders and, in the case of Bear Stearns and Northern Rock, the taxpayer.

3.4 TRADERS' DILEMMA

It is very important to realise that if we are investing our own money we behave a lot differently than when we invest other people's money. In the case of the former, we attempt to measure risks and compare them against potential rewards. Intuitively, we try to decide if the rewards justify the risks. When institutions who manage our pension funds invest the money they too concentrate on the rewards. A fund, for instance, that performs well means higher fees for the institution and of course if an institution outperforms its peers, there will be even higher rewards as past performance does attract new business. But how do these institutions

---

[1] 'O'Neal pays a price', *Financial Times*, 2 November 2007.

measure risk? The answer is that a number of them don't bother because the regulators are not looking closely enough at them, or at least they go through the motions of measuring risk without paying much attention to the results. The accountants add to the problem by not always reporting the losses properly and the credit rating agencies may be tempted to give a high rating despite the fact that the investments could be risky. Where profits are very high, the bank's chief executive gets a huge bonus as well as plaudits on Wall Street for being an outstanding banker. However, where huge losses are made, the chief executive effectively walks away from losses by 'retiring' and receives a hefty compensation package for his loss of earnings. His ego might indeed suffer from the substantial losses but with a compensation package of sometimes around $200 million, the adverse publicity will not cause excessive hardship.

Chuck Prince, the former Chief Executive and Chairman of Citibank, 'retired' in November 2007 in a week when Citibank announced additional losses of $11 billion due to the credit turmoil. According to John Gapper of the *Financial Times*, 'Citibank may have used the word "retire" rather than the less dignified "resign" or "sacked" because a chief executive who "retires" can get a more generous payoff than one who is sacked or forced to resign'.[2] Also, Mr Gapper commented on the departure of Stan O'Neal from Merrill Lynch, 'Merrill Lynch's rules said that Mr. O'Neill, had his departure been described as a resignation rather than a retirement, would not have been eligible to collect the restricted shares which he had not yet got his hands on'. Most corporate governance specialists would have described the bonuses of both banks as rewards of failure. Clearly, a bonus system that rewards success as well as failure is bound to encourage banks to take excessive risks with shareholders' funds. In his article in the *Financial Times*, Raghuram Rajan exposed a problem with Merrill Lynch: 'For example, Morgan Stanley announced a $9.4 billion charge-off in the fourth quarter and at the same time increased its bonus pool by 18 per cent.'[3] Rajan went on to comment, 'Indeed, compensation practices in the financial sector are deeply flawed and probably contributed to the ongoing crises'. Rajan also laid bare the attractions of Collateralised Debt Obligations (CDOs). Although these bonds produced excess returns compared with similarly rated corporate bonds, the excess return was compensation for the 'tail' risk of the CDO, 'a risk that was no doubt perceived as small when the housing market was rollicking along, but which was not zero'. Rajan continued, 'if all the manager had disclosed was the high rating of his investment portfolio he would have looked like a genius, making money without additional risk, even more so if he multiplied his "excess returns" by leverage'.

3.5 MORAL HAZARD

The problem with inappropriate bonus systems is that chief executives act in a manner that enhances their own bonuses while destroying shareholder value. It came as no great surprise to corporate governance specialists in the City of London that City bonuses reached record levels of GBP 8.8 billion only months before the same financial institutions were forced to recognise huge losses. The moral hazard arises because when City institutions make huge profits, traders and chief executives take the lion's share of those profits but when losses are

---

[2] 'Sadly, it pays to retire disgracefully', *Financial Times*, 8 November 2007.

[3] Raghuram Rajan, 'Bankers' pay is deeply flawed', *Financial Times*, 8 January 2008.

made, traders and chief executives simply move out of the firm (after receiving a generous bonus package).

An accountant or regulator who does not understand this relatively simple but dangerous relationship between risk and bonuses runs the risk of helping shareholders to lose money. Clearly, a chief executive who is in this position is unlikely to give it up lightly. Therefore, the temptation to inflate profits and hide losses is overwhelming. The trick is to use complex structured products such as 'inverse floaters', CDOs and structured investment vehicles. In many cases, the accounting profession will have difficulty in valuing these instruments and so they are effectively kept off-balance sheet. Losses are therefore hidden and so bank chief executives can enjoy handsome bonuses even when they are causing a huge destruction of shareholder value.

Banks have attempted to align bonuses with the long-term as opposed to the short-term performance of their share price. The logic behind this is that the bonuses of directors are aligned with those of the shareholders, particularly long-term shareholders. However, unfortunately, there is evidence that boards of directors often allow chief executives to claim their entitlement to unvested stock when things go wrong. What is worrying too is that this is a recent phenomenon. When Salomon Brothers collapsed following a treasury bond scandal in 1991, Warren Buffet – who stepped in as chief executive – blocked the severance payoff of its former risk-taking chief executive. Neither was he allowed to exercise options he held on shares. What appears to be happening therefore is that bonus schemes are becoming less and less effective. Option traders realise that the more volatile the earnings of a bank are, the more valuable the call options on the shares of the company are. If shareholders continue to grant options to directors, the directors are motivated to make the earnings more volatile and are therefore motivated to take more risks. Unfortunately, both the credit rating agencies and the accounting profession, who in theory should act as watchdogs against this abuse, are in fact encouraging it by failing to disclose the risks and losses that shareholders suffer.

3.6 CREDIT RATING AGENCIES I

There is a substantial body of evidence suggesting that innovation in the financial markets is doing little more than allowing banking directors and traders to participate in profits but walk away from losses. In November 2006, the financial press wrote extensively about investment institutions buying complex financial credit products which they most likely didn't understand.

CPDOs (Constant Proportion Debt Obligations) are one case in point. They are extraordinarily complex and most probably overpriced but nevertheless very profitable for the issuers. What is extraordinary is that the rating agencies gave these lethal products a triple-A rating. Fixed income managers are interested in anything that has a triple-A rating and pays a high yield. In the case of CPDOs, the yield was two percentage points over Libor and therefore fixed income managers could effectively borrow at Libor and earn a net yield of 2%. The increase over Libor is due primarily to the fact that the exposure is 15 times leveraged (an indication of how risky the product is). The small print also focuses on the fact that once purchased, it may be difficult to sell before maturity (known as liquidity risk). The rating agencies, along with the issuers of such an instrument, will argue that all the risks were disclosed in the small print. That may be the case, but the big question is why someone would buy these products? The answer is probably that they are spending other people's money. If all goes well, they will make a profit but if things go badly, they can walk away from the losses.

3.7 SHAREHOLDER DEMOCRACY

Another factor that may be contributing to the corporate governance problem is the lack of shareholder democracy. There are two issues here. Firstly, not all shareholders are treated equally. Complex rules within some banks and corporates mean that some shareholders have more power over their company than others, an area that EU Commissioner Charlie McCreevy tried unsuccessfully to address.[4] However, even if this problem is solved, there is another issue. Many pension funds, insurance funds and trade unions have voting power but very often they either don't use it or, if they do, they don't always disclose how they use it.

Consider a situation where an investment bank buys a substantial shareholding in company X on behalf of a pension fund which it manages. The bank, since they control the shares, would of course have voting rights but since they are holding the shares in trust for the pension fund, they do not have a beneficial interest. In effect this means that if the share price falls it is the pension fund that suffers and not necessarily the bank.

In theory, the bank should use its votes in the best interests of the pension fund. Therefore, if the directors of the company are underperforming, the investment bank should consider firing the directors, or at least implementing a bonus scheme that penalises the directors if they underperform. However, in reality, the investment bank may have some other relationship with the company that they have invested in. They may, for instance, be trying to obtain corporate finance work or they may be clients from the derivative desk. The investment bank therefore may vote in a manner that suits itself and not the pension fund. The example above illustrates that shareholder democracy doesn't necessarily work in practice all the time. The largest shareholders of any company are pension funds and insurance companies, and those exercising the votes may not feel inclined to vote in the interests of their beneficial owners. Small shareholders of course have both a beneficial as well as a voting interest in their shares, but they are too small to make an impact.

There is growing concern that the explosion in share lending and unregulated equity futures and CFDs is hampering good corporate governance. A study carried out by Professors Henry T.C. Hu and Bernard Black of the University of Texas suggested that the divorce from beneficial ownership and voting has had an impact on shareholder value. Consider a situation where a hedge fund buys credit protection on a company and also 'rents', from a pension fund, a substantial voting block. The hedge fund may use its power to encourage the company to take on more and more risk. The hedge fund could, for instance, influence the board of directors to acquire (and overpay) for another company financing the takeover by borrowings. The hedge fund benefits because the value of the credit insurance increases substantially as the company becomes more risky. The entity running the pension fund also benefits because it receives a fee for 'renting' its voting rights. It is the pensioners themselves – i.e. those with a beneficial interest in the economic performance of the shares – that suffer, along of course with the other shareholders in the company that the hedge fund has targeted. Even if the regulators do understand what is going on, it can be very difficult for them to take action. Often the transfer of voting power is done through private agreement between the hedge fund and the pension

---

[4] 'Brussels drops shareholder plan', *Financial Times*, 4 October 2007.

fund. Neither the regulator nor the other shareholders know what is going on. And, while the company directors may suspect that something underhand is happening, they may not have enough clout or independence to do anything about it. There is evidence that the regulators are, however, trying to grapple with the problem. The UK Takeover Panel now requires certain derivative holders to disclose their identity, in certain instances, where their stake exceeds 1%. The US regulators are also examining instances where a change in disclosure rules would help corporate governance.

In 2007, Perry Corp (a hedge fund) owned 7m shares in King Pharmaceuticals. Another company, Mylan Laboratories, agreed to buy King at a substantial premium. However, Mylan shares dropped on the announcement, threatening the deal. Perry therefore bought 9.9% shares in Mylan to support the transaction but neutralised the beneficial interest by hedging. Perry therefore had a large voting block in Mylan and also, through their ownership of shares in King Pharmaceuticals, would have benefited if Mylan overpaid for the shares in King. Here there was a clear conflict of interest. Perry could, of course, force Mylan to overpay for King Pharmaceuticals and allow the hedge fund to simultaneously benefit from the deal while causing the shareholders of Mylan to suffer a share price drop.

The same hedge fund was also involved with a New Zealand company, Rubicon (a biotechnology and timber company). In June 2001, the hedge fund said that it held less than 5% of Rubicon. In July 2002, however, it announced holding 16% of Rubicon. The hedge fund bought the shares but also entered into a derivative contract whereby it passed on the economic interest to UBS and Deutsche Bank. It was therefore left with voting power and no economic interest. The hedge fund was able to vote on shares that they did not effectively own.

The corporate governance damage should be glaringly clear. Borrowing shares to vote with them without any economic interest is very dangerous. There is a severe shortage of regulation, particularly US regulation, which means that those who have a vested interest in bringing a company down can do so quite easily and legally.

Charlie McCreevy, the European Commissioner responsible for developing Europe's single market, attempted to correct a flaw in shareholder democracy but faced huge protests. He eventually had to abandon his fight facing (according to the *Financial Times*) opposition from big businesses and several governments. His concern was to align shareholder voting power with shareholder beneficial interest. Apparently, other member states such as Sweden, France and Spain opposed the move. In the UK and Ireland, one share/one vote is the norm and is considered good corporate governance practice. According to Guy Jubb, Head of Corporate Governance at Standard Life Investments, 'It is a principle which provides a level playing field for all shareholders and it provides an incentive for them to exercise their ownership rights'. The problem with giving shareholders voting rights disproportionate to their beneficial interest is that they can immunise companies against takeover, protect weak management and incubate inefficiencies. Often, too, companies can launch takeovers at inflated prices, thus destroying shareholder value. Not only are they prevented from stopping such a deal, they may also not see the true extent of the losses, since in many cases companies that acquire other companies at inflated prices can bury their losses in goodwill.

3.8 STRUCTURED PRODUCTS

As stated earlier, there is the possibility of a link between poor corporate governance and the use of complex structured products. People are quite happy to buy structured products with other people's money but, unless they did not know what they were doing, would not buy these products with their own money. In general, complex structured products are difficult to understand and this lack of transparency allows the manufacturers of these products to make huge fees from their customers without disclosing them. It is also important to realise that structured products by their nature are inefficient. They create huge operational risks both for the manufacturer and the buyer, and involve a lot of expensive resources for their construction. The costs (of the manufacturer), along with their huge fees, are passed on to the naive purchaser. Needless to say, because of their complexity, they are very risky and illiquid. Therefore, in times of difficulty, the purchaser has difficulty in selling them. What appears to have happened, in the current credit crises, is that banks themselves bought these products, financed them through short-term loans and kept them in structured investment vehicles (i.e. off-balance sheet). Many people will be surprised that they could get away with this. The technicalities of structured products and their accounting are discussed in a later chapter.

If structured products are complicated, illiquid, expensive and dangerous, why are sophisticated financial institutions motivated to buy them? The answer may be simple. If the credit rating agencies give them a seal of approval (a triple-A rating), the purchaser will make the assumption (wrongly) that they are not risky. It may be that the purchaser knows from experience that structured products are 'weapons of mass destruction', but if the rating agencies say they are not then the banker can rely on this seal of approval to convince shareholders that he did not act improperly in buying them. What makes structured products attractive to anyone investing other people's money is the 'reward now/risk later' phenomenon. At the risk of oversimplification, a structured product salesperson can tell a potential investor 'if you buy this product now you will see an instant increase in your bonus. In the long term it may prove risky, but if it goes up in value you can cash it in and if it falls in value the loss can be hidden in some offshore vehicle.'

For decades, financial institutions have lost small fortunes from the use of structured products and continue to do so. The accounting standards have responded in a positive manner. There are special 'bifurcation rules' contained in IAS 39 which effectively require purchasers of structured products to recognise a loss immediately if they overpay for a structured product; the technicalities will be discussed later. There are two reasons, however, why it is difficult to implement these rules in practice. Firstly, as pointed out, structured products are complex and often beyond the accountant's comprehension. The IAS 39 rules require that the accountant identifies the derivatives used to create the structured product and identifies their market or fair value. As a general guideline, however, if the structured product is exposed to market risk, i.e. interest rate, foreign exchange rate or equity price changes, then bifurcation is possible, even if difficult. The same cannot be said for credit risk where data is difficult to obtain, owing to the relatively low incidence of credit default. There is a possibility, therefore, that banks have moved away from structured products with market risk to structured products with credit risk. Bifurcation is more difficult, so there is a strong likelihood that the accountant will get the accounting wrong, leaving them off the balance sheet, which is what many bankers want. In addition, the increased complexity allows for greater fees which are harder for the investor to identify.

Orange County

The scandal that caught the attention of the accounting standard setters in America was the bankruptcy of Orange County, California where the 70-year-old treasurer was responsible for

$1.7 billion in losses, mainly through gambling with structured products. Needless to say, many questions were raised as to what happened. A contributor to the losses was the fact that fee-hungry structured salesmen from Wall Street had found an investor, in charge of a huge budget, who was prepared to invest other people's money in complex structured products that he didn't understand. The rating agencies raised a few eyebrows by giving these structured products a triple-A rating. The banks therefore had little difficulty in selling these products, which were 'structured' to get around the oversimplified investment guidelines devised by Orange County. The main types of structured products used were 'inverse floaters'. These bonds, whose market prices are extremely sensitive to changes in interest rates, are suitable for investors who want to speculate on interest rates falling. If, for instance, interest rates do fall, the inverse floaters could make a lot of money for the investor because of their leveraged nature. However, if interest rates rise, the losses can be substantial. There are, of course, huge fees loaded on to these products which, because of their complexity, the investor is unaware of. Frank Partnoy[5] described the treasurer of Orange County, Robert Citron, as 'a big, public version of Jim Johnsen of Gibson Greetings, the company that unknowingly paid more than $10 million in fees from the interest-rate bets it bought from Bankers Trust'. The problem for both Orange County and Gibson Greetings was that interest rates rose and because the structured products were very leveraged, both entities lost colossal amounts of money. A Merrill Lynch structured products salesman described Mr Citron as 'a highly sophisticated, experienced, and knowledgeable investor, I learned a lot from him'.

The rating agencies came in for criticism for this episode. They earned substantial fees for rating Orange County's bond. They received more fees for rating the structured products that Orange County invested in. Also, there is evidence that they were aware of Orange County's difficulties more than six months before Orange County's bankruptcy. They failed to adjust their ratings of Orange County despite this knowledge. According to Partnoy:[6]

> the rating agencies collected substantial fees for rating Orange County's bonds. They collected even greater fees for rating structured notes. The fees raised questions about whether the agencies had been objective in assessing Orange County's risks. More than six months before Orange County's bankruptcy, the agencies had learned about Citron's losses on structured notes, but they kept this information secret and didn't adjust their ratings in response.

Ten years later one would have hoped that the vicious cycle of naive investors, using other people's money to buy products they don't understand from fee-hungry structured derivatives salesmen, would have stopped – apparently not. Recently, JP Morgan found itself in hot water when the Greek government launched an investigation into a deal under which four Greek pension funds became involved in the purchase of €280 million of structured bonds.[7] The bonds were apparently sold at an unfavourable price to the pension funds through a chain of deals involving a number of financial institutions, including North Asset Management, HypoVereinsbank (a German lender) and Acropolis (a local Greek brokerage). A complaint was launched against JPMorgan with the US Securities and Exchange Commission. The complaint, brought by a Greek trade union, alleged that JPMorgan was 'deeply involved' in the sale of a complex financial instrument to unsophisticated buyers. Most Greek

[5] Frank Partnoy, *Infectious Greed*, Profile Books Ltd, 2003, p. 116.

[6] Frank Partnoy, *Infectious Greed*, Profile Books Ltd, 2003, p. 119.

[7] Kerin Hope, 'JPMorgan settles Greek bond dispute', *Financial Times*, 24 August 2007.

state pension funds are managed by trustees who are political appointees as opposed to finance professionals. Commenting on the Greek scandal, Gillian Tett observed:

> But these bonds were bought by local Greek pension funds at a price that will almost certainly produce future hefty losses. .... It transpires that Greek funds have bought numerous similarly overpriced instruments in recent years. In their defense, JPMorgan said it behaved in good faith and had decided not to sell bonds to the Greek pension funds because of the possible reputation risk.[8]

It appears that fee-hungry salesmen have also discovered that municipal authorities in Norway are quite happy to invest taxpayers' money in structured products that they don't understand. They invested €65 million in bonds designed by Citigroup and sold to them by Terra Securities, affiliated to one of Norway's big banking groups. The officials who bought these bonds attempted to defend their position by blaming Terra Securities. Arne Sorensen, employed by the municipal authority in Norway, suggested he was badly served by Terra. Apparently, he received two documents, one in Norwegian and one in English, and commented 'we only read the Norwegian one but it seems there is a huge difference between the two as the Norwegian document didn't contain all the risks'. Citigroup and Terra claim they disclosed all the risks to the Norwegian authorities. There is a simple solution to the Norway and Greece crises: don't spend other people's money on products you don't understand. If you are relying on fee-hungry salesmen to disclose all the risks in a clear and concise way, you are putting local authority and pension money at risk.

3.9   REVENUE RECOGNITION

A recent article in the *Financial Times* suggests that banks may be openly flouting the revenue recognition rules of IAS 18.[9] According to James Mackintosh, investment banks are offering subsidised loans to 'vulture funds' on improved terms if the money is used to buy debt from them. Some banks are keen to sell leveraged buyout debt and are looking for ways to get these risky loss-making securities off the balance sheet. According to one hedge fund manager who recently set up a 'vulture fund', 'the banks are offering different terms depending on whether you take their loans or other people's loans'. The risk from an accounting perspective is that by hiding the discount, the loan is overpriced and so the bank may be able to avoid recognising a loss or impairment. A second problem is that if the vulture fund relies exclusively on the bank selling the loans for finance, the bank may have to consider consolidating the vulture fund. The accounting rules surrounding this are at best grey – they are discussed in more detail in Chapter 9.

Revenue recognition, or at least premature revenue recognition, is an issue that has caused the accounting standard setters many problems. In the lax day of the dot.com era part of the explosion in technology share prices arose from the ability of accountants to inflate sales revenue figures. They were, for instance, able to record as sales revenue projected sales and instances where companies claimed they had sold assets or services at inflated prices even though the alleged purchaser made no commitment. So serious was the problem that the American regulators who found the FASB a little slow on this matter themselves wrote a type of

---

[8] Gillian Tett, 'Beware Greek pension funds bearing risk', *Financial Times*, 4 May 2007.

[9] James Mackintosh, 'Banks tempt "vulture funds" to shift $200bn debt backlog', *Financial Times*, 5 October 2007.

accounting standard on revenue recognition entitled SAB 101. The document was designed to remind accountants to use their common sense when deciding what constitutes a sale. Outlawed as a sale, for example, are instances where the entity lends money to the customer and tells the customer that if he buys an asset and the asset falls in value, the seller will simply take back the product and forgive the loan. The rationale behind this is that the owner has not lost beneficial interest in the asset sold in those circumstances. The FASB eventually devised revenue recognition rules, as did the International Accounting Standards Board. IAS 18.14 only permits entities to record revenue when the entity transfers to the buyer the risks and rewards of ownership. It also assumes that the 'fair value' used to calculate the revenue is the amount for which an asset could be exchanged, or a liability settled, between knowledgeable, willing parties in an arm's length transaction.

Another area where the revenue recognition rules may be breached is where banks buy complex triple-A rated bonds and simultaneously buy credit protection from an insurance company. A complex bond might produce a yield of, say, 10% over five years and a bank may be able to borrow at 6% and buy insurance protection against credit risk of 1%. This gives an additional yield of 3%. Can the bank take that 3% to the Profit & Loss account each year, or can it take the full 15% (3% per year for five years – ignoring discounting) up-front. Apparently, a lot of banks feel that they can do the latter, i.e. take the profit up-front and they also believe that they can pay bonuses based on these profits. The trades are called negative carry trades because the carrying costs (5% + 1%) are less than the yield (10%). These trades increased in volume over the last few years and insurance companies ended up insuring each other in order to recognise profits up-front. So, insurance company A could buy a bond and get cheap insurance from insurance company B, and B would do likewise. A lot of these deals were done on bonds issued by utilities, and often too the bonds had a life of up to 25 years, allowing entities to take a substantial profit and bonus up-front. A key question in deciding the accounting treatment is to determine who would suffer if the value of the bonds fell and the insurance company went bust. If the answer is the entity, then the entity cannot record profits up-front since the entity would end up retaining a lot of the risks and rewards of ownership. Therefore, it is probable that the economic benefits and losses (the beneficial interest) will flow to the entity. In early 2008 a lot of entities suffered huge losses on these transactions as the monoline insurance companies got into difficulties. As Paul J. Davies pointed out in the *Financial Times*:[10]

> The problem is that if monolines are downgraded and their protection becomes effective, profits booked up-front need to be reversed. Restating earnings is a very tricky area for investment banks – not least because the traders involved will have long ago pocketed their bonuses.

3.10 NON-CONSOLIDATION

Introduction

There is very clear evidence that the accounting rules[11] regarding how banks account for off-balance sheet interests are not working properly. The rules apparently allow banks to hide

---

[10] Paul J. Davies, 'New danger appears on the monoline horizon', *Financial Times*, 7 February 2008.

[11] Jennifer Hughes, 'Accountancy rules broken "irretrievably" ', *Financial Times*, 9 April 2008.

trillions in assets on off-balance sheet vehicles, meaning that they escape close scrutiny by both regulators and investors. What is worrying is that it took a severe credit crisis to reveal what was going on. This breakdown does suggest that corporate governance is not as strong as it should be. Corporates like Enron therefore continue to hide risks, and the investor will eventually find out about these abuses when the banks are forced to disclose huge losses.

We illustrate here how off-balance sheet abuses work. Suppose a company buys an asset for £1m using £1m of borrowings and months later the value of the asset falls to £800,000. Clearly, the company has made a loss and also has a liability of £1m which, depending on the size of the company, could put it into a very dangerous predicament. A potential solution to the company's problems is to take the asset and associated liability off the balance sheet. The company could set up a smaller company (the subsidiary) and get the smaller company to borrow money, say £1.1m, which the main company guarantees. Since the main company controls the smaller company, the main company can force the smaller company to buy the loss-making asset for £1.1m. The asset therefore comes off the balance sheet. The £1.1m proceeds are then used to pay back the existing loan of £1m and the remainder (£100,000) could be booked as a profit. The company therefore can show an accounting profit of £100,000 when in reality it is sitting on a loss of £200,000. One of the roles of consolidation (the opposite of off-balance sheet) is to prevent this abuse. If a company is controlled by a parent entity, the parent entity is, under IFRS 3, obliged to 'consolidate' the company. This in effect means that the assets and liabilities of the controlled company must be merged with those of the parent company. The illustration in Table 3.1 shows the difference between consolidation and non-consolidation.

Table 3.1   Consolidation vs. non-consolidation

Parent company			
No consolidation			
Assets	£10,000,000	Shareholders' Funds	£10,000,000
Cash	£100,000	Profit & Loss	£100,000
Consolidation		Liabilities	£1,100,000
Assets	£10,800,000	Ordinary Shares	£10,000,000
Cash	£100,000	Profit & Loss	−£200,000
	£10,900,000		£10,900,000

In the non-consolidation case the entity can show a profit of £100,000 and hide liabilities of £1,100,000. In the consolidation case, which shows things in a truer and fairer way, the liability appears on the balance sheet and the accounting profit of £100,000 turns into an accounting loss of £200,000, which represents the true economic position. It is easy to see why there is a temptation to keep assets and liabilities off-balance sheet. It becomes clear too why the standard setters devised IFRS 3, which in broad terms covers instances when consolidation is necessary.

However, despite the rules, we still have off-balance sheet problems. Many banks use structured investment vehicles to borrow money, which is then used to buy risky assets. Both the assets and liabilities are kept off-balance sheet. The technical issues surrounding consolidation are covered in a later chapter. For the moment we will focus on why the accounting profession has not yet solved the 'off-balance sheet issue'.

If the term 'off-balance sheet' was a recent phenomenon one could have sympathy with the accounting profession. However, the topic has been around for some time and it appears that creative accountants are still exploiting it. In 1991, a former Head of Company Research at UBS Phillips & Drew, Terry Smith, wrote a report entitled 'Accounting for Growth' which later became a best-selling book, one apparently that lobbyists tried to ban.[12] One of his chapters focused on the topic Off-balance Sheet and revealed how entities were exploiting the fact that they were able to control companies, force them to buy assets at inflated prices, and record an artificial profit as well as hide losses. Smith borrowed a quote describing off-balance sheet finance as 'The creative accounting trick which improves companies' balance sheets', which itself was taken from the *Guardian* in 1987. As the *Guardian* is not a specialist finance paper, we must assume that the off-balance sheet phenomenon was well known outside the finance and accounting world.

Enron – off-balance sheet

Months after Arthur Levitt's departure from the SEC, the greatest off-balance sheet scandal erupted. Enron, the energy company, filed for bankruptcy in 2001, causing billions of dollars worth of losses for shareholders. The employees of Enron suffered not only from the loss of their jobs, but it seems that for many their personal savings along with their pensions were tied up in Enron shares, which of course became worthless. Enron became expert at using companies which they clearly controlled but did not consolidate. In the words of Levitt:[13]

> The FASB has been dealing with the question of how to account for SPE's for nearly twenty years. Because of fierce business lobbying, the FASB were unable to reach a consensus on a new standard. If one had been in place, Enron might not have occurred.

Bawag – hidden losses

In March 2006 Bawag, the fourth largest bank in Austria, admitted that it had hidden liabilities and losses (presumably by keeping loss-making derivative transactions off-balance sheet) of approximately €1.3 billion for five years. The supervisory board of Chairman Mr Gunter Weninger said he had not revealed the losses as he was worried about a possible run on the bank. Mr Weninger claimed that he was acting with the law, having taken advice from legal experts, which he did not disclose as well as KPMG, auditors to Bawag. The losses arose because of business with Ross Capital, a derivatives specialist run by Walter Flottl, son of a former Bawag chief executive. The bulk of the loss arose from a bet on Japanese rate swaps during the Asian financial crises.[14]

Banks tempt vulture funds

One other way of keeping risky loans off-balance sheet is to offer a discrete subsidy to hedge funds so that the hedge funds will buy distressed debt at above market prices without these

---

[12] Terry Smith, *Accounting for Growth*, Century Business, 1992, p. 76.

[13] Arthur Levitt, *Take on the Street*, Pantheon Books, 2002, p. 140.

[14] Haig Simonian, 'Bawag concealed Euro 1.3 bn losses for five years', *Financial Times*, 25 March 2006.

hedge funds suffering a loss. During the credit crises in the summer of 2007, the *Financial Times*[15] carried a report showing how banks were attempting to hide losses. The article stated that investment banks were offering finance to 'vulture funds' on improved terms if the money was used to buy debt from them. The banks concerned were keen to shift over $A200 billion of leveraged debt and were willing to lend money to the vulture funds as long as they bought the debt at high or inflated prices. The financing was described in the article as 'hidden discounts'. If the deal succeeded, the banks could have minimised public discounts and therefore hidden losses. Another advantage of this approach was that banks could clear the decks and start lending afresh. According to one hedge fund that was raising money for a 'recovery fund', 'the banks are offering different terms depending on whether you take their loans or other people's loans'. Bankers apparently were of the opinion that there was nothing wrong with offering cheaper or longer-dated finance tied to LBO debt, comparing it to branded car loans. Banks tying finance to the sale of such loans remain exposed to potential defaults. The funds will nevertheless bear the first loss. This is yet another example of banks exploiting the accounting standards to hide the extent of their losses. IAS 39 contains rules on effective interest rates and beneficial interest which would prevent banks from taking such loans off the balance sheet. Furthermore, the revenue recognition rules prevent companies from inflating the price of assets (and profiting from those assets) where the assets concerned are subject to vendor financing at subsidised rates. Yet, that banks even thought about this is a clear indication that firstly, shareholders don't know what is going on and secondly, voting power is split from beneficial interest.

3.11   CREDIT RATING AGENCIES II

Even before the sub-prime collapse, the reputation of credit rating agencies was under pressure. There are similarities between credit rating agencies and accounting firms. Both industries are monopolistic, or at least oligopolistic, in the sense that they are few in number and enjoy regulatory protection. Many investors are, for instance, prevented from buying investment products unless the rating agencies give them a seal of approval. In the same way, shareholders cannot object if the audit quality is poor. An audit is a legal requirement and shareholders in reality have no say over which auditors are appointed. Although auditors are formally approved at the AGM, it is usually the directors and not the shareholders that appoint them. The problem with being protected by regulation is that reputation damage is not linked to a loss of revenue. The likelihood is that credit rating agencies will continue to operate as before and although some changes in their procedure may be necessary, most of the conflicts of interest are likely to remain. Even before the credit crises emerged, the reputation of credit rating agencies was in difficulty. In his book *Infectious Greed* (Profile Books Ltd), Frank Partnoy commented as far back as 2003:

> The financial-market innovations that began in 1987 were about to take a few more twists and turns. Credit ratings were central to the changes. Although few financial market participants understood why at the time, a decade later, credit ratings would be even more

important, and would play a central role in the collapse of several companies including Enron.

The reason for the monopolistic and powerful status of the rating agencies was that few companies could expect to sell bonds that they had issued unless they could acquire a rating above BBB, which was the all-important investment grade. As bankers will realise, a bond with a good credit rating is one which is given preferential regulatory treatment. Mutual funds were also affected by the credit rating agencies. They were prevented from buying bonds with a rating below investment grade. In 1996, a financial commentator made the observation:

> There are two superpowers in the world today in my opinion. There's the United States and there's Moody's bond rating service. The United States can destroy you by dropping bombs and Moody's can destroy you by downgrading your bonds. And believe me, it's not clear sometimes who's more powerful.

So powerful were the rating agencies that they often created opportunities for hedge funds and investment banks to make easy profits. Some traders, for instance, observed that the yields on bonds that the rating agencies didn't approve of were unusually high. Very often the rating agencies did not measure risks properly, allowing fund managers to profit by buying certain non-investment grade bonds with little risk and earning a very attractive return. Two important 'industries' grew from the power of the credit rating agencies. One was the structured product industry. These were complex bonds that paid a high yield. Banks were able to manufacture these bonds, pay to have a good rating and then sell them to investors who were attracted by the high rating and high yield. Very often these structured bonds deserved their rating, but as they became more complex there was a risk that the rating agencies were not examining all the risks and so were motivated to give the important triple-A rating to questionable products and receive a fee for doing so. The second 'industry' to emerge was the structured finance or securitisation industry as we know it today. Banks found a way to bundle together a number of assets that were deemed risky and then sell the entire package to willing investors. Often, insurance companies took some of the risk, with the result that the combined portfolio was less risky than the individual assets within the portfolio. Again, many of these deals were legitimate but structured product manufacturers began to realise that investors concentrated on the AAA rating and the high yield and did not seek a second opinion on whether the credit rating was justified. The credit rating agencies therefore, tempted by fees, may have applied the all-important AAA stamp of approval to questionable and complex deals.

In trying to determine whether the credit rating agencies were responsible for the credit crunch of 2007, Partnoy observed (back in 2003):

> Another reason involved [in the growth in the CDO industry] involved the all-important credit-rating agencies. Beginning in the 1970s, regulators had given up trying to keep pace with modern financial markets. Instead of making substantive decisions about which securities financial institutions should be permitted to buy and sell the regulators had deferred to the credit rating agencies.

The problem with any monopoly is that the motivation to please the customer is not paramount and if the rating agency is discredited in the eyes of the general public, it doesn't matter so long as they have regulatory approval. The customer (i.e. the investor) doesn't have a choice. Two key factors therefore caused the reliability of the rating agencies to deteriorate. Firstly, as pointed out, they had a monopoly and secondly, they were being paid by bankers originating the complex deal and not the investor. The risk therefore is that for the rating agencies, convincing the regulators that the rating process was important was paramount in their minds. Getting the quality right was less so. Partnoy unsympathetically suggests that 'The analysts at the three rating agencies were perfectly nice people, but they were not – to put it charitably – the sharpest tools in the shed'. Partnoy finally observes, 'Not only had the rating agencies given Orange County and Pacific Gas & Electric their highest ratings just before those entities became insolvent, they more recently had given high ratings to Enron, Global Crossing, and WorldCom and stuck to those ratings until just before the companies filed for bankruptcy'.

The recent credit crises suggest that nothing has fundamentally changed. Immediately before the credit crunch ABN Amro launched a complicated product known as the CPDO. The product gave a return of Libor + 2%, but gave the investor an exposure to credit risk. What was surprising was that although the deal was a highly leveraged bet on the creditworthiness of companies, at least one of the rating agencies gave it the AAA seal of approval.

3.12   ACCOUNTING STANDARDS AND LOBBYING

While some may take the view that the credit rating agencies have let the investor down, a similar view could be taken of the accounting standards. For a period of time in the 1980s, financial institutions were allowed to hide the extent to which they were using derivatives. Needless to say, the Financial Accounting Standards Board in America became concerned with this practice. Unfortunately, so too did the lobby groups looking after the interests of derivative dealers. According to Partnoy,[16] the International Swap Dealers Association was formed to 'organize before any problems arise'. Apart from producing standardised documentation which would make dealing in swaps much easier, the association lobbied against new accounting regulations (the equivalent of IAS 39). There is evidence that despite the appearance of IAS 39 and the American equivalent FAS 133, the lobby groups (not necessarily ISDA) did succeed in developing accounting standards that would obscure from the investor what really was going on. In the early 1990s the Chairman of Ernst & Young warned that 'we can expect to see even fatter and more unreadable annual reports in the future. Readers will decide to ignore them, as many people already do'. This was certainly true in the case of Enron.

There were a few accounting initiatives that Arthur Levitt, the long-serving SEC Chairman, attempted to introduce but to much opposition. On 25 September 2000, for instance, a number of American politicians wrote to him regarding his efforts to limit the extent to which auditing firms could earn fees outside of auditing. They wrote:

We are writing concerning the Commission's proposed rules to limit the range of services provided by accounting firms. While we share your belief that auditor independence is

---

[16] Frank Partnoy, *Infectious Greed*, Profile Books Ltd, 2003, p. 47.

critical to meeting the economy's need for reliable financial data, we are not convinced that this level of regulatory intervention is appropriate at this time.[17]

It was not the only source of lobbying that he was exposed to. When trying to devise rules to force directors to treat stock options as an expense (the equivalent to the IFRS 2 rules), he observed 'Dozens of CEOs and Washington's most skillful lobbyists came to my office to urge me not to allow this proposal to move forward'. He eventually advised the FASB to back down and regarded his failure to support the FASB on this matter as 'my single biggest mistake during my years of service'.[18]

In the eyes of many regulators, the accounting standards are very important, placing pressure on auditors to guarantee the quality of their work. Shareholders are unable to take important corrective action, such as selling the shares of poorly managed or underperforming companies, if they are kept in the dark by the auditors. In the past this work was compromised by those auditors who used auditing as a 'loss leader' – a means to get their foot into the door of more lucrative consulting work. New regulations now prevent the auditor from relying on consultancy work and this improvement in independence has led to better-quality audits. However, the pressure to deceive has not disappeared. Auditors are still in a type of conflict of interest because although they effectively report to shareholders about the performance of their directors, it is the director and not the shareholder who influences their appointment. Many corporate governance experts comment that the desire for short-term performance is quite strong for certain bonus schemes and so directors often force auditors to hide losses or recognise revenue prematurely, despite the accounting standards. If the accounting standards were black and white and clear-cut, this problem might not be so severe. The problem is that what auditors put on or take off the balance sheet is still a bit subjective. Levitt spent a lot of time as Governor of the SEC trying to protect the FASB from interference by the lobby groups who, at one stage, tried to secure the appointment of a 'friendly' chairman. The experience of dealing with auditors and the lack of support they gave Levitt led him to conclude that auditors supported the demands of their corporate clients and became advocates. He remarked,[19] 'I would forever look upon the accounting profession differently after this episode'.

3.13 INVESTMENT ENTITIES

A pitfall of shareholder democracy is that we tend to trust institutional investors with our funds. We assume that these investors have not only the competence and experience to select good companies, but also have enough voting power to force directors to encourage good corporate governance and sound accounting practices. In theory, the accounting standards should improve because this will allow powerful institutional investors to use more reliable information when selecting stocks. Reality is often different. Investment institutions like bankers make a lot of their money from earning fees, and often a conflict emerges between fee maximisation and shareholder interest. Eliot Spitzer, the former New York State Attorney General, uncovered a number of undesirable practices with mutual fund brokers. Some mutual funds

---

[17] Arthur Levitt, *Take on the Street*, Pantheon Books, 2002, p. 301.

[18] Arthur Levitt, *Take on the Street*, Pantheon Books, 2002, p. 11.

[19] Arthur Levitt, *Take on the Street*, Pantheon Books, 2002, p. 115.

allowed a certain group of investors to buy and sell units and change the dates. As an example, a 'privileged' customer could put on a trade on say 1 April but record the trade date on say 28 March. The trader would then be able to pick units that went up in value between 28 March and 1 April and so make a profit (at the expense of the other small shareholders in the firm). It is, of course, illegal but was practised by some funds. Market timing occurs when an investor exploits the time differential. For instance, if stock markets crashed in Asia it would take some time before the crash featured in the calculations of certain unit trust prices, mainly because of the time difference between Asia and America. Therefore, traders could use this new information and trade at old prices to make a profit. Unlike late trading, there is nothing illegal about market timing, however the tendency was to allow only privileged investors (such as hedge funds) access to market timing trades. The result was that the small shareholder suffered once again. Clearly, it is really only the institutional investors that can force entities to implement sound accounting practices. In practice, some investment funds may decide that fees can be maximised by looking after the interests of privileged investors rather than the general investor, and so their eye is taken off the ball of finding sound investments with good accounting disclosures. This potentially could be a further impediment to the development and improvement of the accounting standards. In Britain, scandals such as split capital funds, which exposed investors to huge undisclosed risks and provided handsome fees for investment managers, also reveal that occasionally investment fund managers have other things to think about than looking after the interests of their investors. Unfortunately, some fund managers have identified ways to maximise fees without trying to outperform the market and looking after their investors.

Deutsche Bank[20] was challenged by the SEC when it failed to disclose a material conflict of interest when it used its voting power to push through a hotly contested merger between Hewlett-Packard and Compaq Computer Corporation. Deutsche Bank, through its investment banking division, was retained by HP to advise on the proposed merger. The investment arm requested that Hewlett-Packard have an opportunity to present its case to the asset management division (who had voting power). Clearly, intervening in the voting process may prevent the asset management arm from acting in the best interests of its client.

3.14 CONCLUSION

One clear trend emerging in the financial world is that people are not learning from past mistakes. As this chapter has shown, the rating agencies along with the accounting profession gave investors and the government false assurances on certain financial institutions. What is worrying is that they have given these false assurances before. However, for those on the right side of flawed incentive or bonus schemes, there is clearly an incentive to let sleeping dogs lie. Indeed, as Arthur Levitt has shown, the lobbyists have made very strong representations (and threats) to keep things as they are. The incentive scheme works as long as banks are not only allowed to take huge risks but also to hide them. This phenomenon may explain why weak, vague accounting rules continue to dominate the structured finance industry.

Complexity is apparently king. As long as the structured products industry keeps financial instruments complex, the accountants and credit rating agencies can avoid litigation by hiding behind complexity and as long as they are earning fees, there may be an incentive to leave

---

[20] http://www.sec.gov/litigation/admin/ia-2160.htm

things as they are – save a little tinkering to give the impression that they are responding to events. One point can be made with reasonable certainty. Investors will face more and more complexity in the future and equally, the incentive schemes operated by banks will remain complex. As long as this complexity exists, the shareholder will suffer. Ideally, the shareholder could use their voting power to prevent this but in reality, as this chapter has shown, those with voting interests are often unaffected by bad decisions (and in extreme cases – through credit derivatives – benefit from shareholder destruction). One can hardly expect the accounting standards to improve under this environment.

In the interests of avoiding increased regulation the world's leading bankers accepted, on 9 April 2008, that they were largely responsible for the credit crises. The Institute of International Finance, which represents the major financial companies across the world, acknowledged 'major points of weaknesses in business practices, bankers' pay and the management of risk'.[21] A report produced by the Institute of International Finance (IIF) accepted that over-reliance on models and a lack of protection against liquidity risk contributed to the problem. One of the areas that the IIF will be looking at is instances where they may pay less to bankers who have taken on big risks with shareholders' money and struck lucky. Senior accounting experts have also acknowledged that the rules which allowed banks to hide trillions in assets are 'irretrievably broken'. A report concluded that new rules were necessary but may not be available before mid-2011. It appears that because of staff shortages and relative inexperience, the project to amend the off-balance sheet rules has lost momentum.[22]

APPENDIX: CONSTANT PROPORTION DEBT OBLIGATIONS

There are a number of problems with the credit rating agency model. As mentioned, these include conflicts of interest, lack of transparency and complexity. Rating agencies charge much higher fees to rate complex structured products than they would for ordinary, straightforward corporate debt. This leaves them in a very tempting situation. They might be tempted to maximise fees by being more generous with the triple-A rating for structured products as this will almost certainly attract new business. The complexity, of course, leads to a lack of transparency. Occasionally, even the credit rating analysts themselves don't fully understand – relying too heavily on the 'black box' mentality, i.e. feeding data into a computer system and accepting what the computer says without fully understanding what the computer is doing. This leads to the problem of complexity. Investment bankers are often tempted to maximise fees by selling risky products to customers and concealing the risks involved. Thus, an investor might get a return of say Libor + 2% when, given the risks involved, the return should be say Libor + 8%. This gives an investment bank an opportunity to earn huge fees by keeping the excess. To do this, they need the cooperation of the credit rating agencies. Paying high fees to the rating agencies doesn't necessarily secure their cooperation, but the temptations are obvious. One cannot conclude that the rating agencies are incompetent or will risk allowing their reputation to suffer by chasing fees and misinforming the customer. However, the risk is there, as illustrated by the rating of CPDOs. These derivative instruments were designed at the height of the credit bubble. They offered very high returns and, judging by their credit rating (triple-A), contained very little risk. What puzzled the financial community,

[21] Krishna Ghua, 'Blame us for crisis, says leading bankers', *Financial Times*, 10 April 2008.

[22] Jennifer Hughes, 'Off-balance sheet rules for banks "irretrievably broken" say experts', *Financial Times*, 10 April 2008.

including rival credit rating agencies, was how these complex products were able to produce such a high return but with very little risk. What is interesting is that these products were sold to experienced institutional investors who presumably were investing other people's money. An important question here is how these products affected the bonuses of those institutional investors. Did they get a bonus on the excess return, i.e. borrowing at Libor and receiving Libor + 2%? More importantly, when these investments turned sour, losing up to 60%, did the losses feature in the same bonus calculations?

For a long time, people wondered how CPDOs were able to achieve high ratings and high yields simultaneously. It sounded too good to be true. In May 2008,[23] the puzzle was solved. Moody's were forced to admit that they awarded an incorrect triple-A rating to billions of dollars worth of CPDOs. The mistake was traced to an incorrect computer code. According to the *Financial Times*,

> some senior staff within the credit agency knew early in 2007 that products rated the previous year had received top-notch triple A ratings and that, after a computer coding error was corrected, their ratings should have been up to four notches lower.

This leads to a very important question, why did it take until May 2008 to correct an error that was discovered in early 2007?

CPDOs allow investors to take a 'leveraged' bet on the performance of corporate debt issued by American and European companies. They are generally constructed through the use of credit derivatives and indices of credit derivatives. Investors received a premium but in turn had to pay out money if a credit event occurred, such as bankruptcy. A key feature of the structure is that it would, through leverage, earn high fees in the early period and this would enable the CPDO to build up a cash reserve which would cover later payments. The structure was also designed so that leverage would fall if there was a lot of excess cash but if losses occurred, the structure would build up leverage and increase the premium to cover these losses. Apart from Moody's, S&P also got involved in the ratings but they claimed that their models were robust and made available to the investment community.

Destructive Incentive Schemes – Barclays

In November 2008, approximately 18 months into the credit crunch, the *Financial Times* revealed a story suggesting that the complexity of financial instruments, conflicts of interest and inappropriate bonuses are still a potential problem, despite the huge losses that shareholders within banks have suffered in the past. Under a deal with the British Government, Barclays along with other large banks agreed to inject more capital with a view to reducing risk and enhance the ability of these banks to absorb losses. The government gave the banks a choice, they could either raise money themselves, through existing shareholders or other new investors, or they could avail of a government initiative whereby they could issue preference shares to the government. In return for this, the government required a relatively high yield but also wanted to place restrictions on executive remuneration and dividend payments to ordinary shareholders.

---

[23] Sam Jones, Gillian Tett and Paul J. Davies, 'Moody's shares tumble on rating error', *Financial Times*, 20 May 2008.

To the dismay of shareholders, Barclays did not take up the government offer. Instead, according to the *Financial Times*,[24] they opted for 'a complex £7.3 bn capital raising, which will result in Middle East Investors holding 32% of the bank if all warrants are exercised'. These securities not only paid a relatively high coupon but also resulted in a considerable dilution for existing shareholders. Many investors and politicians felt that Barclays imposed this unnecessarily heavy dilution on its shareholders because the government's more generous offer would place restrictions on bonus payments that Barclay's paid to its executives. The Liberal Democrat Treasury spokesman described the deal as a 'scandal of mammoth proportions'. Some of the large shareholders agreed with Mr Cables' view. One said 'we didn't expect such a blatant flouting of pre-emption rights'. James Eden at BNP Exane said[25] 'Clearly it would have been cheaper to raise the money through the government scheme. There is a question whether one factor of doing this is to ensure management can pay itself bonuses'. Barclays however felt that the government scheme would restrict their ability to reward shareholders by resuming dividend payments. They also felt that strategic benefits would arise from the involvement of the Middle Eastern investors. John Varley, chief executive of Barclays also argued that with no government involvement, it would be better able to control its own destiny.

The deal involved raising approximately £5.8 billion from Saudi Arabian investors and another £1.5 billion from other institutional investors. The big problem for existing shareholders however is that the investors have the right to convert their loans into shares or exercise warrants which could result in an extra 4.2 billion shares being issued. This represents a considerable dilution – the Middle Eastern investors are expected to own up to 32% of Barclays if the dilutions go ahead. Barclays used two types of instruments to structure the deal. £4.3 billion of Mandatorily Convertible Notes were issued along with £3 billion of Reserve Capital Instruments/Warrants. The combined coupon on these products is about 14% but, because of the tax break, the effective cost to Barclay's shareholders is approximately 10.5%. The options given with these products are however a major cause of concern to existing shareholders.

Over the years there has been a growth in the number of complex products used by banks to raise capital. These include convertible bonds and hybrid instruments which are effectively loans but have an element of equity risk. The problem for the shareholder is that the extent of the dilution or the loss is not immediately obvious. IFRS 3 – *Share Based Payments* to some extent covers the issues of convertible options and warrants. If a shareholder suffers a dilution because an entity has issued an option on its shares to say employees, the value of the option must be computed and treated as an expense to the Profit & Loss account. It is unclear however, whether complex convertible instruments used to raise finance are treated in the same way. The risk is that the complexity of the instruments will lead to variability and a lack of consistency in the accounting treatment which creates accounting arbitrage opportunities and misleads shareholders.

---

[24] Jane Croft, 'Decision to opt for "high price" deal over bail-out questioned', *Financial Times*, 1 November 2008.

[25] Jane Croft, 'Decision to opt for "high price" deal over bail-out questioned', *Financial Times*, 1 November 2008.

4

Hedge Accounting

4.1 INTRODUCTION

The previous chapter looked at the problems of corporate governance and in particular how those corporate governance problems encouraged lobbying and pressure to allow the weaknesses in the standards to remain, or at least to produce rules that allow accountants to use their discretion with sometimes worrying consequences, particularly when assets and liabilities are kept off the balance sheet. In Chapter 2 we looked at the 'architecture' or foundations under the accounting standards. That chapter focused on the fact that the accounting standard setters have developed a 'mixed model' approach which not only gives accountants flexibility in what they show on their balance sheets, but also creates considerable confusion. The result of this weak foundation is that the accounting standards have great difficulty in coping with financial instruments and off-balance sheet vehicles. Their solution is to develop a lot of rules to smooth over the cracks rather than to correct the foundations, an unfortunate choice. This chapter is quite technical, focusing on how IAS 39 deals with financial instruments, particularly those that qualify for hedge accounting. The mixed model approach, where some assets are shown at cost and others at market value, has serious side-effects, particularly where financial instruments are involved. These side-effects are examined below.

Many entities such as companies use derivatives for hedging purposes, i.e. to reduce their exposure to various external factors. An airline, for instance, might be exposed to say the dollar rising against the euro (perhaps because it leases aircraft from overseas), rising oil prices and rising interest rates. This airline might attempt to reduce the volatility of its earnings so that it can pay a regular, predictable dividend to its shareholders. A foreign currency forward contract can be used to hedge against the dollar rising. The airline might use an interest rate swap to lock in future interest rates and commodity futures to agree today an oil price that they will pay in the future when they purchase oil. Although derivatives often have a bad reputation, they can, when used properly, create value for the shareholder as they can reduce the volatility of the cash flows and accounting profit, thus allowing a company to pay a regular dividend. There are, of course, two problems. Financial instruments are often misused in order to hide losses and risks (as discussed in the previous chapter), and the accounting standards can often paint a very misleading picture for the shareholder. This is because the accounting standards don't always permit hedge accounting, even if the entity is using the derivative for hedging purposes. One argument of the EU was that the accounting rules were far too restrictive, leading to the famous 'carve-outs' which we discuss in detail in Chapter 11. The problem is that an entity may use a derivative for hedging purposes but the strict accounting rules often force the auditor to conclude that the derivative is being used for speculative or gambling purposes. The result is that the accounting profit is a lot more volatile than the economic profit, and so the accounts are misleading.

One of the fundamental principles of accounting is the 'matching concept', i.e. an accountant should recognise revenues and their associated costs in the same accounting period. Often, creative accountants ignore that principle by recognising revenue prematurely, i.e. recognising revenue in one accounting period and costs in a later period. It is important to realise, however, that because of the strict rules associated with hedge accounting, even the honest accountant is prevented from applying the matching concept properly in certain circumstances.

4.2 ACCOUNTING FOR FORWARD CONTRACTS

The American FASB produced an example to illustrate how the hedge accounting rules apply in practice. The example below is based on this American interpretation. Although there are some differences between FASB and IASB, the example below can also apply to the IASB.

We start with a very simple situation where a company is set up with shareholders' funds of £1,000,000 and immediately buys inventory on 1 January 2009 (Table 4.1). Three months after purchase, the inventory goes up in value by £100,000 and the company decides to lock in this profit by entering into a forward contract.

Table 4.1   Opening balance sheet

Assets	
Cash	£1,000,000
Shareholders' Funds	
Ordinary Shares issued	£1,000,000

Under a forward contract, the company effectively agrees to sell the inventory for £1,100,000 (today's market price) at some fixed date in the future regardless of what the market price is on the date of sale. It follows that when inventory prices rise, the forward contract will lose money and if they fall, the forward contract gains. A summary of the transaction is shown in Table 4.2.

Table 4.2   Transaction details

01-Jan-09	Entity purchases inventory	£1,000,000
31-Mar-09	Value of inventory	£1,100,000
	Entity locks in price with forward contract	
31-Dec-09	Value of inventory	£1,075,000
	Value of forward contract	£25,000
28-Feb-09	Inventory sold	£1,075,000

As Table 4.2 shows, the value of the forward contract has gone up by £25,000 between March and December, reflecting the fact that the value of the inventory has fallen by the same amount over the same period.

The first question we address is how the balance sheet should look at 31 December 2009. IAS 2.28 states that the value of inventory must be recorded at the lower of cost or net realisable value. Therefore, in this case, as the value of the inventory is always above cost, the cost is used as opposed to the fair value. As regards the forward contract, in the days before

IAS 39's special accounting rules, it was possible to keep these forward contracts off-balance sheet, with the result that creative accounting opportunities were available. We look at this below.

4.3 ACCOUNTING PRE-IAS 39

It is clear that on 31 March 2009, the company has made a profit of £100,000 (£1,100,000–£1,000,000). However, as the inventory is recorded at cost on the balance sheet, the standards would not permit the company to recognise this profit in the accounts until the inventory is sold. Prior to IAS 39, the derivative would have been kept off-balance sheet, i.e. ignored. There is nothing inherently wrong with keeping the profit on the derivative off the balance sheet, since the standards do not allow the entity to recognise the profit on the inventory. Therefore, one mistake cancels out the other – it is a practical solution. However, some creative accountants under pressure to 'manufacture profits' developed an accounting methodology which allowed them to recognise the gain on the derivative without recognising the reduction in value on the inventory. They were able to do this by cashing in the derivative at 31 December and taking the cash received to the Profit & Loss account. The same creative accountants would avoid cashing in loss-making derivatives, where they exist, and therefore losses were kept off-balance sheet. Table 4.3 illustrates the creative accounting opportunity that was available. If the entity did not close out or cash in the derivative, the profit would be zero but if the derivative was closed out at 31 December, the creative accountant could 'manufacture' a profit of £25,000.

Table 4.3   Closing balance sheet prior to IAS 39

	Derivative not cashed in	Derivative cashed in
Assets		
Inventory	£1,000,000	£1,000,000
Additional cash from broker		£25,000
Shareholders' Funds		
Ordinary Shares issued	£1,000,000	£1,000,000
Retained Profits		£25,000

This problem became widespread. Many entities found that if they gambled with derivatives they could manufacture huge profits, and give the directors a significant bonus as long as they were permitted to keep them off the balance sheet. Needless to say, the losses would later be discovered but usually well after the bonuses were paid. The accounting standards responded with IAS 39. In essence, this standard states that under IAS 39.9, virtually all derivatives must appear on the balance sheet at fair value. However, the new IAS 39 rules are inconsistent with the existing rules. For instance, the rule in IAS 2.28 states that the treatment of inventory remains unchanged. In the simplest application of IAS 39, the change in the derivative must appear on the balance sheet at market value but the change in the underlying inventory must not be recorded. This has created a misleading phenomenon known as artificial volatility, one of the side-effects of an inconsistent or mixed accounting model.

Table 4.4 shows the situation where the balance sheet must show the derivative at fair value but the inventory is shown at cost. The result is that the Profit & Loss account changes as the

Table 4.4   Closing balance sheet on 31 December 2009 (simple application of IAS 39)

	Derivatives on balance sheet
Assets	
Inventory	£1,000,000
Forward Contract	£25,000
Shareholders' Funds	
Ordinary Shares issued	£1,000,000
Retained Profits	£25,000

derivative changes, i.e. by £25,000, suggesting to the shareholder that the entity is speculating with derivatives. In other words, the entity is not allowed to match the loss on the inventory over the period (£25,000) against the gain on the inventory. This clearly violates the 'matching principle' as discussed above, but it is perfectly acceptable under IAS 39. In summary, a simple application of IAS 39 creates artificial volatility in the Profit & Loss account and this could make the published accounts misleading to the shareholder.

For the sake of completeness, we show in Table 4.5 how the balance sheet should look when the inventory is eventually sold in February.

Table 4.5   Closing balance sheet on 28 February 2010

	Derivatives on balance sheet
Assets	
Cash	£1,100,000
Forward Contract	£–
Shareholders' Funds	
Ordinary Shares issued	£1,000,000
Retained Profits	£100,000

The value of the asset at the date of sale was £1,075,000, however, as the entity has locked in the sales price at £1,100,000 and the cost was £1,000,000, this becomes the profit figure.

4.4   ARTIFICIAL VOLATILITY

Artificial volatility is one of the main weaknesses of IAS 39, making entities look more risky than they actually are. To recap, according to IAS 39 virtually all derivatives must appear on the balance sheet at market value and the change must generally go through the Profit & Loss account. However, the hedged asset must be shown at cost on the balance sheet and not fair value. This inconsistent treatment causes the artificial volatility and is a major headache for entities like banks. The accounting standard setters have tried to get around this problem with complex hedge accounting rules, but these rules are very difficult to implement and very bureaucratic, with the result that many entities find that they cannot cope with these complexities and end up implementing IAS 39 in its simplest form, even though it could be misleading.

4.5 HEDGE ACCOUNTING RULES

To eliminate or reduce this misleading artificial volatility, the standard setters under IAS 39.86 state that a derivative or financial instrument can qualify for hedge accounting treatment if it falls under any of three headings:

- Fair value hedge.
- Cash flow hedge.
- Hedge of a net investment in foreign operations.

Fair value hedge. These hedge accounting rules are designed so that entities can use derivatives to lock in the 'fair value' of assets or liabilities on the balance sheet. Where a derivative qualifies as a 'fair value hedge', the entity is allowed to adjust the value of the underlying asset or liability by the change in the derivative. The result is that the derivative does not cause volatility in the Profit & Loss account. The example below illustrates this.

Cash flow hedge. Occasionally, entities do not want to hedge an underlying asset or liability but instead a future cash flow. For instance, an entity may decide to buy oil in four months' time and use a forward contract to lock in the price today. In the absence of hedge accounting, the change in the value of the derivative would have to go through the Profit & Loss account. However, under IAS 39, an entity can reduce or eliminate artificial volatility in the Profit & Loss account by putting any change in the fair value of the derivative into a temporary reserve account (known as the Equity Reserve). As with fair value hedges, the rules can get very complex and are better understood with the examples below.

Hedge of a net investment. Occasionally, entities make investments in foreign entities and, as the value of the foreign investment is exposed to foreign exchange movements, entities often hedge the exposure by entering into a forward foreign exchange agreement. Provided the hedge meets certain conditions, the change in the forward contract does not have to go through the Profit & Loss account. Instead, like the cash flow hedge, the change can go through the Equity Reserve account, thus eliminating artificial volatility in the Profit & Loss account.

Speculative derivatives. Where a derivative fails to meet the requirements of the three headings above, the entity is required to put any changes in the derivative through the Profit & Loss account. In short, if you cannot prove you are hedging the standard setters assume you are speculating. They are anxious that any changes in the value of the derivative are put through the Profit & Loss account so that entities will not speculate and hide losses simultaneously.

Illustration: Fair value hedge accounting

To see how these rules apply, we return to the American example above. In that case the entity, by applying a simple application of IAS 39, is forced on 31 December to show the derivative on the balance sheet at market value and the change in the value of the derivative must go through the Profit & Loss account, even though the derivative is not yet cashed in and the underlying asset is not yet sold. The profit recognised on the transaction at 31 December 2009 is £25,000. By applying the hedge accounting rules, the company can defer recognising the gain on the derivative until the underlying asset (i.e. the inventory) is sold; in other words, it can apply the matching concept. Under the fair value hedge accounting rules, the company is permitted to change the value of the underlying asset (in this case the inventory) so as to eliminate the artificial profit. The revised balance sheet is shown as Table 4.6.

Table 4.6   Simple application of IAS 39 vs. fair value hedge: balance sheet on 31 December 2009

	IAS 39 without hedge accounting	IAS 39 with fair value hedge
Assets		
Inventory	£1,000,000	£975,000
Forward Contract	£25,000	£25,000
Shareholders' Funds		
Ordinary Shares issued	£1,000,000	£1,000,000
Retained Profits	£25,000	

Table 4.6 shows how the standard setters have achieved the combined objective of keeping derivatives on the balance sheet at market value while at the same time eliminating the recognition of profits too prematurely. Unfortunately, in trying to solve one problem they have created another. The figure for inventory on the balance sheet is £975,000, which is simply the cost of the inventory as adjusted for the change in the hedging derivative. However, this figure represents neither the cost nor the market value of inventory. Some might argue that it doesn't really matter. Perhaps for the typical manufacturing company the rules could be classified as inconvenient but tolerable. For financial institutions, however, where hedging is very complex, accountants have a tendency to get too tied up on irritants like this and occasionally they don't understand what is going on, leading to mistakes. In summary, where the derivative qualifies for hedge accounting, it must appear on the balance sheet at market value and the difference must go through the Profit & Loss account. However, the entity is allowed to adjust the underlying hedged asset so as to eliminate artificial volatility.

In reality, there is no such thing as a perfect hedge. It is very hard to select a derivative which matches the underlying exactly. In the case of the example above, suppose the derivative only climbed by £22,500 while the underlying fell by £25,000; the difference is known as 'ineffectiveness' and the standards generally require that ineffectiveness must be recognised immediately in the Profit & Loss account as soon as it occurs.

Table 4.7 illustrates this problem. The underlying must fall by the full amount, i.e. £25,000 and the derivative can only be shown at its current market value, £22,500. The difference goes through the Profit & Loss account.

Table 4.7   Fair value hedging ineffectiveness

	IAS 39 with fair value hedge, 31 December 2009
Assets	
Inventory	£975,000
Forward Contract	£22,500
Shareholders' Funds	
Ordinary Shares issued	£1,000,000
Retained Profits/(Losses)	−£2,500

What is interesting about the first case is that if the entity did not hedge, the entity would not be required to show an accounting loss on 31 December of £2500. By hedging, the company has increased its real profits by £22,500 (the change in the value of the derivative) but is required to show an accounting loss! This is unfortunately only one of the many confusing instances that the current accounting regime throws up.

The retained profit in this case, –£2500, simply represents the margin of error because the derivative has not tracked the underlying 100%. This situation applies in most markets. To reaffirm the point, suppose the derivative increased in value from 0 to £27,000 and the underlying fell by £25,000, the balance sheet on 31 December would look as in Table 4.8.

Table 4.8   Fair value hedging ineffectiveness 2

	IAS 39 with fair value hedge
Assets	
Inventory	£975,000
Forward Contract	£27,000
Shareholders' Funds	
Ordinary Shares issued	£1,000,000
Retained Profits	£2,000

For completeness, we look at how the balance sheet and Profit & Loss account will appear on 29 February 2010. The combined profit is £100,000, as expected. The derivative is cashed in and the profit is calculated as the proceeds (£1,075,000) on the sale of the inventory less the carrying costs (£975,000), giving a balance sheet as in Table 4.9.

Table 4.9   Closing balance sheet on 28 February 2010

	IAS 39 with fair value hedge
Assets	
Cash	£1,100,000
Forward Contract	£–
Shareholders' Funds	
Ordinary Shares issued	£1,000,000
Retained Profits	£100,000

Cash flow hedge accounting

As discussed above, an alternative to fair value (FV) hedge accounting is cash flow (CF) hedge accounting. Like FV hedging, the CF hedging rules are designed to ensure that derivatives are brought on to the balance sheet at fair value and simultaneously, ensure that artificial volatility in the Profit & Loss account is eliminated. The difference between the FV and CF rules, however, is that the FV rules are designed to hedge existing assets and liabilities on the balance sheet whereas the CF rules are designed to hedge future cash flows which are uncertain. Sometimes, but not always, an entity has a choice to use either FV or CF rules. In theory, the choice of hedging rules will not have an impact on the Profit & Loss account. In reality, the choice occasionally will, as we shall see below.

The entity referred to above could have, if it wished, hedged not the FV of inventory but the cash flows that the asset generates when the asset is sold. Under the CF hedge accounting rules, any gain or loss on the derivative is temporarily stored in an account known as the Equity Reserve account. This operates similarly to a 'Deferred Profit & Loss' account, i.e. a gain is made but not recognised immediately. In essence, the derivative has made a profit but the profit is not recognised immediately, it is deferred until the underlying asset is sold. The balance sheet in Table 4.10 (at 31 December 2009) reveals how CF hedge accounting works. There are two important differences. Firstly, the entity is not allowed to adjust the underlying asset or liability. With FV hedge accounting, of course, the underlying item is adjusted. Secondly, the Equity Reserve account is used to temporarily store any gain or loss on a derivative that qualifies for hedge accounting, whereas the Equity Reserve account is not used at all for FV hedges.

Table 4.10   Simple application of IAS 39 vs. fair value hedge: balance sheet on 31 December 2009

	IAS 39 without hedge accounting	IAS 39 with cash flow hedge
Assets		
Inventory	£1,000,000	£1,000,000
Forward Contract	£25,000	£25,000
Shareholders' Funds		
Ordinary Shares issued	£1,000,000	£1,000,000
Equity Reserve		£25,000
Retained Profits	£25,000	0

This time the inventory is carried at its original cost (£1,000,000). When the inventory is sold, any balance in the equity reserve is transferred to the Sales Revenue section of the Profit & Loss account. Therefore, the Profit & Loss account will show Sales Revenue (which also represents cash proceeds) of £1,075,000+£25,000 and the Cost of Sales will be £1,000,000, giving a profit of £100,000.

Using CF as opposed to FV hedge accounting, the closing balance sheet on 28 February 2010 would look as in Table 4.11.

Table 4.11   Closing balance sheet on 28 February 2010

	IAS 39 with cash flow hedge
Assets	
Cash	£1,100,000
Forward Contract	£–
Shareholders' Funds	
Ordinary Shares issued	£1,000,000
Retained Profits	£100,000

In summary, entities that use derivatives, either to take on an exposure or to neutralise an exposure, must show them on the balance sheet at market or fair value. The creative opportunities associated with 'cherry-picking' off-balance sheet items are, as a result, reduced. However, there are practical implementation problems, since under FV hedge accounting entities are allowed to adjust the carrying value of assets on the balance sheet. This can cause confusion.

Effectiveness under cash flow hedge accounting

Cash flow hedge accounting is not without its 'design' problems. For instance, IAS 39.96 states that the amount that an entity can place into the Equity Reserve account in respect of a CF hedge is limited to the lessor of the change in the derivative and the change in the underlying. To illustrate: suppose in the above example the value of the derivative increased only by £22,500 whereas the underlying fell by £25,000. Then only the lower of these two figures would go into Equity Reserve, as shown in the balance sheet in Table 4.12.

Table 4.12   Cash flow hedge accounting ineffectiveness I

Assets	
Inventory	£1,000,000
Forward Contract	£22,500
Shareholders' Funds	
Ordinary Shares issued	£1,000,000
Retained Profits	£–
Equity Reserve	£22,500

If, on the other hand, the derivative outperformed the underlying, i.e. the derivative went up by £27,000 while the underlying fell by £25,000, then once again the lower of these two figures would go into Equity Reserve and the ineffectiveness of £2000 would go through the Profit & Loss account (Table 4.13).

Table 4.13   Cash flow hedge accounting ineffectiveness II

Assets	
Inventory	£1,000,000
Forward Contract	£27,000
Shareholders' Funds	
Ordinary Shares issued	£1,000,000
Retained Profits	£2,000
Equity Reserve	£25,000

Conclusion

In cash flow hedge accounting, if the derivative underperforms, the ineffectiveness is broadly ignored since only the lower of the change in the derivative and the change in the underlying goes through the Profit & Loss account. However, if the derivative outperforms the underlying, then ineffectiveness must be recognised and released through the Profit & Loss account. For fair value hedge accounting, ineffectiveness is realised in both cases, where the derivative underperforms and overperforms. This is summarised in Table 4.14.

Table 4.14   Ineffectiveness

	Dealing with ineffectiveness	
	Fair value	Cash flow
Derivative underperforms	Recognise through P&L	Don't recognise through P&L
Derivative overperforms	Recognise through P&L	Recognise through P&L

4.6   EXAMPLE: FORWARD RATE AGREEMENT

We now show how the fair value and cash flow hedge accounting rules are applied to more complex financial instruments. We start with a Forward Rate Agreement (FRA). On 1 January 2010 an entity locks into an FRA under which it will pay floating and receive fixed. The purpose of the FRA is to hedge the floating interest rate from a deposit of £10,000,000 which it expects to receive on 30 June 2010. The entity will raise this money from the issue of shares and will not spend it until 30 September. For the sake of clarity, we will assume that the FRA is cashed in at the end of September as opposed to the start of the FRA period, which is the normal procedure. The details of the deposit are given in Table 4.15.

Table 4.15   FRA term sheet

		No. of days
Date of agreement	01-Jan-09	
Notional	£10,000,000	
FRA start date	30-Jun-09	180
FRA end date	30-Sep-09	272
Agreed fixed rate (received by entity)	5%	

This swap would qualify as a cash flow hedge because the entity is hedging deposit interest which it has not yet received. Hence, it is hedging a future cash flow (in this case the interest income) which is uncertain. The purpose of the hedge therefore is to lock in the interest at 4% between the end of June and the end of September. The total interest is £126,027, calculated as follows: £10,000,000 × 5% × (272 − 180)/365.

Assume that the opening balance sheet is as shown in Table 4.16 on 1 January 2009.

Table 4.16   Opening balance sheet

Assets	
Cash	£100,000,000
Shareholders' Funds	
Ordinary Shares issued	£100,000,000

Between 1 January and 31 March the FRA increases in value from 0 to £6000. IAS 39 requires that this derivative be shown on the balance sheet at market value and since it is a cash flow hedge, any change must go through Equity Reserve. See Table 4.17.

Table 4.17   Balance sheet on 31 March 2010

Assets	
Cash	£100,000,000
FRA	£6,000
Shareholders' Funds	
Ordinary Shares issued	£100,000,000
Equity Reserve	£6,000

Assume that interest rates turn out to be 4%. We must value the derivative on 30 June 2010. The valuation in Table 4.18 estimates what the payoff will be at 30 September and then discounts back to 30 June 2010.

Table 4.18   FRA valuation: 30 June 2010

Interest rate	4%
Estimated payoff at 30 September	£25,205
Discount Factor	0.990018444
Present Value	£24,954

The payoff on the FRA is $(5\%–4\%) \times £10,000,000 \times 92/365 = £25,205$. As this payment is due at the end of the FRA period, we discount it at the current market rate of 4%. The discount factor is therefore $1/(1 + 4\% \times 92/365) = 0.9900$, giving a present value of £24,954.

The balance sheet in Table 4.19 reflects the increase in the value of the FRA and also the £10,000,000 received on 30 June.

Table 4.19   Balance sheet on 30 June 2010

Assets	
Cash	£100,000,000
Deposit account	£10,000,000
FRA	£24,954
Shareholders' Funds	
Ordinary Shares issued	£110,000,000
Equity Reserve	£24,954

The balance sheet shows that the derivative has made a profit between 1 January and 30 June but, since the derivative is classified as a cash flow hedge, the change in value (i.e. the profit) must go through Equity Reserve.

Between June and September we accrue the interest on the loan and the FRA. The interest on the loan goes through the Profit & Loss account and the interest on the FRA temporarily goes through the Equity Reserve. See Table 4.20.

The accrued interest on the loan is $£10,000,000 \times 92/365 \times 4\% = £100,822$ and for the FRA, $£24,954 \times 4\% \times 92/365 = £24,954$.

The balance sheet on 30 September (after the accrued interest) looks as in Table 4.21.

The balance sheet is then adjusted to show that the FRA was cashed in and the Equity Reserve was transferred to the Profit & Loss account. The result is that we end up crediting to

Table 4.20 Interest accrual, loan and FRA

Deposit account	£10,000,000
Interest days	92
Libor rate	4%
Interest accrued (and paid)	£100,822
FRA valuation: 30 June 2010	£24,954
Interest days	92
Libor rate	4%
Interest accrued	£252

Table 4.21 Balance sheet on 30 September 2010 (part I)

Assets	
Cash	£100,000,000
Deposit account	£10,100,822
FRA	£25,205
Shareholders' Funds	
Ordinary Shares issued	£110,000,000
Equity Reserve	£25,205
Profit & Loss	£100,822

the Profit & Loss account the original locked-in figure of £126,027, i.e. £10,000,000×5%× (272–180)/365. See Table 4.22.

Table 4.22 Balance sheet on 30 September 2010 (part II)

Assets	
Cash	£100,025,205
Deposit account	£10,100,822
FRA	
Shareholders' Funds	
Ordinary Shares issued	£110,000,000
Equity Reserve	£–
Profit & Loss	£126,027

4.7 CONCLUSION

Accounting for simple transactions like a forward commodity contract and a forward rate agreement should be easy to understand and straightforward. The problem with the accounting standards is that the rules make simple transactions complex and cannot cope with complex transactions. As this book will later reveal, accounting for structured products is quite inadequate, resulting in the potential for banks to hide losses and more importantly to conceal risks. Furthermore, the shareholder is losing value through option-style incentive schemes that transfer wealth from them to the directors/employees and are not captured under IFRS 3, *Share Based Payments*.

Illustrative Examples: Hedge Accounting

5.1 INTRODUCTION

It is with interest rate swaps that practitioners have most difficulty dealing with the detailed requirements of the accounting standards. Very often, accountants get it wrong, or they may be tempted to take short-cuts with confusing and possibly, though rarely, disastrous consequences. In this illustration, we look at a detailed example of how a swap can be used as a fair value and cash flow hedge. We also look at the unique problems with foreign exchange contracts and touch on the demanding documentation requirements. The credit spread is an area that causes a lot of practical problems, with the American accounting treatment being different from that of the IASB.

Cash flow or fair value hedge

Accountants are sometimes confused as to whether they should apply cash flow or fair value hedge accounting when they use a swap to hedge a loan. In broad terms, where an entity is converting a fixed loan to a floating loan, fair value hedge accounting is used, while cash flow hedge accounting is used to convert a floating loan to a fixed loan.

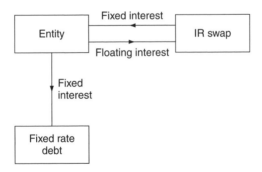

Figure 5.1   Fair value hedge

With fair value hedge accounting, the 'fair value' of the fixed loan on the balance sheet changes as interest rates change. Therefore, fair value hedging is appropriate. On the other hand, a floating loan does not change in value when interest rates change; so, the hedge of a floating loan really only relates to locking in future cash flows which are uncertain.

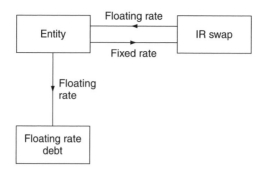

Figure 5.2   Cash flow hedge

5.2   ILLUSTRATION: FAIR VALUE HEDGE

Introduction

Accompanying the FASB publication on FAS 133 is a list of practical examples to aid auditors and accountants. Example 2 in appendix B of that publication covers how the hedge accounting rules apply to interest rate swaps. In practice, this example has caused a lot of confusion. The illustration below is based on that example but modified a little to make explanations easier. In this example, the entity issues a fixed bond for a notional of $4,000,000 and a coupon of 6.41%. The coupon is paid quarterly and the bond has a maturity of two years. The entity has a policy of converting all fixed interest exposures to floating exposures and so enters into an interest rate swap whereby it pays floating and receives fixed. In this simplistic example, the yield on the bond happens to be the same as the yield on the swap and so the hedge qualifies to be 100% effective. The terms of the loan and the terms of the swap are given in Table 5.1.

Table 5.1   Swap and bond term sheet

	Interest rate swap	Fixed rate debt
Trade date and borrowing date	01-Jan-10	01-Jan-10
Termination and maturity	31-Dec-11	31-Dec-11
Notional	$4,000,000	$4,000,000
Fixed interest rate	6.41%	6.41%
Settlement	end quarter	end quarter

Effectiveness

The first point to notice is that the swap and the bond are 100% effective. The notional is the same, the yield on the bond happens to be Libor and the dates coincide. If any one of these three variables were different, a change in interest rates would cause the swap to change by a normally greater – but occasionally lesser – amount than the underlying loan. In reality, the yield on the bond will usually be greater than Libor, which means that the swap will always outperform the bond. This is a matter we will look at later. Before identifying the necessary accounting treatment, it is important to calculate, intuitively, the values that will appear in the Profit & Loss account, for each of the eight quarters. To decide on the charge, we need to obtain the floating rates of interest, which are shown in Table 5.2.

Table 5.2   Libor and swap rates

From	To	Period number	Libor rates	Swap rates
01-Jan-10	31-Mar-10	1	6.41%	6.41%
01-Apr-10	30-Jun-10	2	6.48%	6.48%
01-Jul-10	30-Sep-10	3	6.41%	6.41%
01-Oct-10	31-Dec-10	4	6.32%	6.32%
01-Jan-11	31-Mar-11	5	7.60%	7.60%
01-Apr-11	30-Jun-11	6	7.71%	7.71%
01-Jul-11	30-Sep-11	7	7.82%	7.82%
01-Oct-11	31-Dec-11	8	7.42%	7.42%

In this table the Libor rates and the swap rates are the same. This suggests that the yield curve is flat; in other words, the market believes that interest rates in the future will not be different from what they are at present. In reality, the yield curve is upward-sloping a lot of the time and occasionally downward-sloping. An upward-sloping yield curve suggests that long-term interest rates are higher than in the short term – this would be the case if economists predicted higher inflation in the future. However, in order to avoid unnecessary complexity, we have assumed that short-term rates and long-term rates are the same. Since the interest rate in the first quarter is 6.41%, the charge to the Profit & Loss account is simply $4,000,000×6.41%×3/12=$64,100. The charge for the second quarter is $63,200, etc. Obviously, by converting a fixed loan to a floating loan we change the yield from fixed to floating and therefore it is the floating interest rate that is used to determine the profit and loss charge. Table 5.3 shows the charge for each of the quarters for the combined swap and loan.

Table 5.3   Charge to Profit & Loss account for each quarter

Notional	$4,000,000		
Period number	Libor rates	End period swap rates	Profit & Loss charge
1	6.41%	6.48%	$64,100
2	6.48%	6.41%	$64,800
3	6.41%	6.32%	$64,100
4	6.32%	7.60%	$63,200
5	7.60%	7.71%	$76,000
6	7.71%	7.82%	$77,100
7	7.82%	7.42%	$78,200
8	7.42%		$74,200

Valuation of swaps

As indicated in previous chapters, virtually all derivatives must appear on the balance sheet at fair value. Therefore, at the end of each quarter, we must value the swap and at the same time adjust the loan's value with the change in the value of the swap. Table 5.4 shows how the swap is valued intuitively, while Table 5.5 shows how the adjustment to the bond is obtained.

Table 5.4   Fair value of swap at the end of the first quarter

| | Notional | $4,000,000 | | | |
| | Time period | 0.25 | | | |
	Swap rate	Locked-in rate	Difference	Discount factor	Present value
1	6.48%	6.41%	−$700	0.9841	−$689
2	6.48%	6.41%	−$700	0.9684	−$678
3	6.48%	6.41%	−$700	0.9529	−$667
4	6.48%	6.41%	−$700	0.9377	−$656
5	6.48%	6.41%	−$700	0.9228	−$646
6	6.48%	6.41%	−$700	0.9081	−$636
7	6.48%	6.41%	−$700	0.8936	−$626
				6.5676	−$4597

This table shows the market swap rate at the end of the first period is 6.48%. The company has therefore made a loss on the swap. It has agreed to receive 6.41% but if it entered into the swap at the end of the first period, it would receive the going swap rate which is 6.48%. This gives a difference of about 7 basis points or 0.07%, which equates to −$700 per year ($4,000,000 × 3/12 × 0.07%). When this figure is multiplied by the annuity factor 6.568, the value of the swap becomes −$4597. We then compare the change in the swap to the change in the underlying bond. The fair value of the underlying bond is calculated in Table 5.5.

Table 5.5   Fair value of underlying liability: end first quarter

| | Bond | $4,000,000 | | |
| | Time period | 0.25 | | |
	Time period	Fixed coupon	Discount factor	Present value
1		$64,100	0.9840583	$63,078
2		$64,100	0.9683707	$62,073
3		$64,100	0.9529331	$61,083
4		$64,100	0.9377417	$60,109
5		$64,100	0.9227925	$59,151
6		$64,100	0.9080816	$58,208
7		$4,064,100	0.8936052	$3,631,701
			6.567583	$3,995,403

It is obvious that the swap in this example is 100% effective. The swap has reduced in value from 0 to −$4579 while the bond liability has reduced by $4579 from $4,000,000 to $3,995,403. As explained earlier, in reality it would be difficult to obtain 100% effectiveness mainly because the yield on any corporate loan is normally above Libor; the difference is normally known as the credit spread.

To see the impact this has on the balance sheet, we start, as usual, with an opening balance sheet and then consider the impact of the swap and the loan combined. For this example, we will assume that the company raised $6,000,000 from shareholders and a loan (as above) for $4,000,000, and used the total proceeds to buy a rental building which has an annual yield of 6% giving total quarterly rental earnings before interest of $150,000 or $10,000,000 \times 6\% \times 3/12 = \$150,000$. The opening balance sheet is shown in Table 5.6.

Table 5.6   Opening balance sheet on 1 January 2010

Assets	
Building	$10,000,000
Cash	$0
Liabilities	
Loans	−$4,000,000
Shareholders' Funds	
Ordinary Shares issued	$6,000,000
Profit & Loss (current quarter)	
Retained Profits (previous quarters)	

The closing balance sheet together with the Profit & Loss account for the first quarter is shown in Table 5.7.

Table 5.7   Balance sheet on 31 March

	Assets	
	Building	$10,000,000
	Cash	$85,900
	Liabilities	
	Loans	−$3,995,403
	Swap	−$4,597
	Shareholders' Funds	
	Ordinary Shares issued	$6,000,000
	Profit & Loss	$85,900
Rental yield	6%	
Profit & Loss		
Rental income	$150,000	
Interest expense	−$64,100	
Profit after interest	$85,900	

The increase in cash represents the rental income less the interest payments. The negative value of the swap is shown as a liability in the balance sheet and of course, under fair value hedge accounting, the entity is allowed to eliminate artificial volatility by changing the value of the underlying loan.

Occasionally, the swap may not qualify for hedge accounting. For instance, the auditors may not be satisfied with the documentation or the swap may fail certain hedge effectiveness tests that are regularly performed. If the swap failed to qualify as a hedge, the entity would not be allowed to adjust the fair value of the loan on the balance sheet. This means that the loan would be carried at the original cost and therefore changes in the value of the swap would cause volatility in the Profit & Loss account. See Table 5.8.

Table 5.8 Balance sheet on 31 March 2010, simplified IAS 39

Assets	
Building	$10,000,000
Cash	$85,900
Liabilities	
Loans	−$4,000,000
Swap	−$4,597
Shareholders' Funds	
Ordinary Shares issued	$6,000,000
Profit & Loss	$81,303

Rental yield	6%
Profit & Loss	
Rental income	$150,000
Interest expense	−$64,100
Profit after interest	$85,900
Loss from speculation	−$4,597
Total profit after interest	$81,303

In the illustration above, the entity has entered into a swap which does not qualify for hedge accounting and so is assumed to be speculating with derivatives. The change in the value of the derivative must therefore appear in the Profit & Loss account. Artificial volatility is created in this example because as the swap changes value, so too does the profit and loss. This gives the shareholder the impression that the entity is using swaps to speculate on interest rates, which is not the case in this example. The purpose of hedge accounting is to reduce this volatility.

Shortcut valuation procedures

The value of a swap can be calculated more quickly by the following simple formula:

$$\text{Notional} \times (\text{locked-in rate} - \text{current swap rate}) \times \text{CDF}$$

The CDF is the cumulative discount factor. In the above case, the CDF is simply the sum of the discount factors or can be calculated as follows:

$$\text{CDF} = (1 \times \text{DFN}) / \text{swap rate}$$

As Table 5.9 shows, we firstly calculate the discount factors and use these to calculate the cumulative discount factors. We can then value the swaps and bonds for each period.

To calculate the discount factor for the third period, it is simply $1/(1 + 0.25 \times 6.32\%)^5 = 0.9246$.

The cumulative discount factor is $(1 - 0.9246)/(6.32\% \times 0.25) = 4.7715$. The swap valuation is obtained by taking the difference in the rates, i.e. $(6.41\% - 6.32\%) \times \$4,000,000 \times$

Table 5.9   Swap and bond calculations

	Time period	0.25					
	Coupon	6.41%					
	Notional	$4,000,000					
Period number	Periods remaining	End period swap rates	Discount factors	Cumulative discount factors	Swap valuation	Bond valuation
1	7	6.48%	0.8936	6.5676	−$4,597	$3,995,403
2	6	6.41%	0.9090	5.6774	$0	$4,000,000
3	5	6.32%	0.9246	4.7715	$4,294	$4,004,294
4	4	7.60%	0.9275	3.8170	−$45,422	$3,954,578
5	3	7.71%	0.9443	2.8880	−$37,543	$3,962,457
6	2	7.82%	0.9620	1.9428	−$27,394	$3,972,606
7	1	7.42%	0.9818	0.9818	−$9,916	$3,990,084
8	0		1.0000	–	$0	$4,000,000

4.7715, to give $4294. Finally, the bond valuation is the coupon multiplied by the cumulative discount factor plus the notional times the zero discount factor, i.e. 6.41% × $4,000,000 × 0.25 × 4.7715 + $4,000,000 × 0.9246.

Accounting treatment

The balance sheets for the second and third periods are shown below.

The rental income for the second period, i.e. to 30 June 2010, is $10,000,000×6%×6/12 = $300,000. The swap at the end of period 2 has gone from a value of −$4597 to zero. How this change is treated in the Profit & Loss account depends on whether the swap qualifies for hedge accounting in the second period. If the swap does qualify, the change in the swap value has no impact on the Profit & Loss account, as Table 5.10 shows. Table 5.11 shows the situation where the swap does not qualify for hedge accounting.

In Table 5.11 we use the retained profits figure of $81,303 taken from Table 5.8 (where the swap does not qualify for hedge accounting).

Tables 5.12 and 5.13 show the situation where the hedge qualifies (5.12) and does not qualify (5.13) for the third period to 30 September 2010.

For Table 5.13, the retained profits figure is taken from Table 5.11.

As before if, for whatever reason, the swap did not qualify for hedge accounting, then the entire change in the swap would end up going through the Profit & Loss account and the loan would appear as $4,000,000 on the balance sheet. It would not be adjusted for changes in the value of the swap.

5.3   CREDIT SPREADS

Introduction

The above treatment applies where the swap is 100% effective, i.e. when interest rates change, the impact it will have on the swap will be the same as that on the loan. Unfortunately, this is seldom the case in reality. Most borrowers pay an additional yield to compensate the lender for the credit risk. Consider a company that wishes to borrow $4m for two years at a time when the two-year swap rate is 6.41%. In theory (but not necessarily in practice), the lender will

Table 5.10   Balance sheet on 30 June 2010

Balance Sheet	**30-Jun-10**	
Period 2		
Entity qualifies for hedge accounting		
	Assets	
	Building	$10,000,000
	Cash	$321,100
	Liabilities	
	Loans	−$4,000,000
	Swap	$0
		$6,321,100
	Shareholders' Funds	
	Ordinary Shares issued	$6,000,000
	Profit & Loss	$235,200
	Previous retained profits	$85,900
		$6,321,100
Rental yield	6%	
Profit & Loss for period		
Rental income	$150,000	
Interest expense	−$64,800	
Profit after interest	$85,200	
Total profit after interest	$85,200	

Table 5.11   Balance sheet on 30 June 2010

Balance Sheet	**30-Jun-10**	
Period 2		
Entity doesn't qualify for hedge accounting		
	Assets	
	Building	$10,000,000
	Cash	$171,100
	Liabilities	
	Loans	−$4,000,000
	Swap	$0
		$6,321,100
	Shareholders' Funds	
	Ordinary Shares issued	$6,000,000
	Profit & Loss	$239,797
	Previous retained profits	$81,303
		$6,321,100
Rental yield	6%	
Profit & Loss for period		
Rental income	$150,000	
Interest expense	−$64,800	
Profit after interest	$85,200	
Speculative Profit (Swap)	$4,597	
Total profit after interest	$89,797	

Table 5.12 Balance sheet on 30 September 2010

Balance Sheet	**30-Sep-10**	
Period 3		

Entity qualifies for hedge accounting

	Assets	
	Building	$10,000,000
	Cash	$514,425
	Liabilities	
	Loans	−$4,004,294
	Swap	$4,294
		$6,257,000
	Shareholders' Funds	
	Ordinary Shares issued	$6,000,000
	Profit & Loss	$85,900
	Previous retained profits	$171,100
		$6,257,000
Rental yield	6%	
Profit & Loss for period		
Rental income	$450,000	
Interest expense	−$256,675	
Profit after interest	$193,325	
Total profit after interest	$193,325	

Table 5.13 Balance sheet on 30 September 2010

Balance Sheet	**30-Jun-10**	
Period 3		

Entity doesn't qualify for hedge accounting

	Assets	
	Building	$10,000,000
	Cash	$257,000
	Liabilities	
	Loans	−$4,000,000
	Swap	$4,294
		$6,518,719
	Shareholders' Funds	
	Ordinary Shares issued	$6,000,000
	Profit & Loss	$197,619
	Previous retained profits	$321,100
		$6,518,719
Rental yield	6%	
Profit & Loss for period		
Rental income	$150,000	
Interest expense	−$64,100	
Profit after interest	$85,900	
Speculative profit (swap)	$4,294	
Total profit after interest	$90,194	

attempt to estimate the probability that the entity will go bankrupt in a year and then charge an additional yield on top of Libor (often referred to as the credit spread). If, for instance, the lender believes that there is a 2% chance that the entity will default and if it does default the borrower will lose the entire loan, then the borrower should charge at least Libor + 2%, i.e. a total of 8.41%. In practice, of course, the lender will try to make a profit margin on top of this breakeven rate and so may charge an additional couple of basis points to the yield.

In Chapters 7 and 8 we will see that in practice banks have, because of competition, not calculated the credit spread correctly, with the result that risky borrowers were not charged a correct premium and in effect, bank shareholders and, in some cases, taxpayers ended up footing the bill. Under Basel 2 regulations, there are rules that give supervisors the power to penalise banks if they adopt this unsound practice. These points will be examined in more detail later. For the moment, we will focus on the hedge accounting implications. To see the impact that the credit spread has on credit effectiveness, we look at a simple example.

Credit spread example

Entity X borrows $1,000,000 for five years at 10% at a time when the five-year swap rate is 10%. At the end of year 1, the swap rate moves from 10% to 11%. Table 5.14 shows that there is no ineffectiveness.

In this simplified example, the company borrows at a fixed rate of 10%, which happens to be the swap rate. The company's policy is to convert fixed loans to floating loans, and it enters

Table 5.14   Loan and swap effectiveness without credit spread

Loan advance	$1,000,000	
Term	5	
Yield	10%	
Swap notional	$1,000,000	
Term	5	
Fixed rate	10%	
Entity receives fixed		
End year 1	Swap rate 11%	Swap rate 9%
Cash flow on bond		
1	$100,000	$100,000
2	$100,000	$100,000
3	$100,000	$100,000
4	$1,100,000	$1,100,000
Yield	10%	10%
Present value	$1,000,000	$1,000,000
Yield	11%	9%
Present value	$968,976	$1,032,397
Impact on P&L	$31,024	−$32,397
Swap		
1	−$10,000	$10,000
2	−$10,000	$10,000
3	−$10,000	$10,000
4	−$10,000	$10,000
Swap value	−$31,024	$32,397

into a swap where it receives fixed and pays floating. At the end of the first year, with four years remaining life left in the loan and the swap, the relevant swap rate changes from 10% to 11%. The company has borrowed at a fixed rate of 10%, the 'fair value' of the loan drops from $1,000,000 to $968,976. A reduction in a liability does of course increase economic or true profit, but the accounting standards generally do not allow an entity to recognise this profit in their accounting Profit & Loss account.[1] If, however, the entity adopts fair value hedge accounting on this transaction, it is permitted to recognise the profit.

The swap of course has made a loss. The entity has agreed to receive 10% throughout the life of the swap. However, if it wanted to unwind the swap, it would have to pay 11% while receiving only 10%. This represents a loss of 1%, which equates to $-$10,000 per annum or, in present value terms, $31,025. Thus, the loss on the swap matches the gain from the reduction in the liability and therefore there is no ineffectiveness.

There will also be no ineffectiveness if, at the end of the first year, interest rates fall by 1%. This time the fair value of the liability on the loan increases by $32,397, representing a loss for the entity but the swap gains by an equivalent amount.

Table 5.14 is now reconstructed to show the impact of the credit spread. Normally, when entities borrow money, they must pay an increased yield above Libor to reflect the fact that they are generally riskier than banks. Banks themselves tend to lend to each other at Libor. Where there is a credit spread present, there will always be ineffectiveness. Table 5.15 shows that when a bond is discounted at a different yield to that of a swap, ineffectiveness always arises. In this case, the swap is discounted at Libor (as always) while the bond is discounted at Libor plus a credit spread of 1.5%.

As can be seen, regardless of whether interest rates go up or down, the swap will always outperform the underlying bond. This is always true when the credit spread is positive. In the rare cases when the credit spread is negative (i.e. where borrowers can borrow at yield below Libor), the swap will underperform the underlying loan or bond.

FASB vs. IAS 39 accounting treatment

There appears to be a difference between the way that the American accounting standards board (FASB) and the IASB deal with interest rate swaps. In broad terms, there are two accounting treatments – the short-cut method and the long method. The short-cut method is generally used where the swap is deemed to be 100% effective. The treatment is straightforward. Any swap settlements are transferred to the Profit & Loss account and any change in the market value of the swap is assumed to qualify for hedge effectiveness. The result is that the journal entries are relatively straightforward. However, if ineffectiveness arises, both the international and American accounting standard setters tend to require a more complex bookkeeping system, known as the 'long method'. There are broadly three tests that the IASB requires to determine if the swap is 100% effective. Firstly, are the principals the same? Secondly, are the dates on the swap as the dates of the underlying loan and thirdly, is the yield on the loan equal to Libor? As a broad guideline, if the answer is no to any of these three questions, the hedge is not 100% effective. Therefore, the long method must be chosen. This is quite a complicated system but it is designed to ensure that the correct ineffectiveness is identified and released to the Profit & Loss account immediately.

---

[1] The exception is the fair value option discussed in Chapter 11.

Table 5.15 Loan and swap ineffectiveness with credit spread

Loan advance	$1,000,000	
Term	5	
Yield	11.50%	
Credit spread	1.50%	
Swap notional	$1,000,000	
Term	5	
Fixed rate	10%	
Entity receives fixed		
End year 1	Swap rate	Swap rate
	11.0%	9.0%
Cash flow on bond		
1	$115,000	$115,000
2	$115,000	$115,000
3	$115,000	$115,000
4	$1,115,000	$1,115,000
Yield	11.50%	11.50%
Present value	$1,000,000	$1,000,000
Yield	12.50%	10.50%
Present value	$969,944	$1,031,359
Impact on P&L	$30,056	−$31,359
Swap		
1	−$10,000	$10,000
2	−$10,000	$10,000
3	−$10,000	$10,000
4	−$10,000	$10,000
Swap value	−$31,024	$32,397
Ineffectiveness	−$968	$1,039

Short method vs. long method

To decide between the short-cut method and the long method, three questions must be addressed.

1. **Are the principals the same?** In the above example, the principals are the same at $4,000,000.
2. **Are the dates the same?** If the swap settlements date was not the same as the coupon dates, there would be periods when the entity would temporarily have excess cash or a shortage of cash which it would have to reinvest. Therefore, the hedge would not be 100% effective.
3. **Is the yield on the swap (often Libor) the same as the yield on the bond?** Generally, the yield on the swap is Libor whereas the yield on the bond is usually Libor + spread. The American accounting standards broadly ignore this but the IASB says that if the yield on the bond is different from the yield on the swap, the entity cannot assume 100% effectiveness.

Under IASB, to assume 100% effectiveness the entity must be able to answer 'yes' to all three questions. If the entity cannot assume 100% effectiveness, the 'long method' (discussed later) must be used.

For FASB, the entity must only answer 'yes' to questions 1 and 2.[2]

---

[2] A discussion on the 'short-cut method' can be found at http://www.iasb.org/NR/rdonlyres/C01AB860-68CE-4396-8D9E-3F16EAAA5CF1/0/ObNotes_SME0609ob15a.pdf

On the basis of illustrative examples, produced by the American accounting standards board, it is possible to assume that a swap qualifies for the short-cut treatment even though there may be a credit spread present. This basically means that under the American accounting standards the entity may be allowed to use the short-cut method inappropriately. The result is a slight loss of accuracy but, arguably, this is counterbalanced by a lot less trouble. In reality, the FASB is probably twisting logic to the point where it becomes very confusing. The IASB, on the other hand, argues that if there is a credit spread present, no matter how small, the long method must be used so that ineffectiveness can be calculated properly and more importantly, the correct interest rate is charged to the Profit & Loss account.

FASB 138

In a document entitled 'Examples Illustrating Application of FASB Statement no 138, Accounting for Certain Derivative Instruments and Certain Hedging Activities', the FASB attempted to deal with the issue of credit spreads.[3] Unfortunately, the document raised more questions than it answered, and left some practitioners confused. The example is discussed below.

On 3 April 2010, Global Tech issued a $100 million five-year loan with a coupon of 8% payable semi-annually. The company had a policy of converting fixed loans to floating loans and so entered into a swap which qualified as a fair value hedge, converting a fixed loan to a floating loan. Under the swap arrangement, the entity received a fixed rate of 8% and paid floating of Libor + 78.5 basis points, i.e. 0.785%. The FASB would permit the short-cut method to apply in this case because the principal on the loan and the swap are the same, at $100 million. The dates of the loan and the swap also coincide. In both cases, the tenor is five years, the swap starts at the same time as the loan, 3 April 2010 and the settlements for both the swap and the loan are semi-annual. However, it is the presence of the credit spread that causes the problem. The yield on the bond is 78.5 basis points higher than Libor. Hence, the discount rate on the bond will be higher than that of the swap, leading to ineffectiveness. The FASB attitude appears to be to 'turn a blind eye' to this and use the short-cut method, while the IASB approach is to insist on the 'long method' because of this credit spread differential.

Figure 5.3 shows how the case is presented. Since the swap rate is the same as the fixed rate on the bond, the impression is given that there is no ineffectiveness but, as Figure 5.4 shows, there is an 'economic' difference in the fixed rates. See Table 5.16 for details.

The first problem with this example (though minor) is the PV01 figure calculations. The term PV01 presumably refers to the change in the present value of the financial instrument, assuming a 1% change in interest rates. Therefore, if interest rates went up by 1%, the value of the bond/loan would fall by $4.14 million whereas the value of the swap would change by $4,060,000. The entity has entered into a fair value hedge under which it pays floating and receives fixed. So, if interest rates were to rise, the entity would make money from the reduction in the value of the liability and lose money on the swap. However, the PV01 calculations suggest that the swap is LESS sensitive to changes in interest rates than the bond. This will NEVER be the case as long as the credit spread is positive, as discussed earlier. In other words, if the yield on the bond exceeds Libor, the swap will always be more sensitive to interest rate changes than the loan. Presumably, therefore, the FASB simply estimated the

---

[3] The example can be downloaded from http://www.fasb.org/derivatives/examplespg.shtml

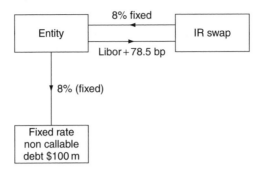

Figure 5.3   Fair value hedge of $100m loan

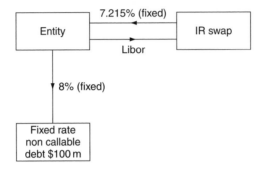

Figure 5.4   Alternative presentation

Table 5.16   Term sheet and sensitivity of bonds and swap

Loan details	
Loan amount	$100,000,000
Fixed interest	8.0000%
Tenor (no. of years)	5
Credit spread	0.7850%
PV01 bond	$4,140,000
PV01 swap	$4,060,000
Swap details	
Notional	$101,970,443
Implied swap rate	7.2150%
Tenor	5

figures rather than calculating them. The error, though minor, can cause confusion. We will continue, however, to analyse the example on the assumption that the figures are correct.

What the FASB suggest is that the notional on the swap should be adjusted to recognise that (in this case only) the loan is more sensitive to interest rate changes than the swap. For instance, if we divide $4,140,000 by $4,060,000 we get 1.0197. Therefore, we adjust the notional of the swap to reflect the fact that it has a lower sensitivity. In theory, the FASB are quite correct, one can improve the hedge effectiveness of the swap by adjusting the notional to take into account the differences in the sensitivities. However, by their own definition, if the notional on the loan is not the same as the notional on the swap, we end up with ineffectiveness according to the FASB criteria (since the notionals and the time periods of the hedging item and the underlying must match).

The second point is that in the example, the FASB appear to turn a blind eye to the fact that if a swap is discounted at Libor and a bond is discounted at Libor plus a credit spread, there will always be ineffectiveness even if the entity adjusted the notional of the swap to reflect different interest rate sensitivities. In this example, the FASB calculated two journal entries to reveal the fair value treatment, as shown in Table 5.17.

Table 5.17   Journal entries, FASB

Debit loan	$3,775,620	
Credit profit & loss		$3,775,620
Debit earnings	$4,016,000	
		$4,016,000
Difference		$240,380

The journal entries show how the FASB interpreted fair value hedge accounting for the above transaction. In this example, the FASB do not give details of all the calculations – however, they are not important. The swap has declined in value by $4,016,000 as a result of an increase in interest rates. The debt has fallen by $3,775,920. The loss resulting from the change in the value of the swap is recognised in earnings, as is the gain from the reduction in the liability. There is a difference of $240,380. The FASB indicate that the difference arises due to 'some imprecision in the calculated hedge ratio'. This, of course, is not quite correct. The change arises because the bond is discounted at Libor plus the credit spread whereas the swap is discounted at Libor. Unfortunately, therefore, while changing the notional can improve the effectiveness of the hedge, it doesn't eliminate entirely the ineffectiveness.

5.4   CASH FLOW INTEREST RATE SWAPS

Introduction

The FASB has produced another example involving interest rate swaps, and appears once again to have sidestepped the credit spread issue, leading to potential confusing consequences. The example can be found in the Implementation Guidance FAS 133 (appendix B, example 5). Unlike the previous examples, where we looked at how we accounted for a hedge that converts a fixed loan to a floating loan, we now look at a situation where an entity buys a floating coupon bond and is worried about interest rate volatility, so enters into a swap arrangement whereby the entity receives floating and pays fixed. The term sheets summarising the transaction are given in Tables 5.18 and 5.19.

Before attempting to understand the accounting treatment, it is important not to lose sight of the economics of the transaction. The entity in this case has bought a bond for $10,000,000. The bond pays a coupon of Libor plus a credit spread of 2.25%. The company has a policy of reducing its exposure to interest rate fluctuations and so enters into a swap arrangement whereby it pays Libor and receives a fixed swap rate of 6.65%. The total yield on the bond

Table 5.18 Term sheet for bond and swap

	Interest rate swap	Corporate bonds
Trade date and borrowing date	1 July 2001	1 July 2001
Termination date	30 June 2003	30 June 2003
Notional amount	$10,000,000	$10,000,000
Fixed interest rate	6.65%	Not applicable
Variable interest rate	3-month Libor	3-month Libor+2.25%
Settlement dates and interest payment dates	End of calendar quarter	End of calendar quarter
Reset dates	End of calendar quarter through 31 March 2003	End of calendar quarter through 31 March 2004

Table 5.19 Libor rates

Reset date	3-month Libor rate
01-Jul-01	5.56%
30-Sep-01	5.63%
31-Dec-01	5.56%
31-Mar-02	5.47%
30-Jun-02	6.75%
30-Sep-02	6.86%
31-Dec-02	6.97%
31-Mar-03	6.57%

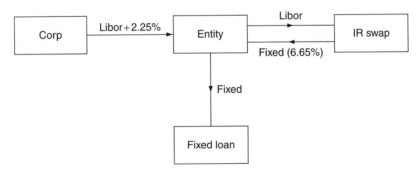

Figure 5.5 Cash flow hedge of corporate bond

is therefore 8.9%. The coupon on the bond is $890,000, or $225,000 per quarter. This is the income that the entity earns and so will be credited to the Profit & Loss account each quarter, regardless of whether the interest rate changes or not. Therefore, for the period July to September, the interest income will be $222,500 and will remain at $222,500 for each subsequent period.

From an accounting perspective, the swap transaction would be classified as a cash flow hedge on the grounds that the purpose of the swap is to make future cash flows more certain. The coupon cash flows are variable or uncertain before the hedge, and become fixed or certain after the hedge. To recap, for cash flow hedge accounting the accounting treatment is such that the swap must appear on the balance sheet at market value and any change in the swap value (apart from settlement at each coupon date) must go through the Equity Reserve account, in order to avoid or eliminate artificial volatility in the Profit & Loss account.

Unfortunately, any gains or losses on the swap will not match 100% the gains or losses on the underlying bond since the swap is discounted at Libor in order to reach market or fair value while the bond is discounted at Libor plus the credit spread of 2.25% in this case. The FASB nevertheless allow the short-cut treatment despite this ineffectiveness.

Short-cut method

Under the short-cut method (assuming that the entity is allowed to apply it), any interest paid on the loan account is charged to the Profit & Loss account. Similarly, any swap settlement is charged to the Profit & Loss account as well. As Table 5.20 reveals, the overall charge to the Profit & Loss account remains at $222,500 regardless of the interest rate.

Table 5.20   Interest income in Profit & Loss account

Bond	$10,000,000				
Swap fixed rate	6.65%				
Bond spread	2.25%				
Quarterly coupon	0.25				
Period from	Period to	Interest rate	Loan interest	Swap settlement	Charge to P&L
01-Jul-01	30-Sep-01	5.56%	$195,250	$27,250	$222,500
30-Sep-01	31-Dec-01	5.63%	$197,000	$25,500	$222,500
31-Dec-01	31-Mar-02	5.56%	$195,250	$27,250	$222,500
31-Mar-02	30-Jun-02	5.47%	$193,000	$29,500	$222,500
30-Jun-02	30-Sep-02	6.75%	$225,000	−$2,500	$222,500
30-Sep-02	31-Dec-02	6.86%	$227,750	−$5,250	$222,500
31-Dec-02	31-Mar-03	6.97%	$230,500	−$8,000	$222,500
31-Mar-03	30-Jun-03	6.57%	$220,500	$2,000	$222,500

As Table 5.20 reveals, the coupon on the bond for each period is simply $10,000,000 × (Libor + 2.25%) × 0.25. In the first period, Libor is 5.56%. The settlement of the swap for each quarter is $10,000,000 × (6.65% – Libor) × 0.25 = $27.250. The journal entries necessary to put this in place are therefore relatively straightforward. As this swap qualifies as a cash flow hedge, the value of the swap at the year end must appear on the balance sheet and any change in the value must go through the Equity Reserve account. Unfortunately, in the example produced by the American FASB, there is insufficient information to calculate the swap, however this is not important when discussing the accounting entries. In this case, the yield curve is upward-sloping, meaning that there are different interest rates for different periods and so we will have to assume that their figure of $24,850 is correct. We show in Table 5.21 the entity's balance sheet before the bond is purchased and the balance sheet at the end of the first quarter.

In this example, the entity has paid out $10m cash to purchase a bond and has taken out a swap to convert the floating yield to a fixed yield of 8.9%. The profit increases, therefore, by the yield of 8.9% per annum or 2.225% per quarter. The swap's value at the end of the period is $24,850, and as it qualifies for a cash flow hedge the difference goes to Equity Reserve.

Table 5.21   Balance sheet extracts

	Opening balance sheet	Balance sheet at 30-Sep-01
Assets		
Cash	$10,000,000	$222,500
Bond	$0	$10,000,000
Swap	$0	$24,850
Shareholders' Funds		
Ordinary Shares issued	$10,000,000	$10,000,000
Equity Reserve		$24,850
Profit & Loss	$0	$222,500

5.5   TIME VALUE VS. CHANGE IN INTEREST RATES

There are two reasons why a swap changes in value. One is the 'time value' change. This means that as time goes by, the present value gets closer to the future value. Accountants often refer to this as the 'unwind of the discount'. This should not qualify for hedge accounting as it is an expected as opposed to an unexpected change. The short-cut method merges the unexpected change with the expected change, causing slight inaccuracy where the swap is a little ineffective. However, no inaccuracy arises where the swap is 100% effective.

Table 5.22 shows the adjustments necessary at the end of the first period using the long method. As the swap has a zero value to begin with, we don't need to worry about the time value of the swap. We simply accrue the interest on the bond and put it through the Profit & Loss account. However, any settlement on the swap is transferred to the Equity Reserve and not the Profit & Loss account as in the short-cut method. The balance sheet is then adjusted for changes in the market value and, as with the swap settlement, this is transferred to Equity Reserve. The total balance in the Equity Reserve account is therefore $27,250 + $24,850 = $52,100. This in fact represents the total profit on the swap and the entire amount is transferred to the Equity Reserve account. The final adjustment reflects the fact that if we convert a floating bond to a fixed bond, the yield that must appear in the Profit & Loss account is $222,500. We have only credited $195,250 so, to bring the Profit & Loss account up to $222,500, we must extract $27,250 from the Equity Reserve account to the Profit & Loss account.

We now look at the adjustments necessary to get from the first period to the second period (Table 5.23) and then discuss the advantages (and disadvantages) of using the long method over the short-cut method. Here a distinction must be made between the 'time value' change and the unexpected change.

Unlike the short-cut method, interest is accrued on the swap as well as the bond. The interest accrued on the swap (according to the FASB) qualifies for hedge accounting, and is therefore transferred to the Equity Reserve. The swap settlement, along with the adjustment to reflect the change in the market value of the swap, as well as the adjustment to the Profit & Loss account, follow the same convention as before.

One area that is confusing in the above example is why the FASB believe that the interest accrued on the swap qualifies for hedge accounting. The interest in this case is $330. Unfortunately, there is very little information in the example to verify the $330 figure, nevertheless, the calculation is not important. What does matter is that the accrued interest is transferred to the Equity Reserve, and this is inconsistent with other examples produced by

Table 5.22 Long method adjustments period 1 to period 2

	Opening balance sheet	Purchase bond	Accrue interest	Settle swap	MTM swap	Adjust P&L
Assets						
Cash	$10,000,000	$0	$195,250	$222,500	$222,500	$222,500
Bond	$0	$10,000,000	$10,000,000	$10,000,000	$10,000,000	$10,000,000
Swap	$0	$0	$0	$0	$24,850	$24,850
	$10,000,000	$10,000,000	$10,195,250	$10,222,500	$10,247,350	$10,247,350
Shareholders' Funds						
Ordinary Shares issued	$10,000,000	$10,000,000	$10,000,000	$10,000,000	$10,000,000	$10,000,000
Equity Reserve	$0	$0	0	$27,250	$52,100	$24,850
Profit & Loss	$0	$0	$195,250	$195,250	$195,250	$222,500
	$10,000,000	$10,000,000	$10,195,250	$10,222,500	$10,247,350	$10,247,350

Table 5.23 Long method adjustments period 2 to period 3

	Opening balance sheet	Accrue interest swap	Accrue interest loan	Settle swap	MTM swap	Adjust P&L
Assets						
Cash	$222,500	$222,500	$419,500	$445,000	$445,000	$445,000
Bond	$10,000,000	$10,000,000	$10,000,000	$10,000,000	$10,000,000	$10,000,000
Swap	$24,850	$25,180	$25,180	-$320	$73,800	$73,800
	$10,247,350	$10,247,680	$10,444,680	$10,444,680	$10,518,800	$10,518,800
Shareholders' Funds	$0					
Ordinary Shares issued	$10,000,000	$10,000,000	$10,000,000	$10,000,000	$10,000,000	$10,000,000
Equity Reserve	$24,850	$25,180	$25,180	$25,180	$99,300	$73,800
Profit & Loss			$197,000	$197,000	$197,000	$222,500
Retained P&L (previous)	$222,500	$222,500	$222,500	$222,500	$222,500	$222,500
	$10,247,350	$10,247,680	$10,444,680	$10,444,680	$10,518,800	$10,518,800

the FASB where the time value is identified and released to the Profit & Loss account, even for derivatives that qualify as hedges. The rationale behind putting the accrued interest through the Profit & Loss account is that the time value of a swap (particularly when used as a cash flow hedge) should not qualify for hedge accounting, only the unexpected change should. Therefore, an alternative treatment (or a proposed correction) to the FASB example is given in Table 5.24.

In this example, the interest accrued on the swap and the interest accrued on the bond are both recognised in the Profit & Loss account, giving a total amount of $197,330. However, the amount that should be transferred to the Profit & Loss account is once again $222,500. It is important to recognise why the swap has changed in value from $24,850 to $73,800. The difference arises because of the change due to time value $330, the change due to settlement $25,500, and the change because of unexpected interest rate movements $74,120. It is only the change that arises from unexpected interest rate movements that qualifies for hedge accounting. The short-cut method, if used inappropriately, therefore distorts (though only slightly) the Equity Reserve account and, as a result, the Profit & Loss account.

To recap, there are two reasons why the swap changes value. The first is the unwind of the discount and the second is the unexpected change in the interest rate. In broad terms, the unwind of the discount doesn't qualify for hedge accounting but the change caused by a change in the interest rate does. Only the latter should qualify for hedge accounting, not the former. The short-cut method doesn't make this distinction, and so a slight inaccuracy could arise.

There is an important logical flaw with the American example. It arises because the FASB turn a blind eye to instances where ineffectiveness is caused by the credit spread. Under IAS, it is almost 100% certain that not all of the $74,120, i.e. the change on the swap due to unexpected interest rate movements, would qualify for hedge acccounting. This is because, under IAS 39.96, the lower of the change in the swap and the change in the underlying bond goes through the Profit & Loss account. This is for reasons mentioned earlier, namely that the discount factor on the swap will always be lower than that of a bond (with a positive credit spread). It follows that there will be a lot of ineffectiveness on the swap (given the size of the credit spread of 2.25%), and this must be released to the Profit & Loss account.

The inaccuracy that arises when using the short-cut method inappropriately is summarised in Table 5.25. As mentioned, the interest accrual of $330 does not qualify for hedge accounting and, under the long method, it is identified separately and released to the Profit & Loss account. The long method therefore breaks down the swap between the unwind of the discount and the unexpected change in the interest rate. The short-cut method merges the two together.

5.6 LONG METHOD FAIR VALUE HEDGE

We finish this chapter by looking at the long method for fair value hedge accounting. We return to the example in Table 5.18. The FASB use the bond and swap in Table 5.26 (which we looked at earlier) to show how the long method may be applied. Unfortunately, this example does not contain a credit spread and so the comparison between the long method and the short-cut method is difficult to make. However, we will examine the approach in detail so that we can see how the FASB interpret the long method and then discuss the implications. The journal entries for periods 1 and 2 are listed in the table.

Table 5.24 Long method adjustments period 2 to period 3

	Opening balance sheet	Accrue interest swap	Accrue interest loan	Settle swap	MTM swap	Adjust P&L
Assets						
Cash	$222,500	$222,500	$419,500	$445,000	$445,000	$445,000
Bond	$10,000,000	$10,000,000	$10,000,000	$10,000,000	$10,000,000	$10,000,000
Swap	$24,850	$25,180	$25,180	-$320	$73,800	$73,800
	$10,247,350	$10,247,680	$10,444,680	$10,444,680	$10,518,800	$10,518,800
Shareholders' Funds						
Ordinary Shares issued	$10,000,000	$10,000,000	$10,000,000	$10,000,000	$10,000,000	$10,000,000
Equity Reserve	$24,850	**$24,850**	$24,850	$24,850	$98,970	$73,800
Profit & Loss		**$330**	$197,330	$197,330	$197,330	$222,500
Retained P&L (previous)	$222,500	$222,500	$222,500	$222,500	$222,500	$222,500
	$10,247,350	$10,247,680	$10,444,680	$10,444,680	$10,518,800	$10,518,800

Table 5.25   Long vs. short method

Opening valuation	$24,850	
Interest accrual	$330	
Change due to interest rate movements	$74,120	qualifies for hedge accounting
Cash settlement	−$25,500	
Closing balance	$73,800	
Opening balance	$24,850	
Change	$74,450	qualifies for hedge accounting
Cash settlement	−$25,500	
	$73,800	

Table 5.26   Long vs. short method cash flow hedge

Start		
Debit cash	$4,000,000	
Credit loan		$4,000,000
Period 1		
Debit P&L	$64,100	
Credit loan		$64,100
Debit loan	$64,100	
Credit cash		$64,100
Debit P&L	$4,597	
Credit swap		$4,597
Debit loan	$4,597	
Credit P&L		$4,597
Period 2		
Debit P&L	$64,100	
Credit loan		$64,100
Debit P&L	$74	
Credit swap		$74
Debit loan	$64,100	
Credit cash		$64,100
Debit swap	$700	
Credit cash		$700
Debit P&L	$626	
Credit loan		$626
Debit swap	$3,972	
Credit P&L		$3,972
Debit P&L	$3,972	
Credit loan		$3,972

These journal entries are relatively straightforward. The $74 in period 2 represents the change in the time value of the swap, i.e. $1,149 \times 6.48\% \times 3/12 = 74. The $626 is referred to in FAS as the 'amortisation of basis adjustment'. We compare the amount that should be charged to the Profit & Loss account against the amount that is charged. The amount that should be charged is $4,000,000 \times 6.48\% \times 3/12 = $64,800$ and the amount that is charged is $64,100 + 74, giving a difference of $626.

It is helpful to see the difference between the long and short method for fair value hedging, and this is analysed in Table 5.27 for period 2.

Table 5.27   Long vs. short method fair value hedge

Opening valuation	−$4597	
Interest accrual	−$74	
Change due to interest rate		
movements	$3972	qualifies for hedge accounting
Cash settlement	$700	
Closing balance	$0	
Opening balance	−$4597	
Change	$3897	qualifies for hedge accounting
Cash settlement	$700	
Closing balance	$0	

As before, the long method breaks down the change in the value of the swap between the expected change $74 and the unexpected change $3972. The short-cut method merges the two together, creating a slight level of inaccuracy. The difference is immaterial where the swap qualifies to be 100% effective.

5.7   FOREIGN EXCHANGE HEDGE

Introduction

As pointed out earlier, many financial institutions along with corporates are forced to apply the complexities of hedge accounting when they hold assets and liabilities which they wish to hedge and those assets and liabilities are not normally shown at cost on the balance sheet. Where hedge accounting is used, extensive documentation is required. Given the complexities of some transactions, documentation can often prove difficult and it is reasonable to say that some entities are applying hedge accounting without the appropriate documentation or using documentation that is flawed. Many practitioners have complained that there is a shortage of guidance on the appropriate type of documentation. This section will attempt to address this shortfall. Below, we look at an example of how the American FASB deal with cash flow hedges on a foreign currency transaction. We then discuss weaknesses with this example and why it might be misleading, and conclude by giving guidelines on how the documentation for such a transaction would look. We also discuss hedge effectiveness testing. We start by looking at foreign exchange basics.

Foreign exchange example

Table 5.28 illustrates a term sheet (agreement) between a bank and a company. The company is British and expects to import $2,100,000 worth of equipment in two years' time. Obviously, the company is worried about the dollar getting stronger and so enters into a forward currency agreement whereby it receives $2,100,000 and pays GBP 1 million in two years' time regardless of what the exchange rate turns out to be.

Normally such contracts are entered into at zero cost, i.e. the value of the forward contract on the date is agreed is zero for both sides. In reality, of course, there are transaction costs

Table 5.28 Forward contract term sheet

Company pays	£1,000,000
Forward exchange rate	$2.10
Company receives	$2,100,000
Expiry	31-Dec-08
Agreement date	31-Dec-06

but we will ignore this for the moment. Therefore, the value of the forward contract on 31 December 2006 is zero.

One year later, on 31 December 2007, the market value of the forward contract would, as we expect, move away from zero. The value depends on how the spot exchange rate changes; the forward contract value will also be influenced by changes in the interest rate of both countries, i.e. Britain and America. The value is important for accounting purposes since the forward contract meets the definition of a derivative and therefore the market value must be ascertained. In order to do this we obtain details of the interest rates and the exchange rate on 31 December 2007. The details are shown in Table 5.29.

Table 5.29 Market rates at 31 December 2007

		Discount factor
Spot	$2.02	
Interest A	4.50%	0.956937799
Interest B	5.00%	0.952380952

The current spot rate is $2.02 to GBP 1 and the interest rate in America is 4.5%, while in Britain it is slightly higher at 5%. The discount factors are shown for each interest rate. Since the maturity is one year, the calculation is straightforward, i.e. $0.9569 = 1/(1 + 4.5\%)$.

Table 5.30 shows the two methods to value a forward contract at 31 December 2007 when there is only one year to expiry on the contract.

Table 5.30 Valuation of forward contract

BP receives		Present value	Conversion to sterling
Asset	$2,100,000	$2,009,569	£994,836
Liability	−£1,000,000	−£952,381	−£952,381
			£42,455
Market forward	$2.010381		
Gain	$89,619.05	$89,619.05	
Discounted	$85,759.85		
Conversion to sterling	£42,455		

Under the first method we simply get the present value of both the asset and the liability by using the appropriate discount factors. We then choose a common currency (sterling) and take the present value of the liability away from the present value of the asset to leave a value of GBP 42,455. The second approach uses the spot exchange rate along with the interest rates of both countries to obtain the current market forward rate. In this case, the forward rate is simply the spot rate multiplied by (1 + the American rate)/(1 + the British rate). Therefore, 2.02×(1 + 4.5%)/(1 + 5%) = \$2.010381. We then compare the market forward rate to the one that we locked in, i.e. \$1,000,000×(2.02 − 2.010381) = \$89,619. This represents the future profit, expected in one year's time on settlement date. Finally, we get the present value and exchange to sterling at the spot rate.

What causes problems for accountants is that the forward contract changes not only because the spot exchange rate changes but also because of interest rate change. Very often, the interest rate changes are not recognised in the accounting profit (particularly for periods of less than a year), and so it is normal practice for entities who use forward contracts to split out the intrinsic value from the time value. The intrinsic value represents the change in the forward contract's value that arises from a change in the spot rate, and the time value represents any other factors that cause the forward contract's price to change. Later, we will see how the intrinsic value is distinguished from the time value. Generally, when currency forward contracts are used for hedging purposes, it is the intrinsic value only and not the time value that qualifies for hedge accounting.

Borrowing expenses with foreign loans

A question that has vexed accountants is what the most appropriate interest charge should be in the Profit & Loss account when an entity uses a foreign loan. A British company, for instance, may borrow money in America when interest rates are 3.5% and convert the money into sterling where the equivalent interest rates are 5%. Should the interest charge on this loan be 3.5% or 5%? The answer without doubt is the higher of the two figures, 5%. The American loan may look attractive superficially but, in reality, the difference between the forward and spot exchange rate compensates for the difference in interest rates. To put this another way, what the entity gains on the interest rates it loses on the foreign exchange rates. In the past, however, many companies were tempted to use the lower of the two rates to calculate the interest charge. In his book *Accounting for Growth*, published in 1992,[4] Terry Smith highlighted some of the creative accounting tactics that entities use when interest rates between two countries are different. In 1991, for instance, the average Libor rate in sterling was 12.8% whereas in America the equivalent rate was about 8.9%. Therefore, many British companies who needed sterling borrowings instead borrowed in dollars. Although this introduced a foreign exchange exposure, the risk being that the dollar might appreciate, many companies claimed that they were able to charge the equivalent of 8.9% as borrowing costs in their accounts instead of 12.8%. Anyone with even a vague understanding of foreign exchange will realise that there is generally no economic advantage to borrowing in a foreign currency compared to the domestic currency, even if there is an interest rate differential, unless the borrower wants to deliberately take on the foreign exchange exposure. In short, what the entity gains on the interest differential it loses when it tries to unwind the loan. Many companies were able to take the gain on the time value through the Profit & Loss account but hide the loss on the loan translation. Hiding losses in this manner is now more difficult since, as we shall see later, IAS 21, *The Effects of Changes in Foreign Exchange Rates* requires that monetary liabilities be shown on the balance sheet at the closing rate on the balance sheet date with any difference going through the Profit & Loss account. In addition, IAS 39 requires that for cash

---

[4] Terry Smith, *Accounting for Growth*, Century Business, 1992, p. 169.

flow hedges, the time value must be distinguished from the intrinsic value with the change in the time value going through the Profit & Loss account.

A simple example will illustrate that there is no economic advantage in borrowing in a foreign currency and, as a consequence, there should be no accounting advantage.

A British entity wishes to borrow £10m for three years and is undecided between a straight-forward sterling loan and borrowing in JPY and converting to sterling. For comparison purposes, we will assume that the entity does not want a foreign currency exposure and there-fore locks in the currency exposure by entering into a three-year forward contract. The details of the loan, the spot rate and interest rates of both countries are shown in Table 5.31.

Table 5.31   Details of loan and interest payments

Zero coupon loan	£10,000,000
Spot rate	JPY 100.00
Interest UK	6.000%
Interest Japan	0.500%
Term	3

The discount factors for each of the currencies are shown in Table 5.32.

Table 5.32   Economic cost of loan and interest payment

	Sterling	Yen
Zero coupon loan	£10,000,000	JPY 1,000,000,000
Spot rate	100	
Interest UK	6.000%	0.8396
Interest Japan	0.500%	0.9851
Term	3	
Payable at maturity		
Sterling	£11,910,160	
Yen		JPY 1,015,075,125
Forward rate	1	JPY 85.23
Sterling equivalent	£11,910,160	£11,910,160

Again they are calculated using the normal compound interest convention. Therefore, $0.8396 = (1 + 6\%)^3$. The company wishes to borrow GBP 10,000,000 today and pay it back in three years' time. The question the company has to address is whether it should borrow in sterling or borrow in yen and convert to sterling. If the accounting standards are ignored and the borrower is keen to calculate the true economic cost, there is no economic difference between borrowing in sterling or borrowing in yen (and hedging the yen exposure with a forward contract). The calculations below reveal this. However, prior to the rules in IAS 39, *Financial Instruments: Recognition and Measurement* and IAS 21, *The Effects of Changes in Foreign Exchange Rates* it was possible to show cheaper borrowing costs on foreign loans, provided the foreign interest rate was lower. Therefore, many companies used foreign loans to replace domestic loans. Some companies even borrowed in a foreign currency and placed it on deposit in the domestic currency and extracted an accounting profit. The trade was known as the 'carry-trade'.

Table 5.32 reveals that there is no economic gain to borrowing in a foreign currency.

If the entity was to borrow GBP 10m using a sterling lender, the amount payable at maturity would be GBP 11,910.160 calculated as £10,000,000×$(1+6\%)^3$. If the entity had instead borrowed in Japanese yen and converted to sterling using the spot market, then interest to the Japanese lender would be calculated by reference to the Japanese as opposed to the British exchange rate. Therefore, the amount payable to the Japanese lender at maturity would be JPY 1,015,075,125. However, when this is converted at the agreed forward rate of 85.23, we end up paying (in sterling terms) the equivalent amount, i.e. JPY 1,015,075,125/85.23 = GBP 11,910,160, giving a cost of finance of £1,910,160.

However, despite the fact that there is no economic advantage from borrowing in yen, many creative accountants assumed there was and ended up charging the yen interest rate in the Profit & Loss account instead of the British one, i.e. 0.5% was charged as opposed to 6%.

The IFRS curbed this type of accounting in two ways. IAS 21 states that 'Monetary liabilities must be converted on the balance sheet at the "Closing rate" and any difference between the closing value and the opening value must go through the Profit & Loss account'. Furthermore, as stated before, IAS 39 generally requires that the time value of the forward contract be identified and released to the Profit & Loss account.

IAS 39 requires, in some instances, any change in the time value of a forward contract to be identified and released to the Profit & Loss account. The remainder, provided it meets certain conditions, can be transferred to the Equity Reserve account. The example below illustrates this in more detail.

IAS 21.16 defines a monetary asset or liability as the right to receive or the obligation to pay a fixed or determinable number of units of currency. Broadly, it is defined as cash or near cash and would therefore exclude assets such as goodwill, intangible assets, inventories, property, plant and equipment, etc. The treatment of monetary and non-monetary assets is different. Non-monetary assets are effectively carried at cost on the balance sheet or, to put it in IAS 21 language, 'non-monetary items that are measured in terms of historical cost in a foreign currency shall be translated using the exchange rate at the date of the transaction' (IAS 39.23). Foreign currency monetary items cannot be treated in this manner since it would give rise to the creative accounting treatment discussed above. IAS 21.23a states that 'foreign currency monetary items shall be translated using the closing rate'. The standard also states that exchange differences shall be recognised in the Profit & Loss account in the period when they arise. The result of this ruling is that the entity is not able to exploit the artificial advantage of borrowing overseas. To illustrate this we continue with the example we looked at previously.

A company has an opening balance sheet as shown in Table 5.33.

Here, the entity buys an asset worth GBP 18,000,000 and finances it with shareholders' funds of GBP 8,000,000 and a foreign Japanese loan of GBP 10,000,000. Prior to the IFRS, a company was able to accrue interest at the Japanese interest rate of 0.5%. The calculations for the loan measurement and the balance sheet value at the end of the first year are shown in Tables 5.34 and 5.35.

To value the loan at the end of the first year, we assume that the spot rate has not moved unexpectedly. It follows that the spot rate at the end of year 1 will simply be the one-year forward rate at the start of the year. To calculate the one-year forward rate we multiply the spot rate 100 by (1 + the JPY interest rate)/(1 + the GBP interest rate), to get 94.81. The value

Table 5.33   Opening balance sheet

Assets	
Physical asset	£18,000,000
Liability	
Loan	−£10,000,000
	£8,000,000
Shareholders' Funds	
Ordinary Shares issued	£8,000,000
Equity Reserve	
Profit & Loss	£–
	£8,000,000

Table 5.34   Loan valuation

One year discount factor	
GBP	0.9434
JPY	0.9950
Forward rate end year 1	JPY 94.81
Value of loan in JPY	JPY 1,005,000,000
Value of loan in STG	£10,600,000

Table 5.35   Balance sheet at end of first year

		Alternative treatment	IFRS treatment
Assets			
Physical asset	£18,000,000	18,000,000	£18,000,000
Liability			
Loan	−£10,050,000	−10,600,000	−£10,600,000
	£7,950,000	£7,600,000	£7,600,000
Shareholders' Funds			
Ordinary Shares issued	£8,000,000	£8,000,000	£8,000,000
Equity Reserve		−£550,000	£–
Profit & Loss	−£50,000	−£50,000	−£600,000
	£7,950,000	£7,400,000	£7,400,000

of the loan outstanding in JPY terms is simply the opening balance JPY 1,000,000,000 plus interest at 0.5% to give JPY 1,005,000,000. When this is divided by the then spot rate 94.81, we get the monetary value of the loan at the closing rate GBP 10,600,000.

Prior to the recent accounting changes, the only charge to the Profit & Loss account was 0.5%, i.e. £50,000. There were two ways that entities accounted for the loan. They either left the loan at cost on the balance sheet, or they adjusted for the closing rate but the difference went to Equity Reserve. The Equity Reserve calculation simply shows the foreign exchange (FX) movement. JPY 1,005,000,000/100 − JPY 1,005,000,000/94.81 = £55,000 represents the FX movement. Under IFRS, the FX difference must go through the Profit & Loss account and so the creative accounting opportunity is eliminated. The charge to the Profit & Loss account is 600,000, being 6% of £10,000,000.

American example

The American FASB has produced an example illustrating its interpretation of the cash flow hedge accounting rules.[5] We examine this illustration in detail below.

Assume today is 1 January 2008. Entity X, an American company with the US dollar as its functional currency, expects to receive three cash flows from a foreign customer, being a payment under a royalty agreement. The payments, three equal installments of foreign currency (FC), are 1,000,000 each at the end of January, February and March, the total is therefore 3,000,000. The company is worried that the foreign currency will depreciate against the dollar, therefore leaving the future cash flows (in dollar terms) uncertain. To hedge this risk, the company enters into a SINGLE forward contract for FC 3,000,000 on 1 January. The contract is due to expire on 30 April 2008. The term sheet for the contract is shown in Table 5.36.

Table 5.36 Term sheet forward currency agreement

Notional	FC 3,000,000
Entity pays	FC
Entity receives	USD
Expiry	31-Dec-08
Agreed forward rate	
Rates at 1 January	
Spot rate	0.6019
Forward rate on 30 April	0.6057

The company has agreed to pay over FC 3,000,000 and receive $1,817,100 (3,000,000 × 0.6057) on 30 April. Since the purpose of the hedge is to lock in a future cash flow which is uncertain, the derivative would qualify as a cash flow hedge. Therefore, any changes in the derivative's value (on the assumption that it qualifies as a cash flow hedge) is initially transferred to the Equity Reserve account. This amount is then transferred to the Profit & Loss account when the underlying payment is received. There are, however, some complexities that the entity must address before complying with IAS 39. Firstly, the dates for the underlying payments do not coincide with the forward contract payment. The underlying payments come in at the end of January, February and March, while the forward contract is settled in April. Secondly, the forward contract will be exposed to changes in the spot rate as well as the time value changes. As discussed previously, the changes in the forward contract that result from time value (i.e. non-spot rate changes) are released to the Profit & Loss account since they don't qualify as hedges. Figure 5.6 illustrates the accounting treatment.

At the end of the first month, both the forward rate and the spot rate have changed. The FASB calculations and accounting treatments are revealed below.

Table 5.37 reveals the spot rates and the forward rates for each of the months. The discount factors are calculated on the assumption that American interest rates remain at 6% throughout the life of the forward contract. The discount factor at 28 February 2008 is calculated as follows: $0.9899 = 1/(1 + 6\% \times 61/360)$. In America, the normal interest rate convention is to assume that there are 360 as opposed to 365 days in the year.

---

[5] Example 3 – Financial Accounting Standards Board Original Pronouncement as Amended Statement of Financial Accounting Standards No. 133, Accounting for Derivative Instruments and Hedging Activities.

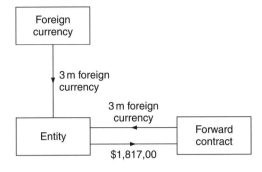

Figure 5.6   Foreign exchange cash flow hedge

Table 5.37   Market rates

Notional	3,000,000			
Discount factors	Number of days to maturity	6%	Spot	Forward 30-Apr
01-Jan-09	119	0.9806	$0.6019	$0.6057
31-Jan-09	89	0.9854	$0.5970	$0.6000
28-Feb-09	61	0.9899	$0.5909	$0.5926
31-Mar-09	30	0.9950	$0.5847	$0.5855
30-Apr-09	0	1.0000	$0.5729	$0.5729

Accounting treatment on 31 January 2008 is shown in Table 5.38.

Table 5.38   Forward valuation

Locked-in rate	0.6057				
Spot rate	$0.6019				
Notional	3,000,000				
Time value	11,400				
Dates	Number of days to maturity	6%	Spot	Forward 30-Apr	Forward valuation
01-Jan-09	119	0.9806	$0.6019	$0.6057	$0
31-Jan-09	89	0.9854	$0.5970	$0.6000	$16,850
28-Feb-09	61	0.9899	$0.5909	$0.5926	$38,904
31-Mar-09	30	0.9950	$0.5847	$0.5855	$60,299
30-Apr-09	0	1.0000	$0.5729	$0.5729	$98,400

On 31 January the value of the forward contract is $16,850. This is calculated by comparing the locked-in forward rate with the current market forward rate. In January, the market forward rate is 0.6000 – which means that if the entity entered into the forward contract at the end of January as opposed to 1 January, it would only receive $1,800,000 instead of the $1,817,100 that it is contracted to receive. The difference of $17,100 represents a profit which we must discount back to 31 January: £17,100 × 0.9854 = $16,850.

Time value

As pointed out earlier, the time value of the forward contract must be identified and any changes released to the Profit & Loss account. The example produced by the American FASB does not indicate how the time value is calculated, however, there is strong evidence to suggest that its method for calculating the change in the time value is incorrect. Table 5.39 reveals the time value as calculated in the American example.

Firstly, the total difference is $11,400. In other words, on the date that the entity entered into the forward contract the spot rate was 0.6019 and the forward rate was 0.6057. The difference between the spot and the forward multiplied by the notional $3,000,000 comes to $11,400. As this difference has nothing to do with unexpected changes in the spot rate, it fails to qualify for hedge accounting and therefore must be released to the Profit & Loss account. It is effectively the 'time value' of the forward contract. The FASB calculated this figure correctly, but appear to have made a mildly inaccurate but very confusing error in the calculations. The figures in the last column show how the $11,400 is released through the Profit & Loss account. In the first year, the FASB calculate $2365 but doesn't reveal how the calculation is done. Table 5.39 was constructed to get the result that the FASB used, but it appears to be ($11,400 – $9000) × 0.9854. The second figure is ($11,400 – $5100) × 0.989 = $6237. As this is a cumulative figure, we deduct $2365 to arrive at $3872 for the second month. The figure $9000 is the spot forward differential calculated at the end of January, i.e. $9000 = $3,000,000 × (0.6000 – 0.5970). As stated earlier, the time value appears to be incorrect, a suggested approach is shown in Table 5.40.

In January the value of the forward contract is $16,850, as calculated previously. The change in the market value arises for two reasons: firstly, the change in the underlying spot rate and secondly, the 'time value' change. The change in the underlying spot rate is straightforward to calculate. Between 1 January and 31 January the spot rate moved from 0.6019 to 0.5970. If we take the difference (0.0049) and multiply it by the notional, we get $14,700. This amount qualifies for hedge accounting and the remainder ($2150) represents the change in the spot rate which in this case does not qualify for hedge accounting.

Accounting treatment

As explained above, the foreign exchange contract qualifies as a cash flow hedge. We start with an opening balance sheet on 1 January 2009 and compare it with the balance sheet on 31 January 2009 (see Table 5.41).

On the opening balance sheet an entity has raised $10m from shareholders and invested in an asset worth $10m. At the end of the first month, the entity receives one of three payments in the foreign currency, i.e. FC 1,000,000 and immediately converts it into the functional currency (which is the dollar) at the prevailing spot rate on 31 January 2009, which is 0.5970 giving $597,000. As this represents income, both the cash and the retained profit are increased. The derivative requires a bit more work. Obviously, under IAS 39 the derivative must appear as an asset on the balance sheet, hence $16,850 is shown on the asset side. However, the time value doesn't qualify for hedge accounting and so is released to the Profit & Loss account. The remainder, $16,850 – $2365 = $14,485, does qualify as a cash flow hedge. This profit relates to three payments, one of which was received at the end of January. Therefore, we recognise one-third of the $14,485 (i.e. $4828) immediately and the remainder (i.e. $9656)

Table 5.39 Time value FASB calculation

Valuation dates	Discount 6%	Spot	Forward 30-Apr	Remaining time value	Cumulative difference	Cumulative difference discounted	Change in time value
01-Jan-09	0.9806	$0.6019	$0.6057	$11,400			$2,365
31-Jan-09	0.9854	$0.5970	$0.6000	$9,000	$2,400	$2,365	$3,872
28-Feb-09	0.9899	$0.5909	$0.5926	$5,100	$6,300	$6,237	$2,719
31-Mar-09	0.9950	$0.5847	$0.5855	$2,400	$9,000	$8,955	$2,445
30-Apr-09	1.0000	$0.5729	$0.5729	$0	$11,400	$11,400	
							$11,400

Table 5.40 Time value alternative calculation

Dates	Discount 6%	0.6	Market value	Cumulative spot movement	Cumulative time value	Change in time value
01-Jan-09	$0.6019	$0.6057	$0			
31-Jan-09	$0.5970	$0.6000	$16,850	$14,700	$2,150	$2,150
28-Feb-09	$0.5909	$0.5926	$38,904	$33,000	$5,904	$3,754
31-Mar-09	$0.5847	$0.5855	$60,299	$51,600	$8,699	$2,794
30-Apr-09	$0.5729	$0.5729	$98,400	$87,000	$11,400	$2,701
						$11,400

Table 5.41 Balance sheet on 1 January and 31 January

	Opening balance sheet	Payment received	Derivative adjustment	Balance sheet 31-Jan
Assets				
Physical asset	$10,000,000			$10,000,000
Cash	$0	$597,000		$597,000
Forward contract			$16,850	$16,850
	$10,000,000			$10,613,850
Shareholders' Funds				
Ordinary Shares issued	$10,000,000			$10,000,000
Equity Reserve			$9,657	$9,657
Profit & Loss (ineffectiveness)			$2,365	$2,365
Profit & Loss	$0	$597,000	$4,828	$601,828
	$10,000,000			$10,613,850

is deferred in the Equity Reserve for future periods. Non-accountants will understandably complain that this is an awkward procedure for booking a relatively simple transaction.

As explained previously, for a derivative to qualify as a cash flow hedge there are detailed requirements contained in the accounting standards. Where these requirements are not met, the entire change in the derivative must go through the Profit & Loss account. IAS 39.88 contains details of those requirements. Proper documentation must be in place on the date that the derivative is taken out. The hedge must relate to a future transaction that is highly probable. The effectiveness of the hedge can be reliably measured and must be assessed on an ongoing basis. A typical test is the 80%/125% test, i.e. does dividing the change in the derivative by the change in the underlying give a ratio between 80% and 125%? If the ratio falls outside this range, the entire derivative fails to qualify for hedge accounting and so the change must go through the Profit & Loss account, creating profit and loss volatility. In the example above, the change in the derivative that qualifies for hedge accounting is $14,485, since the change in the time value does not qualify. The change in the underlying is $3m×(0.5970 − 0.6019) = −$14,700. Dividing $14,485/$14,700 gives 98.5% or, if the change in the underlying is divided by the change in the derivative, we get the reciprocal which is 102%. Both figures are well within the 80%/125% bands and so only the change in the time value is released to the Profit & Loss account. What is confusing about this example, however, is that there is no reason why the derivative should not qualify as 100% effective (at least for the month of January) when the time value is stripped out. In Table 5.42, we show the balance sheet assuming that the alternative calculations from Table 5.40 are used. Effectiveness of 100% is achieved with the revised figures.

There are two things to notice from Table 5.40. Firstly, the part of the derivative that qualifies for hedge accounting is 100% effective. This time, the change in the derivative is $16,850−$2150 = $14,700. The change in the underlying is, as previously calculated, $14,700 as well. So the derivative (after excluding the time value change) is 100% effective. The second point emphasises that the FASB approach is possibly incorrect. The credit to the Profit & Loss account is $601,900, which is basically $1,000,000 × 0.6019. The figure of 0.6019 is the spot rate at the date the hedge was taken out, and therefore $601,900 appears more correct than the FASB figure of $601,828 in Table 5.41.

Accounting for options

Entities that write options, i.e. sell options and receive the premium, are normally unable to obtain hedge accounting treatment. Therefore, the entire change in the option is released to the Profit & Loss account. A possible exception is where an entity sells an option to hedge a long option position, i.e. an entity using a call option to hedge the equity component of a convertible bond.

It is possible, however, to obtain hedge accounting on certain options that are purchased. For instance, an entity might buy a swaption to hedge a loan where the issuer guarantees a fixed rate. Where, however, an entity uses an option to hedge a non-option position, the accounting standards allow the entity to break down the option between the intrinsic value and the time value. Only the intrinsic value qualifies for hedge accounting. The intrinsic value in broad terms means the payoff that the entity will receive if the option is exercised immediately. The time value is the remaining part of the premium.

Example. An entity buys a call option on the purchase of inventory in one year's time. The premium on the call option is $10, the strike of the option is $100 – which happens to be

Table 5.42 Balance sheet on 1 January and 31 January

	Opening balance sheet	Payment received	Derivative adjustment	Balance sheet 31-Jan
Assets				
Physical asset	$10,000,000			$10,000,000
Cash	$0	$597,000		$597,000
Forward contract			$16,850	$16,850
	$10,000,000			$10,613,850
Shareholders' Funds				
Ordinary Shares issued	$10,000,000			$10,000,000
Equity Reserve			$9,800	$9,800
Profit & Loss (ineffectiveness)			$2,150	$2,150
Profit & Loss	$0	$597,000	$4,900	$601,900
	$10,000,000			$10,613,850

the expected forward price of the underlying inventory. If exercised immediately, the option would pay nothing so, at the date the option is purchased, the intrinsic value is zero and the time value – which is the remaining part of the premium – is $10. After six months, the value of the option climbs to $12 and the value of the underlying inventory climbs to $105. At the six-month stage, the intrinsic value of the option is the current inventory price less the strike, i.e. $5. The time value is the remaining premium, $12 − $5 = $7. The total change in the intrinsic value (which would probably qualify as a cash flow hedge) is $5, but the change in the time value, which would not qualify, is $3 and would end up going through the Profit & Loss account.

Fair value hedge accounting follows the same treatment. In the above case, suppose the option was a put option qualified as a fair value hedge, i.e. hedging the value of existing inventory on the balance sheet, the entire change in the option would go through the Profit & Loss account, i.e. $2 would actually increase the profit. But, the change in the intrinsic value would qualify for hedge accounting so the profit would be reduced by the intrinsic value $5, leaving a net $3 charge in the P&L which is the same as the change in the time value.

APPENDIX: DOCUMENTATION

For a derivative to be classified as a hedge, an entity must meet the requirements of IAS 39.88. In particular, there must be in place at the inception of the hedge 'formal designation and documentation of the hedging relationship and the entity's risk management objective'. The purpose of this appendix is to suggest guidance that entities might use when setting up a structure to document derivatives.

The auditor would expect to see the following matters in the documentation:

- Item being hedged.
- Risks that will affect the P&L.
- Risks that are being hedged.
- Derivative used.
- Breakdown between part of derivative that qualifies and part which doesn't.
- Conclusions on effectiveness.
- Procedure for testing effectiveness.
- Record of effectiveness.

We now apply these headings to the American example discussed previously.

Introduction

The entity's functional currency is the US dollar. Its customer ZYX's functional currency is the euro. ZYX agrees to pay DCF a royalty of €1,000,000 every month for the next three months, i.e. 31 January 2004, 28 February 2004 and 31 March 2004. To hedge the FX risk the entity has, on 1 January 2004, entered into a forward contract to sell €3m at a rate of 0.6057. The spot rate at today's date is 0.6019. The spot forward differential therefore is 11,400.

Item being hedged

The entity is hedging the cash flow uncertainty that will arise when it receives three payments of €1,000,000 each at the end of January, February and March.

Risks that will affect the P&L

At the date of receipt each of these payments will be exchanged into the functional currency (the dollar). There is the market risk that the currency will fluctuate and the credit risk that the amounts will not be paid or that the debtor will suffer a downgrading.

Risks that are being hedged

DCF wish to hedge the FX exposure only.

Derivative used

The derivative used will be a forward contract whereby DCF agrees to pay €3m and receive $1,817,100 on 30 April 2001.

Breakdown between part of derivative that qualifies and part which doesn't

The derivative will change in value for three reasons. Firstly, the expected exchange rate on 30 April may vary; secondly, both the euro interest rate and the dollar interest rate may change; and thirdly, the counterparty to the forward contract may become a credit risk and suffer a downgrading at the same time.

Only the FX risk will qualify for hedge accounting, the remaining risks will not qualify and, where relevant, will be released into the P&L. Therefore, changes in the spot forward differential, i.e. 11,400, will be released into the P&L over the life of the derivative. One-third of the derivative will be de-designated as non-hedging for the month of February. Two-thirds of the derivative will be de-designated in March and (where applicable) 100% in April will be classified as de-designated.

Conclusions on effectiveness

The hedge is expected to be highly effective because the principal amount of the underlying risk and the derivative are the same. However, the dates do not coincide, which will result in hedging ineffectiveness. Nevertheless, we believe that the hedge should qualify within the 80%/125% range. Any change in the value of the derivative between 31 March and its expiry will be deemed for trading only and therefore released into the P&L.

Procedure for testing effectiveness

The underlying 'debtor' will be measured by changes in the FX rate prevailing at 30 April 2004 and will not be discounted. The credit risk will not be measured unless there are grounds for impairment.

Record of effectiveness

None so far.

6

Accounting for Structured Products (Market Risk)

6.1 INTRODUCTION

Structured notes and structured bonds are, broadly speaking, bonds whose payoff is based on a complex formula. They are often constructed by buying a straightforward bond and then attaching a number of complex derivatives to it in order to give the complex payoff that investors have demanded over the years. Given the fact that they are often difficult to construct and misunderstood, they are challenging to price and once an investor purchases them, they are often forced to hold them to maturity, because, unlike simple derivatives or simple bonds, there is not a huge number of buyers and sellers for the different types of structured products that exist. An important question is why investors are willing to buy these difficult and complex instruments? It is a feature of today's market that investors often buy products that they don't understand, and thus expose themselves to huge potential losses or at least their shareholders to such losses. From a regulatory and accounting point of view there is the worry that the people buying these products are not doing so with their own money. This increases the risk that the shareholder is deceived and puts pressure on the accounting profession to disclose to the shareholder exactly what is going on.

There are two types of structured products: those exposed to market risk, i.e. interest rate, foreign exchange, equity and commodity risk and those exposed to credit risk. We must treat the two categories separately. The accounting standard setters have developed rules that effectively force entities to recognise losses up-front, where they exist, on certain market risk structured products but they have had less success with structured products based on credit risk. This chapter deals with those structured products that are exposed to market risk and the next few chapters look at credit risk in detail, in particular structured credit products.

Over the years, press stories about structured products have not been highly complimentary. In 1995, for instance, Orange County, California suffered record losses of $1.7 billion as a result of a 70-year-old treasurer Robert Citron whose investment strategy involved buying structured bonds. The bonds were structured in such a way that they met the investment guidelines that Orange County was using at the time. Unfortunately, those guidelines were perhaps oversimplified and therefore effectively ignored the risks that presumably Orange County was trying to prevent. According to Partnoy,[1] Citron was a colourful character: 'instead of developing computer pricing models, he consulted psychics and astrologers for advice about interest rates'. Orange County was not unique in clocking up huge losses. Governments continue to invest in structured products, often with disastrous consequences. So do investment funds, insurance companies, hedge funds and pension funds.

---

[1] Frank Partnoy, *Infectious Greed*, Profile Books, 2004, p. 116.

The growth in the structured product industry arose for a variety of reasons. Firstly, sometimes regulation is quite weak and can often have harmful side-effects. For instance, trustees of pension funds are restricted in the products in which they can invest. This causes two problems. The demand for the permitted products increases, pushing up prices and lowering returns, thus exposing the fund to greater risk, and the permitted products face an increase in demand making them more expensive – the restriction may prevent entities from diversifying properly. This is possibly the case in Nigeria at the minute, where recent rules on pensions restrict the type of products that pension funds can invest in. The restriction may place too much demand on Nigerian government bonds, pushing down yields and restricting diversification opportunities. The irony, therefore, is that those regulations designed to reduce risk end up increasing risk. The same is generally true, though to a lesser extent, of the overall pension industry. Recently, changes in the accounting rules (in the case of IFRS, IAS 19 requires entities to disclose their pension deficits), along with the appointment of a Pensions Regulator in Britain, has altered the way that pension funds invest their money. These accounting requirements, along with regulation, have forced pensions to reconsider investment classes and one of the consequences of the change in rules is that pension funds have migrated to long-term government bonds en masse. The result is that they may end up taking on more risk because the high price pushes down the yield and, when yields fall, so too does profitability for the pension fund. Also, diversification opportunities are reduced if there are unnecessary investment restrictions placed upon fund managers. In these cases, structured products have a legitimate role in getting around the unnecessary restrictions.

A second motivation driving the growth of structured products is that fund managers and companies want to take additional risks without letting the investors know that they are taking those risks. Again, we return to the theme that if investors are investing their own money, they will be very careful about setting risk limits and will not take on products they don't understand, even if the credit rating agencies give them a seal of approval. However, if they are investing other people's money, it makes rational sense to take on as much risk as possible since the rewards to the fund manager will be higher, as we discussed in Chapter 1. In theory, investors can place restrictions on the type of risks that the fund manager takes. In reality, certain fund managers (for instance hedge funds) can take on huge amounts of risk through complex structured products and very often the fund manager is in a position to conceal the amount of risk that the shareholder ultimately takes on. A third motivation for complex structured products is that an investment portfolio manager has more control over the Profit & Loss account and therefore more control over his bonus. In other words, he can recognise profits when structured products turn profitable but if he suffers losses, he can exploit the accounting standards and hide those losses, often for long periods of time. A treasurer or fund manager can, for instance, change his job and leave the new incumbent to suffer the discovery of losses that he has created well after he has received an inappropriate bonus which usually cannot be returned. Hidden losses are, of course, a huge problem for the accounting standard setters. Naturally, they want to prevent a situation where investment managers, traders or treasurers speculate with shareholders' money and hide losses when they arise.

6.2   RISK ADJUSTED RETURN ON CAPITAL

In Chapter 1, we examined the rewards for risk and in particular the ability of certain financiers to keep the rewards for taking on risk themselves and pass on to the shareholder/investor the risks or potential losses that may arise. We saw that if a fund borrowed money, the risks increase but the fee system rewards the investment manager disproportionately. If, however, the investors place borrowing restrictions on the investment manager, the investment manager can still enhance his rewards and increase risk by leveraging up the portfolio with derivatives. Where there are restrictions placed on derivatives, investment managers may use structured products to get around the regulations as well as the accounting disclosure requirements. Needless to say, if they can hide losses as well this is an extra bonus. The next section looks at how the regulators and accounting standards setters have responded to the problem. It would be tempting to say that the accounting rules on structured products have resolved the issue and that the risk of someone like Robert Citron re-emerging is limited. Unfortunately, as discussed later, although the accounting standards setters and the regulators have made progress, they certainly have not eliminated the problem.

As was revealed in previous chapters, one problem with financial centres – i.e. New York and London – is that the bonus or fee system actually encourages risk. In theory, through the Risk Adjusted Return on Capital (RAROC) calculation (see below), traders are penalised if they take on too much risk but if risk is difficult to measure, it is very hard to perform the RAROC calculation. So, in theory, directors of banks and companies should ensure that risk is measured and reported to the shareholders, regulators, etc. In reality, things are quite different.

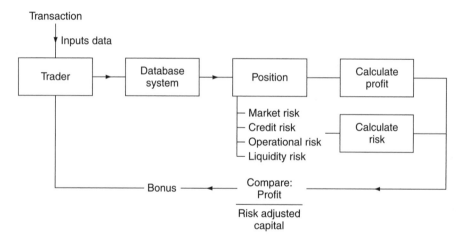

Figure 6.1   RAROC system

Risk Adjusted Return on Capital

Banks are usually not in a position to hold traders accountable for losses for the simple reason that they cannot award 'negative' bonuses. Therefore, if banks are unable to hold traders accountable for the losses they make, the next best thing is to hold traders accountable for the risks that they take on. There are a number of regulatory pressures upon banks to measure risks, including the Basel rules. What the RAROC model attempts to do is measure the risks of a trade on the date that the trader has bought or sold a financial instrument. If the trade is risky, the trader's bonus is reduced. This incentive to reduce risk is indirectly what the Basel committee are trying to achieve.

A simple example of RAROC follows.

A trader buys a 'vanilla' bond and one structured bond for £1,000,000 each. The vanilla bond pays a yield of 6% and the structured bond pays a yield of 8%. The structured bond is three times

(Continued)

more risky than the vanilla bond. Assume that the risk-free rate of interest is 5%. How should the bank calculate the trader's bonus?

A simple analysis shows that 8% is greater than 6%, and so the structured bond will contribute more to the trader's bonus than the first bond. However, if RAROC was to be employed, the capital would be adjusted to reflect the risk. Therefore, the bank calculating the bonus should 'adjust' the capital for the structured product by increasing it according to the risk.

Under the RAROC system, the capital for the structured product might be adjusted by a factor of say three, reflecting the fact that the structured product is three times riskier than the vanilla product. Therefore, the trader buying the structured product is only getting a return of 2.666%, i.e. 8%/300, while the first product is producing a return of 6% as before. It follows that if the RAROC model is implemented properly, the trader will evaluate the risks against the return and this may discourage him from buying structured products.

RAROC should not only measure the sensitivity of the bond to changes in interest rate (known as market risk), but also measure credit risk, operational risk and liquidity risk. While market risk is easy to measure, the same cannot be said for credit risk, operational risk and liquidity risk. Where risk is difficult to measure, RAROC is difficult to implement. This may partially explain why traders are more willing to take on complex structured products with a credit exposure. They do, of course, pay a higher return but the risks are substantial and more importantly, difficult to measure. The result is that because of complexity, banks cannot implement the RAROC system correctly so traders find that their bonuses do not suffer.

As we shall see below, the accounting standards have, along with the regulator, devised rules which force entities to recognise losses and risks associated with an exposure to changes in interest rates, foreign exchange rates, equity and commodity price changes. They have had less success with complex products that have an exposure to credit risk, liquidity risk and operational risks.

6.3 BIFURCATION RULES

The solution to the structured products problem devised by the accounting standard setters was to introduce rules (known as bifurcation rules) whereby, if a structured product was unnecessarily complex – i.e. the complexity was not clearly and closely related to the underlying business or product – both the purchaser and the seller were required to identify the derivative components, calculate their market values and show them on the balance sheet at that value. Any future changes in the market value would normally go through the Profit & Loss account. Unfortunately, implementing this part of the standard is easier said than done, and the likelihood is that many banks and companies are not doing it correctly all the time. The risk to the auditing profession is that they have to pass an opinion on whether structured products are accounted for correctly, without fully understanding how the structured product is valued or constructed.

Banks are, as we have seen during the credit crises, very heavy investors in structured products. This has surprised many investors since, prior to the credit crises, many of these investors believed that the regulations were very tight, thus preventing banks from investing in complex products that they didn't understand. The investors also believed that the accounting profession had adapted their accounting standards in light of the Enron experience. However, it now transpires that many banks operated 'offshore vehicles' where they invested in complex structured products. The regulators, under the Basel 1 rules, were not able to look at these products and measure the risks and the accounting profession have almost admitted that the off-balance sheet issue still remains a big problem for them. Thus, banks were motivated to buy complex structured products that paid a high yield and finance them with short-term loan or overdraft facilities which required a low yield. They were able to take profits (based on the difference between the yield and the loan interest charges) to the Profit & Loss account without applying RAROC correctly, since they did not bother to measure adequately the market, credit, operational and liquidity risks.

6.4 THE REWARD FOR RISK

If auditors or accountants come across structured products within a bank, corporate or investment fund, an important question that they must first attempt to address is why has the entity used the structured product? A treasurer may respond that he simply wants to get a higher return. However, given the extraordinary cost of setting up a structured product, the treasurer has a better chance of making profits by buying straightforward products such as bonds or equities, or even simple derivatives such as forward or future contracts. If the treasurer feels that the return is not high enough on these products, then a simple solution is to borrow additional money and increase his exposure by buying additional shares or bonds. In essence this is all that the structured product maker does. A motivating factor behind most structured products is, as discussed earlier, to take on a huge risk or exposure and hide it from the shareholder. The structured products are normally structured in such a way that the investor can get around regulations or avoid having to reveal the risks to the shareholder.

As we discussed in Chapter 1, if a fund manager is on a 2/20 fee scheme he is given an incentive to expose the shareholder to huge amounts of risk and conceal what he is doing. To recap, a fund manager who has raised £10m from shareholders will have a 'funds under management' fee of 2%, giving £200,000 per year. If he borrows an additional £10m and invests it, the total funds under management fee grows to 2% of £20m, or £400,000. He can increase his fee even further by making the portfolio more volatile. He benefits by taking 20% of the extra profits when the markets do well but can walk away from losses when the markets do badly. If he decides to use straightforward derivative products, i.e. forwards and futures, to leverage his portfolio the additional risk will be picked up on the VaR (market risk measurement) models and so the investor or shareholder will know about it. However, if he uses structured products, where the risks are more difficult to measure, he can make any claim he likes about the risky nature of the portfolio and neither the shareholder nor the accountant/auditor will be in a position to challenge him.

6.5 PROTECTION FOR SHAREHOLDERS

One can clearly see the attractions of using derivatives. What have the accountants and regulators done to protect the investor from such losses? From a regulatory perspective there are a number of rules. Basel 2, for instance, indirectly protects shareholders by forcing banks to measure and disclose the risks that they are taking on. This is known as the Pillar 3 requirement. The benefit for the regulators is that if shareholders see that banks are taking on too much risk they will abandon the shares, causing problems for the bonuses of the bank's directors. Of course, the primary role of the Basel committee is to prevent banks from going bankrupt. By forcing banks to disclose the risks they undertake, the committee ends up protecting shareholders.

As far as the accounting standards are concerned it would be very obvious, from any annual report, if a fund manager or company decided to gear up its portfolio through borrowings. Under IAS 32, for instance, the term 'liability' is defined as an obligation to deliver cash in the future. IAS 39.10 is a relatively new rule which forces banks to identify the derivatives embedded in a financial instrument and account for them separately. Virtually all loans would meet this IAS 32 definition. The use of derivatives is, of course, covered under IAS 39. Although IAS 39 was unwelcome to many accountants, on the grounds that it is difficult to implement, it did constrain treasurers, traders and bank directors from taking on too much risk and hiding losses.

Some traders tried to get around the restrictions of IAS 39 by including derivatives within contracts or within bonds and not calling them derivatives. Suppose a treasurer wants to speculate on the dollar depreciating further against the euro. He could enter into a forward contract, but the auditors would require him to show the derivative at its market value on the balance sheet and allow the change in the derivative to go through the Profit & Loss account. This means that the auditor cannot hide losses. Furthermore, he is forced under IAS 32 and IFRS 7 to reveal to the shareholder the additional risk that the shareholder faces as a result of taking out the forward contract. A more convenient solution is to say to a supplier of, for example, machinery 'can you include a provision in the contract that pays us a lot of money if the dollar depreciates against the euro and we will undertake to pay you if the opposite happens?' For the supplier, anxious to close the deal, this requirement would not pose a problem since the supplier himself can take out a forward currency contract to hedge this additional risk. In addition, the forward contract, though it may cause a bit of administrative convenience, would probably qualify as a hedge so there would be no impact on the Profit & Loss account. So, suppliers found a new marketing tool to help them sell products. They simply said to the treasurer that if he wanted to gamble on foreign exchange, equity or interest rates, it was still possible to do so by putting an extra clause into the contract and keeping it off the balance sheet despite the requirements of IAS 39.

The standard setters therefore introduced rules known as the 'embedded derivative' rules. If there was evidence of a contract containing clauses which would allow an entity to speculate and hide both the risks and losses from the shareholder, the embedded derivative rules would force the accountant or auditor to review all contracts and bonds/loans, extract the embedded derivatives and treat them as they would treat ordinary derivatives – i.e. bring them on to the balance sheet and recognise losses or profits correctly.

6.6   ILLUSTRATION: THE STRUCTURED PRODUCTS PROBLEM

The problem associated with structured products is better illustrated by an example. A structured products salesman approaches an investor and offers him a product with the terms shown in Table 6.1.

At the time of issue, the one-year Libor rate is 4%. The structurer would probably have little difficulty in selling this product to customers, particularly in the days when splitting the embedded derivative was not required (i.e. before IAS 39 and its American equivalent, FAS 133 existed). The coupon appears to be quite generous. An investor could effectively

Table 6.1 Term sheet for structured product

Notional	£10,000,000
Coupon	24.3%–3×Libor
Libor	4%
Tenor (years)	8
Cap	Principal protected
Issuer	AA-rated bank

borrow £10,000,000 at Libor and invest it in this particular bond which would pay a coupon of 12.3% (24.3% − 3 × 4%) in the first year. The risk managers would be happy as well; from a market risk perspective, losses are capped since the coupon cannot turn negative. This, in effect, means that if interest rates move up (and against the wishes of the investor), the investor will still receive his principal at the end of the term. Also, the issuer is an AA-rated bank and so the risk of default is negligible. There are other advantages. If interest rates go up, not only are profits virtually unlimited but there is a very good leverage factor. Although the term sheet shows a leverage factor of three, the actual leverage factor (as we shall see below) turns out to be a lot higher. So a small decrease in interest rates could lead to a substantial increase in profits. But that's not all, there is an accounting advantage as well. If, for instance, the interest rates move in an unfavourable direction, the investor may not be obliged to show the loss (particularly in pre-IAS 39 days). This is because the investor could classify the bond as Loans & Receivables and therefore record it at cost on the balance sheet, ignoring any changes in market value.

So, if the product looks attractive, pays a high yield, has limited risk and also has an accounting advantage, what would motivate a structurer to issue such a product? Surely, what the investor gains, in terms of a generous yield, the structurer loses. In reality, the structurer would probably earn a handsome fee from this particular deal.

The structurer would have access to additional market data, not necessarily available to the investor (or his accountant). Suppose the following information is available, from the trading desk of the structurer at the time of the deal:

8-year swap rate		7.00%	
Cap price	8.1%	0.58%	8 years

The current market swap rate for an eight-year tenor is 7%. The fee for a cap at 8.1% is 58 basis points. This, in effect, means that on a loan of £10,000,000 the structurer can pay £58,000, which protects him against losses due to interest rates rising above 8.1%. The protection is restricted to a loan size of £10,000,000.

In order to see how much the trader has made in fees from the deal, it is important to identify the three parties in the transaction and their cash flows. The three parties, as identified in Figure 6.2, are the investor, the issuer (in this case an AA-rated bank) and the party standing in between, the structurer. The investor pays a notional of £10,000,000 for the structured product, which in turn is passed on to the issuer (the party that wants to borrow the money). The issuer, being AA-rated, would probably pay Libor. In return for the investor's principal, he would receive (as agreed) 24.2% less 3 × Libor.

The structured product leaves the structurer exposed in two ways. Firstly, if interest rates fall, the structurer could lose 4 × Libor. Secondly, the structurer is short a cap, or to put it more precisely, he has given away a free option to the investor. In effect, this means that if interest

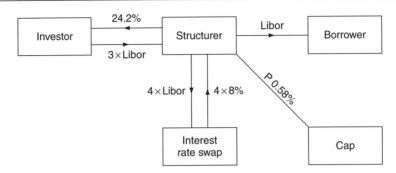

Figure 6.2 Structured products

goes above a certain level, the structurer loses money. The structurer can hedge both risks by taking out four swaps whereby he pays floating and receives fixed, and he also takes out a cap (or more precisely, an interest rate put option) to protect himself against interest rates rising too much. To see the interaction we will hedge the structured product and then look at how we might apply the cap.

Figure 6.2 illustrates how the swap hedges the interest rate exposure. All the Libor inflows now match the Libor outflows. What is noticeable is that the fixed rates which the structurer receives are in total 28%, whereas he is only required to pay out 24.3%, giving a total profit of 3.7% per year. Table 6.2 illustrates the total profit (before the cap is paid for).

Table 6.2 Profits to the structurer

	Structurer receives	Structurer pays	Difference	7% Discount swap rate	Present value
1	£2,800,000	−£2,430,000	£370,000	0.9345794	£345,794.39
2	£2,800,000	−£2,430,000	£370,000	0.8734387	£323,172.33
3	£2,800,000	−£2,430,000	£370,000	0.8162979	£302,030.21
4	£2,800,000	−£2,430,000	£370,000	0.7628952	£282,271.23
5	£2,800,000	−£2,430,000	£370,000	0.7129862	£263,804.89
6	£2,800,000	−£2,430,000	£370,000	0.6663422	£246,546.62
7	£2,800,000	−£2,430,000	£370,000	0.6227497	£230,417.40
8	£2,800,000	−£2,430,000	£370,000	0.5820091	£215,343.37
			Off market swap		£2,209,380.45
			Cap cost		−£174,000.00
					£2,035,380.45

The gross fee before the cap is therefore a very high £2.2m (over 20% of the value of the investment). There is, however, a risk for the structurer; namely if, after the swap is put in place, and interest rates go up, the increase could not only reduce the structurer's profit but also expose him to unlimited losses. The solution is to buy protection. The potential losses are shown in Table 6.3.

Table 6.3 shows that a cap with a strike of 8.1% and a notional of £30,000,000 can offset the shortfall that arises when interest rates go above 8.1%. The cost of this option is 58 basis points (it allows protection for eight years). The overall profit on the deal is therefore £2,035,380.

Table 6.3 Option payoff profile

Interest rate	Notional Rate £10,000,000 24.30%		Libor leverage Swap rate 3 / 7%			Cap Strike £30,000,000.00 8.10%	
	1	2	3	4	5	6	
	Structurer receives from investor	Structurer pays to investor	Structurer pays to swap counterparty	Structurer receives from swap counterparty	Structurer receives from issuer	Overall profit per year	Payoff cap
7.00%	£2,100,000	−£2,430,000	−£2,800,000	£2,800,000	£700,000	£370,000	0
7.10%	£2,130,000	−£2,430,000	−£2,840,000	£2,800,000	£710,000	£370,000	0
7.20%	£2,160,000	−£2,430,000	−£2,880,000	£2,800,000	£720,000	£370,000	0
7.30%	£2,190,000	−£2,430,000	−£2,920,000	£2,800,000	£730,000	£370,000	0
7.40%	£2,220,000	−£2,430,000	−£2,960,000	£2,800,000	£740,000	£370,000	0
7.50%	£2,250,000	−£2,430,000	−£3,000,000	£2,800,000	£750,000	£370,000	0
7.60%	£2,280,000	−£2,430,000	−£3,040,000	£2,800,000	£760,000	£370,000	0
7.70%	£2,310,000	−£2,430,000	−£3,080,000	£2,800,000	£770,000	£370,000	0
7.80%	£2,340,000	−£2,430,000	−£3,120,000	£2,800,000	£780,000	£370,000	0
7.90%	£2,370,000	−£2,430,000	−£3,160,000	£2,800,000	£790,000	£370,000	0
8.00%	£2,400,000	−£2,430,000	−£3,200,000	£2,800,000	£800,000	£370,000	0
8.10%	£2,430,000	−£2,430,000	−£3,240,000	£2,800,000	£810,000	£370,000	0
8.20%	£2,430,000	−£2,430,000	−£3,280,000	£2,800,000	£820,000	£340,000	£30,000
8.30%	£2,430,000	−£2,430,000	−£3,320,000	£2,800,000	£830,000	£310,000	£60,000
8.40%	£2,430,000	−£2,430,000	−£3,360,000	£2,800,000	£840,000	£280,000	£90,000
8.50%	£2,430,000	−£2,430,000	−£3,400,000	£2,800,000	£850,000	£250,000	£120,000
8.60%	£2,430,000	−£2,430,000	−£3,440,000	£2,800,000	£860,000	£220,000	£150,000
9.00%	£2,430,000	−£2,430,000	−£4,000,000	£2,800,000	£1,000,000	£200,000	£570,000

Procter & Gamble

In order to reduce their borrowing costs, Procter & Gamble entered into a contract with a bank whereby they would make money if interest rates did not rise but would lose money if interest rates did rise. They settled for a leverage factor of 25. Subsequently, interest rates did rise and, in February 1994, Procter & Gamble ended up losing approximately 14% per annum over a five-year period.[2]

6.7   THE ACCOUNTING TREATMENT UNDER EMBEDDED DERIVATIVE RULES

As explained above, under the embedded derivative rules, derivatives that are not 'clearly and closely related' to the underlying contract/asset must be identified and treated separately in the accounts. Below, we compare the old accounting method (i.e. pre-embedded derivative rules) with the post-embedded derivative rules. As usual, we assume that the entity has raised £10,000,000 from the issue of shares. Therefore, its opening balance sheet is as in Table 6.4.

Table 6.4   Opening balance sheet

Assets	
Cash	£10,000,000
Shareholders' Funds	
Ordinary Shares issued	£10,000,000
Profit & Loss	£–

As soon as the bond is purchased, the investor would probably classify it as Loans & Receivables under IAS 39.9. This means that it would be carried at cost on the balance sheet. The embedded derivatives would be ignored. On the date of purchase, therefore, there would be no impact in the Profit & Loss account (Table 6.5).

Table 6.5   Accounting for structured product (old method)

Assets	
Bond	£10,000,000
Shareholders' Funds	
Ordinary Shares issued	£10,000,000
Profit & Loss	£ –

Under the new rules, the investor would need to break down the structured bond into its individual components, i.e. a swap, an option and a bond. The swap is 'off market' in the sense that it was locked in at 24.30%, which is not the market rate (the market rate being $7\% \times 4 = 28\%$). The investor is therefore losing 3.7% per annum, as discussed above, and

---

[2] Richard Flavell, *Swaps and Other Derivatives*, John Wiley & Sons, p. 308.

Table 6.6   Accounting for structured product (new method)

Assets	
Bond	£10,000,000
Option	£174,000
Liability	
Swap	−£2,209,380
	£7,964,620
Shareholders' Funds	
Ordinary Shares issued	£10,000,000
Profit & Loss	−£2,035,380
	£7,964,620

therefore recognises the swap as a liability. The option is an asset for the investor and is shown on the balance sheet as such. The closing balance sheet, on the assumption that the embedded derivative rules apply, would be as in Table 6.6.

Table 6.6 shows that the investor is forced to reveal that he has made a loss on the transaction and must also admit under the disclosure requirements that he is taking speculative positions on interest rate movements through the swap and the bond. The embedded derivative rules have, as a result, reduced the demand for structured products. Had Orange County adopted the equivalent of the embedded derivative rules, it is likely that the treasurer would have been forced to disclose losses a lot earlier and of course his trading activities would have ceased, saving Orange County huge amounts of money.

6.8 PAST MISTAKES

In 2007, JPMorgan reached a deal with four Greek state pension funds over four complex structured bonds worth an estimated €280 million. The Greek government also launched an investigation into six other similar deals. As is common with many deals involving structured products, some Greek pension funds bought them at an unfavourable price through a chain of transactions involving a number of banks and brokerage firms. According to the *Financial Times*, a settlement against JPMorgan and other banks left them with a bill of €20m. The six other bonds that the Greek government decided to investigate included those underwritten by banks including Calyon, Morgan Stanley, HSBC, BNP Paribas and Deutsche Banks. These bonds were sold by brokerage firms to Greek pension funds at what were believed to be inflated prices. ADEDY, the Greek civil servants union, filed a complaint against the banks involved. According to the complaint, JPMorgan was involved in the sale of complex financial instruments to unsophisticated buyers. JPMorgan, however, argued that they did nothing wrong in underwriting the transaction. Without getting involved in the complexities of the transaction or who precisely was at fault, it is clear that 12 years after the Orange County fiasco, unsophisticated buyers are still continuing to buy products they don't understand while acting as trustees of other people's money. Ideally, the accounting standards would force entities to recognise the losses on structured products immediately. However, the likelihood is that some pension funds may not have to report under the IFRS standards and even if they did, the auditor would have to fully understand the pricing and risk sensitivities of the structured product before accounting for them correctly. There is evidence therefore that people are still not learning from past mistakes, and while the regulators and accountants recognise the problems, the solutions that they have in place are difficult to apply. According to the *Financial Times*, most Greek pension trustees are political appointees, not financial professionals armed with sufficient knowledge to see the dangers of sophisticated structured products. Unsophisticated trustees spending other people's money are a natural target for commission-hungry structured product sellers. As mentioned elsewhere in this book, Norway taxpayers suffered when a municipal authority invested €65 million in bonds which turned out to be loss-making. The authorities blamed Terra Securities on the grounds that there were translation problems in the documents they received advising them of the risks that they were taking on.

6.9 CONCLUSION

There is little doubt that the IAS 39 rules on embedded derivatives have changed the landscape for structured product originators. In the past, derivative banks had little difficulty in selling complex structured products and were able to hide significant fees they earned. Investors were not troubled by this and very often didn't even bother to calculate the fees that were inherent in the structured products; they didn't have to. The investors were probably aware that they were making losses but as long as those losses could be buried, the investor could concentrate on the 'regulatory' benefits of structured products; namely that if they were profitable, the investor could cash them in and show a profit, but if they were loss-making, the investor could hide losses.

Under the new rules, the auditor is expected to understand and break down the structured product into its individual components. By unwinding the product he ends up recognising the hidden fee which must be charged to the Profit & Loss account. Also, under IFRS 7, he is obliged to identify the derivatives and report on how these derivatives change the risk profile of the entity.

We have seen in this chapter the advantage of keeping the fair value of items on the balance sheet along with simultaneously taking risk but concealing from the shareholder the amount of risk that the entity is taking. We have also seen the response of the accounting standards. IAS 32 requires an entity to reveal, on the balance sheet, the extent to which it is financed by loans. If an entity tries to leverage up the balance sheet by using derivatives, IAS 39 requires that such derivatives be shown on the balance sheet at market value, thus reducing the tendency to hide losses, and IFRS 7 requires detailed disclosure on the risk profile of the derivatives. Finally, where entities attempt to conceal derivatives in complex structured products or contracts, the embedded rules require that the entity scans all contracts, loan agreements and bonds with complex features. If there are derivatives present, they must be isolated (or bifurcated) from the main contract or bond and accounted for as derivatives.

A number of important developments have taken place since the embedded rules were introduced. Firstly, banks have almost stopped selling structured products to entities that have to comply with IAS 39. They have moved away from corporates and more towards governments. Also, retail banks have focused their selling on retail customers, i.e. complex customer deposits. This has caused problems in the UK, where naive investors have lost a lot of money on 'precipice bonds' and split capital funds. In the case of entities that have to comply with IAS 39 or the American equivalent FAS 133, banks have focused on selling these entities structured credit products. As will be revealed in the next chapter, since these products are difficult to price, they contain the usual advantages of being treated off-balance sheet with the result that entities, including banks, continue to be able to hide losses.

APPENDIX 6.1: OVERVIEW OF EMBEDDED DERIVATIVE RULES IN INTERNATIONAL ACCOUNTING REPORTING STANDARDS

IAS 39.10 defines an embedded derivative as 'a component of a hybrid instrument that also includes a non-derivative host contract with the effect that some of the cash flows of the combined instrument vary in a way similar to a stand-alone derivative'.

IAS 39.11 requires that the embedded derivative be separate from the host contract if three conditions are met:

1. The economic characteristics and risks of the embedded derivative are not closely related to the economic characteristics and risks of the host contract.
2. A separate instrument with the same terms as the embedded derivative would meet the definition of a derivative.
3. The hybrid instrument is not measured at fair value with changes in the fair value recognised in the Profit & Loss account.

Consider a case where an entity borrows money at Libor+50 basis points. The entity also agrees with the bank that if the value of the FTSE index climbs over the period of the loan, the principal repaid at maturity will be reduced by the increase and if the FTSE declines, the principal repaid will be increased by the percentage decline. In essence, a borrower would only want such a complex deal because he wants to gamble on the FTSE rising while keeping the speculation off-balance sheet, i.e. hiding the risks and losses from the shareholder. The deal meets the three conditions. The clause in the loan contract has nothing to do with the loan, i.e. it is not 'clearly and closely related'. A separate instrument with the same features would meet the definition of a derivative, i.e. the FTSE clause is similar to a forward contract on the FTSE which is a derivative, and the hybrid instrument would most probably be treated as a loan on the balance sheet and therefore be classified as Loans & Receivables under IAS 39.9.

APPENDIX 6.2: INTRODUCTION TO DERIVATIVES

Derivatives are financial contracts whose price is influenced by a market or credit variable. The market variables are interest rates, foreign exchange rates, exchange rates and commodity prices. The credit variables include credit default risk and credit migration risk (the risk that a bond loses its credit rating). What distinguishes derivatives from other financial instruments, however, is that a trader of derivatives can easily lose more money than he puts down, or, to put it in other terms, the exposure is a lot greater than the initial deposit. What distinguishes a derivative from an ordinary contract too is the concept of net settlement. With an ordinary contract, one asset is effectively exchanged for another. There is usually physical delivery. Thus, if someone wants to buy a house he usually signs a contract to take physical delivery of the house in return for the agreed consideration. Derivatives, however, generally do not involve physical settlement. Instead, at an agreed date, the trader compares the price of the asset that he is buying with the amount he has agreed to pay. If the asset goes up in price only the profit is paid over to the trader. On the other hand, if the underlying asset falls in price this new price is compared against the existing liability and, once again, the difference is paid over to the counterparty.

Derivatives can be divided into three categories: futures, forwards and options.

- **Future transactions**. These are standardised derivative transactions. Both parties to a future agreement only have to negotiate one variable – the price. They are often, but not always, the simplest type of derivative and easy to understand. This simplicity is the key to their success. Simple derivatives are easy to price and more importantly are liquid. Furthermore, when banks deal in future contracts, they are required to pay a margin (known as variation margin) when they make a loss and receive variation margin when they make a profit. Again, this margining system makes life easier for the accountant because in a bank where there are weak controls and traders try to hide losses, the margining system often exposes those traders because they are forced to pay variation margin in the form of cash when they lose money. There are, however, two problems with future transactions. Firstly, future derivatives often contain a cash flow risk. If an entity takes out a future contract on, say, the dollar/sterling exchange rate and the dollar moves against the entity, the entity has virtually 24 hours to make good the losses. Sometimes this urgent call for cash at short notice overwhelms the treasurer, with the result that he may default on the variation, causing his entity to suffer. The second disadvantage with future contracts is that because they are standardised, as opposed to tailor-made, they will never achieve the objective of hedging an exposure 100%. This doesn't matter in the real world since traders very seldom hedge something 100%. However, for accountants, not being able to achieve 100% hedging means that applying hedge accounting can be bureaucratic, confusing and time-consuming under IAS 39 (the accounting standard for financial instruments that covers the hedge accounting rules).

Illustration

Today is 1 January 2008. An entity intends to borrow £10m at the end of March and repay it at the end of September. The entity is concerned that interest rates could rise in the meantime and so decides to lock in interest rates by using derivative contracts. The contract that is probably most suitable is the three-month sterling future contract. The term sheet for this contract is illustrated in Table 6.7.

Table 6.7   Term sheet 3-month future contract

Three-month sterling interest rate future	
Unit of trading	£500,000
Delivery months	March, June, September, December
Delivery day	First business day after the last trading day
Last trading day	Third Wednesday of the delivery month
Quotation	100.00 less the rate of interest
Minimum price movement	0.01 tick size £12.50 tick value

As we will see later, if an entity buys a future contract and interest rates rise by 1%, the entity loses £500,000 × 1% × 3/12 = £1250. On the other hand, if interest rates fall by say 1.5%, the entity would lose £500,000 × 1.5% × 3/12 = £1875.

In this case the entity is concerned about interest rates rising because, if they do, the planned loan of £10m between March and December will lose £10,000,000 × 1% × 6/12 = £25,000. So, the entity wants the hedge to make £50,000 if interest rates rise by 1%.

Future contracts are a bit like bond prices, if interest rates go up, both bond and future prices fall and if interest rates go down, the opposite happens. The entity wants the hedge to make money if interest rates rise, so it will 'short' a number of future contracts. What this means is that the entity sells future contracts today with the intention of buying them back in the future.

The next question is to decide how many contracts to buy. As illustrated above, if interest rates rise by 1% the future contract loses £1250. Therefore, if an entity is 'short' 40 future contracts and interest rates rise by 1%, the entity gains £50,000 which equates to the loss on the underlying loan. Table 6.8 illustrates this.

Table 6.8   Profit & Loss future contract

Underlying loan	£10,000,000
Expected rate	5%
Tenor of loan	0.5

Interest rate sensitivity	Profit/(Loss)
4.00%	£50,000
4.50%	£25,000
5.00%	£–
5.50%	−£25,000
6.00%	−£50,000
6.50%	−£75,000
7.00%	−£100,000

No. of future contracts	−40
Current price	95

Interest rate sensitivity	Future price	Sale price	Ticks per contract	Ticks gained/lost	
4.00%	96.00	95.00	100	−4,000	−$50,000
4.50%	95.50	95.00	50	−2,000	−$25,000
5.00%	95.00	95.00	0	–	$–
5.50%	94.50	95.00	−50	2,000	$25,000
6.00%	94.00	95.00	−100	4,000	$50,000
6.50%	93.50	95.00	−150	6,000	$75,000
7.00%	93.00	95.00	−200	8,000	$100,000

Table 6.8 shows the interest rate sensitivity of the underlying loan of £10m for half a year. The entity will, of course, benefit if interest rates fall but lose money if interest rates rise. As the entity is interested in reducing its exposure to interest rate changes it takes out a hedge which behaves in exactly the opposite way to the loan. As can be seen from the table, the entity 'shorts' 40 future contracts and when interest rates fall, the future contract position loses money but when interest rates rise, the entity makes money from its future position. The point to realise, however, is that every time the loan makes a gain the future position makes

a loss and since the losses match the gains exactly, the entity is not concerned about interest rate movements.

The future price is always quoted as 100 – the rate of interest. So, for instance, when interest rates are 5% the price of the future contract is 95. On the date that the entity took out the contract, interest rates were 5% so the sale price (because the entity sold the futures before buying them) was 95. When interest rates go down to 4% the future price goes to 96. The entity would therefore make a loss on the future contract of 4000 ticks, i.e. -40×100. Each tick is 0.01%.

Unfortunately, as discussed earlier, future contracts are subject to variation margin payments. This means that if the future contracts make losses, the variation margin must be paid before the benefit of the reduction in interest rates is realised on the loan. The cash flow mismatch therefore causes a slight inaccuracy in the hedging relationship and, while this is not a problem in practice, it does cause headaches for accountants. In general, when the derivative is 100% effective, the hedge accounting rules are easy to deal with. Complications, however, arise when the derivative is partially ineffective. It is this cash flow problem that encourages entities to use forward contracts as opposed to future contracts for hedging purposes.

Futures are used not only to hedge interest rates but also foreign exchange exposures, as well as equity and commodity risks.

A typical foreign exchange future contract is shown in Table 6.9.

Table 6.9   Term sheet foreign exchange future contract

Sterling foreign currency future	
Unit of trading	£62,500
Delivery months	March, June, September, December
Minimum price movement	0.01c or $0.0001 tick size $6.25 tick value

This contract could be used by hedgers and speculators. As an example, a trader might have the view that sterling is going to appreciate against the dollar and so goes 'long' a sterling contract. This means that if sterling appreciates against the dollar, the trader benefits but if sterling depreciates, the trader makes a loss. Suppose the trader wants a £2,000,000 sterling position. He will buy £2,000,000/£62,500 = 32 future contracts. Suppose he takes out this contract when the exchange rate is £1/$2 and subsequently the exchange rate goes to $2.10. This means that the trader has gained $2,000,000 × (2.10–2.00) = $200,000. The exchange will simply calculate the number of ticks, which from the above contract is ($2.10–$2)/$0.0001 = 1000 ticks per contract. The trader has used 32 contracts and so has gained 32,000 ticks at $6.25, i.e. $200,000. If, on the other hand, the trader believed that sterling was going to fall against the dollar he would simply short the sterling future contract, which means that he would make money if sterling fell.

Hedgers use future contracts as well. Rather than take on an exposure, the aim of hedgers is to neutralise or reduce an exposure.

- **Forward transactions**. These are like future transactions but the terms are tailored to suit the needs of one or both parties. Typically, a forward transaction is used where, say, a company is due to export goods to America and is worried that when it receives payment the dollar will fall against sterling, which means that its revenue will decline. The entity might consider taking out a forward contract which compensates the entity for the loss arising from the dollar's depreciation. Normally, the entity will arrange with the bank to tailor the exposure so that the loss on the underlying is matched by a gain in the future and vice versa. They will also arrange a settlement date to coincide with the expected receipt of dollars on the underlying transaction. Therefore, the entity gets a 100% perfect hedge and no cash flow risk, since the derivative is settled when the foreign remittance is received. There are two disadvantages, however. Firstly, as the forward contract is tailor-made, the bank will want to charge a fee. Therefore, the transaction costs are higher using a forward than a future contract. Secondly, for both parties, the forward contract is a potential credit risk, since no variation margin is paid by either party. From an accounting perspective, a derivative that is 100% effective requires little or no documentation or testing for hedge effectiveness. However, from a control perspective, it is often the case that traders conceal losses for a period of time on forward transactions since no variation margin is payable. This is effectively what John Rusnik did with Allied Irish banks in 2002.

Illustration

An entity borrows £10m on a floating rate basis for five years. Worried about an expected increase in interest rates, the entity enters into an arrangement with a swap counterparty whereby it agrees to pay a fixed rate over the next five years and receive floating. In effect, the entity has converted a floating loan into a fixed loan and has therefore removed interest rate uncertainty. In entering into the swap, the swap counterparty (usually a bank) has taken on a risk exposure. The bank has a variety of ways of hedging this exposure, and normally uses a combination of swaps or future contracts to hedge the exposure of a portfolio of swaps. The other task the bank has to undertake is to price the swap. We address this next.

The starting point, when pricing a swap, is to download the current Libor yield curve. The Libor rate is the average rate that banks use when they borrow and lend to each other.

Table 6.10 illustrates the yield curve and discount factors. The figure of 0.8492, for instance, is the discount factor for year 3. If £849.20 was placed on deposit for three years at the current Libor rate of 5.6%, the amount at maturity would be £1000. Therefore, multiplying the future value £1000 by the discount factor gives the present value £849.20. Table 6.11 merely confirms that £849.20 placed on deposit for three years at 5.6% gives £1000.

Table 6.10   Libor rates and discount factors

	Yield curve	Discount factors
1	5.2500%	0.9501
2	5.4000%	0.9002
3	5.6000%	0.8492
4	5.7500%	0.7996
5	6.0000%	0.7473

The figure for year 2, £50.22, is simply the opening balance at the start of year 2, £896.75 × 5.6%.

When pricing a swap contract, the bank is effectively trying to estimate what the one-year Libor rate will be each year over the next five years. Obviously, a crystal ball is needed to determine what the forward rates will be, but banks can get a good estimate of what forward

Table 6.11 Compound interest calculation

Future value	£1000	
Value today	£849.20	
Interest year 1	£47.56	5.6000%
	£896.75	
Interest year 2	£50.22	5.6000%
	£946.97	
Interest year 3	£53.03	5.6000%
	£1000.00	

rates are expected to be by looking at the implied forward rate from the yield curve rate. We use the discount factor in year 3 to illustrate how the forward rate is derived in this manner.

Suppose a bank agrees to lend £1,000,000 to a customer at the start of year 3 for one year and the customer wants to lock in the rate. What rate should the bank charge? By agreeing to take on this deal, the bank is taking on an asset and a liability. The asset is the principal plus interest that the bank receives at the end of year 3, i.e.:

$$£10m + £10m \times F$$

The liability is simply £10m, the amount of money that must be handed over at the start of year 3.

On the assumption that the bank wants to break even on this deal, i.e. neither make nor lose money, its task is to find a fixed rate which makes the present value of the asset equal to the present value of the liability. Therefore, we multiply the asset by the discount factor for year 3 and the liability by the discount factor for year 2 and allow the two to equal each other as shown below:

$$(P + (P \times F)) \times DF3 = P \times DF2$$

In other words, the present value of the asset must equal the present value of the liability. A little algebraic manipulation of the above equation shows that the left can only equal the right when $F = DF2/DF3 - 1$. Using the above example, the forward rate for year 3 is simply $0.9002/0.8492 - 1 = 6.0011\%$.

The remaining forward rates are calculated in a similar manner.

In Table 6.12 the bank has estimated what the floating rate is going to be over the next five years and, based on this, calculated its expected liability on the assumption that it enters into a swap contract with a company whereby it pays floating and receives fixed. In year 4, the bank expects the floating rate to be 6.2013% and so the liability of the floating leg of the swap is simply the principal multiplied by the floating rate, namely £620,128. The present value of this liability is obtained by taking £620,128 and multiplying it by the discount factor, 0.7996, to give £495,861. The total of the liabilities for the five years is £2,527,418.

An intuitive way to understand the figure of £2,527,418 is to realise that it is simply the value of a floating bond minus a zero coupon bond, as illustrated in Table 6.13.

The value of a zero coupon bond is simply the notional £10,000,000 times the discount factor for five years, that is £10,000,000 × 0.7473 = £7,472,582. Subtracting the value of a zero coupon bond from the face value gives the value of the floating cash flows, i.e. £10,000,000 − £7,472,582 = £2,578,418. Therefore, a quick way to calculate the present

Table 6.12   Libor rates and discount factors

Notional	£10,000,000			
Tenor	5			
Swap rate				
	Yield curve	Discount factors	Forward rates	
0		1		
1	5.2500%	0.9501	5.2500%	£525,000	£498,812
2	5.4000%	0.9002	5.5502%	£555,021	£499,607
3	5.6000%	0.8492	6.0011%	£600,114	£509,615
4	5.7500%	0.7996	6.2013%	£620,128	£495,861
5	6.0000%	0.7473	7.0059%	£700,592	£523,523
					£2,527,418

Table 6.13   Fixed coupon bond

Year	Cash flows: floating bond			Cash flows: less zero coupon
1	£525,000	0.9501	£498,812	£525,000
2	£555,021	0.9002	£499,607	£555,021
3	£600,114	0.8492	£509,615	£600,114
4	£620,128	0.7996	£495,861	£620,128
5	£10,700,592	0.7473	£7,996,105	£700,592
			£10,000,000	£2,527,418

value of the floating side of a swap is $P \times (1 - DFn)$, i.e. £10m $\times (1 - 0.7473) = £2,527,418$ (subject to rounding).

The next task of the bank is to calculate the fixed rate that gives a present value of the cash inflows equal to the present value of the cash outflows, namely £2,527,418. The schedule in Table 6.14 shows the cash inflows that the bank expects to receive from the swap at the breakeven fixed rate.

Table 6.14   Fixed side of swap

	Notional	£10,000,000		
	Swap rate	5.9520%		
	Yield curve	Discount factors	Expected fixed receipts	Present value
0		1		
1	5.2500%	0.9501	£595,199	£565,510
2	5.4000%	0.9002	£595,199	£535,773
3	5.6000%	0.8492	£595,199	£505,441
4	5.7500%	0.7996	£595,199	£475,927
5	6.0000%	0.7473	£595,199	£444,767
		4.2463		£2,527,418

Table 6.14 reveals that the breakeven swap rate is 5.9520%. For both the bank and the company, the present value of the asset side of the swap and the present value of the liability of the swap will be the same, meaning that the swap is fair to both sides. In reality, banks act as market makers and so quote a bid–offer spread around the breakeven rate. So, if the breakeven swap rate is 5.592%, the bank might quote 5.57% as a bid and 5.61% as an offer. This means that if the company enters into a swap and wishes to receive fixed, the bank will pay 5.57% but if the company wishes to pay fixed, the bank charges 5.61%.

As can be seen from the table, the present value of the fixed side of a swap can be calculated using the formula $P \times CDFn \times$ swap rate, i.e. £10m $\times$ 4.2464 $\times$ 5.9520% = £2,527,418. As emphasised above, the swap rate is initially chosen so that the present value of the fixed side equals the present value of the floating side, i.e.:

$$P \times (1 - DF5) = P \times S \times CDFn$$

Again, a little bit of algebra reveals that the swap rate is simply $S = (1 - DF5)/CDF5$, where DF5 represents the discount factor (in this case 0.7473) and CDF5 (4.2463) represents the cumulative discount factor. Therefore, the swap rate is simply $S = (1 - 0.7473)/4.2463 = 5.9520\%$.

We now illustrate how swaps are valued in practice.

A bank has entered into a six-year swap with term sheet details as in Table 6.15 on 1 January 2008.

Table 6.15   Swap term sheet

Swap notional	£100,000,000
Fixed rate (bank receives)	8%
Start date	01-Jan-08
End date	31-Dec-13

On 31 December the bank wishes to value the swap, in accordance with IAS 39. Obviously, at the year end there are five years left running in the swap. There are two ways to value the swap. The first is to compare the present value of the asset against the present value of the liability. The second is to anticipate the future cash flow payments and to determine the present value of those payments. We look at the first method in Table 6.16.

The present value of the asset is simply $P \times S \times CDFn$ = £100m $\times$ 8% $\times$ 4.2463.

The present value of the liability is $P \times (1 - DFn)$ = £100m $\times$ (1 − 0.7473) = £25,274,183. Since the present value of the asset exceeds the present value of the liability, the swap will appear as an asset on the balance sheet.

The second approach is to estimate the future cash payments. A practical way to do this is to assume that the current market swap rate is the average Libor rate for the next five years. Table 6.17 shows that based on current swap rates, the bank expects to receive £2,048.011 on average each year for the next five years. The figure is calculated as the difference between the rate agreed 8% and the current swap rate 5.5920% multiplied by £100,000,000. Once again, we get the present value of the future cash flows to give us a market swap value.

Table 6.16   Swap valuation first method

Swap notional		£100,000,000
Fixed rate (bank receives)		8%
Start date		01-Jan-08
End date		31-Dec-13
Yield curve		Discount factors

	Yield curve	Discount factors
0		
1	5.2500%	0.9501
2	5.4000%	0.9002
3	5.6000%	0.8492
4	5.7500%	0.7996
5	6.0000%	0.7473
		4.2463

Present value asset	£33,970,737	
Present value liability	−£25,274,183	
	£8,696,554	

Table 6.17   Swap valuation second method

	Market swap rate	Locked-in rate		
1	5.9520%	8%	£2,048,011	£1,945,853
2	5.9520%	8%	£2,048,011	£1,843,533
3	5.9520%	8%	£2,048,011	£1,739,164
4	5.9520%	8%	£2,048,011	£1,637,611
5	5.9520%	8%	£2,048,011	£1,530,393
				£8,696,554

- **Option trades**. Unlike future and forward derivatives which are simple as they only involve either exchanging one asset (or cash flow) with another, option-based contracts are a bit more complex to price. Unlike future and forward contracts, option contracts require one counterparty to pay a premium to the other. The person who receives the premium buys either a call option or a put option. A call option gives the holder (or the party who paid the premium) the right but not the obligation to buy an asset, whereas a put option gives the holder an option to sell a particular asset. Obviously, for the purchaser of the option, the risk is contained since the most he loses is the premium that he pays. Nevertheless, on buying the option, the purchaser of an option experiences a lot of volatility since a small movement in the underlying can lead to a substantial movement in the value of the option. For the seller of the option the risks are relatively unlimited. The big challenge for option traders is trying to value the option. Where options are very liquid and standardised, pricing is relatively straightforward. The difficulty arises when the option is tailor-made and not very liquid. In these cases, accountants who wish to comply with IAS 39 must use a sophisticated pricing model (usually Black–Scholes). The problem with these models is that they require assumptions and judgements, which means that the valuation is quite subjective and therefore open to various forms of manipulation.

7

Accounting for Credit Risk

7.1 INTRODUCTION

If a layman was asked to guess the two most important skills that a banker needs, he would probably state that credit skills would be one and the ability to manage cash flows another. Banks have lent money for generations, building up quite a lot of experience and so are perhaps in a better position to assess the risk that someone who borrows money will default. As regards liquidity risk, based on various glossy brochures that banks occasionally issue they will often sit down with a small business owner and help him to plan his business, identifying the expected cash flows and budget accordingly. The advantage, of course, is that with good budgeting a small business manager can anticipate instances where he may need to borrow and therefore put his well-prepared case to borrow money in good time and reassure the bank manager that he is anticipating problems rather than reacting to them. The same layman might also conclude that the credit rating agencies will help banks and investors where they lack expertise, again passing on the benefit of their years of experience, and the layman might also believe that after the Enron scandal accountants have worked hard revamping the accounting standards to stop the 'off-balance sheet' deceptive practices that Enron and others used a decade ago. Finally, the layman might take comfort from the fact that financial institutions are heavily regulated so, even if there was a breakdown in the way that banks conducted their business, the regulators would act as a safety net. There may be occasions when banks assess credit risk incorrectly and/or find that their liquidity needs are overwhelmed by external events, but these should be rare and the amount of losses or shortage of cash should be small. As we now know, banks have lent recklessly, creating huge losses. The credit rating agencies did not anticipate these problems and continued to allow triple-A ratings despite evidence of severe credit risk. The accounting standards were interpreted in such a way that banks felt they had a licence to keep risky investments off the balance sheet and the regulators had difficulty in supervising liquidity risk.

Over the next few months, as pressure mounts on various governments to regulate banks better, one question that everyone will ask is why banks were able to amass such huge losses given their expertise in credit risk measurement and liquidity management. A possible answer is the ease with which banks were able to use shareholders' money to gamble, allowing traders and banking directors to take the lion's share of the profits when their bets were successful and forcing the shareholder and taxpayer to subsidise the losses when things went badly. To maintain this ideal position, directors and traders came up with complex structured products which had the attraction of not being understood so the shareholders and the government could not see what was going on. As explained in the previous chapter, structured products were once exposed to market risk but the auditors developed bifurcation rules under IAS 39 which made life difficult for those entities that were attracted by the accounting treatment. Unfortunately, the standard setters were not as successful in bringing structured products exposed to credit risk onto the balance sheet. This failure might have indeed encouraged the explosive growth in complex credit products. Regulators had the same problem. They used Value at Risk (VaR) models to identify the market risk associated with these structured products and penalise banks accordingly. Structured products associated with credit risk, however, are more difficult to measure and indeed it is reasonable to say that the risk measurement rules for credit risk are more difficult to implement compared to market risk. This is certainly true in the case of complex securitisations. The result was that banks could continue to hide risks and losses until the money ran out or, as the Citibank former chairman put it, 'until the music stops'. Some auditors and regulators, along with the credit rating agencies who suffered severe conflict of interest problems, all gave false reassurance to shareholders and the government, with the result that the flawed model was used for a lot longer than it should have been.

In April 2008, the International Monetary Fund suggested that losses from the sub-prime crisis could reach $945 billion.[1] Clearly, banks were not measuring credit risk correctly. They had a tendency to advance what were termed 'covenant lite' loans, i.e. loans with very few restrictions, reducing the quality of loans advanced. This applied to some extent to corporate loans, but certainly applied to mortgages where the assumption amongst borrowers and lenders was that property prices could only go one way – up. This assumption, of course, allowed lenders to earn huge fees and generate significant profits. In March 2008, the UK Treasury Select Committee launched a scathing attack on investment banks and credit rating agencies.[2] The Committee found flaws with the rating agencies for their 'inherent and multiple conflicts of interest' as well as flaws in their rating methods. Banks were criticised for selling 'ludicrously complex' products that senior managers themselves did not fully understand. The report stated 'If the creators and originators of complex financial instruments have only a limited understanding of these products then it raises serious questions about how investors. . . can possibly understand such complex products and the risks involved'.

Few can doubt that the credit rating agencies contributed in some small way to the credit crises, but another contributor was the banks themselves. In the past, banks originated loans and then held on to them, usually until maturity. It was in their interest, therefore, to make sure that the loans were of good quality. The tendency now is to originate loans and sell them. This introduces a 'moral hazard' problem because the entity that originates the loan is not ultimately responsible for the credit risk associated with the loan. Therefore, the temptation is to act recklessly and originate as many loans as possible regardless of their quality. The investors clearly paid little or no attention to the risks involved, perhaps a symptom of investment managers not investing their own money but other people's money. Eventually, banks started buying loans off each other and holding them in special investment vehicles. The benefit of these structures is that the accountants and auditors may regard them as off-balance sheet, with the result that they did not trouble the shareholder with details of the risks and possible losses contained in these loan portfolios. The regulators were unfortunately caught on the back foot since they did not pay close enough attention to the fact that banks were, in their eagerness to expand, 'overtrading' – i.e. buying complicated illiquid assets such as a portfolio of (often poor quality) loans and financing them with short-term overdraft facilities. The challenge for accountants is that if they are involved in the auditing of investment banks but don't fully understand the problems with the credit markets, then they may end up misleading the shareholders about the true profitability (as required under IAS 39) and the true

---

[1] http://dealbook.blogs.nytimes.com/2008/04/09/imf-warns-that-credit-losses-could-approach-1-trillion/

[2] Jennifer Hughes and Jane Croft, 'Credit rating agencies "flawed" claim MPs', *Financial Times*, 3 March 2008.

risks (as required under IFRS 7). Unfortunately, too, there is evidence that entities may be able to comply with the accounting standards and simultaneously mislead the shareholder – in other words, a flaw in the standards.[3] One could stretch this point by stating that a risk manager who is impartial and eager to inform the shareholder of the true position could easily do so without any understanding of the accounting standards. This in effect makes the standard somewhat redundant since, because of their complexity, standardised reporting is very difficult. However, this criticism is confined to accounting for financial instruments only. Outside of this, the accounting standards appear to work well.

Credit risk, credit derivatives, structured credit notes and financial guarantees have proven to be one of the biggest growth areas and simultaneously one of the most challenging areas for accountants and auditors. Unlike market risk products (i.e. those financial instruments exposed to interest rate, foreign exchange, equity or commodity risk), credit risk products are often difficult to value, their accounting treatment is confusing, and entities like credit rating agencies are operating under worrying conflicts of interest. It is for these reasons that financial entities have managed to hide substantial losses. Many practitioners in the credit market claim that the substantial innovations within their industry have resulted in a safer financial system because credit risk is not confined to one bank but spread across the world, over a number of banks along with non-banking financial entities such as insurance companies, hedge funds, pension funds and even individual traders. The theory is that if one area of the market gets into difficulty the burden is shouldered by all the banks and so the risk of an individual bank going bankrupt is remote. There is an element of truth in this. Banks are not particularly worried about the occasional loan going bad. What they are worried about is a number of loans defaulting at the same time. If there is a high correlation amongst loans, i.e. because they are all in the same industry, then if one loan turns bad (perhaps because of a property downturn) a number of loans will turn bad at the same time. A potential solution to the problem is to spread the risks of a particular loan portfolio (say a loan portfolio exposed to the Irish property market) amongst a number of international banks. The result is that banks become more diversified and therefore less risky. They pass on some of the risk from the loans that they originate and in turn take on the risk of foreign banks. This trend would explain why a large number of European banks suffered when the American sub-prime market got into difficulty in 2007. However, the argument is oversimplified. The credit markets are a lot more concentrated than we think. The American sub-prime market raised questions about the moral hazards inherent in the 'originate and sell' loan model, with the result that the flaws of the securitisation industry were exposed across the world and not just in America. Therefore, when American banks suffered, banks around the world suffered. A number of European banks, for instance, found that their market capitalisation halved during the credit crises despite having minimal exposure to the American sub-prime crisis. There are, of course, harmful side-effects when a bank can originate loans and then pass on the risk to another bank. The bank originating the loan is not too worried about taking on risky loans. The bank buying the loan, in theory, should worry about the inherent risks but, in the past, the task of measuring this risk was farmed out to credit rating agencies, a process that has certainly not worked well all the time. One thing is certain from this innovation. Banks have lent carelessly and have operated on the assumption that credit cycles, i.e. boom periods followed by bust periods, were a thing of the past. Prior to the 2007 credit squeeze, credit spreads (the extra yield on a loan to reward a bank for credit

---

[3] Jennifer Hughes, 'Off-balance sheet rules for banks "irretrievably broken" say experts', *Financial Times*, 10 April 2008.

risk) were very low, indicating that banks were happy to take on credit risk without measuring it properly. The interest charged on some corporate loans was barely higher than that payable on government bonds – banks did not distinguish risky loans from relatively risk-free loans. In other words, they lent carelessly. The accounting rules were not helpful. It was possible for banks, for instance, to keep losses from loans off-balance sheet by failing to impair loans in a timely manner. As we shall see, loans were kept off-balance sheet and therefore losses were hidden and, since the credit rating agencies were reluctant to downgrade loans, banks were in a better position to simultaneously take on more risk and hide losses.

7.2 LOAN APPROVALS

Three to four decades ago, the lending industry was a lot more localised than it is today. There were fewer people involved. The bank manager in a local town would know most of his customers, their earnings potential and their ability to repay loans. Job hopping amongst bank managers was not as common as it is today, therefore if a bank manager made a bad loan he knew that it would rebound on him at some stage in the future. Today, the process is more distant. Typically, with say mortgages, a customer approaches an independent financial advisor, who for a commission applies on the customer's behalf to a bank. The bank originates the loan and may in turn securitise that loan, i.e. package a number of loans into a portfolio and then sell tranches of that portfolio to various types of investors. Often, the loans are bought by an intermediary who in turn repackages them, again setting up a portfolio which buys tranches from existing portfolios (a type of 'fund of fund' arrangement known in the markets as a CDO squared). This in turn is bought by a hedge fund which has, as its investors, a number of pension funds. In short, therefore, if the customer defaults, it is not the intermediaries who suffer but the pensioner down the line, who is in a remote country. One can clearly see the dangers. Firstly, if there are too many intermediaries, they all have to extract a fee which is ultimately borne by the pensioner. Obviously, in the case of straightforward loans, if too many middlemen are taking commission the ultimate value of the pensioner's investment deteriorates considerably, raising alarm bells. The solution is to make the loan more leveraged and more risky. This means the rewards are higher, allowing everyone to extract a fee and leaving the unfortunate innocent pensioner with a huge amount of risk. There are two factors here that affect the accounting profession. Firstly, if a company or a financial institution buys one of these products, as opposed to a pensioner, how does the auditor report the risks that the shareholder faces under IFRS 7? The second question is how does the auditor ensure that the correct profit or loss is revealed to the investor? The answer is that, in many cases, the auditor is prevented from meeting his responsibilities to the shareholder owing to the sheer complexity of the transaction. The credit rating industry, on which the shareholder also depends, is similarly constrained from doing its job properly. The result is that the shareholder takes on a lot more risk than he is even aware of, and of course suffers a huge potential loss.

An article in the *Financial Times*[4] revealed that the 'sub-prime' market accounted for 8% of loans, but the real problem was mainstream lenders taking on risky loans, i.e. sub-prime lenders masquerading as ordinary lenders, giving out over-leveraged loans to people who can't afford them, using over-priced property as collateral. The article went on to give some examples of poor credit quality control in the lending market. Examples included a seasonal worker

---

[4] Jim Pickard, 'Contagious ready-to-lend mindset spins tales of woe', *Financial Times*, 10 September 2007.

who presented to his bank pay slips in the summer months and got a hefty mortgage on the assumption that the summer months reflected his average monthly earnings. An IT consultant and his pregnant girlfriend obtained a mortgage at three times their combined annual salary, at a time when interest rates were at an all-time low. A taxi driver raised approximately 5% of his deposit by borrowing heavily on his credit card, to purchase a rental investment. The developer also gave him a 'discount' so that he could meet the deposit criterion of 15%. This technique was, and probably still is, used by property clubs in order to meet the deposit criterion. The fourth case involved someone who earned less than £30,000 being able to borrow 10 times that amount, again financing the deposit from discounts offered by the developer. These practices are not isolated incidents and, although the lending criterion has, for most banks, become more strict after the summer 2007 credit crunch, the question remains as to why bankers do not use the experience they have built up over the years to spot these problem loans in advance. As explained earlier, the answer is complex but part of the problem is that these loans are securitised and therefore some pensioner or insurance company shareholder somewhere ends up taking the brunt of the losses. These end users rely on the intermediaries to measure and disclose risk properly and ensure that their investments are safeguarded. In practice, the intermediaries are more focused on fees and bonuses. In short, if there is a willing borrower and a willing investor and high fees, the deal gets done regardless of the risk. If the investor is not measuring the risk or doesn't know how to measure the risk, it is his problem. Unfortunately, there seems to be little incentive for the accounting profession to understand the complexity of these deals and to report losses and risks accurately. Indeed, this problem may have allowed losses to escalate to the extent they did.

The problem isn't confined to the 'risky' end of the mortgage market. Corporate loans are following the same route. The logical conclusion of some lenders is that if no one is measuring the risk and fees/bonuses can be earned through risky loans, then originate as many risky loans as possible. The former star fund manager for Fidelity, Anthony Bolton, spoke of a new type of loan known as 'cov-lite' in a farewell speech when he left the organisation.[5] Mr Bolton referred to special loans offered to the growing private equity industry, where poorly performing publicly quoted firms were bought by private consortiums using loan finance and a small equity injection. Like many other commentators in early 2007, before the credit crunch, he warned 'it is only a question of when rather than if [things go wrong]'. His comments were echoed by Paul Tucker of the Bank of England, who described cov-lite loans as a 'slow fuse'.

Loan covenants are clauses in loan agreements designed to protect the lender against excessive risks. Traditionally, they bound the borrower in such areas as cash flow coverage, interest coverage and leverage. Cash flow covenants basically allow the lender to reclaim the loan if the cash flows of the borrower are below certain targets. These targets also restrict the borrower from borrowing elsewhere. To make sure that a company has sufficient profits to pay the interest due on loans, certain interest cover covenants are set. These are similar to rental income covenants set in the 'buy-to-let' market where, for instance, rental income divided by interest payments must exceed 125%, etc. With covenant lite loans, no such covenants are set and therefore the lender has difficulty in identifying risky or loss-making loans. This problem is on top of that imposed by the accounting standards where, as we shall see later, banks are generally not allowed to recognise immediately the loss on a deteriorating loan which has not yet defaulted. Also, through the accounting treatment of securitisations, banks are often able

---

[5] Paul J. Davis and Gillian Tett, 'Shiny new "cov-lites" show signs of tarnish – news analysis – Questions are being raised about the relatively new loan instruments favoured by private equity groups', *Financial Times*, 16 May 2007.

to keep risky loans off the balance sheet, again hiding risks and delaying the recognition of losses. The deals can get very complex and display the willingness of banks to take on more and more risk. In one deal, for instance (KKR's deal for Boots), banks were asked to underwrite a lot of the equity in the deal. The banks then intended to sell on these deals to their 'favoured clients'. As the investments would not carry voting rights, corporate governance complexities might arise. Another trend that was growing prior to the credit squeeze of 2007 was that private equity forms were able to attract senior loans without having first to attract too much in junior loans or equity. In the event of default, it is the equity and junior note holders that bear the brunt of the first losses. However, if their holding is small, it makes the senior loans more risky. The truth is that investors who buy into these leveraged and risky leveraged loan deals do so because they believe they can sell them on at a mark-up. They are not worried about the risks if the ultimate buyer of the loans doesn't measure the risks. There is another group of investors who will hold the loans perhaps to maturity. Even they are satisfied with the covenant lite approach. In the words of the *Financial Times*, 'In this view, investors that are struggling to find enough deals to buy are almost complicit in the loosening of lending standards'. To put these words in other terms, 'it suits us to buy risky loans and not to measure those risks'.

7.3   CREDIT SPREADS

In theory, when a bank is considering a loan it must perform two calculations: firstly, identify the estimated probability of default (PD) and secondly, the amount of money lost if there is a default – the loss given default (LGD). From this the bank can calculate the credit spread and then price the loan correctly. Obviously, the bank will need to make a margin on the loan and this too is factored into the price of the loan.

This is illustrated below.

Bank X is approached by company Y that wants to borrow £10,000,000. Bank X would firstly do a credit score analysis and consider a number of factors, including:

- Whether the customer is an existing or a new customer.
- Track record with previous loans.
- Loan covenants.
- Income of the entity.
- Interest cover.
- Length of time in business.
- Barriers to entry in the industry.
- Stability of earnings.

The bank would then use this information to put the customer in an appropriate category. We will assume that the bank uses a rating scale of 1 to 8. The next step is to value the collateral. Some loans, of course, are well collateralised with liquid assets repo transactions which tend to use government bonds as security. At the other extreme are loans which are unsecured. The LGD figure is based on the value of the collateral and the liquidity of the collateral if there is a forced sale, etc. More sophisticated banks would try to calculate the correlation between the prospects of the lender defaulting and the value of the collateral falling at the same time.

Table 7.1 shows the various categories of loans. The bank would, based on its practical experience, identify the number of historical loans that have defaulted in that category and

Table 7.1 Loan pricing

Category	Defaults	No. of loans	Probability of default
1	2	1000	0.200%
2	6	1100	0.545%
3	8	1200	0.667%
4	9	1400	0.643%
5	5	400	1.250%
6	12	800	1.500%
7	15	900	1.667%
8	17	700	2.429%

Category	Value of security	Loss given default
A	90%	10%
B	55%	45%
C	20%	80%

Loan notional	10,000,000
Libor	5%
Margin	1%

express this as a percentage of the total number of loans advanced to that category. From this the probability of default is estimated. This, in effect, is what the new regulatory rules (Basel 2) are trying to encourage. If the regulators are satisfied that banks are categorising their loans correctly and keeping proper records of default experience, banks will be allowed not only to calculate their own probability of default, but also the Basel 2 weightings (see Chapter 11) and use these to determine how much shareholders' funds (tier one) capital they need. In broad terms, the amount of shareholders' funds needed is about 4% of the loans granted (the PD figure is used to identify the risk weighting). The LGD figure is influenced by the value of the collateral. Where a loan defaults and the collateral (when sold) only provides 20% of the value of the loan, the remainder is the loss suffered by the lender.

In order to price the loan the bank effectively calculates the loss if there is a default and the probability of losing that money (PD) and from this determines the 'breakeven' credit spread. Adding on a margin of 1% and Libor then gives the price of the loan, as shown in Table 7.2.

If banks lend below Libor plus the credit spread, i.e. 6.093%, they are in effect underpricing the loan and should therefore recognise an up-front loss as soon as the loan is granted. The bonus for the lending officer should be based on his ability to attract a yield above Libor

Table 7.2 Loan yield

Loan categorisation	8B
Loss given default	£4,500,000
Expected loss	£109,286
Breakeven credit spread	1.093%
Alternative calculation	1.093%
Libor	5.000%
Credit spread	1.093%
Margin	1.000%
	7.093%

plus the credit spread. A practical difficulty with this application is that the probability of default is estimated, or to put it more precisely, the past is expected to be a good guide to the future. In reality, markets go through credit cycles and so during a boom period, when credit defaults are low, the expected probability of default might end up being much lower than actual experience. The same could be true, of course, if we go from a period of high bad debts to a recovery period. It follows, therefore, that banks should collect information on bad debt experiences over a long period of time so that the PD figures capture both boom periods and periods where the credit markets are very tight.

Practical experience suggests that the credit markets are not working as they should. At the extreme, the sub-prime experience in America suggests that many banks made the assumption that property prices can only go one way – up. Therefore, the value of the collateral would always be much higher than the loan, so no risk of default. Across the world, there is evidence that banks have lent money cheaply because they placed more emphasis on trying to acquire market share than pricing a loan correctly. Also, as mentioned throughout the book, if banks found that they could sell loans immediately after origination (i.e. through a securitisation), the moral hazard problem becomes prominent.

7.4 ACCOUNTING STANDARDS

If a bank calculates that a loan should have a credit spread of say 2% at a time when Libor is 5%, then the bank would have a breakeven yield of 7%. There is an economic loss, therefore, to the bank if they decide to subsidise the loan – i.e. lending at 6.5%. From a common sense point of view the value of this subsidy should be treated as a loss in the Profit & Loss account. The value of the financial instrument would clearly be less than the cash paid out if the true yield on the loan was less than the coupon.

One of the reasons why the implementation of Basel 2 was delayed was that banks did not keep sufficient data on past default experience. The result is that they were not able to estimate the probability of default. Banks advanced risky loans, receiving coupons (annual interest payments) that did not reflect the amount of risk they were taking on. Needless to say, if they did not estimate the PD correctly, there was a high probability that they did not measure the risks correctly. Their incentive schemes did not encourage them to do so. A failure to measure PDs meant that they did in fact subsidise loans and failed to recognise the losses on the balance sheet. The only time, therefore, that shareholders get to hear about bad decision lending criteria is when the loans actually default.

There is a second problem with the accounting of loans. The accounting standard setters are understandably concerned about situations where banks speculate, make huge profits and then hide those profits, placing them in 'cookie jars' and using them to prop up accounting profits in future periods when bonuses are under threat. Banks often created a general provision for bad debts in good times and released them in bad times. There is nothing inherently wrong with this if it is done correctly, but some banks were motivated by poorly designed incentive schemes and so 'overprovided' in good years and 'underprovided' in bad years. This had two benefits. Firstly, directors could get around badly flawed incentive schemes by giving themselves a bonus every year rather than some years and secondly, the banks could give the impression that their Profit & Loss account was a lot less volatile than it really was.

IAS 37, *Provisions, Contingent Liabilities and Contingent Assets* now has very strict rules on provisions. In essence, a bank must have clear evidence of default (known as trigger factors) before the bank can write down the loan. In theory, therefore, if a bank lends to a customer and the customer's credit rating drops, the market value of the loan drops and, as a result, the bank makes a loss. Yet, the bank may not be allowed to recognise that loss because although the customer may have become more risky and although the probability of default may have increased, the customer has not yet defaulted.

The only exception to this is the collective impairment provisions contained in IAS 39, paragraphs 58–70. The rules allow for an additional charge to bad debts on top of write-offs for individual loans. In essence, loans may be 'grouped on the basis of similar credit risk characteristics that are indicative of the debtor's ability to pay all amounts due according to the contractual terms'. Paragraph IAS 39 AG 89 states that future cash flows in a group of financial assets that are collectively evaluated for impairment are estimated on the basis of historical loss experience for assets with credit risk characteristics similar to those in the group. The standard gives an example. A bank, for instance, would be allowed to impair a portfolio of credit card loans if it could prove that it had statistical evidence that when people died, the risk of credit default grew. Therefore, the entity could make a general provision against all credit card holders who died, even though the bank may not yet have recognised individual instances of default. These types of losses are known as Incurred But Not Reported Losses (IBNR).

In summary, the accounting rules would be prudent if they allowed banks to write off specific instances of bad debts, i.e. where a customer alerts the bank to his inability to repay, and general instances of bad debts, i.e. where a bank lends money to a customer whose credit quality subsequently deteriorates but who has not yet defaulted. The bank is allowed to write off specific instances of bad debts but is not always allowed to write off a general provison for customers whose credit quality has deteriorated, subject to the collective provision rules contained in IAS 39 AG 89.

7.5   CREDIT RATING AGENCIES

One feature of the credit markets in 2007 was the extent to which reliance was placed on the role of the credit rating agencies. Throughout 2007, there was a huge influx of structured credit products which had a triple-A rating, even though a number of companies found it increasingly difficult to maintain the AAA status. The obvious question is why the structured credit industry is able to create triple-A rated products from non-AAA rated loans. There is a surplus of the former and a shortage of the latter. According to the *Financial Times*,[6] 99% of the triple-A credit market is composed of structured products as opposed to loans. Clearly, investors are eager to obtain the higher yield that structured credit products can offer. The obvious question is, how can structured products offer such high yields? Structured products are expensive to develop and there is a shortage of AAA loans to construct these products. No one quite knows how both the bank structurers and the rating agencies are able to pull this off. There is the argument that structured products offer diversification and therefore a portfolio of loans is less risky than individual loans. Although this argument has some merit, it is often over-egged. Another reason is that monoline insurance companies were used by securitisation structurers to insure a portfolio of loans. Again, this argument has some justification but what

---

[6] Saskia Scholtes and Richard Beales, 'Securities appeal to the risk-adverse – Issues mushroom to $5000 bn in New York', *Financial Times*, 16 May 2007.

subsequently emerged during the credit crises was that monoline insurance companies were overextending themselves, taking on too much risk – a fact that was not picked up by the rating agencies. What is worrying is that the rating agencies are in a type of monopoly position, have a very important role in the sale and distribution of structured products and are often immune from court action seeking damages where they give a risky structured product a high rating. Also, as Partnoy noted (discussed in Chapter 3) their reputation suffered long before the 2007 credit crises emerged. The growing complexity of the market means that investors are unable to do their own analyses. They are relying on the rating agencies and keeping their fingers crossed. It follows that the lack of liquidity, transparency and past data on defaults, together with the increased complexity, means that only a few institutions have the resources to deal with structured products. Credit rating agencies therefore have opened the doors for novice or ill-informed investors to play a very complex and dangerous game with other people's money. A cynic might argue that many bankers realise both their own limitations and those of the rating agencies, but still go ahead since the products offer a high yield and, if losses do occur, the directors can walk away from them, leaving the shareholder and sometimes the government to suffer. Senior investors of major investment banks were often keen purchasers of what are known as 'super-senior' investment products. These products are a type of bond issued from a securitisation. They are termed super-senior because when it comes to payment, they rank senior to all the other bonds/tranches issued by a securitisation. What makes them attractive is that they pay a high yield (above Libor) and have a triple-A rating. Their most important advantage, however, is that the regulators consider them close to risk-free so banks can acquire them in large quantities without the regulator becoming unduly worried about the risks involved. They offer what bankers term a 'regulatory arbitrage opportunity'; namely, they allow banks to take on an exposure (or create volatility in their Profit & Loss account) but the regulators and accountants consider them to be safe so the risk is not reported correctly to the shareholders. According to Tett,[7] 'banks such as UBS and Merrill have been cramming their books with tens of billions of super-senior debt – and then booking the spread as a seemingly never-ending source of easy profit'. Hedge funds have also played this game, and these hedge funds are often financed by banks such as UBS and Merrill. It became clear, however, at the start of the credit crises the reason why the structured notes paid a high yield. They were risky. They suffered liquidity risk and probably more credit risk than their name 'super-senior' implied. Experienced bankers should have known that the credit rating agencies don't always get it right and that they are conflicted, but perhaps it was convenient to their Profit & Loss account to assume that the rating agencies never get it wrong.

7.6   CREDIT DERIVATIVES

Credit Default Swaps

Credit Default Swaps (CDSs) allow banks to transfer credit risk to other banks or to hedge funds or other institutional investors. The bank transferring the risk (the transferor) pays a premium, which is closely related to the credit spread of a particular loan. The transferee receives the premium and undertakes to make good any loss suffered by the transferor on the reference loans.

---

[7] Gillian Tett, 'Super-senior losses just a misplaced bet on carry trade', *Financial Times*, 18 April 2008.

The CDS market, like the derivative market, in general includes both hedgers and speculators. Banks often use CDSs to transfer credit risk since these derivatives are treated as credit enhancers by the regulators and so the bank does not need to hold capital to protect loans on which they have bought protection. However, more recently, many banks and hedge funds have used CDSs to speculate on the credit spread. If, say, a hedge fund thinks the credit spread is too low they will buy protection (cheaply) and sell protection, i.e. receive the premium, if they feel that the premium or credit spread is above what it should be.

Few could doubt that, if used properly, credit derivatives are a positive influence on the financial markets. Banks that don't want to turn away business but also don't want to take on too much credit risk find that they can issue loans and then buy protection against the loans defaulting. The result is that banks earn a fee for originating the loan and the investor who buys the loan has a chance to diversify his exposure away from, say, equities and property.

However, to the uninitiated, derivatives can have side-effects. We discussed at length earlier the moral hazard problem that arises when one party originates the loan and another party effectively takes on the risk. There is another problem. A hedge fund might buy credit default protection on, say, company X and might also buy (or rent) voting shares in the same company. The hedge fund is therefore in a position to add value to the credit default derivatives by using its voting power to increase risk. The hedge fund might therefore encourage the company to borrow more and expand, and also encourage the company to make its Profit & Loss account more volatile by using complex derivatives.

Royal Bank of Scotland

There is little doubt that shareholders of the British bank Royal Bank of Scotland suffered while credit default protection buyers benefited from the strategic plan which RBS implemented. In early 2007 it negotiated the purchase of ABN Amro at what many analysts considered to be an inflated price, and also invested heavily in structured products linked to American sub-prime debt. Both of these initiatives would, of course, have made their Profit & Loss account more volatile, making RBS one of the most leveraged banks in Europe. As was stated in the *Financial Times*,[8] 'The decision to buy ABN, on the other hand was questionable at the time, and is looking worse by the day. The suspicion was that Sir Fred wanted the deal at any cost.'

The beneficiaries, apart from those who shorted RBS shares, would have included the managers and directors – since volatility increases the value of incentive schemes, which allows the beneficiaries to walk away from losses if they arise. Holders of credit default protection would also have enjoyed their enhanced value, since the aggressive strategies of RBS would have increased the risk of default. The losers were the shareholders and the British government. Any increase in volatility leads to a transfer of wealth from the shareholders to those on huge bonuses, and the British government was forced to accept mortgages as collateral so that RBS, along with other British banks, would find it easier to borrow money.

---

[8] The Lex Column, *Financial Times*, 10/20 April 2008.

(Continued)

In April 2008, RBS was forced to tap shareholders for £12 billion – the biggest rights issue ever, at the worst possible time (when its share price lost more than 50% in the space of a few months). This issue represented a significant U-turn in RBS's strategic plan, and one that was bound to worry corporate governance experts. At the Annual General Meeting on 23 April 2008, shareholders expressed anger at having watched their shares halve in value over a year and were critical of senior executives' pay packages, which included a special bonus for Sir Fred for his work on the ABN Amro deal.[9]

Although in the above case there is nothing to link Sir Fred Goodwin's risky decision to credit default swaps, there is little doubt that like option incentives, which pass value from the shareholder to the directors when the entity becomes riskier, the use of credit default swaps may also encourage actions detrimental to the shareholder. As pointed out earlier, the credit default market is much bigger than the actual bond markets that they protect. A person who buys, say, £100m of CDS protection and £20m of bonds from the same entity clearly has an incentive to make the company more risky. The owners of credit default protection might, therefore, use their voting power to make the company more risky, perhaps encouraging the directors of the company to engage in an expansion strategy regardless of cost and issue bonds to finance the strategy. Worse still, if the company is in difficulty, the owner of the bond may vote against a restructuring if he also holds credit default swaps. A study by the University of Texas[10] revealed the problem of credit default swaps: 'the vexing thing is that these seemed the only fairly simple and benign corner of the credit derivatives jungle. But as it turns out, they can have perverse results.'

Credit Default Swap

How an entity accounts for a CDS is not entirely clear. It would appear that if an entity (such as a bank) buys a credit default swap with the intention of hedging a loan, the entity may classify the CDS as a financial guarantee and therefore keep it off-balance sheet. On the other hand, if an entity enters into a CDS arrangement but there is no underlying loan, the entity must treat the CDS as a straightforward derivative and show it on the balance sheet at market value. The topic is discussed in the IAS 39 Implementation Guide (Questions and Answers): 'Question 1-2 Credit derivatives financial guarantee contracts that provide for payment to be made if the debtor fails to make payment when due are excluded from IAS 39.' So, if a credit derivative cannot be distinguished from a financial guarantee contract, it is excluded from IAS 39 and therefore not shown on the balance sheet at market value. A credit derivative that guarantees against the quality of the loan deteriorating, i.e. a credit downgrading, apparently falls outside the scope of a financial guarantee and so must be shown on the balance sheet at market value.

---

[9] Peter Thal Larsen, 'Apologies missing as RBS board defends decision', *Financial Times*, 24 April 2008.

[10] Tony Jackson on Monday, 'Derivatives is an industry tainted by its side-effects', *Financial Times*, 4 February 2008.

7.7 ACCOUNTING FOR LOANS

In this section we look at the accounting rules for loans and later discuss the rules for credit derivatives.

Prior to IAS 39, *Financial Instruments: Recognition and Measurement* and IAS 37, *Provisions, Contingent Liabilities and Contingent Assets* the accounting standards permitted companies and banks to charge both specific bad debts and also a general provision to cover expected future bad debts. For example, a bank might have say 1000 loans at £1,000,000 each on its books. Assume that in a particular year, 40 loans defaulted, without any recovery, and the bank believes that the value of the remaining loans is 3% lower because of the difficult credit environment. The charge to the Profit & Loss account is therefore £40,000,000 in relation to the specific provision and a further 3% of the remaining loans (£960,000,000) would be charged as the general provision – £28,800,000. The total charge to the Profit & Loss account would therefore be £68,800,000. See Table 7.3.

Table 7.3 Old method of loan provisioning

Loan size	£1,000,000
No. of loans	1000
No. of loans in default	40
Provision on remaining loans	3%
Loan value	£1,000,000,000
Specific bad debts	−£40,000,000
	£960,000,000
General provision	−£28,800,000
Carrying value of loans	£931,200,000

Although this is a theoretically correct way to account for potential bad debts, practical problems arose. Firstly, loans were normally carried at cost on the balance sheet and the decision to write down loans varied from entity to entity. A simple example in Table 7.4 illustrates this.

Table 7.4 Loan cash flows

Notional	10,000
Fixed coupon	8%
01-Jan-06	−£10,000
31-Dec-06	£800
31-Dec-07	£800
31-Dec-08	£800
31-Dec-09	£10,800

A bank originates a loan with a customer on 1 January 2006 for £10,000. The customer undertakes to pay a fixed interest of £800 each year for the next four years with the final principal at the end of year 4, i.e. 31 December 2009. After the first year, the bank will accrue interest and credit the Profit & Loss account. Therefore, the balance on the customer account at the end of the first year, immediately before the interest is paid, is simply £10,000 plus accrued interest

£800. Suppose the customer misses the first coupon payment because he is in difficulty and arranges with the bank to repay the loan as in Table 7.5.

Table 7.5   Restructured cash flows

31-Dec-07	£800
31-Dec-08	£800
31-Dec-09	£11,600

As mentioned, the treatments under the old accounting rules were varied. Some banks would take the view that the expected cash flows (in this case £13,200) were still greater than the book value (i.e. £10,000) and therefore impairment was not necessary. Other banks would have reduced the value of the loan since if the customer demands a restructuring, he is in difficulty. The new rules under IAS 39, as we shall see shortly, try to standardise the approach by taking the present value of the future cash flows and comparing them with the book value. If the present value is below the book value, impairment is necessary.

The second problem with the old approach was the general provision. Financial institutions were often able to hide losses (and in some cases hide profits) as well as disguise true volatility by increasing or reducing a provision as necessary. A simple example illustrates how lucrative this could prove for banking directors. Suppose the board of a particular bank is awarded substantial bonuses if the profits of the bank are above £1,000,000,000 in a particular year. In year 1 the bank makes £1,200,000,000 and in year 2 £840,000,000. Left unmanipulated, the directors would receive a bonus in year 1 only. However, by creating a 'general provision', the bank could reduce profits in year 1 to say £1,000,100,000 by increasing the bad debts general provision. The general provision could then be released to the Profit & Loss account in the following year as Table 7.6 demonstrates.

Table 7.6   Reserve accounting

	Year 1	Year 2
Profits before provision	£1,200,000,000	£840,000,000
(Creation)/release provision	−£199,900,000	£160,500,000
Reported profits	£1,000,100,000	£1,000,500,000

The judicious use of reserve accounting, as shown above, can guarantee directors a bonus every year. In America, this is known as 'cookie jar' reserve accounting. Both the international accounting standards and the American standards have tightened up rules in relation to this area. IFRS, for instance (through IAS 37), places restrictions on what companies can and cannot do in relation to provisions. For example, IAS 37 sets out three conditions for setting up a provision. In broad terms, the event leading up to the potential liability must have taken place, there must be a high probability of a cash outflow and the liability must be reliably estimated (IAS 37.14). Provisions for loans are also covered in IAS 39, which in essence restricts a company from recognising losses on loans. We discuss this in more detail below.

A third problem is the use of off-balance sheet trusts and special purpose vehicles for loans. Sometimes they are accounted for as trading assets, therefore any change in the market value goes through the Profit & Loss account. Sometimes they are treated as 'Held to Maturity', in which case they will be recorded on the balance sheet at cost. Another categorisation is 'Available for Sale', whereby they are shown on the balance sheet at market value (though any change in profit does not go through the Profit & Loss account but instead through Equity Reserve). Finally, they are often kept off the balance sheet altogether and so the profit (or in many cases loss) is hidden.

7.8   CHANGES IN THE ACCOUNTING STANDARDS

The new accounting standards now address many of these issues though, as usual, the new rules do have some important side-effects, are often difficult to implement and, judging by the use of off-balance sheet structures to invest in corporate loans, are implemented in a misleading fashion.

Firstly, in relation to 'specific' provisions for bad debts, IAS 39.58 restricts circumstances when a bad debt can be recognised. There must, for instance, be evidence that the borrower is in significant financial difficulty. Alternatively, the borrower must be in breach of a contract such as default in a payment when it falls due. A restructuring of the loan would also act as a trigger for impairment. If there is evidence that the borrower will enter into bankruptcy or observable data indicating that the borrower is in considerable difficulty, these too give rise to default. Once the loan satisfies the requirements under IAS 39.58, the next step is to determine the value of the loan after the impairment event has occurred. The standard lays down that the entity must try to anticipate the future cash flows that it is entitled to receive. This is then multiplied by the probability of recovery (which must be estimated) and discounted at the original effective interest. The difference between the carrying value and the book value on the balance sheet is then charged to the Profit & Loss account.

The illustration below reveals how this is achieved. We return to the fixed coupon loan that we looked at in the previous section. For the sake of simplicity, we will assume that the bank is 100% confident that it will recover all the money that it is legally entitled to, despite the missed payment. The details of the loan are given in Table 7.7.

Table 7.7   Original and revised loan agreement

Original agreement	
Notional	10,000
Fixed coupon	8%
01-Jan-06	−£10,000
31-Dec-06	£800
31-Dec-07	£800
31-Dec-08	£800
31-Dec-09	£10,800
Restructured agreement at 31 December 2006	
31-Dec-07	£800
31-Dec-08	£800
31-Dec-09	£11,600

On 31 December 2006 the borrower owns the principal and accrued interest, £10,800 in total, but defaults on a payment. The default, along with the restructuring, would trigger an

impairment under IAS 39.58. The standard requires that the entity identifies the future cash flows and multiplies them by the probability of recovery. Therefore, if the expected probability of default was 2%, the recovery rate would be 98% so each of the cash flows would be multiplied by 98%. In Table 7.8, however, we will simplify the situation by assuming that there is a 100% chance of recovery.

Table 7.8   Revised value of loan

	Loan valuation 31 December 2006 Probability of recovery		100%	
		Future cash flows as per contract	Expected cash flows	Discount factors
				8%
1	31-Dec-07	£800	£800	0.925925926
2	31-Dec-08	£800	£800	0.85733882
3	31-Dec-09	£11,600	£11,600	0.793832241
		£13,200		£10,635

In this example there is no difference between the contractual cash flows and the expected cash flows. All the cash flows are discounted using the compound discount method, i.e. the discount factor for year 2 is simply $1/(1 + 8\%)^2$. Since the present value of the cash flows is below the book value, an impairment of £165 is charged to the Profit & Loss account. The new carrying value of the loan is therefore £10,635. Table 7.9 illustrates how the income is calculated for future years.

Table 7.9   Revenue recognition

	Opening balance	Income	Cash flows	Closing balance
Year 1	£10,635	£851	−£800	£10,686
Year 2	£10,686	£855	−£800	£10,741
Year 3	£10,741	£859	−£11,600	£−
	£10,635	£2,565	−£13,200	

The opening balance at the start of 2007 is £10,635. The loan will produce total cash flows of £13,200 and therefore the difference, £2565, represents the bank's profit on the restructured loan. This is allocated to the Profit & Loss account using the effective interest method, i.e. 8% of the opening balance. Therefore, for year 2, 8% of the opening balance of £10,686 is £855. At the end of the first year, the carrying value of the loan will be £10,635 + £851 − £800 = £10,686.

We now illustrate how the figures appear on the balance sheet. We start with an opening balance sheet as in Table 7.10.

In this balance sheet, the bank has advanced a loan of £10,000 at the start of the year. During the year, interest income is recognised (even though not yet paid). Therefore, the Profit & Loss account shows a balance of £800. Table 7.11 illustrates the impact of recognising an impairment of £165. The book value of the loan drops to £10,635 and the loss is recognised immediately in the Profit & Loss account.

Table 7.10   Opening balance sheet

Balance sheet 31 December 2006	
Assets	
Loan	£10,800
Cash	£–
	£10,800
Shareholders' Funds	
Ordinary Shares issued	£10,000
Profit & Loss	£800
	£10,800

Table 7.11   Balance sheet after impairment

Assets	
Loan	£10,635
Cash	£–
	£10,635
Shareholders' Funds	
Ordinary Shares issued	£10,000
Profit & Loss	£635
	£10,635

The final balance sheet (Table 7.12) at 31 December 2007 shows the situation at the end of the next year. As Table 7.9 reveals, during the year, interest income of £851 was earned, bringing the total profit to £1486 and the carrying value of the loan to £10,686 (taken from Table 7.9).

Table 7.12   Balance sheet at end of second year

Balance sheet 31 December 2007	
Assets	
Loan	£10,686
Cash	£800
	£11,486
Shareholders' Funds	
Ordinary Shares issued	£10,000
Profit & Loss	£1,468
	£11,486

The idea behind the new rules in the accounting standard is that banks can now recognise bad debts and interest income on a consistent basis, which in turn allows for comparison.

An important change is that impairment can only take place when there is clear evidence that a borrower is in difficulty, i.e. he fails to make contractual payment when due or asks for a restructuring. Once a loan is picked for impairment, there is an element of subjectivity since the probability of recovery percentage must be estimated. The cash flows are always discounted at the original effective interest rate, even if the yield on the loan changes. This may sound counter-intuitive, since the value of a loan is always related to the loan's yield. However, the change in the credit spread is captured by estimating the probability of recovery.

7.9 ACCOUNTING RULES ON CREDIT DERIVATIVES AND FINANCIAL GUARANTEES

In the past, credit derivatives were treated similarly to insurance companies. Suppose bank X lent £10,000,000 to entity Y. The regulators would naturally be worried about the potential credit risk that bank X faces and so bank X might decide to hedge away the credit risk through a CDS. Under this arrangement, bank X would pay a premium to another counterparty willing to 'insure' the credit risk. We will assume that the counterparty charges a premium of 96 basis points. In effect, this means that the counterparty agrees to charge a premium of £96,000 to protect the loan for one year. Prior to the recent changes in IAS 39, both entities would simply accrue the fee income over the year to the Profit & Loss account, the protection seller as income and the protection buyer as a type of insurance expense.

In August 2005, IAS 39 was amended for financial guarantees. Entities that, prior to August 2005, treated financial guarantee contracts as insurance in nature could continue to account for them by simply recognising the premium or fee through the Profit & Loss account, as discussed above. However, there was concern that too many insurance companies were offering credit derivatives and financial guarantees at too cheap a premium. Perhaps the motivation behind this was that these entities were able to keep financial guarantees off the balance sheet and so hide potential losses. The IASB therefore responded by treating financial guarantees and credit derivatives in general as pure derivatives. Therefore, they came under IAS 39 as opposed to IFRS 4, the insurance accounting standard. The rules for financial guarantees were slightly different from credit derivatives. The practical effect of this was that generally, financial guarantees (particularly loss-making ones) were now shown on the balance sheet at fair or market value as opposed to cost, and so it became more difficult to hide losses. Needless to say, this rule change did bring about more volatility in the Profit & Loss account.

7.10 STRUCTURED CREDIT PRODUCTS: AN EXTRA LAYER OF COMPLEXITY

Experts now recognise that when it comes to structured credit products, the accounting rules are inadequate. The confusion allows banks to hide what they are doing and the rating agencies are only slowly getting around to recognising the huge risks that banks face. That the regulated banking and investment industry could lose (according to the IMF) close to $900 billion of shareholders' money is an indication that the regulators are losing their grip on the problem as well. According to Jennifer Hughes in the *Financial Times*,[11] 'the rules which have allowed

---

[11] Jennifer Hughes, 'Off-balance sheet rules for banks "irretrievably broken" say experts', *Financial Times*, 10 April 2008.

trillions in assets to escape close scrutiny, have come under attack in the wake of the credit crises as banks have been forced to disclose huge losses on these holdings'.

Few can doubt that credit derivatives have had a severe impact on the recent destabilisation of the capital markets. It isn't too difficult to see why. Consider the following series of transactions:

Mr X has very little income and no deposit. He is anxious nevertheless to buy property for £300,000, so he approaches an independent financial advisor. The independent financial advisor, anxious to earn a fee, gets around the lack of deposit by encouraging the builder (or seller) to finance the deposit. The builder does this by pushing the price of the house up to £360,000 and giving the customer a cash refund of £60,000, which the customer can then use as a deposit. The independent financial advisor overcomes the problem of little or no income by allowing Mr X to 'self-certify' his expected income. Mr X therefore certifies earnings of £100,000 per annum. To minimise the risk of default, a mortgage with a 'teaser rate' is selected. This means that Mr X pays a very low rate of interest for the first two years and is then moved on to a higher rate, which reflects the subsidy of the first two years. The independent financial advisor then passes the application form to the mortgage company, after earning his fee. The mortgage company notes that the customer has put a 17% deposit up-front (financed by the builder) and the income multiple is 3, and therefore approves the application and advances the loan. In theory, the mortgage company should make proper checks to ensure that Mr X has the intent and ability to pay, but since the loan is going to be sold on, it is not of prime concern to the mortgage company and in any event the independent financial advisor has made the appropriate checks on income multiples and deposits. The mortgage company includes this loan together with a number of other loans in a portfolio where it is sold to an investment bank, in a process known as securitisation. The originating mortgage company sells the loan for slightly less than £100,000 to cover the costs of originating the loan and then charges a fee for administering the loan. The entity buying the loans (probably an investment bank) sets up a special company which issues bonds. The bonds are sold to investors and the money is used to finance the purchase of the loans. The investors of these bonds are often other securitisation structures (known as CDO squared). In turn, these securitisations issue bonds which are bought by hedge funds and the hedge funds themselves may be partially owned by pension funds. Therefore, the individual pensioner or saver is ultimately responsible for the risk.

People reading the above might form the view that the loan market is very inefficient. It is. But the chief problem is that everyone is motivated to let the deal go through and few people are prepared to measure the risks. They are not motivated to do so. The chief problem is that as the loan passes through each stage, complexity emerges and where complexity emerges the middlemen are able to take fees, leaving the ultimate owner of the loan with a huge amount of risk which he or she does not have the resources to measure. Instead, that person relies on the regulators to make sure that the financial system remains stable. He relies on the accounting profession to ensure that where losses are incurred in the process they are identified immediately, and relies on the rating agencies to measure the risks involved. Unfortunately, as the last credit crises revealed, an investor who relies on the rating agencies, the accounting rules and to some extent the regulator will have received very false reassurances.

8

Accounting for Structured Products
(Credit Risk)

8.1 INTRODUCTION

Securitisations have suffered quite a lot of bad press recently. We discuss below what they are and how they are constructed. There are two principal reasons for the negative publicity. Firstly, through securitisations, banks were able to approve and advance loans and then sell them to either other banks, hedge funds or pension funds. This ability to transfer risk created a moral hazard problem. Banks became a little lax about measuring credit risk, knowing that they would not be held accountable for the bad debts. The second reason for the bad publicity was the complexity. As stated earlier, the more complex a structure the easier it is to earn fees. Many creators of securitisations realised that investors in securitisations were not measuring the risk properly. They therefore ended up buying complex structures which were loaded with risks. The complexity also enabled these investors to take a profit up-front and hide the true risks that they were taking on. Obviously, with the severe credit crunch of 2007 and 2008, investors became very aware of how much risk they were taking on and more importantly, the dangers of investing in complex products became very visible. The result was that for a period of time, there was a shutdown in the securities market. Everyone wanted to sell these complex products but there were few buyers. Some commentators even predicted an end to the securitisation industry.

In reality, securitisation is a very positive financial innovation. The problem is that this financial innovation proved to be profitable and so was taken to the extreme. The innovation that brought a simple securitisation to the very complex animal that it sometimes is today was possibly motivated by the need for structured product salesmen to confuse the investor, the accountant and the regulator so that they could earn high fees and conceal the risks that the ultimate investor was taking on. As stated earlier, in its simplest form securitisation can often work to the benefit of everyone. The major commercial banks have branches in almost every high street and, together with their strong brand name, they are in a position to originate and process loans. However, unlike other companies and certain financial institutions, the risk of a bank going bankrupt could have very detrimental side-effects for the entire financial system (as Northern Rock has shown). To overcome this, banks are exposed to heavy banking regulation known as the Basel rules. In effect, these rules place restrictions on the amount of risk and therefore loans that a bank can take on. It seems logical, therefore, that those banks should continue to originate loans as they normally do and then sell the excess loans through a securitisation to other banks, entities or investors. This is what securitisation does. The advantage for the investor is that he can diversify away from property or equities (particularly when there is the perception that these two asset classes are overpriced). Economically, securitisations can be justified because they are simply a form of transferring risks from those who can't bear them to those who can. The other advantage is that risk is not concentrated but spread out amongst a number of financial institutions around the globe, hence the sub-prime crisis in America affected a lot of European banks as well. The irony is that the dependence by the banking system on securitisation caused many banks to suffer and included casualties such as Northern Rock and Bear Stearns. Securitisation clearly has a place in the financial world, but because it grew so fast and became so complicated so quickly and was relatively unregulated, the financial community was reluctant to measure the risks that it was generating, as exposing this too early might have had a negative impact on the fees that most investment bankers and credit rating agencies generated from it. Needless to say, the failure to measure the risk of securitisations properly was eventually revealed in the form of huge losses to shareholders. In some cases banks suffered a 50% reduction in share value and then tapped the shareholder to invest extra funds, through a rights issue. Shareholders paid dearly for the mistakes of their directors.

What was very unique about securitisation was that corporates were having difficulty obtaining triple-A ratings on their loans. Yet, when these loans were bought by securitisation vehicles, the vehicles themselves were able to obtain a higher rating. In fact, at one stage, structured products – i.e. securitisations – accounted for around 99% of the triple-A ratings. There was probably a legitimate reason for this. Securitisations are able to diversify their exposure, which presumably helps their ratings. They were also in a position to buy insurance protection from monoline insurance companies. Finally, they were able to issue different tranches of bonds (which we discuss below), which meant that some of the safer tranches were able to avoid the first, say, 2% of losses. However, the reality is that traders within financial institutions who invested money took the view that if the rating agencies gave the instruments a triple-A rating it was not necessary to ask further questions. There is growing evidence, however, that the rating agencies were out of their depth and unable to deal with the complexities of 'advanced' securitisations. They were also motivated to earn fees. The *Financial Times* put it succinctly:[1]

> Moody's for example, made 44 percent of its revenue last year from structured finance deals. Such assessments also command more than double the fee rates of simpler corporate ratings, helping keep Moody's operating margins above 50%.

There is little doubt that at the peak of the securitisation industry, the fees that rating agencies earned were a lot higher than those earned from rating corporate bonds and loans. Even if one could argue that the rating agencies had procedures in place to act independently, they were paid by investment institutions anxious to sell as many securitisations as possible and therefore were not independent. Credit rating agencies suffer from the same problems that auditors suffer. They, in theory, act on behalf of the shareholder/investor but are paid by those they regulate (i.e. the board of directors) and not the shareholder/investor to whom they report.

8.2 SECURITISATION OVERVIEW

The example below illustrates how securitisation operates. A bank has issued £400,000,000 worth of loans and finds that there is a demand for more loans. The bank's regulators constrain

---

[1] 'Falling grades? – why regulators fear credit rating agencies may be out of their depth', *Financial Times*, 17 May 2007.

the amount of loans that the bank may take on, putting pressure on the bank to turn down new customers. The bank sets up a company called SPV (Special Purpose Vehicle). The purpose of this company is simply to issue bonds which will, in turn, be used to finance the purchase of loans. The company will be run by trustees/directors who are, in broad terms, appointed independently of the bank. The SPV then raises £400,000,000 through the issue of five types of bonds (bond A, B, C, D and E). The £400,000,000 is then passed on to the bank who, in return, sells the loan to the SPV. The five tranches of bonds are listed in Table 8.1.

Table 8.1   Tranche structure

Tranche	%	Notional	Rating	Payment over Libor
A	35.00%	£140,000,000	AAA	0.150%
B	30.00%	£120,000,000	A	0.500%
C	15.00%	£60,000,000	BBB	1.000%
D	10.00%	£40,000,000	BB	2.000%
E	10.00%	£40,000,000	NR	Remainder
	100.00%	£400,000,000		

Tranche A is the least risky tranche since defaults must be 65% before it suffers a default. In other words, it is paid first in priority. If there is a default the E tranche is affected first, followed by the D tranche, then the C tranche, etc. Needless to say, the lower tranches get a higher yield because of the risk they take on. Suppose Libor (the inter-bank rate) is 5%, then tranche D would get a yield of 7% as long as there are no defaults and tranche C gets only 6% since it is taking on lower risk.

The quality of the bonds issued by the securitisation is heavily dependent on the quality of the loans purchased by the securitisation structure. This reduces the obvious moral hazard where banks offload all their risky loans through the securitisation. Normally, in the agreement between the bank and the securitisation there are certain parameters set, i.e. only loans with

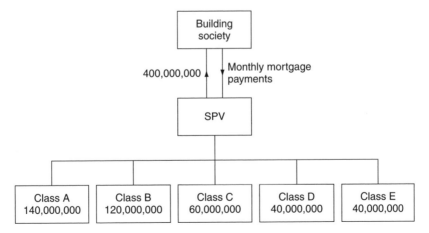

Figure 8.1   Simple securitisation

a grade of AA or better or loans with a credit rating below A– cannot constitute more than 1% of the portfolio. In addition, there are also 'concentration' limits placed on the portfolio of loans, i.e. exposure to countries rated below AA is limited to 10% and there can be no loans to countries rated below A, etc. Unfortunately, these general guidelines, which were designed to protect the investor, have not always succeeded. Even some of the more sophisticated investors such as European investment banks were quite happy to take on exposure to the American sub-prime market through securitisations and structured investment vehicles.

8.3 REGULATORY ARBITRAGE

One undesirable consequence of securitisation is the 'regulatory arbitrage' opportunities that banks take advantage of. As emphasised throughout this book, banks are motivated to take on as much risk as possible (because it represents a transfer of wealth from the shareholders to banking directors and traders on huge bonuses). For a while, securitisation was a means by which banks could take on additional risk – the regulators could not stop them and the accounting rules were not sophisticated enough to report what was going on.

In essence, regulator arbitrage worked as follows:

A bank has £400m of loans where the probability of default is about 2%. Under the Basel regulatory rules, the bank would be required to finance approximately 4% of these loans by shareholders' funds, i.e. £16m and a further 4% financed by long-term subordinated loans. A bank could therefore securitise the portfolio and retain the equivalent of the E tranche itself (assume that the equity tranche is 10% of the entire portfolio). Clearly, the bank has retained virtually all the risk (since if the average bad debts exposure is 2% there is little chance of it exceeding 10%, thus the bank retains all the bad debts risk). According to the regulators, however, the Basel 1 rules simply recognised that the bank's maximum exposure after the securitisation was the value of the E tranche, namely 10% of £400,000,000, i.e. £40,000,000. Therefore, the regulatory equity capital falls to 4% of £40,000,000, that is £1,600,000. Thus, securitisation allowed banks to reduce the regulatory burden without reducing the risk, hence the term 'regulatory arbitrage'. The position has changed significantly under the Basel 2 rules. Broadly, under the new rules, if a bank retains the risky tranche of a securitisation, it must finance virtually all of this tranche either through shareholders' funds or long-term subordinated loans. There are accounting implications here. If the regulators decide that the bank has not transferred the risks and rewards of a particular loan portfolio, the auditor will find keeping the securitisation off-balance sheet a bit more difficult to justify. We discuss this in more detail later.

8.4 PREPAYMENT RISK SYNTHETIC SECURITISATIONS

Occasionally, borrowers whose loans are securitised, i.e. sold by the bank into a securitisation, may want to repay their loans before the due date. This puts pressure on the securitisation to retire some of the bonds it has issued. Investors in securitisations often refer to this as 'prepayment risk'. For instance, an individual might take out a 25-year mortgage which is subsequently securitised by the bank. The individual may then sell his house after two years, forcing the securitisation to reduce the coupons to the tranche holders of the securitisation.

To avoid prepayment risk, securitisation specialists have developed what is known as a synthetic securitisation structure. Here, the bank wishing to transfer the risk simply enters into a credit default swap arrangement with the securitisation vehicle. Under this agreement the bank pays a fee and in return is protected against default. The bank is then free to initiate new loans. The regulators tend to accept the credit default swap as a form of credit mitigation and so will not penalise a bank who takes on a loan and subsequently transfers the credit risk to a securitisation. When the securitisation structure is set up, the funds raised from the issue of the various tranches are used to buy (usually) government bonds. In the event of default, these government bonds are liquidated and the funds are used to pay the bank compensation for any losses it may have.

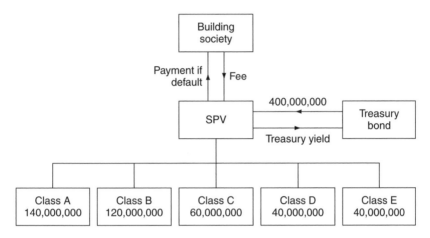

Figure 8.2   Complex securitisation

For a period of about 20 years there was an explosive growth in the use of credit derivatives, particularly credit default swaps and securitisations. Their prime advantage was that they converted illiquid loans into more liquid bonds, ones on which the credit rating agencies were happy to confer a high rating. They also pleased the regulators because usually, the portfolio of loans was well diversified. As we shall see later, the downfall of securitisations occurred when they became so complex that few people knew what was going on. Some banks found that they were able to dump into a securitisation questionable loans which, although they met the simplified parameters, were nevertheless risky and very leveraged. The financial community to some extent put huge pressure on the rating agencies. Their ratings were all-important and so there was a temptation by the rating agencies to please everyone by giving very risky securitisations a high rating. During the period 1990 to 2007, securitisations along with monetary policy allowed people to take a very optimistic view on the world economy. When central banks acquired power from the government to set interest rates, the financial community responded by saying that this marked the end of various credit cycles since central bank governors were more interested in the long-term health of the economy, unlike politicians who meddled with interest rates to survive the next election. The prevailing view, therefore, was that property prices could only go one way – upwards. This view, of course, allowed the securitisation industry to succeed as they could relax their lending criteria. At the same time, there were a lot of investors who complained that they could not achieve diversification in their portfolios. Investing in securitisation structures was the answer.

8.5 ACCOUNTING FOR CREDIT RISK

As pointed out in the previous chapter, the accounting profession and regulators find credit risk a bit more difficult to deal with than market risk. Market risk (i.e. exposure to interest rate, foreign exchange rate, equity and commodity risk) is relatively easy to measure; the process used is VaR (Value at Risk), which is discussed in Chapter 11. The accountants should, in theory, have little or no difficulty in identifying embedded derivatives that are exposed to market risk. Identifying bifurcation credit derivatives is a bit more tricky. Unlike market risk data, where there is plenty of information available on interest rate, foreign exchange, equity and commodity price movements, there is too little information available on instances of customers defaulting. This lack of data gives structured product salespeople the opportunity to value products on the basis of assumptions. In America, for instance, the assumption that property prices can only go up pushed up the value of mortgages and so pushed up the value of structured products based on mortgages. There was also the risk that banks found they could issue, and perhaps securitise, covenant lite loans because they could assume that the credit cycle was a thing of the past, given the new horizon where central bank governors decided interest rate movements and not politicians (who might have been tempted towards short-term targets by reducing interest rates without worrying about inflation).

There are a few areas where the accounting standards could improve the way they report to shareholders. Firstly, they could penalise complexity. This may mean stating in their audit report that a lot of the income of the bank is derived from complex financial instruments whose value is subjective. If a bank is allowed to buy complex structured products that it doesn't understand, and is allowed to keep them off the balance sheet, there will be a lot of mistrust of bankers not only amongst shareholders but even amongst bankers themselves. Throughout 2008, for instance, the Libor rate (the rate at which banks borrow and lend to each other) was a lot higher than the base rate which the central banks set. The difference broadly indicates the poor health of the banking sector – the wider the spread, the greater the risk of banks. For a time in 2008 the gap between Libor rates and base rates was stubbornly high, indicating that banks did not trust each other. There was a risk that banks were hiding from shareholders the details of disastrous and illiquid investments that they made on credit products. Secondly, they could possibly introduce a standard on liquidity as this is very important for Profit & Loss calculation. IAS 39 states that if an entity has the ability and intention to hold an asset to maturity, it can record the asset at cost on the balance sheet and ignore changes in market value. On the other hand, if the entity has borrowed heavily in the short term, the market value of the asset is very important since the bank could easily become involved in a distressed sale situation (as the hedge fund Long Term Capital Management discovered many years ago). The difficulty for the accounting standards is deciding what is liquid and what is illiquid. In the absence of definitive guidance, bankers will attempt to hold complex financial instruments at cost on the balance sheet and then cash them in only if they make a profit (there is nothing inherently wrong with this). However, if a bank does not have enough cash and the assets have fallen in value, then the riskier banks will be forced to sell in a distressed market. So, if the value of the asset is hidden (either shown at cost or kept off-balance sheet), the shareholder will not be aware of the huge losses building up. Experts, for instance, estimated that Citibank had $1.1 trillion of assets off-balance sheet.[2]

---

[2] David Reilly, 'Accounting-rule makers plan to re-examine how banks treat off-balance-sheet vehicles that have played a big role in the credit crunch', *Wall Street Journal*, 29 February 2008.

Triple-A rated CPDOs

Perhaps the signal that the credit markets were getting out of hand occurred in early 2007 when the financial press was confused about how an extremely complex credit derivative could get a triple-A rating from the rating agencies. In the summer of 2006, ABN Amro developed a debt product using complex mathematics. The bond was designed to pay the same yield as 'junk' bonds but have the risk profile of an ordinary bank account. Needless to say, a structured product that pays a high yield and is not risky took the market by storm. The product was titled a Constant Proportion Debt Obligation. It paid 2% above Libor. A moderately educated banker might say that this is too good to be true, yet the credit rating agencies assumed it was true by giving it the all-important triple-A rating. The 'fantastically complex instrument that used a mathematical strategy to make a highly leveraged bet on a pool of credit derivatives' was sold to a wide pool of investors including pension funds, which are often prevented from holding risky investments. Standard & Poor's gave the rating, in the belief that the chance of default was very low. As the *Financial Times* stated:[3] 'Moody's, the rival agency, later also awarded top ratings to similar deals. But some observers were surprised by the high ratings and thought the agencies had been duped.'

8.6 ACCOUNTANTS, REGULATORS AND CREDIT AGENCIES

Complexity prevents accountants, along with regulators and credit rating agencies, from doing their jobs properly. Accountants are responsible for ensuring that losses (where relevant) are recognised immediately. If banks were forced to recognise losses sooner rather than later, the problems of using complex instruments to hide risk would have come to light very quickly. This would have encouraged corrective action. Instead, for a period of years, banks were able to make loans to the sub-prime sector even though there were very clear warning signals that entities were not measuring risks and so problems would emerge later. They nevertheless continued, perhaps motivated by fees and the fact that they were not obliged to disclose the losses and the risks that they were occasionally taking on. In many cases, banks were able to pass on the risks to other banks and to other entities such as hedge funds and pension funds. But, when the music stopped, banks found that they could not pass on these complex instruments and structures and therefore held them in 'off-balance sheet' vehicles and also used accounting procedures which would prevent them from having to realise losses. There are three possible reasons why the accounting of these products contributes to the problem. Firstly, many banks could not sell securitisation structures that they had bought or developed and were forced to keep them. Rather than show these on the balance sheet, the banks set up separate companies and placed the assets there. These separate companies used borrowed money to finance the assets, but there was an implied guarantee or understanding that the bank would take the responsibility for the loans if the assets fell in value. Hence, many banks were forced to bring 'on-balance sheet' assets that were kept 'off-balance sheet' when the lenders became worried. The second contributor was the valuation. Complex financial credit instruments are notoriously difficult to value and require a lot of assumptions along with complex mathematical models. The result is that banking auditors are tempted to show the assets at cost on the balance sheet (that's assuming they have not exploited the off-balance sheet opportunities). They

---

[3] Richard Beales, 'How S&P put the triple A into CPDO', *Financial Times*, 17 May 2007.

are therefore able to hide losses. A third problem with the accounting standards is that entities often classify investments in securitisations as 'Available for Sale'. This means that even if they show these securitisations on their balance sheet, and at their correct value, the change in value does not necessarily have to go through the Profit & Loss account. Instead, it is stored in the Equity Reserve account.

The regulators are charged with the task of making sure that the financial system remains stable. In particular, they are responsible for ensuring that banks are appropriately capitalised for the amount of losses they take on. As explained in previous paragraphs, accountants have a lot to learn from the rules that regulators use to make sure that banks are appropriately financed. In essence, the regulators are more concerned with volatility of profits than the profits themselves, though the underlying profitability of the bank is important. There are mathematical models that the regulators use to measure how exposed a bank is to interest rate, equity, foreign exchange and credit risks. If these models indicate that the underlying earnings of the bank are high, then the regulators require that the banks inject more capital, either through shareholders' funds or through subordinated loans. Company law and accounting rules tend to apply the same rules, but accountants tend to assume that the maximum dividend payments should be based on past profitability. Basel 2 regulators, on the other hand, tend to focus on maintaining the shareholder base by focusing on future volatility.

Unfortunately, there is evidence that regulators are suffering from the same problems as accountants, namely that the products they are trying to regulate are too complex, difficult to price and contain a lot of liquidity risk. There is a strong correlation between complexity and liquidity – the more complex a product is, and the more difficult it is to value, the less liquid it is. One of the biggest stumbling blocks that causes the regulator problems is measuring liquidity risk. Unlike market risk, liquidity risk is difficult to measure. In the case of the hedge fund Long Term Capital Management, despite having on its board academics who won Nobel prizes for their contribution to financial risk management, their failure to measure liquidity risk led to the collapse of the hedge fund, requiring the American government to step in because of its potential impact on other financial institutions. It follows that when there is market turmoil, banks with complex structured products have difficulty selling them. Also, it becomes difficult for the bank to borrow against them. This was a major source of liquidity risk. Banking accounting practices (which effectively allowed them to hide losses) also contributed to liquidity risk because banks were afraid to lend to any other bank exposed to the sub-prime losses, particularly when they used structured products linked to the American sub-prime market. There were two notable casualties of the liquidity risk crises. Firstly, in Britain, the regulators came under severe criticism for failing to spot the problems with Northern Rock. The chief criticism was that Northern Rock was expanding at too fast a pace and was effectively using overdraft (or at least very short-term loans) to finance their expansion. Northern Rock relied on the securitisation industry to alleviate its liquidity problems but, of course, when the American sub-prime crisis erupted, and tainted the entire securitisation industry, Northern Rock suffered as it was unable to sell its loans in the usual way. In the end, the government had to rescue Northern Rock, by effectively nationalising it. The reputation of the City was damaged because they delayed taking this action, resulting in huge queues outside Northern Rock branches as customers with money on deposit with Northern Rock panicked.

In America, the regulators suffered though in a more discreet way. In order to reduce the prospect of America going into recession, banks were allowed to borrow huge amounts of money from the Federal Reserve by using securities which would not have previously qualified as collateral owing to their risky nature. Under the Fed's Term Auction Facility (TAF), banks were able to borrow at relatively attractive rates and this resulted in a huge amount of borrowing. According to Gillian Tett, borrowings reached $50 billion by mid-February 2008.[4] Needless to say, the Fed's willingness to provide extra liquidity facilities at generous terms may be interpreted as a reward for failure: the failure of banks to act responsibly in protecting depositors' funds and the failure of regulators to stop what was going on. Many analysts expressed unease at 'the stress developing in opaque corners of the US banking system and the banks' growing reliance on indirect forms of government support'.[5]

The concerns are understandable. Banks are not as motivated to measure risks if the government continues to bail them out in times of difficulty. Government bail-outs do create a moral hazard problem, which was why the Governor of the Bank of England was reluctant to bail out Northern Rock in 2007. Banking executives want to earn bonuses. Therefore, they will continue to originate risky loans as long as there is a fee to be earned. Typically, they will pass on the risk of these loans through a securitisation structure. However, even if they cannot sell the loans, there is no major problem since they know that if they keep them complex the regulator cannot do an awful lot about it. Then, if the banks do get into difficulty, the Federal Reserves' Term Auction Facility might assist them.

The Fed announced this flexible lending facility in December 2007. They had hoped that other central banks around the world would take a similar line, but there was some unease amongst other banks on this policy and they were not over-enthusiastic about adopting the system. In the past, banks borrowing money from the Federal Reserve had to do so using the so-called 'discount window'. The problem with this approach is that there was a fear that the markets would find out about it and this would lead to the problem of a bank having to own up to its difficulty. Needless to say, the next question is 'how long will the Federal Reserve hold out this safety blanket?' Generally, entities (not only banks) that receive some form of state aid or privilege from the government are unlikely to give it up too easily. There is a risk that banks will invest strongly in lobbying pressure to keep this privilege, even if the markets return to normal. It is a dangerous precedent when structured products become so complex that regulators fail to do their job effectively and so the only avenue left is state subsidy. It is hardly a motivation for banks to reduce complexity and increase transparency. While all this goes on, the accounting profession will suffer as it tries to battle with this clearly growing problem.

In a letter to the *Financial Times* in February 2008[6] the President of Tavakoli Structured Finance in Chicago, Janet Tavakoli, stresses the role that derivatives have played in getting the market into a pickle. In that letter she explains how the security industry operates.

Lend money to mortgage lenders who will use that money to lend to people who cannot pay them back. Securitise these obligations by allowing hedge funds to put up minimal cash for the appearance of taking the first loss in a deal, and allow the hedge fund to hive off the excess income. Then persuade financial guarantors to use a type of credit derivative to 'insure' the 'safest' part of these unstable structures. After that, use credit derivatives to transfer the middle risk that you could not sell, the mezzanine tranche, to yet another

---

[4] Gillian Tett, 'US banks quietly borrow $50bn from Fed via new credit facility', *Financial Times*, 18 February 2008.

[5] Gillian Tett, 'US banks quietly borrow $50bn from Fed via new credit facility', *Financial Times*, 18 February 2008.

[6] Janet Tavakoli, 'Cynical use of derivatives has market in a pickle', *Financial Times*, Letter to the Editor, 31 January 2008.

securitisation. Now do the same thing all over again. You have just destabilised the financial guarantors, because the 'safe' credit derivatives-based structures are now in danger of losing substantial principal. But you are doing fine because you used a credit derivative to buy credit default protection on the financial guarantors from some poor sucker, who was not paying attention.

Most finance professionals reading the above might not have a clue what is going on. However, if you are an internal or external auditor and you come across structured credit products regularly, not understanding the above places you at risk of not auditing these products correctly. It is important to observe that many experienced users of credit derivatives have found a way of passing on risk to those who cannot measure it. Often, it is easy to sell a securitisation if a potential (but naive) investor is told that a major bank or hedge fund will take on most of the risk of default so, if they are prepared to take on the risk so too should the investor be. However, the structure is designed so that the hedge fund only 'appears' to take on the risk by putting risk capital into the structure. In reality, most of the risk capital is put in by the naive investor, and he only realises this when the structure goes sour.

8.7 COMPLEXITY

To understand the complexity and therefore the reason why many corporate governance people describe credit structured products as 'toxic waste', consider the following extracts from the financial press on a day when Barclays bank announced their results in February 2008. Although the results were a lot better than expected, with Barclays 'only' suffering a write down of £1.635 billion and reported profits of £7 billion, journalists directed readers to the small print, namely footnote 18 in a 102-page document. Between January and June 2007, Barclays had reduced their investment in ABS CDO Super Senior products from £7.4 billion to £4.6 billion. Also, 'Other US subprime' decreased from £6 billion to £5 billion. The *Financial Times* commentary was as follows:

> The first query is about Barclays' approach to recognising losses. The bank yesterday reported write-downs of £1.635 billion. However, that included a £685 million gain on the carrying value of the bank's own debt – an accounting sleight-of-hand used widely in the financial sector in recent months.[7]

However, the big question mark was on Barclays' approach to the valuation of its leveraged loans. The bank recognised a £58 million loss on a portfolio of £7 billion, which was much less than that of its rivals (at 90%). The commentary suggests, therefore, that where there is complexity, there are inconsistent valuation procedures between banks, making them difficult to compare. Furthermore, these valuation procedures are not necessarily transparent, yet, given the size of Barclays' investment in sub-prime debt and complicated leveraged loans, their valuation methodology has probably a more important impact on the Profit & Loss account than underlying economic performance. The problem with this opaqueness is that objectivity may be lost. Barclays may, in picking its valuation methodology, focus on maximising bonuses

---

[7] 'All eyes turn to small print of Barclays' results', *Financial Times*, 20 February 2008.

rather than informing the shareholder. John Varley, Barclays' Chief Executive commented 'the risk exposure and the way banks have managed their risk is not generic'. Unfortunately, the same could be said for the way that banks value and account for their positions in these complex products and so the reliability of the Profit & Loss statement is always something that analysts will question, particularly in the middle of a severe credit crunch.

Not only must investors worry about the opaqueness of the pricing and risk management of structured products, the conflicts of interest argument creeps up as well. As the *Financial Times* put it:

> There is a further worry: how can banks manage their own risks, if they can't work out exactly what their positions are? Executives also have to grapple with the vested interests of staff, who may not be in a position to confront the cold hard truth. Now that bonuses have been banked, more problems could be around the corner.

The implication is worryingly consistent, namely that banks will continue to use complex products if they have control over how they are valued. If the external valuer doesn't understand the risks and sensitivities of structured products, they end up allowing the traders to dictate their own bonuses. Traders can do this by exposing banks to huge risks, knowing that neither the risk managers, the internal accountants nor the external accountants fully understand what is going on. Thus the shareholder is left vulnerable and unprotected.

8.8 DISCLOSURE

There is evidence that banks are slowly attempting to make improvements in the way that shareholders are informed about profitability and risk. When Barclays disclosed their results in February 2007, they were careful to include a detailed note on the fair value measurement of financial instruments. This note reminded shareholders that the fair value of a financial instrument is determined by reference to the quoted price and only uses 'appropriate valuation techniques' or marking-to-model approaches where no liquid market exists. There are two types of valuation procedures used where the markets are not liquid. Firstly, some valuation techniques are based on market observable inputs. This means that when pricing instruments using a spreadsheet/model they will use implied volatility figures or credit spreads which may be obtained from the options market or credit derivatives market. The other type of valuation technique relates to valuations where the significant inputs are not observable. In such instances, the financial instruments are price at the 'transaction price' and not adjusted. This means that if there are losses, these can be hidden since the true value of the financial instrument remains off-balance sheet.

8.9 CREDIT SUISSE FIASCO

In February 2007, Credit Suisse benefited from an investment policy of Qatar Investment Authority to invest about $15 billion in US and European banks. According to press reports,[8] the stake was about $500 million which represented approximately 1.5% of the bank's market

---

[8] 'Qatar SWF buys Credit Suisse stake', *Financial Times*, 19 February 2008.

capitalisation. Immediately after signing the deal, Credit Suisse was forced to expose a significant mark-down on its trading positions. The crisis, which led to a loss of $2.85 billion,[9] related to their structured credit positions. In early 2008, the credit quality of complex structured products held by banks across the world continued to deteriorate significantly. Once again, complexity was the root cause of the problem. It appears that a handful of traders failed to update valuations of their structured credit positions. The mispricing was discovered during a routine review of risk procedures. Unlike traders who contribute to the bottom line, risk managers and back-office staff are often classified as administrative staff or, according to some traders, a 'headache that must be endured to comply with regulatory requirements'. The result is that risk managers and accountants are not given the same resources or status as traders and often, where risk managers challenge traders, the enquiry goes cold owing to a combination of factors – the risk manager doesn't have enough clout and, due to a lack of resources, is probably not in a position to handle the complexities of the structured credit market.

Most banks encourage their traders to value their positions on a daily basis. The complexity arises because, where the structured products are illiquid, the traders are obliged to make assumptions about the volatility of earnings and the correlation of loans within the portfolio. Needless to say, this is easier said than done. The role of the middle office (or risk management unit) is to oversee these inputs and make sure that traders are making realistic assumptions, as opposed to assumptions that would maximise their bonus. Most bankers will admit that there is always a tense relationship between traders who contribute to profits and middle-office staff who attempt, amongst other things, to put a break on the amount of risk that a bank takes on. In periods when banks are making huge profits and paying huge bonuses, traders become 'star' quality and can perhaps more easily rebuff enquiries made by middle-office staff. There is the possibility, though remote, that some staff at Credit Suisse were tempted to delay recognition of losses, or whether the losses arose because of errors. One banking executive commenting on the case said it was 'conceivable that Credit Suisse's controllers had not understood the valuation'.[10] The Credit Suisse fiasco has left many questions unanswered and, until answers emerge, the banking sector will be treated with suspicion as long as it continues to use complex illiquid structured products. A reasonable question that an investor may ask when reading the annual report is 'how much of these profits are based on valuations by traders that auditors and middle office people don't understand?' Until a more consistent and transparent accounting procedure is identified, a question mark remains over the usefulness of audited reports where structured products are concerned. It was perhaps a painful experience for Qatar Investment Authority, who committed themselves to approximately $500 million, days before the loss of $2.85 billion was revealed.

An important question is whether bank's investors (shareholders) are in a similar predicament to auditors, risk managers and regulators. A simple answer is 'yes'. If the published accounts are wrong, the investor's decision to invest will perhaps be wrong. This may be true of the ordinary shareholder, who is heavily reliant on annual reports. Could it be true for the more experienced institutional investor, who will have access to senior management at the bank he intends to invest in? Unlike the small investor, the institutional investor has access to the board of directors and of course can pay for research and is therefore not overly reliant on the financial statements. Unfortunately, there is evidence that even the institutional investor does not know what is going on. This situation may arise because those making decisions

---

[9] 'Deference may explain trading failure', *Financial Times*, 21 February 2008.
[10] 'Deference may explain trading failure', *Financial Times*, 21 February 2008.

at the institutional level are not investing their own money but other people's money. It also suggests that there are weak internal controls in relation to risk management and valuation at this level. Obviously, there will be repercussions at the accounting level. The motivation to improve the accounting standards and to hold auditors to account for poor quality audits is quite weak if investors are not overly concerned. As pointed out elsewhere in this book, the problem with institutional investors is that they are investing other people's money and therefore may not have a beneficial interest in the investment (in other words, they are not penalised if they make losses). Ordinary shareholders, of course, usually cannot walk away from losses but are too small to influence the improvement of the accounting standards.

An article titled 'Western banks face backlash as they hand out begging bowl'[11] suggested that banks faced increased difficulty when they 'passed the begging bowl around the sovereign wealth funds'. One Asian commentator noted 'The Chinese are worried they are turning into [the source of] dumb money. There is the risk that Gulf funds may also classify themselves in this manner and so are using the experience of private equity funds as partners in the hope that the experience of the latter will avoid situations similar to the Credit Suisse fiasco.'

8.10 MONOLINE INSURANCE COMPANIES

From the above it is clear that the use of complex products has resulted in regulators, accountants and credit rating agencies failing to do their job properly – another group that has contributed to the lack of transparency is the monoline insurance companies. For years, in return for a premium, many insurance companies were quite happy to insure various CDO tranches, enabling banks to secure a high triple-A rating from the rating agencies. However, as the credit crises deepened in 2007 and 2008, these insurance companies were forced to admit that they were taking on a lot more risk than they should have. For a very long period of time, the supply of companies willing to offer credit protection was so high that credit spreads were at a worryingly low level in the peak of the credit boom. Eventually, the credit rating agencies were forced to downgrade the insurance companies and this had negative implications for banks and other sponsors of CDOs who engaged in what is known as the 'negative carry trade'.

The term 'negative carry' in this context simply means that the rewards for holding a financial instrument are greater than the financing costs. Consider a case where a bank buys a financial instrument (say a CDO bond) which gives a yield of 10%. The Libor costs that the bank faces are 5% (Libor being the inter-bank rate) and, to protect itself against a credit loss, the bank takes out insurance with a monoline insurance company, paying say 82 basis points. The result is that the bank pays a total of 5.82% and earns a coupon of 10%, giving an excess profit of 4.18%. Suppose the bond was to last for five years, and many banks were tempted to take the entire profit up-front. Thus, if they spent £10m on the bond, the profit would be 4.18% per year or approximately 20.3% over the five years (after discounting). Thus, a £10m investment could yield a £2m up-front profit. The accounting standards, particularly IAS 18, would generally not allow this type of revenue recognition (simply because the bank that made the investment would have an ongoing exposure to the underlying bond) and so a diligent auditor would insist that the maximum profit to be taken up-front is zero, and that 4.18% should be accrued each year until the bond matures (rather like the accounting stipulated in the effective

---

[11] Gillian Tett, 'Western banks face backlash as they hand out begging bowl', *Financial Times*, 8 February 2008.

interest rules under IAS 39). However, some banks have drawn the conclusion that if they buy a bond and insure it, they do not carry any of the risks and so are allowed to recognise the profits up-front (and presumably award themselves a bonus on that basis). What happens, however, if the monoline insurance company has extended itself to such an extent that its own credit rating suffers? Then, the bank that has purchased the bond will find, during the credit crunch, that the value of the bond will fall, but the value of the protection (which is of course dependent on the rating of the monoline insurance company) will be close to worthless and so the bank will have to take a significant hit to its Profit & Loss account, without being able to recover the bonuses it paid out. This is exactly what happened during the credit crunch in 2008.

8.11 ACCOUNTING IMPLICATIONS

There appear to be four accounting methods that entities use when accounting for structured credit products. The first, which is probably the ideal one (at least for many investors), is to get the market value of each structured product and compare it with the previous market value, allowing the difference to go through the Profit & Loss account. Here the accounting Profit & Loss account is close to the true economic profit and, therefore, closer to reality. As an example, an entity buys a structured financial instrument at the start of 2007 for 100. By the end of 2007 the value of the instrument has fallen to 80 and by the end of 2008 the value has fallen to 45. The entity would recognise a loss of 20 in 2007 and a further loss of 35 in 2008. The obvious practical difficulty with this is that getting the market value for a complex illiquid instrument is quite difficult. A second accounting approach would be to recognise that the valuation is quite subjective, therefore it is carried at cost on the balance sheet and only the yield or coupon is put through the Profit & Loss account. This approach is quite easy to implement, but as the bulk of the valuation is kept off-balance sheet, it provides the entity with an opportunity to hide losses and, in some cases, to 'cherry-pick' the profit-making instruments where the entity may be able to realise a profit from a sale. A third approach is to classify the instrument as 'Available for Sale'. Here, the entity shows the financial instrument at its market value on the balance sheet but any profit or loss is stored in reserves (or more precisely, the Equity Reserve) and remains there until the asset is sold, in which case it is transferred from the Equity Reserve to the Profit & Loss account. Therefore, an entity can hide losses until the asset is sold. A fourth accounting approach is to classify the financial instrument as off-balance sheet. Here, the bank effectively sets up a company and uses that company to borrow money. The company in turn buys the asset. The interest on the loan is financed from the coupon on the financial instrument. There is an implied understanding that the bank will not allow the company to fail, otherwise the investor putting up the loan would be unwilling to finance the risky asset.

Of the four methods, there is often ambiguity as to which one applies. Very often, therefore, the entity investing in the financial instrument has a choice and will probably choose any one apart from the first. It is the first approach that prevents an entity from hiding losses. All the other approaches allow a trader to conceal losses as they provide the entity with the ability to keep the financial instrument off-balance sheet, or at least in the case of 'Available for Sale' to bring the asset on to the balance sheet but hide the profits or losses in reserves.

What is worryingly clear is that the accounting standards are inadequate. In February 2008, the International Accounting Standards Board discussed the issue of keeping items off-balance sheet and promised to publish a consultation paper in late 2008.[12] The important question is why the accounting profession is only now getting round to discussing a problem which came to light not months ago but decades ago. In 1987, the *Guardian* newspaper (not a specialist accounting publication) revealed the problems of off-balance sheet finance, describing the technique as 'The creative accounting trick which improves companies' balance sheets'.[13] In 1992, a controversial book *Accounting for Growth* by Terry Smith revealed details of companies who kept borrowings and losses off their balance sheet. The author found himself in hot water because of the revelations. The subtitle 'the book they tried to ban' appeared on the front cover and the author subsequently lost his job as a research analyst, perhaps because he offended clients who did not want their shareholders to see what they were doing. In his book, the term 'off balance sheet' is defined as 'the funding or refinancing of a company's operations in such a way that, under legal requirements and existing accounting conventions, some or all of the finance may not be shown on its balance sheet'. This quote was borrowed from the Institute of Chartered Accountants in England and Wales – Technical Release 603.[14] Although this definition is correct, it does not reveal the other side-effect of off-balance sheet activity, namely the ability of companies not only to hide borrowings but also to hide losses. In 2002, the American energy company Enron was not only able to hide loans through off-balance sheet activities, but also to hide losses and report profits – a severe embarrassment to the accounting profession.

8.12   FIRST TO DEFAULT

One of the more popular highly leveraged financial instruments widely used to conceal losses and risks was the 'First to Default' bond. With these bonds an investor places, say, £1,000,000 into a trust fund. That fund hedges, say, ten loans of £1,000,000 each through credit default swaps. This gives a leverage factor of ten times, i.e. an exposure of £10,000,000 for an initial investment of £1,000,000. The investor's funds are wiped out as soon as the first loan defaults. These instruments produce a high yield (perhaps Libor + 320 basis points). If the investor concerned actually borrows money to finance the initial £1,000,000, leverage increases further. Since these products have a high leverage factor, an appropriate accounting treatment is to treat them as a trading instrument, i.e. calculate the true market value and record any changes through the Profit & Loss account. However, some accountants might argue that the bond is going to be held to maturity and so record it at cost on the balance sheet. There is also the risk that some banks might put this bond into a Structured Investment Vehicle which, along with the associated borrowings, is kept off-balance sheet. If a trader is buying such a product on behalf of the investor and is on an asymmetrical bonus scheme (where he can walk away from losses), then the increase in volatility caused by this instrument automatically increases the value of the trader's bonus at the expense of the investor (who is probably unaware of what is going on). A second problem with these types of products is that they are often difficult to bifurcate (i.e. identify how they are constructed). Therefore, the bank which originates or 'manufactures' the product can charge a huge fee without telling the investor. Obviously, the

---

[12] 'Companies face being forced to reveal off-balance sheet vehicles', *Financial Times*, 9 January 2008.
[13] Quoted in Terry Smith, *Accounting for Growth*, Century Publications, 1992, p. 76.
[14] Terry Smith, *Accounting for Growth*, Century Publications, 1997, p. 76.

fee charged by the originator is – broadly speaking – the loss that the investor suffers but often fails to recognise.

8.13   SFAS 157 VALUATIONS

Structured credit products are more difficult to value than structured market products and therefore their accounting treatment is questionable. This is primarily because some of the inputs used to value credit products are assumed rather than taken from the market place. In other words, the incidence of credit default (prior to mid-2007) was quite low, so it is impossible to do a meaningful statistical analysis. On the other hand, there is quite a lot of historical data available to assess market risk. In addition, products based on market risk (such as interest rate swaps and equity futures) are more liquid, so the price is more reliable. The American accounting standards recognise this problem. SFAS 157, for instance, distinguishes between Level 1, 2 and 3 inputs.

Level 1 inputs are quoted prices in active markets. Most simple financial instruments would fall into Level 1. Level 2 inputs are prices which are not available directly and so prices for similar assets and liabilities would be used. For instance, a bank might be able to value tailor-made options by using implied volatility figures obtained from similar exchange traded options. Level 3 inputs are unobservable inputs and therefore the entity is forced to use its own assumptions about what market participants would use to price the asset or liability. Clearly this is a problem area, since traders might be tempted to use assumptions that maximise their bonuses and are therefore directed towards complicated credit structured products where the pricing inputs are unobservable. As we have seen in the recent credit crunch, these are the products that expose shareholders' funds to liquidity, credit and operational risk. SFAS 157 forces disclosure on these products and in theory, therefore, the shareholder or reader of accounts is at least alerted to what could be a very serious problem.

8.14   CONCLUSION

The complex area of securitisation and complex structured products has caused a lot of problems for the accounting profession. Even if we ignore the complexities of accounting, the products themselves have exposed shareholders and the taxpayer to huge risks. Through the securitisation process banks have simultaneously sold loans that they originated and bought loans from other banks even though they were not familiar with the customers of these purchased loans. The cardinal banking rule of 'knowing your customer' was breached, causing a moral hazard problem whereby banks piled into risky sub-prime loans and then passed on the risk to other banks through securitisation. The complexity of securitisation meant that many of the financial instruments used to transfer risk were difficult to value and, as a consequence, the measurement of risk became impossible. This did not, however, prevent certain bankers and traders from awarding themselves huge bonuses – despite the destruction in shareholder value that many of them created.

Needless to say, the accounting for these structured products was weak. The huge fees paid by investors for these products were hidden from the shareholder. So too was the leverage. The accounting profession has responded. Through the American accounting standard SFAS 157, banks are required to disclose more details of these toxic products. Regulators have also recently responded by forcing banks to keep more regulatory capital where complex products are used. In other words, banks must use shareholders' funds as opposed to borrowings to finance the purchase of these risky investments. Furthermore, the Financial Services Authority say they will look into instances where bonuses are based on profits, which themselves are derived from assumptions as opposed to market prices. Clearly, a lot of accounting and regulatory reform is needed in this area.

9
Off-Balance Sheet Accounting

9.1 INTRODUCTION

One question that will continue to occupy the minds of accounting standard setters is how to deal with the age-old problem of off-balance sheet. Indeed, so old is the problem that a more legitimate question is not how to revise the off-balance sheet rules but whether we should overhaul the entire accounting system. Or we could pose the question another way, given the current accounting framework and structure is it possible to devise accounting rules that will make clear to financial institutions and companies when items should be kept off-balance sheet and when they should be brought on? The objective is to develop a set of accounting rules that are easy to apply without misleading the shareholder. Certainly, the problem has become more important than say 20 years ago, when financial instruments were in their infancy and credit derivatives were virtually unheard of. Rather than overhaul the accounting rules, the standard setters have simply meddled with them continuously – introducing rules to deal with casualties when they arise. The profession was reactive as opposed to proactive, with the result that we now have too many confusing rules allowing creative accountants to interpret them as they please. Also, the rules of the American accounting standards board are occasionally different from those of their European counterparts.

Accountants dealing with off-balance sheet issues are now obliged to consider a number of factors. Firstly, they must understand what credit derivatives are and in particular how they are used to hide losses and risks. Then they must come to grips with securitisation and the difficulties associated with their valuation. Finally, they have to deal with the hundreds of accounting rules. They must know a QSPE from an SPE or what a VIE represents. They must also be able to distinguish between ARB 51, SFAS 140 and IAS 27. The accountants are also required to understand the requirements of IFRS 3, *Business Combinations*. Even within those rules there is a lot of complexity, allowing banks to create complex smoke screens to disguise that they are motivated to take on as much risk as possible and to hide those risks. Not all banks, of course, are doing this – but virtually all bankers will agree that if you have a bonus system which rewards risk and an accounting system which disguises what is going on, the temptation is to take as much risk as possible and to conceal it. The rules of accounting that are concerned with off-balance sheet are seriously flawed. In the next section we look at a number of case studies where these flaws have worked against the shareholder. We then look at some of the more important accounting rules surrounding this area.

That the accounting profession must now revisit the problem in 2008, after banks amassed huge losses, is an indication that the off-balance sheet problem is not one that will go away quickly. The *Financial Times* stated in February 'A number of leading banks including Citigroup and HSBC have announced they will be bringing structured investment vehicles back on to their books as a result of the market turmoil sparking questions as to whether they should have been allowed to use the special accounting treatment in the first place'. At present, banks utilise footnotes to disclose their risks but as the Americredit case study discussed later in this book shows, disclosure accounting has its pitfalls and may not be the solution. It is unclear what direction the new rules will take, but the Head of the IASB Sir David Tweedie gave some guidance in February 2008. 'At this stage, we're not trying to zero down to an answer. What we're trying to do is simplify the accounting so banks can say: "If it all blows up, this is what we face, but here are the reasons it won't". That way, people have the information.'

As Paul Davis pointed out in the *Financial Times*:[1]

> When Citigroup announced – hot on the heels of Chuck Prince's departure as chairman and chief executive – additional writedowns of up to $11bn related to subprime mortgages, the most surprising thing was that many of the losses were on $43bn worth of off-balance-sheet exposures.

9.2   OFF-BALANCE SHEET MANIPULATION

The example below illustrates the accounting advantage of keeping items off-balance sheet. Company X bought an IT asset for £100 million two years ago. The market value of the asset is now £60 million but the company is anxious to avoid having to reveal the loss. To get around the problem a special company is formed called 'SPV'. SPV borrows £120 million from a bank which is guaranteed by company X. Company X then sells the asset to the SPV for £120 million. From an accounting perspective the series of transactions can be treated in two different ways: consolidation and non-consolidation. The first treatment in Table 9.1 shows the balance sheet on the assumption that the auditor insists that the SPV must be consolidated with the balance sheet of company X. The second treatment shows the favourable position that would arise if company X managed to convince the auditors that the SPV should be kept off-balance sheet.

Table 9.1   Consolidation vs. non-consolidation

Opening balance sheet	Company X £m	Consolidation £m	No consolidation £m
IT asset	£100	£60	0
Cash	£900	£1020	£1020
Loans	−£700	−£820	−£700
Shareholders' funds	£300	£260	£320
Ordinary Shares issued	£200	£200	£200
Retained Profit & Loss	£100	£60	£120

Company X has a balance sheet (before the sale) which contains the IT asset of £100m and cash of £900m. This is financed by liabilities of £700m and shareholders' funds of £300m. Retained profits are £100m. If the SPV is consolidated, the entity is not allowed to recognise the 'inter-company' sale and would more than likely have to impair the asset from £100m down to £60m. The result is a loss of £40m, which brings retained profits down to £60m.

---

[1] Paul J. Davies, '10Q clue to Citigroup's financial headache', *Financial Times*, 7 November 2007.

The alternative treatment is to regard the SPV as a separate entity, allowing company X to treat the sale of the IT asset as a genuine sale. The company receives £120m, which pushes its cash position from £900m to £1020m, and is allowed to record a profit on the sale of £20m, bring total retained profits from £100m to £120m. The attractions of keeping assets and loans off-balance sheet should be obvious. Apart from profits being higher, the liabilities are of course lower, since the £120m must be treated as a loan in the 'consolidated' but is not recognised as such in the 'non-consolidated' case.

SEC experience – off-balance sheet abuse

The SEC[2] has come across many instances which reveal the efforts that entities are taking to avail themselves of off-balance sheet accounting treatment:

> Although there is debate about whether the guidance in SFAS No. 140 is effective, much of the controversy is caused not by the standards themselves, but by transaction structuring. Issuers often structure transfers in order to achieve or avoid sale accounting, trigger or avoid the recognition of losses (or gains), or change the measurement attribute applied to the recorded assets and liabilities. The Staff believes based on its reviews of issuer filings, that the most frequent structuring goal is to achieve sale treatment without consolidation of any related SPEs [Special Purpose Entities]. While economic motivations for most asset transfers exist, some transfers of financial assets appear to be significantly, primarily, or even solely entered into with accounting motivations in mind.

The SEC also point out that some of this structuring has been undertaken by using Qualifying Special Purpose Entities (QSPEs, discussed below) in situations that appear to be beyond those originally contemplated by the FASB. Basically, if a securitisation qualifies as a QSPE consolidation is not necessary. In broad terms, a QSPE can be constructed in such a way that the transferor/seller of the assets does not control the QSPE in any shape or form. The FASB originally intended a QSPE to be merely a pass-through entity to essentially serve as custodian of the underlying financial assets, and attempted to define it in such a way as to ensure that this was the case. There are restrictions on the types of assets that an SPE can hold while remaining 'qualified', and when it is acceptable for the QSPE to dispose of certain non-cash financial assets.

Although the limitations on the activities of QSPEs do not permit the QSPE to manage the assets on its balance sheet, there are few explicit limitations on managing the balance sheet liabilities. That is, in structures where the QSPE holds longer-term assets and funds the purchase of such assets through the issuance of shorter-term interests to investors, decisions have to be made regarding the nature of the new interests to be issued when the original short-term interests mature. In very broad terms, if a bank buys illiquid long-term assets and finances them through short-term borrowings then the structure should fail to qualify as a QSPE if the bank guarantees the short-term borrowings, since it is effectively taking on a risk of the QSPE or controlling the QSPE. In practice, these decisions are subjective and made by the issuer transferring the financial assets. Accountants and auditors have concluded that the trust holding the assets – despite such management of liabilities – is a QSPE under

---

[2] SEC's June 2005 Report and Recommendations Pursuant to Section 401(c) of the Sarbanes–Oxley Act of 2002 On Arrangements with Off-Balance Sheet Implications, Special Purpose Entities, and Transparency of Filings by Issuers.

SFAS No. 140, and is therefore exempt from consolidation. These and other interpretations of the QSPE guidance have expanded the activities of QSPEs beyond the simple pass-through entities originally forecasted by the FASB. Needless to say, efforts by the SEC to stop this practice were thwarted:

> Despite persistent work by the FASB and the Commission, the Staff considers the accounting for sales of financial assets to be in need of improvement. Indeed, the FASB already has several projects on its agenda relating to transfers of financial assets.

However, this area is challenging to standard setters, in large part because financial structures are virtually limitless and continue to evolve at a rapid pace. Clearly this area is in need of improvement.

Qualifying Special Purpose Entities

Under the FASB accounting standards, the seller of assets into a securitisation structure can classify the structure as a Qualifying Special Purpose Entity (QSPE). These types of trusts are recognised by SFAS 140 as being separate entities and therefore consolidation is not necessary.

A QSPE must be distinct and separate from the Seller of the securitised assets and cannot be dissolved, wound up or terminated by the Seller. The Seller therefore has virtually no control over the QSPE. The QSPE's activities are governed by guidelines set by at least a majority of the beneficial interest holders, other than the Seller and its affiliates. This requirement minimises the Seller's control over the entity's activities on an ongoing basis.

Eligible assets

The QSPE places a lot of restrictions on its relationship with the Seller – namely:

1. The transferred assets do not give the Seller significant influence over the entity's financial and operating policies.
2. Derivative instrument agreements must be entered into at the time of SPE establishment or receivables transfer.
3. The QSPE may hold financial assets that insure against failure by others to service the assets or make payments.
4. The QSPE may hold servicing rights related to the assets that it holds.
5. The QSPE may temporarily hold non-financial assets obtained in connection with the financial assets it holds.
6. The QSPE may hold cash collected from financial assets and investments purchased prior to distribution to beneficial interest holders (investments must be relatively debt-free, without options and mature no longer than the expected distribution date).

9.3 CASE STUDIES: OFF-BALANCE SHEET

Introduction

Financial commentators often associate off-balance sheet 'abuse' with creative accounting. Yet the term 'creative' suggests an original way of accounting. The irony is that off-balance sheet accounting is decades old. As mentioned previously in this book, the UK *Guardian* newspaper was writing about off-balance sheet problems in the 1980s. It is therefore worrying that in 2007 regulated large banks are still copying (though in a slightly different format) an accounting procedure which is three decades old. Clearly, the accounting profession has a lot of work to do. The likelihood however is that, within the current accounting framework, there is no easy solution. Over the last three decades, as we shall see, the accounting profession has devised hundreds of rules and standard amendments to try and tackle the problem. Perhaps the accounting standard setters are not at fault. It could be that banks and other entities are simply ignoring the requirements of the accounting standard setters. However, where the rules are confusing and there are monetary incentives to break the spirit of the rules, it is not too difficult to forecast what will happen. The practice still continues and as yet, there is no solution in sight. The case studies below reveal how entities copy each other with 'off-balance sheet' techniques. The next section illustrates the accounting rules that have tried to curtail this activity.

Dynergy

According to the *Washington Post*[3] Dynergy Inc., a major United States producer of power, was forced to reach an agreement with shareholders who alleged that Dynergy misled them through off-balance sheet activities where the company was able to hide liabilities and inflate profits simultaneously. In 2005, the company announced that it had agreed to pay the plaintiffs led by the University of California $250 million from its own funds and $468 million in company stock. An insurance company also agreed to contribute $150 million towards compensation and costs. Dynergy apparently set up an offshore company and their interpretation of the accounting rules was that Dynergy was not obliged to consolidate this offshore company with their own balance sheet. The result was that Dynergy could offer goods and services to this offshore company and any cash received could go through Dynergy's Profit & Loss account.

The plaintiffs in this case claimed that Dynergy misled investors with a natural gas transaction called Project Alpha. In effect, Dynergy borrowed $300 million through an offshore company. Dynergy then sent an invoice to this offshore company, which was duly paid. When Dynergy received the money it failed to recognise the liability on the balance sheet. Instead, it was recognised as revenue and the company was therefore able to inflate the Profit & Loss account and also claim more market share acquired (because sales revenue was artificially increased). Dynergy was subsequently forced to reduce earnings by $300 million and also paid $3 million to resolve charges brought by the US Securities and Exchange Commission. According to Chris Ellinghaus, an analyst at Williams Capital Group in New York, 'it reflects how angry investors were about the energy industry of the 1990s, how shockingly everything collapsed, and how insistent they were on a large settlement'.

Harold F. Degenhardt, commenting on the Dynergy case, advised accountants, 'Public companies using off-balance sheet, special purpose entities must ensure not only that their accounting treatment complies with GAAP, but also, that they have accurately portrayed the economic realities of the transactions . . . In this case, Dynergy portrayed as operating cash flow what was essentially a loan. As a result, Dynergy investors were deceived.' Clearly this statement reflects a change in attitude by the SEC. In the past, external auditors merely had to

---

[3] http://www.washingtonpost.com/wp-dyn/articles/A57895-2005Apr15.html

comply with the accounting standards, weak as they are. This in itself is a monumental task. Now, the SEC requires that as well as complying with the complex and ever-changing accounting standards on off-balance sheet activities, entities must ensure that the economic realities of the transactions are accurately portrayed. Clearly this means that if an auditor observes that his client is engaged in creative accounting, he must blow the whistle. The statement also puts pressure on the accountant and auditor to accurately portray the risks. Investors might be comforted with this statement. The problem is that this statement was made in September 2002. Since then, a number of major banks have mimicked what Dynergy did by keeping assets off-balance sheet and financing these assets with loans also kept off-balance sheet. The result – very heavy losses, yet the accounting profession has only very recently admitted that the standards surrounding off-balance sheet activities are inadequate.

According to the SEC, energy analysts following Dynergy had noticed a widening gap between Dynergy's net income and operating cash flow. Dynergy had recognised in its net income unrealised gains from forward positions. Since these gains were 'unrealised', Dynergy was showing an increase in profits without a corresponding increase in cash. The Project Alpha deal effectively allowed Dynergy to borrow money and conceal the borrowings. Therefore cash levels (the proceeds from the loan) increased. As the SEC commented:[4]

> Dynergy defrauded the investing public by failing to disclose in its 2001 Form 10-K the true financing, as opposed to operating, nature of the $300 million. In reality, the $300 million was a loan masquerading as operating cash flow on Dynergy's 2001 Statement of Cash Flows. This is particularly significant for two reasons: first, analysts view operating cash flow as a key indicator of the financial health of energy trading firms such as Dynergy; and second, historically, the Statement of Cash Flows has been considered immune from cosmetic tampering.

Elan

Elan, the Irish-based pharmaceutical company, got into difficulty[5] with off-balance sheet problems in 2001. At one stage it was Ireland's biggest business, with a market value of $22 billion. The company's share price suffered after it was forced to write down research into an Alzheimer's vaccine drug. However, it was the probes into its off-balance sheet vehicles that caused the major problem for its shareholders. The auditors KPMG were forced to delay publication of its 2002 accounts, creating a potential risk of default with its bondholders who were owed $2.2 billion. According to *Business Week*, 'voracious deal-making sowed the seeds of Elan's rise ... and fall'. Elan entered into negotiations with approximately 50 companies using complex joint-venture arrangements. The company was careful to ensure that their stake was less than 20%. If the stake was higher, then the American accounting rules would have required Elan to include in their Profit & Loss account and balance sheet details of any losses and liabilities that these 50 biotech companies had incurred. Needless to say, these 'off-balance sheet' biotech companies came under the scrutiny of the SEC in America, where Elan was listed. Through these off-balance sheet companies Elan managed to earn revenue in the form of a $15 million licensing fee which was paid to them by the biotech partner.

---

[4] http://www.sec.gov/news/press/2002-140.htm

[5] 'Elan: One Sick Celtic Tiger', *Business Week*, 15 September 2003. http://www.businessweek.com/magazine/content/03_37/b3849132_mz034.htm

The accounting risks here are similar to that of Enron. If there was evidence that Elan controlled any of the biotech companies and simultaneously kept them off-balance sheet then Elan might have been able to inflate its own profits in a number of ways. For instance, it could have charged the biotech companies for research that Elan carried out at inflated prices. Elan could also have used the biotechs to borrow money and transfer it to Elan. This would allow Elan to treat the cash proceeds from the loan as income, since the liability for these loans would have been parked in the biotechs' balance sheets and not Elan's. Elan could also have charged licensing fees to the biotechs and allowed these companies to suffer huge losses. Elan would, of course, have been ultimately responsible for the losses but might not have informed the shareholders.

In 2003 the *Financial Times* (FT) wrote about the difficulties that Elan faced.[6] It pointed out that Elan had about $2 billion in debt which was used to finance assets of $1.4 billion in cash and $1.6 billion in other financial assets. Unfortunately, these 'other financial assets' were mostly troubled investments in biotechnology companies. Elan apparently had guaranteed another $1 billion to other special purpose entities which were kept off-balance sheet. The FT also commented that Elan was forced to pay over $160 million to some troubled SPVs in order to meet cash flow payments on their loans. Apparently, Elan revealed that it had funded the payment by selling $148 million of financial assets, at a loss, to a purchaser who had raised the money backed by a full guarantee from Elan.

In the words of the SEC:[7]

Elan misled investors about its joint venture program, which generated approximately $490 million of revenue during 2000 and 2001. The company failed to disclose that it required its joint venture partners to engage in 'round-trip' transactions, in which the ventures paid license fees to Elan using money that Elan had provided to the partners.

The SEC also alleged that Elan failed to disclose that none of the partners or joint ventures ever used any of their own assets to pay for the licence fee (most of them did not have the financial resources to do so). Also, the company never sold a licence for its drug delivery technology to any unaffiliated entity at the prices charged to the joint ventures ($10–15 million, in most cases), an indication that Elan charged an inflated price for what was really an inter-company sale. During 2000 and 2001, Elan became heavily dependent on these inter-company sales. They did not sell any such licences other than through the joint venture programme. By failing to disclose these facts, Elan obscured the true demand for the licensed technology and its ability to generate licence revenue in the future. Shareholders were therefore misled about the true characteristics of the sales revenue and cash flows of Elan.

According to the SEC:

During June 2002, Elan facilitated an artificial sale of certain joint-venture related securities between one of its off-balance sheet subsidiaries and an ostensibly independent third party in an attempt to continue favorable accounting treatment. Elan publicly stated that the subsidiary had sold the securities at 'estimated fair value' (approximately $148 million) to an 'unaffiliated third party'.

---

[6] 'Elan', *Financial Times*, 4 July 2003.
[7] http://www.sec.gov/litigation/litreleases/lr19066.htm

The SEC believed that these statements were materially false and misleading. Elan failed to disclose that:

(i) The purchaser was not an 'unaffiliated third party' because Elan created it. The SEC in fact felt that Elan should have consolidated these entities.

(ii) Elan paid the purchaser $1 million to participate in the transaction – an indication that Elan controlled the joint venture/entity and therefore should not have recognised the cash flows as sales revenue and inter-company profits.

(iii) The purchaser did not negotiate the $148 million purchase price, which was fixed by Elan – again further evidence of control.

(iv) The claimed 'estimated fair value' did not reflect what a willing buyer would pay to acquire the securities, which was substantially less than $148 million. Subsequently, in September 2003, Elan restated its financial results due to this transaction, which reduced its 2001 net income by $73.9 million, or 22%.

There are plenty of parallels between Elan's experience in 2003 and the sub-prime banking crises which the world faced in 2007 and 2008. Elan appeared to have some sort of control over the biotech companies, since it was assuming responsibility for their losses but they did not consolidate. In 2007, various banks were able to set up special purpose vehicles where they bought complex structured products and financed them through the issue of commercial paper. When the complex structured products became illiquid, made losses and were difficult to sell, the holders of commercial paper understandably put pressure on the banks to sell the illiquid structured products and accept the loss. The banks did so. In the words of the *Financial Times*,[8] 'First, investors were shocked to discover its exposure to collateralised debt obligations had ballooned, as previously off-balance sheet commitments suddenly turned up on Citi's books. And now, $49 billion worth of assets in off-balance sheet vehicles will be brought on to the balance sheet as well.'

Americredit

In September 2002, Americredit – a large independent middle-market car finance company in North America – was forced to issue a press release informing investors that as a result of changes in its business and accounting policies, they were going to recognise heavy losses previously kept off-balance sheet. The situation is similar to what happened with many banks caught up in the credit crises today. Americredit typically lent to 'customers who are usually unable to obtain financing from traditional sources'; in other words, they operated in the 'sub-prime' market in the car loan sector. In the words of their then CEO Mike Barrington:[9]

Middle market automobile finance can be a complex business and some of our stakeholders have told us they don't fully understand the accounting for our business due to the use of gain-on-sale. So, we've made the decision to move to on-balance sheet securitisations to make it clearer for all our stakeholders to understand our business and assess the financial results over time.

---

[8] 'Citigroup's SIVs', *Financial Times*, 14 December 2007.
[9] Americredit Form 8-K, 16 September 2002.

It appears that the American regulators, the SEC, were not too pleased with off-balance sheet presentations as well. Americredit had previously provided disclosure notes or 'pro forma portfolio-based earnings data' which presented the profitability of Americredit's portfolio, removing the effect of 'gain on sale' accounting. The SEC, however, took a strong stance on entities who relied overly on disclosure notes and asked Americredit not to rely on such disclosure notes in this way. Presumably the SEC's policy on disclosure notes stems from the embarrassment caused by Enron, where Enron kept a large number of assets and liabilities off the balance sheet but disclosed in notes the impact of this accounting policy. Very few people read the disclosure notes, and therefore they are a poor form of accounting. The impact of the change in accounting policy indicates that Americredit might have recognised revenue prematurely:

> The September 2002 quarter's net income guidance of 55 to 60 million dollars, or approximately 62 to 68 cents per share on today's share base, includes the last of the gain-on-sale revenue. We originally offered guidance of a dollar six to a dollar nine in earnings per share for this period. The forecast is now lower because, even though we will record a gain on sale for securitisations in the September quarter, we will also be providing loss provision for a growing on balance sheet portfolio of 54–57 cents pre tax.

There is a question mark as to what precisely went on here. The words 'we will also be providing loss provisions for a growing on balance sheet portfolio' suggests that, like today's bankers, Americredit was forced to bring back on to its balance sheet loans which it had previously sold. The fact that Americredit are providing loss provisions for loans that were previously sold to the SPV suggests that Americredit was in some way exposed to the losses on loans that had sold. This 'guarantee' makes the loans more valuable, and so a greater gain can be recognised up-front. Clearly, however, this form of securitisation contravenes the accounting 'matching concept' because it records profits up-front even though the risk may be spread over a few years.

9.4   ACCOUNTING IMPLICATIONS

Introduction

In this section we look at the American accounting rules that deal with consolidation and then consider the IFRS rules. Unfortunately, owing to the complex nature of the rules, the difference in approach taken by the FASB and the IFRS, and the fact that the rules are as yet unfinalised and about to change, we can only highlight the problems and comment on some of the more controversial rules rather than give definitive guidance on what should/should not appear on the balance sheet.

American standards

As regards the American standards, Accounting Research Board 51 (ARB 51) dates back to 1959 and uses voting rights to determine if a particular off-balance sheet vehicle should be brought on to the balance sheet. Presumably, in the simpler cases, if an entity has more than 51% of the ordinary shares in another company ARB 51 would require consolidation. Originally, in the securitisation world, banks which wanted to sell loans set up SPEs. The objective was to simply isolate the financial risk and provide less expensive financing. For example, a software company might spend £10m to produce software for a government department. Assume that the government department agrees to pay a royalty of £2m each year for the next 10 years. If the software company could only borrow at a credit spread of 3%, then financing the project would be costly. A sensible approach, therefore, would be to set up a SPE which would own the royalty that the government pays for the software. The SPE then borrows £10m, which is paid to the software company and used to extinguish the loan. The lender to the SPE would regard the borrowings as safe, since the only risk of default is if the government defaults. Therefore, the cost of financing would not include the 3% that the software company suffers and so the overall cost of financing would drop considerably. The accounting standards are designed so that the software company can keep both the asset (the government royalty payments) and the liabilities off the software company's balance sheet in those circumstances.

To reduce the prospects of accounting abuse the American accounting standards, in particular SFAS 140, *Accounting for Transfer and Servicing of Financial Assets and Extinguishment of Liabilities* introduced QSPEs to ensure that only legitimate transfers of assets (including their risks and rewards) were kept off-balance sheet. They are often referred to as Variable Interest Entities (VIEs) – a definition established in FASB Interpretation 46. There are various types of transactions which auditors treat as off-balance sheet. These include:

- **Synthetic leases**. Here a shell company is set up and buys an asset which is used by the sponsor. So, for instance, if the airline is a sponsor it might set up a company to buy and own aircraft. The airline would then lease the aircraft from the company. Often the motivation to do this is cosmetic. Airlines want an excuse to keep the planes and their loans off the balance sheet in order to make their balance sheet look healthier. A second motivation may be tax. Where an airline leases an asset the expense may in its entirety be treated as a tax-deductible expense. If the asset is brought on to the balance sheet, however, the depreciation expense may be disallowable.
- **Take or pay contracts**. An electricity company may want to supply electricity to a particular district and may not want the newly built generator or loan on its balance sheet. A solution, therefore, is to set up an SPE and borrow money. The SPE then enters into a contract with the sponsor whereby the latter pays the former a fee for the electricity it uses. The contract is termed 'take or pay', which in effect means that the electricity company guarantees to buy a certain amount of electricity each year.
- **Securitisations**. As discussed, a pool of financial assets such as mortgage loans is bought by an SPE and the interest payments on these mortgages are used to finance the coupon payments on the bonds/tranches issued by the securitisation. The big difficulty here is that the auditor must establish who has control over the assets, i.e. the sponsoring bank or the trustees to the securitisation. The auditor must also attempt to identify the party with the beneficial interest. If the sponsoring bank guarantees the mortgages against default in any shape or form, the auditor may question whether it is appropriate to take the assets off the balance sheet of the sponsoring bank.

As Jalal Soroosh, PhD, CMA, KPMG Faculty Fellow, Professor of Accounting at Loyola College, Baltimore, MD noted, 'The challenge for investors is the difficulty in spotting these transactions. Unfortunately, the magnitude of the dollar amounts involved in these transactions notwithstanding, any available disclosures about them are buried in footnotes.'[10] The main problem for accountants is that the people who structured these securitisations often sold them on the basis that the sponsoring company could maintain control over the assets they transferred. They could therefore force the SPE to buy assets at inflated prices and create an artificial profit. They could also arrange to guarantee loans, thus inflating their value and selling them to the SPE. The result is that they could recognise the reward for credit risk immediately, contravening the matching concept principle in the accounting standards. In other words, they could insure credit risk for, say, four years and receive an up-front premium which they recognised immediately in the Profit & Loss account and not over the four years of protection.

The first hurdle that the creative accountants faced was, as mentioned above, ARB 51 which dealt with consolidated financial statements. This statement simply said that if an entity controls the majority of the voting power (i.e. 51% of the ordinary shares), they must consolidate. Otherwise, they need not. Entities like Enron were able to get around this superficial rule by structuring the deal so that they controlled the company but did not own the ordinary shares. They simply asked a solicitor to set up a company with, say, two ordinary shares. The solicitor would then do exactly what Enron wanted them to do. As Enron was the main financer of the SPE, the solicitor did not really have control even though he owned the ordinary shares. Enron was therefore able to hide loans and create profits. What is worrying about this is that Enron was not the originator of this type of abuse, and is certainly not the last case. The accounting standards are reacting too slowly, perhaps because closing the loopholes involves changing hundreds of pedantic rules within the accounting standards – evidence perhaps that the current accounting system simply cannot cope with the strain of complex accounting systems.

Another 'get out' clause that entities used to avoid consolidation was the '3% rule'. If the entity could prove that an outside independent third party owned at least 3% of the SPE's total capitalisation, then the entity could avoid consolidation. This rule was also changed post-Enron because of accounting abuses.

In 1996 the American accounting standards board issued SFAS 125, *Accounting for Transfer and Servicing of Financial Assets and Extinguishment of Liabilities*. However, as companies and banks were determined to keep things off-balance sheet, they managed to get around the restrictions of SFAS 125 and as a result the standard setters developed a new standard, SFAS 140. In addition to determining when an entity should remove an asset or a liability from the balance sheet, the standard also has extensive disclosure requirements.

Following abuses at Enron, the FASB responded by introducing new interpretations of the existing accounting principle with the aim of consolidating a lot more than was previously consolidated. The exposure draft was a further interpretation of ARB 51, known as 'Fin 46', *Consolidation of Variable Interest Entities, An Interpretation of ARB 51*. Needless to say, not everything went according to plan as companies and financial institutions continued to exploit the opportunities associated with keeping items off the balance sheet. The standard setters responded with Interpretation 46(R) and a few others (FSP Fin 46-3, FSP Fin 46-4, FSP Fin 46-6 and FSP Fin 46-7). The cycle of rules, abuses, more rules, more abuses has not had its intended effect. We have simply ended up with more and more rules, more off-balance sheet activity and more confusion. It seems clear that the accounting standard setters are losing the battle, and perhaps now is the time to abandon a lot of the rules and come up with a new

---

[10] http://www.nysscpa.org/cpajournal/2004/704/essentials/p30.htm

framework which measures risk, measures rewards and ensures that revenue recognition is matched with risk, rather than the current regime where all the rewards are taken up-front and risk is not even measured, making life difficult for accountants who want to apply the 'matching concept' correctly.

Fin 46(R) is quite important. It attempts to focus attention on VIEs. In broad terms, the VIE rules are designed to capture companies that cannot survive on their own and are unable to absorb expected losses without help from a 'parent' company. Where there is evidence that, say, company B is heavily dependent on company A, then company A must consolidate company B with the result that inter-company profits must be cancelled and also, all liabilities and assets on company B's balance sheet must be consolidated with that of company A and published in the annual report. Perhaps the main flaw with these detailed rules is that the auditor and financial controller are required to make subjective decisions. There is the obvious risk, as with all areas of subjectivity, that banks will want to increase risk and hide risk simultaneously, and so might take the view that the VIE does not need to be subsidised. The rules are complex and, for the reader, a detailed account can be obtained in the Jalal Soroosh article.

Clearly, the accounting standards can deal with situations where one company owns more than 50% of the voting shares of another. Consolidation is mandatory in that situation. However, where one company controls another but the controlling company owns less than 50% of the voting shares, the standards have to devise special rules which are unfortunately complex and subjective. This is because entities have found ways to control other companies without owning the ordinary shares. One example might be where company A gives company B a loan on very favourable terms. If company A withdraws the loan then company B goes bust. Clearly, A controls B but may not own any shares.

This is what FASB Interpretation 46(R) attempts to address. Its objectives are to identify VIEs and then determine if such entities should be consolidated. In broad terms, an entity is classified as a VIE if it does not have enough equity to support its operations. So, in the example above, where a company makes a subsidised loan to an entity that entity might be regarded as a VIE since it is heavily dependent on the company that made the loan. In other words, the company that made the loan effectively controls the VIE. If, however, the loan was made on ordinary commercial terms and the VIE would be able to replace the company's loan with a new loan where necessary, then consolidation might not be necessary. Furthermore, if any restriction is placed on the shareholders, i.e. preventing them from voting on major issues, then consolidation might be necessary. Fin 46(R) also focuses on who the beneficial owner of the assets may be. Suppose company A has assets which it sells to company B. There is a complicated relationship between A and B such that if the assets fall in value, then A suffers 60% of the losses and if the assets go up in value, A enjoys 55% of the gain. This would indicate that although A has sold the asset to B, A still has a beneficial interest in the asset and so, under Fin 46(R), A might have to treat B as a VIE and consolidate. Therefore, any profit that A makes when it sells the asset to B must be cancelled and furthermore, if B has borrowings, they must appear on the A consolidated balance sheet in A's annual report.

Entities can avoid consolidation if they can prove that 10% of a company's assets are financed by 'external' shareholders, i.e. shareholders not connected with the main company. It would appear that shareholders' funds must be 10% of total assets. As Jalal Soroosh points out:

The sufficiency of the equity investment must be evaluated at each reporting period. To help determine 'sufficiency', the interpretation increases the 3% threshold to 10%. An equity investment shall be presumed insufficient to allow the entity to finance its activities without relying on financial support from variable interest holders unless the investment is equal to at least 10% of the total assets.

The 10% cut-off appears to be a guideline only. If the entity has, say, 6% of shareholders' funds and can demonstrate that it does not need additional financial support, then consolidation may not be necessary. Conversely, there may be instances when 10% equity finance is not enough.

International financial reporting standards – consolidation

What may confuse investors and readers of accounts, however, is not just the delays but the fact that the accounting standards already have rules in place to prevent off-balance sheet abuse:

IFRS 3, *Business Combinations*
IAS 32, *Financial Instruments: Presentation*
IAS 18, *Revenue*
IAS 39, *Financial Instruments: Recognition and Measurement.*

IFRS 3, Business Combinations

Like the American accounting standards, the IFRS rules on consolidation focus on control and the risk that company A might control company B. Company A may then force B to borrow money to buy A's assets. Obviously, the objectives of the consolidation rules are to prevent the recognition of inter-company profits and the concealment of liabilities. If, for instance, entity A controls entity B and does not consolidate B's balance sheet into its own, i.e. show all the assets and liabilities of B's balance sheet on A's published accounts, abuses could arise. A could sell goods to B at inflated prices or A could get B to borrow money and keep it on B's balance sheet. Alternatively, A could force B to buy an asset worth, say, £20 million for £28 million so that A could show an artificial profit. Through consolidation, A would not only be unable to conceal the borrowings but would also have to ensure that interest paid on any borrowings by B is shown on A's Profit & Loss account. The risk of A fabricating profits by selling to B assets at an artificially high price is also prevented under the consolidation rules, since any 'inter-company' profits must not be recognised until the asset transferred is sold out of the group of companies. So, in a nutshell, IFRS 3 forces the consolidator to recognise liabilities and not recognise inter-company profits if there is evidence that A controls B. This rule is understandable, however, there is a risk that the spirit of IFRS 3 was not always applied by some banks, judging by the recent credit crises where banks revealed substantial losses on assets kept off-balance sheet.

Consider a case where bank A sets up an SIV (Structured Investment Vehicle). The bank buys £100m of risky structured credit instruments and, to compensate for the increased risk, a high coupon is paid – say 8%. The bonds are expected to last for five years. The six-month Libor rate is 4.1% and the five-year swap rate is 6%. The cash flow coming into the SIV each year is therefore £8m and the cash outflow is based on the interest rate, i.e. £4,100,000. The bank manages the fund and charges a fee of £3,900,000 per annum (deliberately set to sweep up the excess cash flows). Unfortunately, for shareholders, a bank might be tempted to classify this as fee income in its Profit & Loss statement and so keep the underlying bond off-balance sheet. The shareholder only sees the fee income, believing that like most income from fees it is risk-free. The high fee income influences the bonus of the banking directors and this, in turn, motivates them to invest heavily in such products. Some risk managers also believe that when assets are kept off-balance sheet the regulators tend to ignore them, particularly under the Basel 1 rules. That said, the regulator will have more power under the replacement rules, Basel 2, which banks are due to implement shortly. Only when the structured product gets into difficulty will the bank consider bailing out the SIV by bringing it on to the balance sheet and informing the shareholder, rather late in the day, of the risks and losses that the bank has suffered from this structure. Do the accounting standards permit this practice? Under IFRS 3, the external auditor has the authority to say 'no', though he might be pressurised by the client to do otherwise. IFRS 3, paragraph 17 states:

> An acquirer shall be identified for all business combinations. The acquirer is the combining entity that obtains control of the other combining entities or businesses.[11]

Although control is difficult to define, IFRS 3, paragraph 19 states that:

> Control is the power to govern the financial and operating policies of an entity or business so as to obtain benefits from its activities.

The word 'benefit' suggests that if an entity has a 'beneficial interest' in an asset, that asset must appear on the entity's balance sheet. In the past, creative accountants were able to get around this stipulation by making sure that they did not own more than 51% of the ordinary shares. However, IFRS 3, paragraph 19 goes on to state:

> Even if one of the combining entities does not acquire more than one-half of the voting rights of another combining entity, it might have obtained control of that other entity if, as a result of the combination, it obtains: power to govern the financial and operating policies of the other entity under a statute or an agreement; or power to appoint or remove the majority of the members of the board of directors or equivalent governing body of the other entity.

It follows, therefore, that no matter how complex the structure is, bank A would probably be deemed to control the SIV if there was any hint, expressed or implied, that the bank was going to bail out or subsidise the SIV. Also, if there was evidence that the bank was responsible for the losses of the SIV, then the bank has an equity-type exposure and may be forced to bring the financial instruments back on to its balance sheet when the instrument incurs huge losses. Once on the balance sheet, the bank is then forced to reveal the risks it takes on. If, for instance, the bank financed a long-term financial instrument from short-term borrowings, it would have to explain itself to the shareholder (IFRS 7 requires detailed disclosures on the impact of financial instruments). Also, the regulators would consider the liquidity risk, credit risk and market risk of such a financial instrument and determine whether the bank is appropriately capitalised or whether it is too heavily dependent on loans (particularly short-term loans).

---

[11] International Financial Reporting Standards, International Accounting Standards Board, January 2007, p. 313.

IAS 32, Financial Instruments: Presentation

Even if a bank successfully manages to convince the auditor that the bank neither has control, nor therefore equity interest, the next stumbling block for the bank (or the next weapon for the auditor) is IAS 32. This standard is very important to any entity (whether banks or corporates) using financial instruments as it attempts to draw a very clear line of distinction between equity and liabilities. The objectives of IAS 32 are set out below:[12]

> The objective of this Standard is to establish principles for presenting financial instruments as liabilities or equity and for offsetting financial assets and financial liabilities. It applies to the classification of financial instruments from the perspective of the issuer, into financial assets, financial liabilities and equity instruments; the classification of related interest, dividends, losses and gains and the circumstances in which financial assets and financial liabilities should be offset.

The objectives section goes on to state that the principles in the standard complement the principles for recognising and measuring financial liabilities in IAS 39, *Recognition and Measurement* and for disclosing information about them in IFRS 7, *Financial Instruments: Disclosures.*

The distinction between liability and equity is very important, though it is often deliberately blurred in practice so that risks can be concealed. As explained elsewhere in this book, whether a company is financed by liabilities or shares is very important. An entity with secure earnings which do not contain too much credit risk could consider loan financing as it maximises returns to the small group of shareholders. However, there are plenty of stories of companies that use short-term loans to invest in assets with volatile unpredictable cash flows. These assets are often exposed to substantial credit risk and are illiquid. When banks are lending to companies they use various ratios to make sure that there is an appropriate amount of equity finance to cover these risks. Yet, judging by Northern Rock and others, it is a cardinal rule that they break themselves and furthermore conceal what they are doing through off-balance sheet mechanics. To recap, when assets are financed by equity, the investor (usually through ordinary shares) cannot withdraw his money from the entity and of course this makes the entity safer as they cannot withdraw in times of difficulty when cash is needed most. Loans are obviously different (even long-term loans). Here, a lender can withdraw money almost instantly and will of course do so if there is any sign of trouble. The hedge fund Long Term Capital Management learnt this very important lesson when the markets turned against it. Understandably, therefore, IAS 32 carefully defines what a financial liability is.

A financial liability is any liability that is a contractual obligation:

1. to deliver cash or another financial asset to another entity; or
2. to exchange financial assets or financial liabilities with another entity under conditions that are potentially unfavourable to the entity.

It is very clear therefore that an entity that borrows money is obliged to deliver cash and therefore has a liability. So, if a bank sets up an SIV and uses it to buy complex financial

---

[12] International Financial Reporting Standards, International Accounting Standards Board, January 2007, p. 1364.

instruments, borrowing money from the commercial paper market to finance the investment, how should this be treated?

The answer appears clear-cut, though not necessarily to some banking auditors. If the bank is responsible for the shortfall between the value of the assets and the value of the loan, then the bank has effectively borrowed money and therefore has a liability. This liability should appear on the balance sheet along with the asset, suggesting that off-balance sheet financing is inappropriate.

On 20 August 2007 a number of German banks announced that they had got into difficulty.[13] What was extraordinary about this was that approximately two weeks earlier these German banks reassured the world that they were not overly exposed to the American sub-prime crisis. Eventually, the German government had a situation similar to the British government with Northern Rock; they had to decide whether a state bail-out should go ahead. Eventually it did, making approximately €17.3 billion available to the Sazony bank to cover an affiliate that was suddenly unable to provide the credit that it had pledged. The problem that the German banks faced was one of liquidity and credit quality. The liquidity problem was similar to that of Northern Rock; the German banks borrowed using the equivalent of overdraft facilities, i.e. short-term paper or 'commercial paper' as it is commonly called. The funds obtained from this source were then used to finance the purchase of more long-term illiquid bonds which were linked to the troubled UK mortgage market. The yields on the illiquid bonds were much higher than the interest payments on the commercial paper. The difference found its way into the Profit & Loss account of the German banks and presumably appeared as 'fee income' since the assets and commercial paper were kept in a trust and were therefore off-balance sheet. Therefore the German banks were, for a period of years, able to show profits in the form of fee income but did not disclose (on the balance sheet) the huge liquidity and credit risk they were exposing the shareholders to.

The situation was described by an analyst as follows:

Even worse, those asset-backed commercial papers (ABCPs) are often issued by affiliates which make no appearance on the mother ship's balance sheet. It was just such an affiliate, known as a 'conduit,' which sent Sachsen LB to the brink. Called Ormond Quay and based in Dublin, Ireland, the conduit ran into liquidity problems as investors began shying away from ABCPs, leaving Sachsen LB in a bind.[14]

Unfortunately, there are a lot of questions unanswered by the auditors of these banks. If a bank retains responsibility for bailing out a 'conduit' then surely it has control over that conduit and therefore should consolidate it under IFRS 3. The consolidation rules would have forced the German bank to bring both the asset (the UK mortgage securities) and the short-term liabilities, the asset-backed commercial papers, on to the balance sheet. Then, both the regulators and the shareholders would have seen the substantial liquidity and credit risks that were building up. The regulators would most probably have urged the bank to either cut back on the risk or raise more shareholders' funds. The shareholders might have noticed that these structured products were difficult to value and therefore the risk of hiding losses was quite high. Presumably, they would have avoided the shares.

---

[13] http://www.spiegel.de/international/business/0,1518,500833,00.html

[14] http://www.spiegel.de/international/business/0,1518,500833,00.html

IAS 18, Revenue

A further weapon open to auditors when dealing with off-balance sheet items is IAS 18. Paragraph IAS 18.14 states that:

> Revenue from the sale of goods shall be recognised when all of the following conditions have been satisfied:
>
> (a) the entity has transferred to the buyer the significant risks and rewards of ownership of the goods;
> (b) the entity retains neither continuing managerial involvement to the degree usually associated with ownership nor effective control over the goods sold;
> (c) the amount of revenue can be measured reliably;
> (d) it is probable that the economic benefits associated with the transaction will flow to the entity; and
> (e) the costs incurred or to be incurred in respect of the transaction can be measured reliably.

The principles behind the paragraph are clear. If an entity retains risks and rewards of ownership, the asset must remain on the entity's balance sheet. A similar treatment should apply if the entity controls the asset. In the case of the banks mentioned above, the banks themselves suffer if losses occur – hence, the risks and rewards of ownership rest with the bank.

On 7 February 2008 the *Financial Times* wrote a story that revealed how the above accounting standards are implemented in practice.[15] The story concentrated on the risk that the monoline insurance companies might lose their rock-solid AAA ratings. These monoline insurance companies provided insurance protection against the risk that structured securitised financial instruments would lose their value as a result of credit events. For instance, bank X might purchase sub-prime investment securities for a yield of, say, 9% and buy protection against a credit event of 1%. Assume that these investments were financed by commercial paper (overdraft facilities), which required a payment of 6%. Could the bank that bought these investments record an up-front profit of 2% per annum and therefore an up-front payment of 10% (subject to discounting) if the bonds were to last for five years?

Superficially, the answer is 'yes'. The bank has, through the insurance company, transferred the risks and rewards of ownership to the insurance company. There might be a risk in that the interest on commercial paper may rise while the five-year swap rate (the rate that presumably influences the five-year bond) could fall. However, some banks may decide to hedge this exposure in the bond market. Banks that do not hedge may still argue that a substantial portion of the risks and rewards have transferred to the insurance company, and so need not be kept on their balance sheet. The volume of the transactions outlined above was, according to the *Financial Times*, quite large – leading to very large risks. These transactions were even more complex. According to the FT:

> These so-called negative basis trades were done in large volumes in recent years. They allowed both banks and monolines to book apparently 'free money' and saw monolines

---

[15] Paul J. Davis, 'New dangers appear on the monoline horizon', *Financial Times*, 7 February 2008.

writing guarantees on each other. If they have to be unwound it will be a costly business for all involved.

Banks, in taking an exposure to complex structured credit instruments, have indirectly taken an exposure to the insurance companies. The reference to 'free money' suggests that the monolines are booking the insurance premiums received in their Profit & Loss account without considering adequately the risks involved. That the monoline insurance companies are 'writing guarantees on each other' does suggest that some of the insurance protection is artificial in nature. What is interesting, and perhaps an indication of the major weaknesses of financial reporting, is that no-one really knows the size of the profits the banks and the insurance companies have booked in relation to these trades. It is clear that the trades were profitable, the yield on the financial instruments that the banks received more than covered their borrowing and insurance costs. In many cases, banks involved in this trade decided that the risks and rewards of ownership were transferred. As the article explains:

> The difference between what the bank paid for the insurance and what it received in yield from the bond could be pocketed as 'risk free' profit – and in many cases banks took the entire value of that income over the life of the bond upfront.

These trades involved billions of dollars and perhaps explained why, for a period of time in early 2008 (with the risk that monoline insurance companies would lose their credit ratings), banks – already suffering from huge off-balance sheet losses – were forced to reveal a lot more. Most of the deals were related to utility and infrastructure debt. These were considered attractive because they were linked to inflation.

The view that borrowing in inflationary times is a no-brainer and therefore not risky is clearly something that needs to be questioned. In Britain, during the 1980s and 1990s, many endowment mortgage holders discovered this to their cost. They were told that the principal of their borrowings could be paid from life assurance policies, which were themselves dependent on equity prices. The sales line was that the life assurance policies would benefit from inflation and it is always a good idea to borrow in inflationary times. The losses suffered by endowment mortgage holders were quite severe.

Banks presumably used this no-risk assumption to book profits up-front. According to one executive (quoted in the FT article):

> On a £100m deal over 25 years, a bank could conservatively book £5m up front – even more if it was index linked.

The monoline insurance companies also recognised up-front profits since they hedged their exposure through reinsurance deals with other monoline companies. These trades potentially unravel when monoline insurance companies themselves start to get into trouble. If the credit rating agencies reduce the rating of monoline insurance companies, there is a risk that the value of any insurance protection they offer will be worthless. The investment banks are then forced into a situation where they have to reverse profits previously booked and record heavy losses. As Davis points out, 'the traders involved will have long ago pocketed their bonuses'.

IAS 39, Financial Instruments: Recognition and Measurement

There is a difference between the way that the American FASB and the IFRS deal with securitisation,[16] which does not help things. Although both FASB and IFRS are anxious to converge the standards, important differences remain. In broad terms, the IFRS appear to be a bit more strict on consolidations than their American counterparts. In the United States, the main accounting standard for securitisations is SFAS No. 140, *Accounting for Transfers and Servicing of Financial Assets and Extinguishment of Liabilities*. The IFRS equivalent is IAS 39, *Financial Instruments: Recognition and Measurement*. As explained above, the key issue is derecognition. The benefit of taking assets off the balance sheet is that, once removed, the entity appears less geared and less risky. There may also be scope for the entity to recognise profits on derecognition, a facility that would not be available under the consolidation rules since it would fall foul of the requirement that inter-company profits cannot normally be recognised. The FASB has developed QSPEs: in broad terms, if a securitisation comes under this definition, the American standard setters may allow non-consolidation but this is not necessarily true of the IFRS, where there is no equivalent to QSPE.

Under the FASB, control of an asset is deemed to be surrendered if certain conditions are met. These conditions, in broad terms, state that if the transferor goes bankrupt, its creditors cannot reclaim the assets transferred. Furthermore, the transferee must be generally free to use the asset as collateral without seeking permission from the transferor. Finally, the transferor must not 'effectively maintain control', i.e. through a repurchase agreement. If control is not passed, then consolidation is necessary. Furthermore, if an asset meets certain QSPE requirements, consolidation is not necessary.

Under the IASB approach there are five steps involved:

1. Evaluate if rights to the cash flows have expired.
2. Determine if the transfer has taken place.
3. Apply risk and rewards approach.
4. Apply control approach.
5. Apply continuing involvement.

In an article in the *Journal of International Financial Management and Accounting* in 2008, Ajay Adhikari and Luis Betancourt[17] compared how the international accounting standards and their American equivalents would deal with various securitisations of Ford Motor Company. They concluded that the accounting treatment is a lot different under US GAAP compared with IAS. Consolidation was not required under the US rules, but necessary under the more strict IAS rules. Under US GAAP, more specifically under SFAS No. 140, only three conditions are required to keep the securitisation off-balance sheet:

(i) Are the transferred assets isolated?
(ii) Can the transferee pledge or exchange the transferred assets?
(iii) Does the transferor maintain control over the assets transferred?

---

[16] Ajay Adhikari and Luis Betancourt (2008), 'Accounting for Securitizations: A Comparison of SFAS 140 and IASB 39', *Journal of International Financial Management and Accounting* **19**(1), 73–105. doi:10.1111/j.1467-646X.2008.01017.x

[17] 'Accounting for Securitizations: A Comparison of SFAS 140 and IASB 39.'

Adhikari concluded that all of the conditions were met, and therefore Ford was able to keep the transferred assets off the balance sheet. Under the IFRS rules (and more specifically the IAS 39 rules), since Ford itself actually set up the securitisation and therefore control is considered to arise, so, initially at least, consolidation is necessary. The next step is to determine if derecognition should apply. Clearly, the cash flows to the underlying assets have not expired, so the next step is to determine if a transfer has taken place. There are three conditions necessary here. Firstly, Ford has no obligation to pay the cash flows unless it actually collects the money from the customer. Secondly, Ford is prevented from selling or pledging the assets and thirdly, the entity has to remit any cash flows it collects without material delay to the securitisation vehicle. The first two conditions appear to be satisfied but the third condition poses a problem. The Ford prospectus states, 'The servicer also will be entitled to receive investment earnings (net of investment losses and expenses) on funds deposited in the bank accounts of the trust'. Therefore, derecognition is not permitted under the IAS approach but would be allowed under US GAAP.

Ongoing accounting for a securitisation, even if treated as a financing, requires many subjective judgements and estimates and could still cause volatility in earnings due to the usual factors of prepayments, credit losses and interest rate movements. After all, the company still effectively owns a residual even though a reader cannot find it on the balance sheet. Securitisations accounted for as financings are often not that much different economically than securitisations that qualify for sale accounting treatment. Therefore, the excess of the securitised assets (which remain on-balance sheet) over the related funding (in the form of recorded securitisation debt) is closely analogous economically to a retained residual.

Double-counting – IAS 39

One area of IAS 39[18] that has puzzled accountants who specialise in securitisation accounting is how to account for retained subordinated interest. In practice, as discussed earlier, if a bank sells a portfolio of loans into a securitisation it usually retains (or buys back) the riskier tranche. This may be for regulatory arbitrage purposes or it may simply be because it cannot sell this risky tranche. There is a question as to how this tranche should be dealt with in the accounts. It would appear from paragraph AG 52 in IAS 39 that the bank concerned would keep as an asset on the balance sheet, the value of the retained interest plus an additional amount to cover the 'continuing involvement' in the assets transferred. Some people argue that this is double-counting. The illustration below reveals the problem.

An entity has on its balance sheet £20,000 of loans. It decides to securitise 85% and receives proceeds of £18,000. In addition, the entity is entitled to 50 basis points each year of all the money it collects. For instance, if interest rates are 6% and the entity collects £1200 on the loans, it only has to remit 5.5% (i.e. £1100) and can keep the remaining £100 itself. The securitisation is expected to last for five years. The entity can therefore expect to receive £100 a year for five years. We will assume that this has a present value of £485. Assume that the loans have a fair value of £21,000. How much should go through the Profit & Loss account?

---

[18] Marty Rosenblatt, Jim Johnson and Jim Mountain, *Securitization Accounting – The Ins and Outs (And Some Do's and Don'ts) of FASB 140, FIN 46R, IAS 39 and More...*, 7th edn, Deloitte, July 2005.

Table 9.2 gives the securitisation details. The fair value of the loans on the balance sheet is £21,000 and the SPV buying the loans is in fact buying the full amount. However, the securitisation is selling 10% of the loans back to the bank. The bank in this case is taking the 'subordination' tranche. If the risks and rewards were divided evenly between all the parties, the accounting would be easy. The bank is effectively selling 85% of the loans and 85% of the sales proceeds is £17,850. The reason that the securitisation is paying an additional £150 is because the bank is taking on a proportionately higher share of the risk. If there are bad debts, for instance of 8%, the bank – which is exposed to the first 10% of losses – will suffer all the losses. The value of the credit enhancement is therefore £150. Table 9.3 illustrates how the profit and loss is calculated.

Table 9.2 Securitisation details

Book value of loans	£20,000
Amount securitised	85%
Present value of spread	£485
Fair value of loans	£21,000
Proceeds	£18,000

Table 9.3 Profit & Loss

Fair value of loans	£21,000
Fair value of loans transferred	£17,850
Value of credit enhancement	£150
Proceeds	£18,485
Cost	−$17,000
Profit	£1,485
Recognise immediately	£850
Defer to future periods	£635

The profit of £850 can be recognised immediately. This is simply 85% of the fair value of the loans less the book value of £17,000. The remainder, £635, relates to the interest spread £485 and the value of the credit enhancement £150. These would end up being recognised roughly evenly over the remaining five years.

The wording in IAS 39, paragraph AG 52 [amended to this example] is as follows:

In addition [to the part of the loan portfolio not sold] the entity recognises a continuing involvement that results from the subordination of its retained interest for credit losses. Accordingly, it recognises an asset of £3,000 (the maximum amount of the cash flows it would not receive under the subordination), and an associated liability of £3,635 (which is the maximum amount of the cash flows it would not receive under the subordination, i.e. £3,000 plus the fair value of the subordination of £635.

This is illustrated in Table 9.4.

Table 9.4   Balance sheet

	Before	After
Assets (loans)	£20,000	£3,000
Additional assets		£3,485
Cash		£18,000
Liability		−£3,635
	£20,000	£20,850
Shareholders' Funds	£20,000	£20,000
Profit		£850
	£20,000	£20,850

One could argue that there is double-counting (namely the £3000 is captured twice) under 'Assets' and 'Additional assets'. However, although the maximum liability is £3000 (in a worse case situation), the subordinated tranche of a securitisation is very risky. So, although the IAS 39 approach is not correct, the value carried on the balance sheet does reflect the risky nature of the asset.

10

Reconciliation

10.1 INTRODUCTION

In early 2008, as the banking sector faced damaging attacks to their reputation for conceal-ing losses on complex financial instruments, the French bank Société Générale was forced to reveal the presence of a rogue trader Jerome Kerviel, who allegedly lost €4.9 billion from unauthorised trading activities. The regulatory world was coming to the worrying conclu-sions that not only were banks unable to report their profit and loss correctly on their annual reports, but they had little or no control over potential fraud opportunities. The issue is one that accountants should feel concerned about since both auditors and accountants involved with Société Générale allowed a situation to develop where both losses and liabilities were kept off the balance sheet.

Charlie McCreevy, the European Union's internal market commissioner, said it was inex-cusable that SocGen had ignored warnings from Eurex, a major derivative exchange, who had warned the bank about the activities of the trader. He said:

> As far as treasury and proprietary trading risk is concerned, it seems to me amazing that, despite all the lessons about controls that should have been learnt from a sequence of multi-billion dollar losses clocked up by rogue traders in several financial institutions around the world over the past decade, a top-class institution has once again been exposed as having fundamental control weaknesses.[1]

His surprise and anger were shared by risk consultants who criticised the adequacy of internal controls and more importantly, SocGen's failure to learn from past mistakes. Approximately 10 years previously a single rogue trader, Nick Leeson, brought a long-established British bank 'Barings Bank' to its knees. Allied Irish Bank had a similar problem with a single trader, John Rusnik, a few years later – though the losses in that case were relatively small. When these losses were reported, banks around the world did invest fortunes into their risk man-agement function. Thousands of people were recruited into what the banks call their 'middle office', whose function is to monitor traders and ensure that their trades are properly recorded as well as ensuring that traders stay within their risk limits. Regulators also strengthened their monitoring teams to ensure that banks put the appropriate checks and balances in place. Indeed, many shareholders of banks assured themselves that the risk of a single trader bring-ing down a bank again was very remote. Many were surprised, therefore, that SocGen was not able to put controls in place to prevent the 'rogue trader' from re-emerging.

According to the *Financial Times*,[2] 'So after Société Générale failed to convince with its initial version of how Jerome Kerviel concealed a trading position that ended up costing the

---

[1] Tony Barber, 'Bank slammed for carelessness', *Financial Times*, 7 February 2008.
[2] 'SocGen unravels "exceptional fraud"', *Financial Times*, 28 January 2008.

bank almost Euro 5 billion, it was yesterday forced to give more details'. The SocGen affair had quite a lot in common with Barings Bank and Allied Irish Bank. In all three cases, the traders were appointed as 'arbitrage traders'. Arbitrage trading is a very junior form of trading and is often the only type of trading permitted by junior traders. It basically involves identifying pricing anomalies and exploiting them. For instance, a trader might see that a bond is priced lower on one market than another. So, he buys at the lower price and sells at the higher price, making a small profit. If this type of trade is carried out in large quantities the bank can make a comfortable profit, though arbitrage traders often realise that as the profit potential is quite low, their bonuses are also relatively low – however, it is very close to risk-free and that of course is important for banks.

A type of trading which is slightly more dangerous is known as 'relative value trading'. This is where a trader is permitted to take a bit more risk than an arbitrage trader. Like an arbitrage trader, the relative value trader buys one asset and sells another similar-type asset (but not identical as opposed to an arbitrage trader). For instance, a trader might buy an ordinary corporate bond and an option on the corporation's shares and simultaneously sell a convertible bond, if he felt that the corporate bond and the option were underpriced and the convertible bond was overpriced. Relative value trading often requires a little more experience than arbitrage trading. The profits are higher but so too are the risks, though the risks are largely contained. Hedge funds, often associated with risky trades, generally prefer 'relative value trading' since what a hedge fund is really trying to ensure is that they are well rewarded for taking risks. They therefore contain – or hedge – the risks they don't want. One of the trades that the hedge fund Long Term Capital Management (LTCM) got involved in was to buy 'old' treasury bonds and sell freshly issued treasury bonds. The yields on the old bonds were higher than the yields on the new bonds, simply because many investors had an appetite for freshly issued bonds. LTCM was therefore able to profit substantially from the differences in the yield, and also benefited from the fact that the 'old' bonds were underpriced while the new bonds were overpriced, but only took a small amount of liquidity and market risk.

The third type of trading is proprietary trading. This is quite dangerous. Proprietary traders are allowed to buy assets which they feel are underpriced. They often hold on to these assets for a long period of time before selling them. Alternatively, they borrow assets which they feel are overpriced, then sell them when the price falls and return them to their original owner – a process known as 'shorting the market'. Proprietary trading is only for very experienced traders, and can be highly lucrative. As traders are occasionally holding on to positions for a relatively long period of time and are not offsetting them by 'short' positions, the market risk is quite high.

The bonus scheme adopted by most banks encourages traders towards proprietary trading. There is a simple explanation for this. If traders can make the portfolio more volatile, they can earn very high bonuses when their trades are right and walk away from huge losses when their trades are wrong. Thus, by making the portfolio more volatile the trader acquires a very valuable asset – a call option over his portfolio, which is in effect a transfer of wealth from the investors to the trader. The investor is usually very much unaware of what is going on, in these circumstances, until the bad news of huge losses hits the headlines. Apart from the bonuses there are other behavioural factors that encourage traders to move from arbitrage-style trading to proprietary trading. The concept of the 'star' trader is important. A 'star' trader is a trader who is making huge profits for a bank. Not only is he revered by other traders, but often his bosses are afraid to lose him (and therefore are tempted to overlook certain transgressions such as breaching limits set by the middle office).

10.2   MIDDLE OFFICE

The role of the middle office is in essence to measure and control risks. The back office are the people responsible for making sure that all trades are captured correctly on their database system. It is not entirely unreasonable to say that in the case of Barings, Allied Irish Bank and SocGen, there were major failings in the middle and back-office functions. There are two important controls that a bank should put in place to discourage and (ideally) prevent rogue trading. The first is to make sure that trades are captured. A rogue trader is, of course, tempted to make bets and then keep quiet about them. Therefore, instinctively, he is looking for weaknesses in the back office with the possible intention of exploiting them. This 'instinct' is not necessarily confined to rogue traders. Even honest and experienced traders can tell of weaknesses in the back office. Often too they are tempted to conceal these weaknesses just in case they need to tap in on them in emergencies. Consider a trader who is not fully alert one morning and puts on an unauthorised trade which causes the bank to lose, say, £100,000 in the space of an hour. The trader concerned could tell his superiors about the incident, spend hours writing a compliance report and being grilled at an interview and may even be prevented from trading for the rest of the day. The alternative is to hide the trade – or to use their jargon, 'park the trade' – in a temporary account. Then, play double or quits to cancel the loss and, if unsuccessful, play double or quits again until the loss is extinguished. The problem for the bank is that if a trader spots this opportunity he may continue to use it. At some stage, if there are many traders in this position, the bank could find itself with a serious problem.

The second type of control, usually carried out at the middle office, is to check the trader's position against his limits. If the trader breaches his limit without justification, this would of course warrant serious disciplinary action. Often the limits are set using VaR, which focuses on the potential losses and risks that a trader takes on rather than monetary or volume limits, which traders can easily get around using highly leveraged financial instruments. Traders who engage in arbitrage trading make a low profit per trade but need to trade in high volumes to justify their existence. Therefore, they would be given a low VaR limit, which contains the risk they can take, but higher volume limits. Relative value traders would be given a VaR limit a bit higher than that for an arbitrage trader. Proprietary trading, on the other hand, involves taking a huge amount of risks and therefore traders need to have more flexible limits and so will have a much higher VaR than their arbitrage trading counterparts.

The conclusion to be drawn from this is that Jerome Kerviel (the SocGen trader), John Rusnik (the Allied Irish Bank trader) and Nick Leeson of Barings would all have been discovered by the middle-office risk management team if VaR had been measured correctly and indeed if correct VaR limits were set and monitored frequently. In all three cases, the middle office would have seen that although given the authority only to engage in arbitrage trading, the VaR calculations would suggest that they were actually speculating heavily. So why did the VaR models not pick this up?

The answer, in all three cases, is that VaR can only work well when the data used to calculate VaR is correct. In all three cases, Barings, Allied Irish Bank and SocGen, it appears that the traders concerned were in some way able to manipulate the data so that they could hide losses. So, although VaR certainly has its weaknesses, it was not a weakness in the VaR system that allowed these banks to amass huge losses. Instead, there was a weakness with data capture. In the case of Barings, Nick Leeson was able to manipulate the back-office data by inputting his own trades. For Allied Irish Bank, there was evidence that either John Rusnik was inputting trades incorrectly or at least manipulating what was on the database. According to SocGen, Mr Kerviel 'hedged his trading position with false contracts, created by hacking into the system using other people's access codes and forged documents'. Mr Kerviel apparently had created fictitious operations that were registered in SocGen's systems but did not correspond with economic reality.

In all three cases, the fraud was due to weak data capture. Risk managers and senior management therefore relied on this flawed data to determine the overall risk that the bank was taking, and also to inform shareholders of its financial performance and risk profile through its annual report. An obvious solution to this is to allocate more resources to the back office so that the data quality is more accurate. However, this is an oversimplification of the problem. There are a variety of conflicts of interest within the banking structure – not only of the three banks mentioned, but of the entire banking system. Once again the problem arises because of complexity and inappropriate bonuses.

It is important to understand the behaviourial difficulties that the middle office, back office, regulators and accountants find themselves in. Efforts by the middle office and the back office to improve controls are not always greeted warmly, either by traders or banking directors. Consider a situation where the board members of a particular bank are on a remuneration package which rewards them for high profits. Naturally, the bank will consider hiring good star traders. Needless to say, if the board of directors allow their bonuses to influence or direct their activities, they will want to introduce as much volatility into their portfolios as possible. The way to do that is to hire proprietary traders of star quality rather than arbitrage traders. The problem, of course, is that the regulators will object to this since high volatility will lead to higher risk for the deposit holders and, unless volatility is contained, a possible run on the bank (similar to that for Northern Rock) would be possible. Equally, the shareholders may object on the grounds that they don't want the risks, and neither would they be willing to invest in a bank where the traders walk away with the bulk of the profits while the shareholders suffer the losses. There is a trade-off, the more a bank invests in its middle office and back office, the higher the costs but also the lower the volatility. Therefore, banking directors might be motivated to take on huge amounts of risk and find ways to conceal from both the regulators and the shareholders what they are doing. One way of doing this is to hire star traders, but tell them that they can only engage in arbitrage trading. In effect, this means that a culture within banks is created where traders are formally told to act as arbitrage traders, but everyone turns a blind eye if they take on proprietary trading positions. Unfortunately, the accounting standards contribute to this deception. For instance, there is no economic difference between borrowing €30 billion and investing in shares or taking a long future position on shares with a notional of €30 billion. Yet the accounting standards treat trades with the same economic risk quite differently. In the former case, the borrowings appear on the balance sheet, making it look very highly geared. In the latter case, the future position is treated in accordance with IAS 39 and therefore only appears on the balance sheet if the trade has made a profit or a loss. No liability is recognised. The trade is shown gross if it is not a derivative, i.e. the asset and the liability are shown gross while the derivative is shown net.

In the case of SocGen, Jerome Kerviel did not borrow money and invest it in equity. Presumably, being a relatively junior trader he would not have been allowed to borrow what the bank was worth, i.e. €30 billion, and conceal it from his board of directors. But apparently this is exactly what he did, though he used derivatives to take his position. The accounting standards are partly responsible for this unusual situation, since the standards allow entities plenty of ways to borrow money and to conceal from shareholders what they are doing.

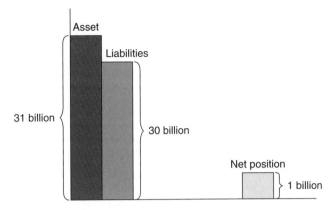

Figure 10.1 Cash position vs. future position

There is the possibility, therefore, that the middle office is seen by boards of directors as a token gesture to keep the regulators satisfied and to reassure the shareholder that the bank is prevented from taking on excessive risks. The middle office manager is expected to measure risks, deal with the Basel 2 requirements and make sure that the appropriate disclosures are in place in the annual report and rubber stamp whatever is necessary. In other words, he is expected to go through the procedure of measuring and controlling risks without doing it very effectively. There are many instances where middle office managers should have objected to the use of off-balance sheet vehicles, and the purchase of complex structured products, and looked out for alarm bells. Unfortunately, there are far too many instances of this not happening, perhaps because the board of directors will not over-encourage anything that might reduce their bonuses. The directors and traders pay only lip-service to the middle office and use it to simply give the appearance of measuring and controlling risk.

There is too little information available to conclude that this is what happened at SocGen, or any other bank, but the perverse conflicts of interest created by a bonus system that does not measure risks properly certainly encourage a bureaucratic approach to risk management, where only the simple risks that are easy to measure are measured – encouraging traders to enter into complex derivative positions that the middle office people don't understand and would not have the resources to control even if they did.

What was worrying about SocGen, therefore, was that the money was lost through simple non-complex products and the middle office team did originally initiate enquiries into Jerome Kerviel's trades but these enquiries did not amount to much. The Head of Corporate and Investment Banking at SocGen told the *Financial Times*,[3] 'he was always rolling one transaction into another. If he was ever caught he just said it was a mistake and would start putting the trade somewhere else'. Unfortunately, these explanations were not enough for suspicious financial commentators. There was the feeling that SocGen did not learn from past mistakes. Neither did it have a middle office strong enough to cope with such a simple fraud.

Another fact that surprised many was that SocGen was known as the top equity derivatives and trading house throughout the world. It held regular client seminars and parties to show how its financial sophistication made it world leader. Perhaps the conclusion that people will draw from the SocGen affair is that derivatives are simply difficult to deal with and, though

---

[3] Martin Arnold, 'SocGen unravels exceptional fraud', *Financial* Times, 28 January 2008.

lucrative, one must expect losses and substantial losses. However, as the remainder of this chapter shows, there are certain reconciliation procedures that banks should carry out to ensure that losses are not hidden or that traders are not trading outside their limits. The control is similar to what accountants call the 'Debtors/Creditors' control account.

10.3   INITIAL AND VARIATION MARGIN

When traders open derivative positions they must normally place a deposit with the exchange – known as the initial margin. This margin stays with the exchange until the position is closed out. In addition there is a variation margin payment, which traders must make to the exchange when a trading position loses money, but they receive variation margin when a trading position makes money. It follows that if a bank is losing money through unauthorised trades, the trader must find variation margin to cover his losses. The purpose of the initial margin is to protect the exchange if a trader or bank misses variation margin payments.

Example

A bank has three traders who are allowed to take proprietary positions on the bank's behalf.

The first trader has a view that the three-month sterling interest rate (Libor) is going to fall between March and June and decides to take a position on a notional of £2,000,000 using the three-month future contract. We will assume that, on the date he takes out the contract, interest rates are 6%. Suppose he puts on the position on 2 January. Three weeks later, on 23 January, interest rates fall to 5.5% and the trader decides to take his profits by closing out the future position. The overall profit will be £2,000,000 × (6% − 5.5%) × 3/12 = £2500.

As Table 10.1 shows, the notional size of each future contract is £500,000. Therefore, as the trader wants to take an exposure on £2,000,000, he would purchase four future contracts. Future contracts are similar to bonds; their price goes up as interest rates fall and vice versa. As he wants an exposure to interest rates between March and June, he will buy four March future contracts. These future contracts track the rate between March and June.

Table 10.1   Trader 1 term sheet

Three-month sterling interest rate future	
Unit of trading	£500,000
Delivery months	March, June, September, December
Delivery day	First business day after the last trading day
Last trading day	Third Wednesday of the delivery month
Quotation	100.00 less the rate of interest
Minimum price movement	0.01 tick size £12.50

The price of the future contract is 100 minus the expected Libor rate between March and June. Therefore, on the date of purchase, the future contract is priced at 94 (100−6). When the trader closes out his position on 23 March, interest rates fall to 5.5% and therefore the new futures price is 94.50. To calculate the profit for each future contract we must identify how many ticks were earned. We subtract the closing price from the opening price and, as the term sheet in Table 10.1 reveals, we divide by 0.01. In this case we bought at 94 and sold at 94.5.

This difference is then divided by 0.01 to give 50 ticks. The trader used four future contracts and so made a profit of 200 ticks, and each tick had a value of £12.50 – so the trader made a profit of £2500. This is how the exchange calculates the profit and variation margin.

The second trader trades on behalf of a client. The client is of the view that the dollar is expected to get weaker against sterling and wants to take an exposure of £2,000,000. The trader will simply enter into a forward contract with the client on 2 January, when the dollar/sterling exchange rate is $2.00. The trader then decides to hedge his position by using future contracts. In this case, the trader will buy 32 future contracts – i.e. £2,000,000/£62,500 = 32. Assume that between 2 and 23 January, sterling, contrary to the client's expectations, actually falls to $1.90. Then, under the forward contract, the client owes the bank money, namely $2,000,000 \times (\$1.90 - \$2) = \$200,000$, and this is the amount of money that the trader receives from the future contract. As the term sheet in Table 10.2 reveals, the tick size is $0.0001 and the tick value $6.25. For each future contract, the purchase price was $2 and the closing price was $1.90. This equates to a loss of $0.10 and since each tick size is $0.0001, the total number of ticks lost per future contract is $0.10/\$0.0001 = 1000$ ticks. The trader took 32 positions leading to a loss of 32,000 ticks and, as each tick value is $6.25, the total loss is $200,000 – which equates to the amount of money that the client owes the trader.

Table 10.2   Trader 2 term sheet

Sterling foreign currency future	
Unit of trading	£62,500
Delivery months	March, June, September, December
Minimum price movement	0.01c or $0.0001 tick size $6.25 tick value

The third position is taken by a trader who has the view that the equity markets are going to rise. The trader wants to take an exposure of £1,200,000. On 2 January, when the index is 6000, the trader puts on the trade. To calculate the number of future contracts that the trader will use, we divide the notional exposure £1,200,000 by (the current index multiplied by £10). £10 represents the value of each index as shown in the term sheet of Table 10.3. The trader in this case would purchase £1,200,000/(6000 × £10) = 20. We will assume that between 2 and 23 January the index falls by 8% to 5520. Clearly, the trader has lost 8% of £1,200,000, i.e. £96,000. From the exchange's perspective, the index has dropped by 480 points. The trader has a position of 20 contracts and so loses 9600 points. As each point is worth £10, the total loss is £96,000.

We will assume for the sake of simplicity that an initial margin of £5000 is paid on each contract.

Table 10.3   Trader 3 term sheet

FTSE 250 index future	
Units of trading	£10 per index point
Delivery months	March, June, September, December
Last trading day	First business day after last trading day
Quotation	Index points
Minimum price movement	0.50 £5

The role of the back office, amongst other things, is to reconcile the variation margin payments with the Profit & Loss account. Where a trader pays variation margin, it can be for either of two reasons: the trader is making a loss or he is trading on behalf of clients who are making losses. If the former, the back-office people will ensure that any variation margin payment is charged to the Profit & Loss account. This is a simple journal entry, debit the Profit & Loss account and credit Cash. If, however, the trader is trading on behalf of clients, then the client bears the burden of the loss and so the client is charged with the loss. The journal entry is altered slightly. Instead of debiting the Profit & Loss we debit the Client and once again credit Cash with the margin payment. Obviously, when variation margin is received, it can be for either of two reasons: the trader makes a profit or he is trading on behalf of clients who are making a profit. The journal entries are therefore a mirror image.

On a daily basis, exchanges will provide details of trades that a bank has entered into. Where the trade has made money, the bank will receive variation margin. The statement will compare the current price with the previous price and then calculate the variation margin. Also, of course, if the trade loses money, variation margin will be paid.

Table 10.4   Variation margin

	Tick size	0.01
	Tick value	£12.50
	Variation margin	
		March 3-month sterling contract
	Quantity	4
02-Jan-08	94.00	
03-Jan-08	94.10	£500.00
04-Jan-08	94.22	£600.00
05-Jan-08	94.20	−£100.00
06-Jan-08	94.23	£150.00
07-Jan-08	94.08	−£750.00
08-Jan-08	93.98	−£495.00
09-Jan-08	93.88	−£495.00
10-Jan-08	93.78	−£495.00
11-Jan-08	93.68	−£495.00
12-Jan-08	93.59	−£495.00
13-Jan-08	93.49	−£495.00
14-Jan-08	93.60	£570.00
15-Jan-08	94.61	£5,050.00
16-Jan-08	94.40	−£1,050.00
17-Jan-08	94.81	£2,050.00
18-Jan-08	95.20	£1,950.00
19-Jan-08	95.63	£2,150.00
20-Jan-08	96.00	£1,850.00
21-Jan-08	95.50	−£2,500.00
22-Jan-08	94.49	−£5,050.00
23-Jan-08	94.50	£50.00
		£2,500.00

Table 10.4 shows how the variation margin would work for the first trader. We have assumed that the trader bought the contract for 94 on 2 January and closed out for 94.5 on 23 January.

Obviously, during these dates, the price will fluctuate. Where the price goes up, it works in the trader's favour so he receives variation margin and of course when the trade loses money, variation margin must be paid. The exchange is not particularly worried if the trader is hedging or speculating; the trader simply pays variation margin if the future loses money and receives variation margin if he makes money.

What banks should consider doing, particularly SocGen and Barings, is to make sure that the reconciliation is carried out by the back office. The back office, for instance, will receive statements from the exchange each day. The first task of the back office is to check these statements against the database that the bank uses to calculate VaR. If there are trades missing, i.e. trades appearing on the broker or exchange statements that do not appear on the database, this potentially indicates that traders have not entered their trades correctly (or in some cases not at all). This should send alarm signals as there is a possibility that the trader is trying to hide the trades.

In the above example, for instance, there are three trades. Suppose the third trader, the equity trader, did not put his trade on the system or manipulated the system in some way, there are two ways that the back office could find out about it. Firstly, they would obtain a statement from the exchange and the exchange would, of course, clearly show that the equity trade had taken place. Secondly, there would be a daily cash settlement to cover the variation margin. This would have an impact on the cash account and, of course, if a trader was hiding huge losses, the back office people would be able to spot it because they would see a huge variation margin payment. It is therefore surprising that SocGen and Barings were not able to spot the huge positions that Jerome Kerviel and Nick Leeson were taking, and taking for prolonged periods of time.

In both cases, much attention focused on their ability to manipulate the back-office system. Mr Kerviel, for instance, was alleged to have stolen passwords to access the system while Nick Leeson was able to open a special account which he called an '88888 account' in order to hide his losses. However, even if they were clever enough to manipulate the back-office system, they could not manipulate statements from the exchange or broker. So, it should have been clear to the back office staff, given the amount of variation margin that was paid and given that trades must have appeared on the statement, that the traders were manipulating the system in some way. What appears to have happened in both cases is that the VaR calculations which checked their positions and limits used a database that the traders could manipulate. Had the middle office simply worked from the statements and kept an eye on the cash account, the internal manipulation would have come to light.

In short, there should be no excuse for allowing rogue traders to lose huge amounts of money from trading in simple derivatives. Many people questioned whether SocGen really lost money from simple products. Writing for the *Financial Times*, Frank Partnoy commented:

> Although SocGen has emphasised that Mr Kerviel was responsible only for 'plain vanilla futures hedging on European equity market indices', the bank's own documents suggest he was involved in more complicated strategies, including quantitative trading, swaps and equity derivative strategies.[4]

Obviously, the more complex the derivative, the greater the risk of operational failure. Exchanges normally tend to concentrate on simple derivatives. They are often known as future

---

[4] Kerviel is just part of a rogue's gallery – Frank Partnoy, 28 January 2008.

contracts and options on future contracts. They are generally very liquid, easy to price and the exchanges require variation margin (and pay variation margin on profit-making trades). In addition, as variation margin is paid over and back, credit risk is mitigated. A bank therefore needs simply to use the broker's statements and exchange statements to calculate VaR and then keep controls in place so that rogue traders can be identified. The real challenge in the middle office is when traders use complex financial instruments. Often these trades are not done through an exchange, so there is no initial or variation margin going over and back.

10.4   EXAMPLE: ILLUSTRATION OF RECONCILIATION

A bank has the balance sheet shown in Table 10.5 at the start of day 1.

Table 10.5   Opening balance sheet

Client accounts	£40,000
Loans to customers	£900,000
Cash	£60,000
Customer deposits Shareholders' funds	£980,000
Shares issued	£8,000
Equity reserves	£10,000
Retained profits	£2,000

The bank acts as a broker/market maker and currently, the clients owe the bank £40,000. Loans to customers consist of bank loans and mortgages. Cash on hand is £60,000. The bank is financed predominantly by customer deposits of £980,000 and shareholder funds of £20,000. The shareholder funds are broken down between shares issued £8000, equity reserves £10,000 and retained earnings £2000. The equity reserves comprise entirely cash flow hedges. In this case, the bank expects to borrow money on a floating rate basis and use it to finance fixed-rate mortgages. If interest rates go up the bank suffers, so the purpose of the cash flow hedge is to reduce the bank's exposure to a rise in interest rates. In this case, the bank shorted four December future contracts. As explained previously, when interest rates rise, future prices fall so a short future contract will make money when interest rates rise. In the above case, the bank profited from the future contract which it closed out in December. The purpose of the hedge was to lock in interest rates between January and March 2008, so the balance in the cash flow hedge will be released to the Profit & Loss account over January to March. Assume that there are 90 days in this period, which means that the bank will release £10,000/90 = £111 each day.

During day 1, the bank undertakes the trades shown in Table 10.6.

Trade 1 was undertaken by a trader in the proprietary trading desk. The trader has the view that sterling will appreciate against the dollar over the next few months. He has taken a position on £1m, which means that he needs to take a long sterling position on 16 contracts. A long sterling position simply means that if sterling rises, the trader profits and of course if sterling falls, the trader loses money. The exchange will normally protect itself against a credit loss by insisting that the counterparty posts collateral, often called 'Initial Margin'.

The second trade was taken by the bank on behalf of a client. The client believes that the equity markets are going to rise and takes on an exposure of £600,000. Again the position

Table 10.6 Trades

		Notional per contract	Quantity	Day 1 market rates	Reason for trade	Initial margin per contract
Trade 1	FX future sterling dollar	£62,500	16	$1.90	Speculative	£1250
Trade 2	Equity future	£60,000	10	6000	Client	£1250
Trade 3	Interest rate future	£500,000	4	4%	Hedge CF	£1250
Trade 4	Swaps/brokerage	£3,000,000	1	5%	Hedge FV	£0

is 'long', meaning that the client benefits if the index rises but loses if the index falls. The notional size of the equities future contract is, as always, the current index multiplied by the point value £10 as we saw in the term sheet earlier. Therefore, the bank goes to the exchange and takes out 10 contracts to create the £600,000 exposure that the client requires. Obviously, the bank does not have a market exposure in this case since they are simply trading on behalf of the client. It is worth noting, however, that the client could lose money if the stock market falls and may also be unwilling or unable to pay his losses to the bank. Therefore, if the stock market does fall, the bank's credit exposure would potentially increase. Obviously, the bank will, in most cases, make sure that there is sufficient collateral from the customer to cover these potential losses.

Trade 3 is a 'fair value' hedge, as defined in IAS 39. Strictly speaking, as we are dealing with future contracts, the hedge will not work 100% and so we should identify the ineffectiveness. However, for the sake of simplicity, we will assume that the hedge works 100%. The hedge is used to lock in the fair values of a fixed loan. As explained earlier, the bank tends to finance itself from floating deposits and uses this to finance fixed coupon deposits. In this case the bank calculates that it will lose money between March and June if interest rates go up and so takes out a short future position that makes money if interest rates rise.

Trade 4 is a swap that the entity has taken with another broker. The swap is a cash flow hedge as defined in IAS 39 and, once again, we will assume that it is 100% effective. The bank proposes to securitise this loan in the future and the purpose of the hedge is to lock in the cash flows on its sale to the securitisation entity. The loan is expected to last for five years and has a coupon of 4% + 2%. The 4% represents the five-year swap rate at the date of issue; the 2% is the credit spread, meaning that the market believes there is approximately a 2% chance that the entity will fail to meet its repayments. The bank believes that the 2% expectation is quite high and is therefore quite happy with the interest rate exposure. However, the bank also believes that the five-year swap rate will rise and as the bond has a fixed coupon, there is the risk that a rise in interest rates will reduce the value of the loan, particularly if the bank securitises the loan before maturity. Therefore, the bank decides to lock in the Libor rate. It does this by entering into a swap whereby it pays a fixed rate of 4% and receives the floating rate. In effect, through the fair value hedge, it is converting a fixed loan into a floating loan. Unlike the other trades, this swap is 'over the counter' (OTC), which means that the swap is taken out with another bank as opposed to the exchange. Therefore, there is no variation margin. This increases the risk slightly since traders do not always have to finance their losses when dealing with other banks as counterparties. When dealing with the exchange, however, the trader does have to pay variation margin on loss-making positions and therefore it is more difficult to conceal loss-making trades.

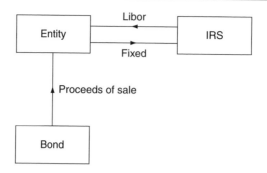

Figure 10.2   Cash flow hedge swap

Table 10.7   Day 2

Trade 1	FX future sterling dollar	16	$1.80	£1000
Trade 2	Equity future	10	5900	£1000
Trade 3	Interest rate future	4	3%	£1400
Trade 4	Swaps/brokerage	1	4%	£0

We now move on to day 2, where the prices have changed a little (Table 10.7).

Sterling has depreciated against the dollar, which means that the trader has made a loss and will have to pay variation margin to the exchange. The second trade has also made a loss, and so the bank must again pay variation margin but this time it is recovered from the customer and so there will be no impact to the Profit & Loss account. The three-month Libor interest rate has decreased from 4% to 3%, which means that the trader will receive variation margin on this trade but, as this trade is classified as a fair value hedge (under IAS 39), the profit will be offset against 'Loans to Customers' as opposed to the Profit & Loss account and finally, the fourth trade makes money. The purpose of this trade was to lock in the cash flows on the sale of a fixed coupon loan. The bank therefore agreed to receive a fixed rate of 5% and pay the relevant floating rate. However, the five-year swap rate has now decreased to 4% – suggesting that the bank will end up paying out less than it receives, over the life of the swap. Unlike the other three trades, this trade is OTC. In other words, the derivative is a private agreement between two banks and therefore will not feature on the exchange at all. The likelihood is that no variation margin will be paid or received.

Once the above statement is received, the first step for the back office people is to ensure that the trades are correctly identified on a database that is hopefully not capable of being manipulated by traders or anyone who has a conflict of interest, i.e. anyone who benefits by concealing losses. In a good control environment, a trader is allowed to enter trades onto a database but is not allowed to cancel them until the trade has been closed out with the exchange. The back office would then use this database to compare against external statements to make sure that it is complete and not exposed to any form of manipulation. One of the major downfalls with SocGen and Barings was that in both cases, the rogue traders with back-office experience were able to manipulate the data. Nick Leeson confirmed his own back-office trades at Barings. Almost 12 years later, it appears that SocGen did not learn the valuable lesson of keeping traders out of the back office. The SocGen press release admitted that Jerome Kerviel had a lot of back-office experience and, it appears, more back-office experience than the entire back-office staff – given that he could effectively borrow the worth of the bank (€50 billion) and conceal this from the back-office staff. The solution is therefore to use exchange statements and prime office broker statements to verify the database and not rely on traders' inputs. Also, though it is stating the obvious, the statements should go direct to the back office without any interference from the trader. This reduces the risk and temptation for traders to hide losses by forging confirmations.

Once the trades are confirmed, the next step is to calculate or verify the variation margin and initial margin payments/receipts. The schedule in Table 10.8 shows how the variation margin is calculated.

Table 10.8 Variation margin

	Previous price	Current price	Quantity	Tick size	Ticks gained	Tick value	Variation margin
Trade 1	$1.90	$1.80	16	$0.0001	−16,000	$6.2500	−£55,556
Trade 2	6000	5900	10	1	−1,000	£10.0000	−£10,000
Trade 3	4%	3%	4	0.01%	−400	£12.5000	−£5,000
Trade 4				N/A		N/A	

For the first trade, the exposure was £1,000,000 sterling. Sterling has, however, depreciated against the dollar so the trade has made a loss of £1,000,000 × ($1.8 − $1.9) = −$100,000. Converted to sterling, the loss is $100,000/$1.8 = £55,556. As far as the exchange is concerned, each sterling future contract has lost 1000 ticks, i.e. ($1.80 − $1.90)/$0.0001. There are 16 long positions, so the total ticks lost is 16,000. Each tick is worth $6.25 and so the total loss is $100,000; using the current rate $1.80, the total loss in sterling terms is £55,556.

In the second trade, the total exposure is £600,000 on the FTSE 100 index. As the index has fallen by approximately 1.67%, i.e. (6000 − 5900)/6000 = 1.67%, the trade has lost £600,000 × 1.67% = £10,000. In terms of the exchange, each future contract has lost 100 points and each point is worth £10. Therefore, the loss per contract is £1000 and the loss on 10 contracts is £10,000.

Trade 3 has gained £5000. The total exposure is £2m. The trade was taken out to protect a deposit of £2,000,000. In this case the bank was worried that a fall in interest rates would dent profits. Interest rates did fall, so the bank made money on the hedge to offset against the reduced interest that the bank would receive on the underlying deposit. The hedging period was three months. Therefore, the gain on the hedge was £2,000,000 × (4%−3%) × 3/12 = £5000. The exchange compares the purchase price of the derivative against the selling price and calculates the number of ticks gained and then, in the usual manner, multiplies the ticks gained by the number of futures and the value of each tick. The purchase price of the derivative was 100 − 4% = 96 and the current price is 100 − 3% = 97. The total ticks gained therefore is (97 − 96)/0.01 = 100. This figure is multiplied by 4 (being 4 futures) and then £12.50 to give £5000. The total variation margin payable is therefore the sum of the three trades, namely −£60,556. There are two possible reasons why this figure is negative. Firstly, the trader is trading on his own behalf and making losses. Secondly, the trader is trading on behalf of clients and the clients are making losses. In this example the bank is actually making a loss on some trades and its clients are making losses on others. The back-office people therefore should charge any variation margin payments to the Profit & Loss account. There are two exceptions, however. If the back-office people can confirm that the client accepts he has made the loss and more importantly, has the capacity to pay, then the relevant portion of the variation margin is charged to the client instead of the Profit & Loss account. If the variation loss relates to derivatives that qualify for the strict rules of cash flow hedge accounting under IAS 39, the losses can be transferred to Equity Reserve (in the case of a cash flow hedge) or used to adjust the carrying value of an underlying asset or liability (in the case of a fair value hedge). We will see later in the example how this is achieved.

As pointed out previously, the exchange often requires payment of an initial deposit or initial margin when the bank takes out a trade (Table 10.9). The reason for this initial margin is to protect the exchange from credit risk. If, for instance, a bank takes out a future contract which subsequently loses money and the bank is unable to meet the variation margin requirement, the exchange can recover any variation margin shortfall from the initial margin account. Normally, there is sufficient money in the initial margin account to cover approximately three days' expected variation margin. Therefore, where a bank misses a variation margin payment, the exchange has approximately two days to close out the relevant future contract without making a loss. The calculation of the initial margin is complex and depends on the expected volatility of the price. However, as the calculation is carried out automatically by the exchange, the method used need not concern us here. What is important, however, is that the exchange may vary the initial margin and require extra payments or possibly return funds to the bank, depending on whether they have increased or reduced the initial margin. In this example, we assume that the initial margin is settled in cash, though in reality the bank may use collateral such as bonds – thus preventing the opportunity cost of tying up cash.

Table 10.9   Initial margin

	Quantity	Existing initial margin	Current initial margin	Change
Trade 1	16	£1,250	£1,000	−£4,000
Trade 2	10	£1,250	£1,000	−£2,500
Trade 3	4	£1,250	£1,400	£600
Trade 4	N/A			
		£37,500	£31,600	−£5,900

One of the practices which exacerbated the credit crises of 2007 and 2008 was that hedge funds and banks suffered increases in their initial margin requirements on certain derivative products. Banks and hedge funds, that were already strapped for cash, were therefore placed in a forced sell situation, pushing the prices down further. This created a spiral effect, since the forced sale created losses which in turn concerned the regulators and this led to a wave of rights issues and further selling.

Table 10.9 shows that the exchange has reduced the initial margin requirements on trades 1 and 2 but increased the requirements on trade 3. The exchange might make this change because of a reduction in the price volatility for the first two trades and an increase in volatility for the third. For trade 1, the reduction in the initial margin is £250 per contract which comes to £2500 for 10 contracts. The cash received/paid to the exchange is therefore summarised in Table 10.10.

Table 10.10

Initial margin refunded	£5,900
Variation margin paid	−£60,556
Total cash paid	−£54,656

Before we can complete the reconciliation we need to calculate the amount owed to the prime broker in respect of the fourth trade. Interest rates increased from 4% to 5% and the bank, though it lost money on the underlying bond, benefited from the swap. For illustrative purposes, the bond is valued before the interest rate change and immediately after the interest rate change (Table 10.11).

Table 10.11

Cash flows		Notional	3,000,000
Yield		Coupon	6%
Libor	4%	5%	
Credit spread	2%	2%	
Coupon	6%	7%	
Year 1	£180,000	£180,000	
Year 2	£180,000	£180,000	
Year 3	£180,000	£180,000	
Year 4	£180,000	£180,000	
Year 5	£3,180,000	£3,180,000	
Present value	£3,000,000	£2,876,994	
Loss		−£123,006	

The bank entered into a swap with a swap counterparty where the bank agrees to pay fixed 4% and receive floating. If the swap rate goes from 4% to 5%, the gain on the swap is shown in Table 10.12.

Intuitively, the value of a swap is simply the present value of the expected future cash flows. Since the swap rate has gone up, the bank expects to receive on average 5% every year for the next five years and pay only 4%, which is the fixed rate it locked into. The notional of the swap is £3,000,000 and so the net cash flow each year is £30,000 or 1%. We simply attempt to anticipate the future cash flows on the assumption that the current swap rate remains constant and discount those cash flows at the prevailing swap rate.

For intuitive purposes, Table 10.13 simply shows that if the counterparty to the swap gave the bank £129,884, the bank would be able to replicate the cash flows of £30,000 per year. The figure of £5.319 represents the balance at the start of the year (£106,379) multiplied by 5%.

One final point for consideration is that the change in the value of the swap (at £129,884) is slightly larger than the loss suffered on the underlying (£123,006). The difference may

Table 10.12   Swap valuation

Swap notional	3,000,000
Bank pays fixed	4%
Bank receives floating	5%
Expected cash flows	
Year 1	£30,000
Year 2	£30,000
Year 3	£30,000
Year 4	£30,000
Year 5	£30,000
Net present value	£129,884

Table 10.13   Illustration of swap valuation

Opening balance	Interest	Flows withdrawn	Closing balance
£129,884	£6,494	−£30,000	£106,379
£106,379	£5,319	−£30,000	£81,697
£81,697	£4,085	−£30,000	£55,782
£55,782	£2,789	−£30,000	£28,571
£28,571	£1,429	−£30,000	£0

seem small, but it causes a huge headache in practice because it suggests that the swap is slightly ineffective in hedging the underlying exposure. Where a hedge proves to be slightly ineffective, the accounting requirements under IAS 39 can be quite cumbersome, requiring very complex journal entries. For this example and in the interests of simplicity, we will make the assumption that the swap is 100% effective.

We can now proceed with the reconciliation. The total gains and losses from exchange traded derivatives and non-exchange traded derivatives are shown in Table 10.14, along with the allocation of those profits.

Table 10.14   Allocation of gains/losses on financial instruments

Cash paid	−£60,556	
Change in prime broker	£129,884	£69,329
Profit & Loss	−£55,556	
Client	−£10,000	
Fair value	£5,000	
Cash flow	£129,884	£69,329

To recap, the bank pays £60,556 to the broker in respect of variation margin (the initial margin will be dealt with later). The prime broker owes the bank £129,884 in respect of the swap.

The Profit & Loss account is charged with the loss on the foreign exchange position (trade 1). The client will pay £10,000 in respect of losses he has made on the equity position (trade 2). The final two transactions represent gains that the bank has made but is not allowed to recognise immediately because the relevant derivatives were designated as cash flow and fair value hedges. To recap, any gains or losses on a cash flow hedge go to Equity Reserve and with fair value hedge accounting, any gain on a derivative is deemed to be matched by a loss on the underlying. In this case, because Libor on the corporate loan is going to be less than initially expected, the underlying loan is adjusted by the gain on the derivative.

Most accountants feel more comfortable with journal entries. So, the journal entries necessary to reflect the above reconciliation are shown in Table 10.15.

Table 10.15

	Debit	**Credit**
Cash		£60,556
Prime brokerage account	£129,884	
Client account	£10,000	
Retained profits	£55,556	
Equity reserve		£129,884
Loans to customers		£5,000
	£195,440	£195,440

There are two further adjustments that we must make to complete the reconciliation. Firstly, we must recognise that the initial deposit (or initial margin) with the exchange has dropped by £5900 and secondly, there is a balance in the Equity Reserve account which must be released to the Profit & Loss account over the next 90 days. This relates to a previous cash flow hedge which was closed out in December. The hedge protected the bank against interest rates falling between January and March. The gain on the hedge was initially transferred to Equity Reserve and now must be taken from Equity Reserve to the Profit & Loss account. The amount to be released per day is £111.11.

Table 10.16 shows the balance sheet after adjustments. The client account has increased by £10,000 because the clients owe more money to cover their losses. The adjustment to the customer loan is a fair value hedge and the cash is reduced by £54,656 – the amount paid to the exchange. The change in the prime brokerage account reflects the profit on the swap. The

Table 10.16   Final balance sheet

	Original balance sheet	Variation/ broker adjustment	Initial margin adjustment	Transfer of hedge	Final balance sheet	
Balance sheet						
Client accounts	£40,000	£10,000			£50,000	
Loans to customers	£900,000	−£5,000			£895,000	
Cash	£21,500	−£60,556	£5,900		−£33,156	
Initial deposit	£37,500		−£5,900		£31,600	
Prime brokerage accounts	£1,000	£129,884			£130,884	£1,074,329
Customer deposits	£980,000				£980,000	
Shareholders' funds					£0	
Shares issued	£8,000				£8,000	
Equity reserves	£10,000	£129,884		−£111	£139,773	
Retained profits	£2,000	−£55,556		£111	−£53,444	£1,074,329

Equity Reserve account changes primarily because of the gain on the swap with the prime broker and the retained profit changes principally because of the speculative position on the foreign exchange contract.

10.5 CONCLUSION

What puzzles many risk managers is why this simple reconciliation was not carried out at Barings and SocGen. Nick Leeson, the Barings trader who was based in Singapore, was forced to ask Barings of London for huge amounts of cash to cover his loss-making positions with various exchanges. Should Barings in London not have asked questions as to why this cash was needed when Leeson claimed he was making profits on his trades? Eventually, as the back office started catching up with him, Leeson was forced to forge faxes from 'clients' suggesting that not Leeson but Barings customers had made losses. Clearly, the back office should have verified these independently and not relied on what Leeson gave them. Similarly, the SocGen trader Jerome Kerviel must have placed SocGen in a situation where they were paying away huge amounts of variation margin but were not recording the payments as losses. Also, initial reports investigating the fraud suggests that like Leeson, Kerviel may have relied on forged confirmations to hide his positions.

11

Moving Towards Mark-to-Market Accounting

11.1 INTRODUCTION

As emphasised in previous chapters, a huge debate exists within the accounting profession on whether they should show assets and liabilities at fair value (i.e. current market value) or at cost on the balance sheet. Showing everything at fair value has the advantage of portraying economic reality, but trying to obtain a correct market value is difficult. A second advantage, one that the IASB recognised when they designed the Fair Value Option (FVO), is that the accounting framework is in line with risk management and regulation – where only the fair value is used and the cost is ignored. Indeed, the EU have clashed with the IASB on this matter, resulting in the EU amending the IAS 39 standard as we discuss below. However, the market value of certain assets and liabilities depends on assumptions and judgements, but the judgements and assumptions used might be those that maximise incentive payments and bonuses rather than portray economic reality or give a true and fair view. Sometimes, shareholders might not benefit from knowing the market value of certain assets and liabilities. If, for instance, an individual or institution has a portfolio of banking shares which it intends to hold for a very long period of time, then the volatility of the current share price is less important (or in many cases, not at all important) than the dividend income. Indeed, showing everything at market value can often have a spiral effect and create unnecessary panics – particularly when auditors become ultra conservative in the midst of credit crises, as has happened recently. That said, if the accounting profession is allowed to hide market values, we end up with off-balance sheet problems and the ability for entities to hide losses and risks which, in part, has led to the current credit crises. In this chapter, we look at the debate between fair value accounting and showing items at cost. We once again look at how accountants have approached the dilemma and consider possible improvements that they could make. We examine how banks measure risks and rewards outside the accounting rules and identify whether accountants should continue to go it alone with their cumbersome and bureaucratic rules to match risk with reward or whether they should instead adopt the methodology that banks have used for decades. Needless to say, the conclusion is that the accounting profession should not work in isolation but instead learn from the risk measurement methodology that banks use – such as VaR and Basel 2 – and then develop accounting standards that match risk with rewards correctly, rather than use their clumsy and confusing approach as currently (i.e. fair value hedge accounting, cash flow hedge accounting, fair value options, testing for hedge effectiveness, carve-out options, etc.).

11.2 LIQUIDITY AND FAIR VALUE

It is understandable that banks would express concern over the IASB's desire to get banks to show everything at market or fair value on the balance sheet. One of the problems with complex financial instruments is that when the markets go into panic mode, there is a spiral effect. When default rates on mortgages increase, the fair or market value of those mortgages drops. So too does the value of securities based on mortgages, such as credit default swaps and bonds issued from securitisations. These falls in value force banks that show assets and liabilities at fair value on the balance sheet to recognise losses. The losses lead to a reduction of shareholders' funds, which attracts the attention of the regulators. In those cases, the regulators will force banks to reduce the risk on their balance sheet by restricting new loans – and this restriction may in turn force the banks to increase the collateral or margin on existing loans. It is unlikely that banks would force corporates and individuals to repay their loans early, but they would have no qualms about forcing hedge funds to do so. The hedge funds that are normally highly leveraged are forced into a quick-fire sale and flood the market with complex securities, and this in turn sets the chain reaction off again. One important contributor to the credit crises of 2007 was the contagion effect, i.e. it doesn't matter how profitable a hedge fund or bank may be, if their borrowings are high, everyone panics and forces even profitable institutions to possible bankruptcy.

One might be tempted to forgive the likes of Citibank and Carlyle Hedge Fund, who clearly found themselves trapped in this spiral. The former was forced to raise more equity at a time when its share price was deflated and to cut back on loans and increase margin calls. Carlyle, on the other hand, was forced to hand over its assets to its lenders, who subsequently sold them at distressed prices. There is certainly an argument that if both entities had been allowed to avoid showing assets at market value on the balance sheet, at least until the market picked up, they might have been able to avoid the heavy losses that were inflicted upon their shareholders.

There are many conservative banks, well financed, that will be able to get through the credit crunch unscathed. At the other extreme are banks that have used the short-term commercial paper market to finance the purchase of long-term illiquid instruments. Clearly, as the value of these illiquid instruments drops, the holders of commercial paper will force the bank to offload their assets at distressed prices. The well-financed bank, however, can continue to enjoy the high yield on these papers. There were probably a lot of hedge funds that, during the credit crises, were making money – i.e. the yields on their investments exceeded their borrowing costs – but because of the panic that engulfed the market, these same hedge funds were exposed to very heavy (mark-to-market) losses. In other words, the value of the assets (as determined by a very panicked market) was under, or if over, only barely over, the value of the liabilities. It is the equivalent of a buy-to-let landlord, say, earning a rental yield of 8% on borrowing costs of 6% – yet the bank is forcing the landlord to sell the property because the market value of the property has gone down. Fortunately, buy-to-let landlords do not have to calculate the fair value of their property on a day-to-day basis and are therefore spared the problems that hedge funds and financial institutions face.

The Japanese experience

One topic considered in the financial press during the credit crunch turmoil was whether the auditors should relax the accounting rules where a credit spiral exists. According to the *Financial Times*:[1]

---

[1] 'An unforgiving eye – Bankers cry foul over fair value accounting', *Financial Times*, 14 March 2008.

During Japan's bank crises a decade ago, the Japanese regulators performed a unified audit of the banks in a bid to offer investors better transparency and prevent market confidence from being damaged by a continual 'drip feed' of bad news.

Softening the accounting rules was a tactic used during the Latin American crises. Regulators knew very well that some losses were hidden from view, but there was an agreement between the regulators and the auditors that the auditors would slow down impairment and adverse impacts on the Profit & Loss account. In a post-Enron environment, however, auditors themselves may be the first to object to instances where they are obliged to conceal losses from shareholders. More than ever, accountants want to appear to have corrected themselves from the Enron-style problems and of course want to avoid the wrath of angry shareholders.

11.3 BANKING VS. TRADING BOOK

Introduction

Banks, along with companies, are required to show certain assets and liabilities at cost and others at market value. This 'mixed model' can create a lot of distortion and confusion. In 2003, these problems came into the public domain when, to the embarrassment of the IASB, the then French President Jacques Chirac complained about the many problems that IAS 39 was creating for the banking community. The EU also informed the IASB that they were unhappy with the IAS 39 standard and went on to alter the standard, by changing certain requirements even when the IASB was reluctant to do so. These changes became known as the 'carve-out' features, adding to confusion by creating two versions of the already complex IAS 39 standard – the amended version, which the EU has adopted and the original version, as prescribed by the IASB.

Banking vs. trading book

Banking book

The Banking book carries on what are known as 'traditional' banking activities, i.e. borrowing from one set of customers (depositors) and lending to other customers. The customer loans are financed not only from deposits, but also through the inter-bank market. Banks usually manage these books with the intention of earning the interest margin as opposed to speculation. The deposits and loans are therefore classified as 'Loans & Receivables' and are shown at cost (as opposed to fair value) on the balance sheet. Only the effective interest, and loan write-offs, go through the P&L.
  Problems with accounting for banking book:

1. Customer loans and deposits are usually shown at cost on the balance sheet, thus hiding some potential losses – such as losses arising from interest rate movements.
2. Derivatives hedging the bank from interest rate, foreign exchange and credit exposure must generally be shown at market value. This mixed model approach creates artificial volatility in the Profit & Loss account.
3. This artificial volatility can be 'cured' through special hedge accounting rules, namely 'fair value' and 'cash flow' hedge accounting – the rules are not simple and can lead to bureaucracy and confusion.

(Continued)

4. These hedge accounting rules are very rigid and cannot deal effectively with 'demandable deposits'. The IASB appear to be in disagreement with the EU on this matter.
5. A further layer of complication arises with the 'fair value option', which in effect means that a bank can now elect to show at fair value certain 'Loans & Receivables'. This was a second area of dispute between the IASB and the EU, but both parties have now reached a compromise solution discussed below.

Trading book

Banks do have traders who 'take positions' on the markets (i.e. speculate) and also engage in market-making activities. Obviously, if a bank is using financial instruments to take positions it cannot classify them as 'Loans & Receivables' or 'Held to Maturity', and so must show them at fair value or market value on the balance sheet, with the difference normally going through the P&L (except for 'Available for Sale' financial instruments which must go through the Equity Reserve).

Problems with accounting for trading book:

1. Some financial instruments are difficult to value.
2. There may be a conflict of interest between the correct or 'true and fair view' value and the value that maximises incentive/bonus schemes.

Banks throughout the world tend to divide their balance sheet between the trading book and the banking book. Although the distinction is not always clear-cut and consistent within banks, the general trend is to confine to the banking book loans made to customers and deposits taken from customers as well as other liabilities (where there are insufficient deposits) to finance loans made. Normally, banks do not 'trade' or speculate in the banking book. Their intention is usually to hold the loan to maturity, though this is not always the case, particularly with banks that securitise their loans. The trading book, on the other hand, comprises proprietary trading (speculation) and market-making activities – i.e. being willing to buy and sell securities to customers who ask for a quote. The profit for such market-making activities is the difference between the bid–offer spread. From an accounting perspective, the general convention is to show everything in the banking book at cost and everything in the trading book at market value. Obviously, the standard setters want to avoid the possibility that banks will speculate and hide losses. In the banking book, the intention is simply to earn the interest margin.

The mixed model problem

As discussed earlier, the accounting standard setters tend to apply a confusing mixed model approach when dealing with financial assets and liabilities. A bank that originates a loan with a corporate tends to record this at cost on the balance sheet; any changes in market value are ignored. Yet, if the bank bought a corporate bond, issued by the same company with the intention of selling it in the short term, then it would probably be classified as trading and would have to be shown on the balance sheet at market value not at cost. A corporate bond has broadly the same value and economic exposure and fair value as a loan (as long as the terms and conditions are the same), but the accounting treatment is entirely different. The main reason for the different accounting treatment is, to a large extent, based on intention and subjectivity. If a bank lends money to a corporate, it normally holds on to this loan for a long period of time, often to maturity, and its intention is not necessarily to speculate on the company's credit spread but to simply provide a banking service. In reality, banks securitise their loans, therefore there is often an intention to sell before maturity, but we will ignore that complication here. Having different accounting treatments for the same type of assets was not normally a problem, either for banks or accounting standard setters who want to avoid or reduce opportunities for creative accounting. However, when banks became heavy users of interest rate derivatives and credit derivatives, in order to hedge the banking book, problems started to arise.

Prior to IAS 39, banks recorded derivatives at 'cost' on the balance sheet. For the majority of cases, the derivative used was an interest rate swap which normally has a zero cost up-front. The result was that derivatives were kept off-balance sheet, and therefore exposed to the usual problems, namely cherry-picking. Credit derivatives were treated in a similar manner. The problem with this accounting is that if the derivative makes money, the bank might be tempted to cash in those derivatives that have made money and release this extra cash through the Profit & Loss account.

Initial IAS 39 solution

To stop off-balance sheet abuse, IAS 39 required that all derivatives be brought on to the balance sheet at market value, regardless of intention. This created an unusual situation in the banking book. The underlying assets (i.e. loans and deposits) were shown at cost while the derivative hedging the exposure was shown at market value. Obviously, if interest rates changed, the market value of the derivative would also change but would be counterbalanced by a change in the underlying, resulting in (provided the hedge was implemented properly) a nil effect on the profitability of the bank. However, under the IAS 39 accounting rules, only the change in the derivative would be recorded on the balance sheet. The entity was not allowed to alter the underlying asset or liability and it was therefore shown at cost.

Artificial volatility

Artificial volatility arises when banks or companies are required, because of obscure accounting rules, to show certain assets at cost and others at market value. The 'mixed model' treatment of showing the underlying assets/liabilities at cost and the derivatives at market value leads to artificial volatility; the accounting profit jumps up and down as interest rates change, in line with the derivative. To overcome this, the accounting standards introduced cash flow and fair value hedge accounting. Under these two rules, a bank could put gains and losses through Equity Reserve (cash flow hedge) or could alter the value of the underlying asset/liability on the balance sheet (fair value hedge). Although these approaches are very bureaucratic, requiring extensive documentation and testing for hedge effectiveness, etc., they did to some extent reduce the problems of artificial volatility. However, many banks have argued that even with fair value and cash flow hedge accounting, the rules do not work well all the time and artificial volatility could result even if the banks availed themselves of these hedging measures. The problem is particularly acute when it comes to deposit accounts and current accounts, where the interest payable is below the current market rate.

IAS 39 carve-outs

Fair value own debt. Recently, the IASB introduced rules that allowed entities to show their liabilities at fair value rather than at cost. The EU objected to this and created an additional 'carve-out' which restricted entities from showing their debt at fair value. In 2005, however, the EU and the IASB came to an agreement whereby certain entities are allowed to show their debt at fair value as opposed to cost provided certain conditions are met – namely artificial volatility would arise if the liabilities were shown at cost on the balance sheet. Also, the entity must prove that it normally uses the fair value and not the book value when measuring and hedging the risk associated with these financial instruments.

Relaxing of hedging rules. The EU asked the IASB to consider rewording some of the hedge accounting rules, particularly in instances where banks hedge deposit accounts. The IASB declined and so the EU came up with an amended version of the standard. Under the amended version, banks are able to apply hedge accounting more leniently – with the result that the published Profit & Loss account is, in some circumstances, less volatile under the amended version compared with the original version.

The principal problem is contained in IAS 39, paragraph AG 99C. Consider a case where a bank receives £1000 from a customer and agrees to pay interest for three years at 4% per annum at a time when Libor is 5%. Clearly, the bank is making a profit margin of 1% on this transaction. Suppose the bank is worried about interest rates rising. It may decide to lock in the margin of 1% by entering into a three-year receive fixed pay floating swap with a notional of £1000. Unfortunately, this swap would not work as the coupon on the swap is effectively the current Libor rate of 5% while the deposit account has a coupon of 4%. A possible solution is to break the deposit down between a hedged value and a residual value and declare the hedged value as the 'hedged item'. The example below illustrates this. Using this approach, 100% effectiveness could be achieved, but on the hedged item only. In this case the 'hedged item' is greater than the cash flows of the underlying. This procedure is prohibited by AG 99C. The result is that entities are only allowed to hedge deposit accounts on an individual basis rather than an aggregate basis. The restricting sentences in AG 99C are:

> If a portion of the cash flows of a financial asset or financial liability is designated as the hedged item, that designated portion must be less than the total cash flows of the asset or liability. For example, in the case of a liability whose effective interest rate is below Libor, an entity cannot designate (a) a portion of the liability equal to the principal amount plus interest at LIBOR and (b) a negative residual portion

Table 11.1 illustrates the situation.

An entity receives a deposit from a customer. For the sake of simplicity, the entity intends to lend this money on the inter-bank market where it will receive Libor. As the deposit rate 4% is less than the current Libor rate 5%, the entity expects to make a profit of about 1% per annum, which it decides to lock in using a swap. The swap chosen is one with a tenor of five years, where the entity receives fixed and pays the floating Libor rate. In theory, it is difficult for the entity to get an exact hedge, so it breaks down the underlying between a deposit account that pays Libor and the residual which is effectively the profit on the deposit account. It then matches the swap with the hedged item (where it achieves 100% effectiveness) and leaves

Table 11.1 Hedging a deposit account with a swap

	Deposit	Swap					
Notional	£1000	£1000					
Deposit rate	4%						
Swap rate Libor							
Tenor	5	5					
Libor		5%					

	Year	0	1	2	3	4	5	
Expected cash flow		£1000	−£40	−£40	−£40	−£40	−£1040	a
Hedged item		£1000	−£50	−£50	−£50	−£50	−£1050	b
Residual		£0	£10	£10	£10	£10	£10	c
Swap		−£1000	£50	£50	£50	£50	£1050	d

the profit element unhedged. This means that the profit element is exposed to interest rate changes, though the amount of the change would be quite small.

Although this is a practical solution, the accounting standards (AG 99C) won't allow this simple treatment. The standard setters argue (with some legitimacy) that if the above approach is chosen, the exposure on the swap is greater than the exposure on the underlying deposit. Therefore, the swap is more exposed to interest rate changes than the underlying deposit. In other words, the underlying position is 'over-hedged'. If the standard setters allowed the hedge to be more sensitive than the underlying, they would open the floodgates to off-balance sheet speculation, which of course they don't want to do. For this reason, they say that the 'hedged item' cannot exceed the underlying cash flows. In effect, line b above cannot exceed line a. It is nevertheless a restriction that creates a huge headache. In December 2006 the EBF[2] suggested an additional set of hedge accounting rules, known as Interest Margin Hedging (IMH). However, the IASB understandably threw cold water on this idea – there are far too many rules as it is. The matter appears to remain unresolved.

11.4 VAR

Introduction

The risk measurement methodology used by the regulators, namely Value at Risk (VaR), offers a potential solution to this problem. Before analysing it, we need to look at the argument about whether the accounting framework which we are currently using needs to be examined. There are plenty of weaknesses in the accounting standards but by and large, outside of financial instruments, they can cope. However, in the world of financial instruments, those weaknesses in the standards clearly show the strain that the accounting standard setters operate under. One main problem is that they have developed a framework for accounting without considering the complexity or sophistication of financial instruments. Therefore, revising the standards to deal with the complexities of financial instruments becomes almost impossible. Although banks employ rocket science for certain areas of risk management, the measurement and control of risk in the banking book is a relatively well-trodden path and unsophisticated compared

---

[2] European Banking Federation, 'IASB exposure – Draft on exposures qualifying for hedge accounting', 10 January 2008, http://www.efrag.org/files/EFRAG%20public%20letters/IAS%2039%20Amendments%20Exposures%20Qualifying%20for%20 Hedge%20Accounting/CL%2014%20Enc-0011-1%20_D0045A-EBFPositionIASBExposureDraftIMH-IAS39_.pdf

with other aspects of banking. However, the accounting standards appear to be having a lot of possibly unnecessary difficulty even with this relatively simple area. Worse, the accounting standards themselves restrict how a bank might hedge, with the result that banks end up being forced to use a convoluted non-portfolio procedure for hedging. Also, they are often forced to use complicated illiquid derivatives rather than simple ones. This, of course, brings about an extra layer of operational and liquidity risk. The irony is that in introducing a standard to measure and control risks, the IASB has simply encouraged a more complicated, confusing and riskier environment that lacks transparency.

Merging VaR and hedging principles

The chief problem with the accounting standards in this area is that they are attempting to measure risk, so that instances where entities increase risk/exposure are treated differently from instances where entities are reducing risk. In short, where entities increase risk they are speculating and the standard setters, in the interests of preventing speculators from hiding losses, require entities to show the fair value of all derivatives on the balance sheet and any changes through the Profit & Loss account. Where entities are reducing risk, i.e. hedging, the accounting standards attempt to match the volatility of the hedging derivative with the underlying transaction (that is, allow entities to avoid artificial volatility by using CF and FV accounting). Few can deny that these are sound principles. What is happening, however, is that the standard setters – through IAS 39 – are rewriting the rules of risk management in an unnecessarily complex way and are not synchronising their efforts with best practices in risk management, though there is evidence that they are slowly moving in the right direction.[3]

The illustration below shows how VaR principles could be used to hedge a portfolio of demandable deposits, without infringing the golden rule of AG 99C where entities are prevented from over-hedging. What VaR aims to do in relation to risk management is to break assets and liabilities down into zero coupon bonds, then collect all the zero coupon bonds with similar risk characteristics together. From this it is possible to identify natural hedges. VaR is then calculated on the remaining exposure and the objective of the accountant is simply to ensure that the entity does not over-hedge or, more precisely, to ensure that derivatives which qualify for hedge accounting are only used in accordance with the entity's risk policies as stated and disclosed under IFRS 7.

In the example in Table 11.2, a bank has borrowed money from a depositor for five years and used the money to buy a corporate bond which also has a tenor of five years and pays 2% over Libor. The bank is worried about interest rate movements and therefore wants to hedge against interest rate falls. Firstly, the interest rate risk is obvious – the bank has a fixed liability, i.e. the deposit from the customer, and is using this to buy a bond which pays Libor plus a spread. A possible solution to the problem is to use a swap to convert the fixed deposit into a floating deposit. However, IAS 39, paragraph AG 99C places restrictions on the type of swap that can be used. This restriction makes portfolio hedging (i.e. hedging a group of deposits collectively rather than individually) difficult. The bank must decide, therefore, to hedge the deposits individually or not to hedge at all. If it does decide to hedge, on a portfolio basis the derivatives may not qualify for hedge accounting and this will lead to artificial volatility.

---

[3] The Fair Value Option allows entities to show assets and liabilities (along with their hedging derivatives) at market value which coincides with current best practice in risk management.

Table 11.2   Cash flow ladder

	Corporate bond								
Credit spread	2%								
Libor	5%								
Deposit margin	1%								
Tenor	5								
Notional	£1000								

	Cash flow bond	1	2	3	4	5			
Credit spread		£20	£20	£20	£20	£20			
Deposit margin		£10	£10	£10	£10	£10			
Deposit Libor		−£50	−£50	−£50	−£50	−£1050			
Net exposure		−£20	−£20	−£20	−£20	−£1020	5%	−£870	
							6%	−£832	£39

In practice, what the risk manager does – in line with current VaR methodology – is to break the asset down between a Libor bond and the extra cash flows. Therefore, the corporate bond could be broken down between the credit spread and a straightforward Libor bond. As the Libor bond is floating, it is not exposed to interest rate change and is therefore ignored for risk analysis purposes. The credit spread, however, represents a future stream of cash and the present value of this cash flow changes when interest rates change. Therefore, it is exposed to interest rate risk and so is broken down into five zero coupon bonds.

Next we deal with the customer deposit, which is a liability. Once again, the deposit is broken down between fixed coupon Libor bonds. A Libor bond is one that has a coupon equal to the current swap rate. As the bond is fixed, it is exposed to interest rate changes so the risk manager must represent it as a series of cash flows – i.e. £50 each year and £1050 in the final year when the principal is repaid. The deposit margin is shown as an asset since it represents the profit (or additional cash flows) that the bank makes because it is paying the customer interest which is below the current market rate.

From this we can identify a net exposure. The figures are the equivalent of being short a bond for five years with a coupon of 2% and a principal of five years. If interest rates go down, therefore, the value of the bond goes up but since it is represented as a negative figure, it follows that if interest rates go down the bank will lose money and if interest rates rise the bank will make money. The benefit of breaking the cash flows down into zero coupon bonds is that the bank can see exactly its overall interest rate exposure and determine the most appropriate hedge.

The final calculation illustrates how the risk sensitivity is calculated. If interest rates are 5% the present value of the cash stream is −£870, and when interest rates rise to 6% the present value goes to −£832. It follows that the bank gains £39 (rounded) when interest rates rise by 1%. If the bank has a policy of hedging its entire interest rate exposure, it will need to develop a portfolio of derivatives with a risk profile which is exactly opposite to the underlying exposure. Table 11.3 shows the hedge.

In practice, the bank will have difficulty getting a swap which pays a fixed coupon of 2% at a time when the current Libor is 5%. So, the bank could consider getting a market swap (i.e. at 5%) and adjusting the notional so that the risk profile of the swap broadly matches the risk profile of the underlying. A swap with a notional of £917 (calculated either by trial and error or Goalseek on Excel) reveals that the most suitable swap is one which has a coupon of

Table 11.3   Hedging solution

		1	2	3	4	5
		−£20	−£20	−£20	−£20	−£1020
Hedge	Net exposure	£46	£46	£46	£46	£962
Exposure after hedge		£26	£26	£26	£26	−£58

Swap	£917
Coupon	5%

5%	£917	
6%	£878	−£39
Sensitivity after hedge		−0

5% and a notional of £917, where the bank receives fixed and pays floating. The sensitivity after the hedge is therefore potentially zero, since the interest rate sensitivity on the swap is opposite to that of the loan.

Unfortunately, despite matching the interest rate sensitivity, the bank still has an exposure. If, for instance, the yield curve changes slope – i.e. short-term interest rates go up but long-term rates (for example, the five-year rate) go down – the bank is left with an exposure. However, with a more sophisticated derivative portfolio, it is possible to reduce considerably this exposure so that the 'Exposure after hedge' line contains a row of zeros or figures close to zero. The role of the accountant is simply to make sure that the hedge sensitivity is close to but cannot exceed the underlying cash flow. Therefore, the entity is adhering to the spirit of paragraph AG 99C but is hedging on a portfolio basis rather than on an individual basis.

The accounting standards appear to have gone off the rails a bit in this area, because they have failed to consider the basic tenets of interest rate risk management. As long as they continue to do so, they will force the banks to use confusing hedging strategies and will run into pressure from various lobbyists including the European Banking Federation, who have written consistently about the practical problems that IAS 39 poses.

Fair Value Option

The FVO (as distinct from fair value hedging) was the second area of disagreement between the EU and the IASB, resulting in the EU 'carving out' the rules in an amended standard. However, this carve-out was intended to be temporary and, following amendments by the IASB, the matter is now resolved. The rule was introduced principally as a means of allowing financial institutions like banks to reduce artificial volatility, particularly when the hedges are legitimate. IAS 39.9 states that under the FVO, an entity is allowed to show certain financial instruments at fair value with any change going through the Profit & Loss account as long as two important conditions are met. Firstly, if the entity can prove that an 'accounting mismatch' or artificial volatility would arise if the financial instrument was carried at cost. Secondly, the risks of the financial instrument are normally measured and controlled by identifying the market value and then the risk sensitivities and hedging accordingly. These two conditions were necessary because the EU was worried about banks having the ability to make a profit if they suffered a credit downgrading. For instance, bank X might originate a loan for £10m for five years at 6%. As soon as the loan is taken out, bank X loses its credit rating and therefore the fair value of the loan drops. If bank X was allowed to show the debt at fair value, it would be able to show a profit as soon as it was downgraded. Also, if the directors' bonus system was poorly designed, a situation could easily arise where a downgrading would lead to an increase in the directors' bonus. This would, of course, encourage the directors to take on more gearing and make the bank more risky. As stated, the FVO can only be used where it is the only way to eliminate or reduce artificial volatility and where the fair value is normally used for risk management purposes. Furthermore, where the fair value is used, IFRS 7 contains detailed disclosure requirements.

VaR

As stated earlier the IASB, through IAS 39, is introducing hedging rules which are quite different from the way risk is measured in practice. In practice, most banks use VaR to measure, control and hedge risks. VaR measures the maximum loss that an entity can suffer over a given time period and over a given confidence level. In practical terms, VaR measures the volatility of the Profit & Loss account of a particular portfolio or entity. Regulators became concerned at the extent to which traders were speculating within various banks and they wanted some means to measure and control the risks. VaR is the preferred method to measure market risk and is now used by the majority of international banks. Where a bank is taking on excessive risks, the regulators will insist that the bank finances itself with more equity. This discourages banks from taking on too much risk and they are therefore encouraged either to cut back on their trading or to hedge some of their exposures. Since accountants are required to disclose the entity's risk profile under IFRS 7, many banks tend to simply disclose their VaR figures in their discussion on risk management. Although VaR was originally designed for the trading book, many banks that have a foreign exchange or interest rate exposure within the banking book use VaR to estimate the risks and to decide an appropriate hedging strategy. Clearly, the best way to hedge is to look for natural hedges as far as possible and then to hedge the remainder. For instance, if a bank buys an asset denominated in dollars and uses a dollar loan to finance 70% of this asset, then the liability acts as a natural hedge to the asset and the risk manager therefore needs derivatives to hedge the remaining 30%. Unfortunately, the accounting standard setters don't always see things so clearly, and often insist that the asset be hedged using one derivative while the liability is hedged with another. This is of course wasteful, expensive and time-consuming. Furthermore, another important difference between risk managers and accountants is that risk managers don't go for 100% hedging. Very often they can use simple standardised derivatives and achieve, say, 95%. The standard setters, however, think differently. They insist on 100% hedging and in cases where 100% hedging cannot be achieved, extensive documenting and testing for hedge effectiveness is required. Very often too, the IASB will put pressure on the entity to use special tailor-made derivatives while risk managers find that standardised derivatives, though not 100% accurate, are cheaper and do a reasonably good job at hedging. There is also the risk that under the IASB rules a hedge may fail its effectiveness test and therefore be reclassified as speculation, even though it achieves its purpose of reducing VaR.

VaR illustration

The illustration in Table 11.4 shows how VaR operates.

A portfolio manager has two assets in his portfolio. Asset 1 has a weighting of 30% and a volatility of 25%. The volatility is effectively a standard deviation calculation and shows the extent to which the asset price moves away from the mean. Needless to say, risky assets

Table 11.4 VaR illustration

Value of portfolio	£1,000,000	
Confidence level	95%	
Time period	1	
	Asset 1	Asset 2
Standard deviation	25%	26%
Weighting	30%	70%
Correlation coefficient		0.70
Variance of portfolio	0.05786	
Standard deviation	24.05%	
No. of standard deviations	1.644853627	
VaR (%)	0.395651411	
VaR (£)	£395,651	

are very volatile. Asset 2 is slightly more volatile and comprises 70% of the portfolio. The correlation between the two assets is 0.7. The first step is to calculate the volatility of the portfolio. If the assets had a correlation of 1 with each other, the volatility of the portfolio would be somewhere between 25% and 26% and given that most of the portfolio is invested in the second asset, we would expect the volatility of the portfolio to be close to 26% (it is in fact 24.7% – see Table 11.5). However, as the correlation is less than 1 it follows (in this case) that the volatility of the portfolio will be 24.05%. The next step is to calculate the maximum loss that the portfolio will make for a given probability. In practice, VaR uses a probability of either 99% or 95% (the regulators prefer 99%). The Normal distribution table tells us that 95% of the time, a variable will not lose more than 1.645 standard deviations. So, multiplying the portfolio size £1,000,000 by the volatility 24.05% and the scalar 1.645, we calculate the VaR of the portfolio to be £395,651. This VaR figure is then used by the regulators under the Basel 2 rules to assist in determining how much shareholders' funds (broadly, tier-one capital) should be used to support the risks. In other words, the maximum loss we expect to make 95% of the time is £395,651.

Table 11.5 shows how the 'undiversified VaR' is calculated. The undiversified VaR assumes that all assets in the portfolio have a correlation of 1 with each other. In other words, the

Table 11.5 VaR illustration: diversification

Value of portfolio	£1,000,000	
Confidence level	95%	
Time period	1	
	Asset 1	Asset 2
Standard deviation	25%	26%
Weighting	30%	70%
Correlation coefficient		1.00
Variance of portfolio	0.06605	
Standard deviation	25.70%	
No. of standard deviations	1.64485363	
VaR (%)	0.42272738	
VaR (£)	£422,727	

undiversified VaR takes the pessimistic (or prudent) assumption that if one asset in the portfolio loses money then all other assets lose money at the same time. Needless to say, the undiversified VaR will always be greater than the diversified VaR.

VaR is not only used by regulators, banks use it for internal risk management purposes. If a bank is considering investing in a hedge fund, it will require details of the potential VaR of the hedge fund in order to ensure that the proposed hedge fund investment fits in with the bank's overall risk appetite. Furthermore, VaR is used by banks to allocate limits to traders. If the bank is well diversified, it has a lower risk profile than one which is heavily concentrated on a particular sector. VaR is designed to measure this diversification. Finally, VaR is often used in the calculation of traders' bonuses. The process is known as RAROC (Risk Adjusted Return on Capital). This process distinguishes traders who take very little risk from those who do – the latter would not receive as high a bonus as the former. In practice, however, RAROC is difficult to implement and it is reasonable to say that it is not implemented correctly in all banks, particularly given the high bonuses that were paid immediately before credit losses were announced in 2007.

We now return to the example in Table 11.2 where we broke down a corporate bond along with a deposit account into a series of zero coupon bonds in order to evaluate the overall risk profile.

Line a in Table 11.6 shows the net exposure to the various interest rates as calculated in Table 11.2. A 'weighting matrix' can be calculated by simply getting the present value of the future cash flows. We have assumed in this case that the yield curve is flat at 5% and therefore use this figure to calculate the present values. If a bank wanted to calculate the undiversified VaR at that point it would simply download the interest volatilities from a data provider (such as Riskmetrics). With the volatilities the bank could calculate undiversified VaR, which in this case is £9.06. The bank could also, if it wished, download a correlation table to identify the diversified VaR – however, we will ignore this complication here.

Table 11.6   VaR for banking book

	1	2	3	4	5	
Net exposure	−£20	−£20	−£20	−£20	−£1020	a
Hedge	£46	£46	£46	£46	£962	b
Exposure after hedge	£26	£26	£26	£26	-£58	c
Volatility	2%	1%	2%	1%	1%	
Yield	5%					
Before hedge						
Weighting matrix	−£19	−£18	−£17	−£16	−£799	
Undiversified VaR	−£0.38	−£0.18	−£0.35	−£0.16	−£7.99	£9.06
After hedge						
Weighting matrix	£25	£23	£22	£21	−£45	
Undiversified VaR	£0.49	£0.23	£0.45	£0.21	−£0.45	£0.93

Once it puts the hedge in place, it now has a new weighting matrix and recalculates the VaR. The hedge has brought VaR down from £9.06 to £0.93. Unfortunately, although the hedge has clearly worked in this example, IAS 39 would probably not allow the swap as a hedge since it generally prevents banks from hedging on a portfolio basis when deposit accounts are involved.

11.5 BASEL 2

Introduction

The international accounting standards have now placed the burden of risk disclosure for financial instruments upon the shoulders of accountants. It follows, therefore, that accountants (at least in theory) should have a good understanding of Basel 2 (the regulatory rules for measuring risk) before commenting on risk matters, as required under IFRS 7. Whether it is a good idea for accountants to be responsible for disclosing risk is debatable. On the one hand, shareholders need to see the risk profile of their investments. There is no point, for instance, in comparing the performance of Barclays with that of HSBC unless some attempt is made to understand the respective risks of each bank. If, for instance, the earnings yield of Barclays was only 20% greater than that of HSBC yet it was taking double the risks, it would make more sense (subject to diversification requirements) for an investor to double his investment in HSBC because he has the same risk profile as investing in Barclays but has a higher profit potential. Therefore, focusing on profits alone would only offer a limited picture. Clearly, what the accounting standards promote is that not only must an entity disclose its profits but it must also disclose the risks taken to acquire those profits. However, although many people would regard the annual report as more valuable and useful if all financial risks were disclosed, many are of the opinion that accountants are not trained in the complex area of risk management and therefore the task of summarising the risks of financial instruments and presenting them in the annual report is an unrealistic ideal. There is the risk that accountants will comply with the detailed requirements of IFRS 7 but at the same time not portray the risks in a manner that is useful and meaningful to shareholders. Auditors could therefore end up giving shareholders false assurances.

Distribution of income

The accounting standards, along with company law rules, constrain a company's ability to return money to shareholders. In broad terms, an entity can only pay money to its owners provided they are financed from accounting profits. It doesn't matter how much cash the company has available, the rules are applied quite strictly. Obviously, the constraint only applies to dividend payments, not other providers of capital – i.e. lenders or bondholders who receive interest payments. There are many reasons for this, but the principal concern is that shareholders might be tempted to speculate and take unusually high risks and then avoid losses by exploiting the laws of limited liability. Creditors and lenders, of course, would unfairly suffer in these circumstances and therefore need protection from such activities. The Basel 2 rules have a similar principle in mind, but its rules are more sophisticated (and probably better suited to a world of complex structured products and financial instruments) compared with the outdated accounting/company law rules. In a nutshell, the Basel 2 rules constrain a company from returning money to shareholders if their risk profile puts the creditors at risk. Unlike the crude rules of the accounting profession, the Basel 2 rules focus exclusively on risk and not past profitability. A loss-making bank can, for instance, technically return money to shareholders (in their language, referred to as reducing tier-one and tier-two capital) by reducing their exposure to risky assets. The problem with the accounting approach is that an entity can transfer value from lenders to shareholders by taking on extra risks. By making the Profit & Loss account more volatile, the shareholders benefit from the excess where the entity makes money but walks away from losses when they get too high. This has to some extent happened in the banking sector, where the market value of their debt has fallen owing to the increased risk. The shareholders of these financial institutions, however, have not necessarily benefited. Instead, through asymmetrical incentive payments, both traders and directors have benefited while lenders and shareholders have lost out. The Basel 2 rules, which we discuss next, are in principle designed to protect the lenders, not necessarily the shareholders. They do so by constraining the risk that banks take on.

Currently, in the main financial markets, there is a trend towards private equity firms buying established companies, getting them to borrow heavily and then returning money to shareholders. Increased gearing is justifiable if the volatility of profits is quite low and is not over-reactive to changes in the economic cycle. However, where profits are hard to predict or are very volatile, the most appropriate financing strategy is through the issue of shares. Many critics believe that private equity deals distort risk because they effectively create high gearing, meaning that a small downturn in the economic cycle could wipe out shareholders and put creditors at risk. Already, one group of powerful creditors – pension fund administrators – are putting blocks on potential private equity deals for that precise reason. A report by the EU has, however, highlighted that while the risks of private equity/high leverage buyouts may not lead to financial disaster they did correctly forecast that if too many deals are done when credit spreads are at an all-time low, problems could arise later on. Gearing and leverage are important. If an entity is highly geared then although it may have the intention to hold certain assets to maturity, it may not have the ability to do so, particularly if they fall in value. Entities therefore that have a liquidity problem or a gearing problem, i.e. where the balance sheet is stretched, should probably show assets and liabilities at fair value as opposed to cost.

The sophistication of financial instruments and the trend towards leveraged buyouts will of course mean that the old accounting rules will not be as effective at protecting creditors as they once were. The fact that a company has built up millions of pounds of profits that it has not yet distributed should not in theory be relevant to whether the company is able to pay a dividend in the future. What is more important is the volatility of earnings. A company with high leverage is much more risky than a company with low leverage, yet this risk may not be picked up under the old accounting rules.

Volatility

The rules of corporate finance should prevail. If an entity makes profits that are not very volatile and predictable then high dividends, high gearing and a lower capital base are probably appropriate. Therefore, such an entity should be allowed to return money to shareholders. The difficulty arises when a company appears safe because it may have, say, £10m of profits on its balance sheet which it has not yet distributed. If that company decides to alter its risk profile through the use of financial instruments then it is clearly taking on more risks, yet the risky company might decide to return money to shareholders thus putting the remaining creditors at risk.

Basel 2 rules

Basel 2 focuses on the volatility of earnings. Where the volatility of earnings is very high, Basel 2 rules require banks to finance more of their activities from equity. On the other hand, if the bank makes 'safe' investments, such as floating government bonds, the Basel 2 rules permit an entity to finance such investments mainly from deposits and other liabilities. Table 11.7 illustrates how Basel 2 operates.

Table 11.7   Basel 2

	Amount invested	Weighting	8% Risk-weighted assets	T1/T2 finance	Deposits
AAA government bond	£1,000,000	0%	£ –	£ –	£1,000,000
B corporate bond	£5,000,000	150%	£7,500,000	£600,000	£4,400,000
Unrated securitisation	£3,000,000	1250%	£37,500,000	£3,000,000	£–
			£45,000,000	£3,600,000	£5,400,000

In this simplified example, a bank finances itself from two sources: shareholders' funds and customer deposits. The bank has invested in three types of assets: an investment of £1,000,000 in AAA government bonds; £5,000,000 in a B-rated corporate bond; and £3,000,000 in an unrated securitisation. Under the Basel 2 rules, a weighting is assigned to each asset class (based on its perceived risk) to calculate the risk-weighted assets. Banks are generally required to hold capital to exceed at least 8% of the risk-weighted assets. The total of the risk-weighted assets is £45,000,000, so the amount of capital needed to support the assets is 8% or £3,600,000. Based on the regulator's view, AAA-rated government bonds are deemed to be risk-free since the risk of a highly rated government defaulting is minimal. The B-rated corporate bond has, of course, more uncertain cash flows since the risk of bankruptcy is much higher than for an AAA-rated government bond and so attracts a weighting of 150%. In this simplified example, we assume that the bank has no subordinated loans and so 8% of the risk-weighted assets must be financed from equity. The remainder may be financed from bank deposits. Unrated securitisations are quite different from government bonds and corporate bonds in that they are very heavily leveraged. This means that if a portfolio of loans suffers bad debt losses of say 1%, the effect on certain securitisation tranches could be as high as 30%, giving a leverage factor of 30 times. Clearly, the cash flows from these bonds would be very volatile and uncertain, hence the very high weighting (1250% is the reciprocal of 8%) – representing the maximum weighting possible. The impact of the weighting is that all of the asset must be financed from shareholders' funds. In theory, therefore, if the value of the securitisation went from £3,000,000 to zero because of a severe bad debts experience, the shareholders and not the deposit holders would suffer. One can see a certain element of logic behind these rules. As loans get closer to default, the predictability of the cash flow becomes less certain and therefore they are very volatile and so require more shareholder as opposed to liability financing. Also, if there is evidence that a particular asset is very leveraged (such as unrated securitisations), the volatility can be quite high – particularly if the credit ratings are very low. Consequently, they acquire the maximum rating. It can be seen from the above that the regulators do not necessarily have the power to stop a bank from investing in very volatile assets. They can only ensure that such assets are financed from equity as opposed to liabilities (particularly customer deposit liabilities). The above example is simplified to illustrate the impact of volatility on the capital structure of a bank. A more detailed discussion of

Basel 2, tier-one capital and tier-two capital follows. A point worth mentioning is that one of the reasons why the credit crises of 2007 emerged was that banks were not constrained sufficiently from investing in risky securitisations under Basel 1 (Basel 1 rules applied in 2007 and 2008). The new Basel 2 rules allow regulators to penalise securitisations and structured credit products by applying a higher weighting. In theory at least, the Basel 2 rules should discourage banks from taking on risky structured products, even if they are kept off-balance sheet.

Table 11.8 shows the ratings used under Basel 2. Some banks, however, will be permitted to calculate their own weightings if they can convince the regulators that their risk measurement process is sophisticated enough to capture credit risk. Under the simplified role, the credit rating agencies do play an important part. There are, of course, questions as to how much regulatory power the credit rating agencies should enjoy – particularly as there are many critics of the rating agencies who believe that inherent conflicts of interest in the rating process contributed to the current credit crises.

Table 11.8   Weightings

	Sovereign	Corporate	Securitisation
AAA	0%	20%	20%
AA	0%	20%	20%
A	20%	50%	50%
BBB	50%	100%	100%
BB	100%	100%	350%
B	100%	150%	1250%
Below B	150%	150%	1250%
Unrated	100%	100%	1250%
Retail portfolios	75%		
Residential mortgages	35%		
Commercial mortgages	100%		
Past due loans	150%		

An unfortunate consequence of regulation is that if the rules are too simple, not all the risks are captured and if they are too complex, they become difficult to implement. The 'standardised' approach, as demonstrated, is considered to be too simple. The regulators tend to compensate for this by using weights and a ratio that are perhaps too high. The consequence of this is that well-run banks who manage their risks properly are probably over-capitalised while badly-run banks are appropriately capitalised. Where well-run banks are over-capitalised they are in a situation where regulatory capital is greater than economic capital. In other words, the amount of money that the regulators require a bank to keep as capital may be greater than the amount of money they would keep aside in the absence of regulation. This could mean that banks focus on regulatory capital when they should focus on economic capital. The Basel committee recognises that a potential solution to this problem is to encourage banks to use internal models in the hope that the gap between regulatory and economic capital gets smaller.

With this in mind, the regulators have developed a more sophisticated model which, in essence, allows banks to calculate their own weightings. An illustration is given below.

In Table 11.9, a bank has a loan whose LGD is 45%. This means that if the loan does default, the bank only expects to recover 55% (perhaps through the sale of collateral) and so loses 45%. The maturity of the loan is 2.5 years and the bank estimates that the probability of default is 0.25%, i.e. a chance of 1 in 400 that the loan will default over the next year. From this data alone it is possible to calculate the expected loss and the credit spread. The expected loss is PD × LGD × loan principal (P). Therefore, it is $0.0025 \times 0.45 \times £19,654,816 = £22,112$. In percentage terms, this is $£22,112/£19,654,816 = 0.1125\%$. A more direct way to calculate the credit spread is simply as PD × LGD $= 0.25 \times 0.45 = 0.1125\%$. When deciding the interest charge that the customer must pay, the bank will take into account the relevant Libor rate (i.e. the rate at which bankers on average borrow and lend to each other). The bank will also charge the credit spread and an additional amount to cover administration and its profit margin.

Table 11.9   Calculation of weights for more sophisticated methods

		Gross	Capital required
LGD	**45%**		
Maturity	**2.5**		
Probability of default	**0.2500%**		
Correlation R	0.2258996		
Maturity adjustment M	0.1996		
Capital requirement	3.95773%		
Weighting	**49.472%**		
Loan	£19,654,815.86		
Expected loss	£22,111.67	£276,395.85	£22,111.67
Unexpected loss		£9,723,560.54	£777,884.84
		£9,999,956.39	
Credit spread	0.1125%		

Banks will automatically provide for expected bad debts if the interest charged to the customer includes the credit spread. However, if the bank subsidises the loan in any form – i.e. charges at a rate which does not recover the credit spread – then the bank will end up underproviding for future expected losses and so will be required to finance this shortfall through shareholders' funds. To calculate the unexpected loss, the Basel formula requires three ingredients: LGD, PD and the maturity adjustment (M). The maturity adjustment reflects the fact that loans with long maturities are more sensitive to changes in the credit spread than loans with short maturities.

Rationale behind Basel 2

Obviously, all banks experience a situation where they make bad loans and suffer losses of both interest accrued and principal. In theory, banks – when deciding the rate they should charge for a loan – calculate what is known as a credit spread and add this to Libor. A profit margin is also included in the total yield. A very simple example illustrates how a loan is priced. A customer's probability of default is calculated as 2%. If a default does occur, the bank expects to lose 80% of the loan outstanding. Therefore, if a bank advances say £1,000,000 the expected loss will be $2\% \times 80\% \times £1,000,000 = £16,000$ or 1.6% of the loan.

If the Libor rate is 5% then the bank will charge (at least) Libor plus the credit spread of 6.6%. Of course, it will include an extra margin to cover administration and other costs, but this amount varies from bank to bank and depends on the market demand for loans at the time. The accounting standards, particularly IAS 18 and IAS 39, require that both the credit spread and the margin be released to the Profit & Loss account over the life of the loan. In theory, if a bank calculates the credit spread with very fine precision then the actual losses experienced will not differ too much from the money earned through the credit spread, and so the risk of the bank defaulting is remote. In reality, actual loss experience can vary considerably from expected losses and the difference 'unexpected losses' (if high) will of course lead to a poorly capitalised bank going bankrupt.

The regulators therefore are not overly concerned about expected losses since they are normally covered by charging a credit spread (though a regulator would be concerned if a bank did not calculate the credit spread properly and offered cheap loans). Indeed, one of the problems that led to the American sub-prime crisis was that banks were so eager to lend money that they charged a credit spread which assumed there was very little risk of default. In other words, banks underpriced loans. Nevertheless, the prime concern with regulators is unexpected losses. Unexpected losses are a direct function of the volatility of actual losses. If actual losses are high, then unexpected losses – the difference between actual and expected losses – will of course be high.

11.6 ACCOUNTING FOR VAR AND IFRS 7

Introduction

There is a strong argument that if accountants are going to influence an entity's policy on hedging (through hedge accounting) and if they are going to report on the risk profile of an entity – a requirement of IFRS 7 – they should attempt to become more knowledgeable on risk management. Furthermore, if auditors want to avoid the tricks of creative accountants, particularly when it comes to structured products, they need to understand how to measure risks. Only then can they apply the matching concept, i.e. match risks to rewards rather than allow rewards to be recognised prematurely and risks kept off the balance sheet. Thus, a sound understanding of risk measurement and management principles is essential. The remainder of this chapter is concerned with how risks are measured and also looks at the requirements of IFRS 7.

There appear to be two objectives behind IFRS 7, *Financial Instruments Disclosures*. According to the standard setters, the first objective is to highlight 'the significance of financial instruments for the entity's financial position and performance'. The second objective is to reveal the nature and extent of risks arising from financial instruments to which the entity is exposed during the period and the reporting date, and how the entity manages those risks. The second objective is very important, particularly in the current financial environment, where banks and financial institutions are clearly taking on more risks but not informing the shareholder about them.

Significance of financial instruments

The significance of financial instruments is covered in paragraphs 7 to 30. In earlier chapters, we emphasised that the accounting standard setters are unsure about what should be shown on the balance sheet at market value and what should be shown at cost. The result is that assets and liabilities are broken down into various headings, as listed under IFRS 7.8.

IFRS 7.8 requires the carrying amounts of each of the categories to be disclosed, either on the balance sheet or in the notes:

1. Financial assets at fair value through profit or loss.
2. Held-to-maturity investments.
3. Loans & receivables.
4. Available-for-sale financial assets.
5. Financial liabilities at fair value through profit & loss.
6. Financial liabilities measured at financial cost.

In summary, some assets and liabilities are shown at cost, while others are shown at market value. To add to the confusion, there are 'Available for Sale' financial assets where the market value is shown on the balance sheet but the change in the market value does not go through the Profit & Loss – instead, it goes through Equity Reserve. In addition, the assets which are shown at market value through the Profit & Loss are broken down between those which are classified as trading and those 'designated as such upon initial recognition'. The methodology used by the IFRS may appear to be very confusing. Unfortunately it is, even to experienced practitioners. It is because of the inconsistency and confusion thrown up by the above rules under IAS 39 that extra disclosure is necessary. In short, the entity needs to reveal to the shareholder more disclosures about what assets are shown at cost and what assets are shown at market value. As pointed out in earlier chapters, the IFRS rules are too complex because they have a mixed model approach, and so the standard setters need to generate loads of rules to ensure that cherry-picking opportunities are reduced or eliminated. They need additional rules to eliminate the inconsistencies that too many rules inevitably throw up and finally, they need disclosures to show how the rules are applied to financial instruments and this seems to be what IFRS 7 is trying to achieve. Another way of viewing the objectives of IFRS 7 is that the entity is given too many choices on how to account for financial instruments and so, to reduce the damage created by these inconsistencies, more disclosure is required. As pointed out earlier, however, over-reliance on too much disclosure is not necessarily good practice. The problem with today's annual reports, particularly those issued by financial entities, is that they calculate the Profit & Loss incorrectly by keeping items off-balance sheet and not showing assets at their correct market value, and then rely on pages and pages of confusing disclosure notes to reveal what the shareholder should know. Instead, however, the shareholder ends up getting confused and is left in the dark about the true financial position.

Held to Maturity investments, along with Loans & Receivables, are normally shown at cost on the balance sheet. Therefore, where a financial institution buys a bond and intends to hold it to maturity, it will appear at cost on the balance sheet with only the yield or interest going through the Profit & Loss account. Loans & Receivables are treated in a similar manner. Where a bank lends money or takes money in on deposit, the market value of these loans is virtually ignored. Available for Sale assets are shown on the balance sheet at market value but the difference does not go through the Profit & Loss account. Instead, it goes through the Equity Reserve and remains there until the asset is eventually sold (and the profit realised). Items 5 and 6: 'Financial liabilities at fair value through profit & loss' and 'Financial liabilities measured at financial cost' are quite confusing. In essence, they relate to situations where a financial institution, worried about the risk profile of certain loans and receivables, decides to hedge and finds that the hedge doesn't qualify for hedge accounting. In those instances, artificial volatility is created and there is a risk that applying IAS 39 strictly would lead to very misleading results. Therefore, where artificial volatility is created, an entity can generally reclassify certain assets and liabilities as financial assets and liabilities at fair value through the Profit & Loss account. The result is that the asset or liability is shown at market value and not cost. The derivative is also shown at market value and so artificial volatiliy is eliminated.

There are broadly speaking two reasons why, for instance, a financial liability will change in value, market risk and credit risk. The market risk changes arise from changes in variables such as foreign exchange rates and/or interest rates. The credit risk refers to the fluctuation in value of a loan or a bond because the issuer has become more (or sometimes less) risky. Ironically, if an entity's credit rating deteriorates and suffers a credit downgrading from the credit rating agencies, its Profit & Loss account could improve, as the illustration below demonstrates.

In the example in Table 11.10, an entity has issued a loan at a yield of 7% at a time when Libor is 5%. The implied credit spread is 2%. As soon as the loan is issued, the entity suffers a downgrading and the credit spread jumps from 2% to 4% while Libor remains unchanged. The new yield on the loan is therefore 9% but the coupon remains at 7%. The value of the loan therefore falls from £10 million to £9,352,056. As the illustration shows, if the FVO is chosen, the loan's new value creats a profit of £647,944 in the Profit & Loss account. IFRS 7 obviously requires this disclosure since the increase in profit is not because the entity was managed well – in fact, the increase in profit possibly arises for quite the opposite reason.

Table 11.10 Profiting from downgrades

Bond notional	£10,000,000	
Libor	5%	
Credit spread (at issue date)	2%	
Current credit spread	4%	
Tenor	5%	
Ordinary shares	£5,000,000	
	Bond cash flows	
	£700,000	
	£700,000	
	£700,000	
	£700,000	
	£10,700,000	
Fair value		
before downgrade	£10,000,000	7%
after downgrade	£9,352,056	9%
Balance sheet	Before downgrade	After downgrade
Assets	£15,000,000	£15,000,000
Liabilities	−£10,000,000	−£9,352,056
Shareholders' funds	£5,000,000	£5,647,944
Ordinary shares	£5,000,000	£5,000,000
Profit & Loss	£0	£647,944
	£5,000,000	£5,647,944

In addition to the above, the entity must also disclose its maximum exposure to credit risk at the reporting date. If credit derivatives or credit insurance are used to reduce (or in some cases enhance) the risk of a credit event, that too must be disclosed. Finally, where the fair value of an asset has changed, the change must be broken down between the market risk and the credit risk and appropriately disclosed. Occasionally, entities reclassify assets from those measured on a cost basis to market value, etc. Obviously, such reclassification will affect the way the profit and loss is calculated and so details of the reclassification, including the reasons, must be disclosed. Reclassification, covered in IAS 39.50 to IAS 39.54, is often necessary because, for instance, of a change in intention. Occasionally, entities will reclassify assets to the Available for Sale category, since this gives the entity more flexibility should it wish to sell the asset. Occasionally too, an asset may be classified at cost because it is difficult to value. However, if subsequently the asset becomes easier to value, the entity may change from carrying the asset at cost on the balance sheet to carrying the asset at market value.

Paragraphs 12–14 of IFRS 7 are more concerned with the disclosure of credit risk, an area that is very important today since many entities caught up in the sub-prime market have failed to disclose adequately the credit risks that they face. Occasionally, entities sell securities to a third party but retain the majority of the risks and rewards of ownership. As an example, through the securitisation process a bank might create bonds from loans that it has and sell these to investors. Obviously, the bonds will fetch a higher price if the bank itself guarantees the bonds, i.e. the bank steps in to compensate the investor if the underlying loan defaults. In such circumstances, understandably, the accounting standard setters do not allow the bank to remove the loans from its balance sheet. The bondholders therefore are treated as a liability on the bank's balance sheet. Needless to say, shareholders would be interested in the risk profile of these assets that fail to qualify for derecognition. Items that must be disclosed include the nature of the asset, in particular the risks and rewards of ownership. Also, the entity needs to disclose the 'carrying value' of the asset.

Credit disclosure

Credit risk is quite a complex area and there is a possibility that the credit disclosures demanded by IFRS 7 are a bit too basic. That is to say, an entity may carry a considerable amount of credit risk but may not disclose this effectively and yet may still be in compliance with the detailed requirements of IFRS 7. Included in the disclosure requirements are details of collateral. For instance, the creditors of an entity would be very interested in instances where the entity pledged its assets to certain lenders. These assets would, of course, not be available to the general creditors if the company got into difficulty. Obviously, the opposite can occur – where the entity holds collateral as security for loans which it has made.

A second area of disclosure relates to bad debts. As indicated in earlier chapters, an entity can only impair a loan (i.e. write down the value of a loan) when a 'trigger event' occurs as defined in IAS 39.59. These trigger events include significant financial difficulty of the issuer, a breach of contract or a loan restructuring. Once a loan is identified for impairment, the entity must identify the contractual cash flows – i.e. the cash flows the borrower has agreed to pay – and calculate the expected cash flows. The expected cash flows are basically the contractual cash flows multiplied by a probability of default. The expected cash flows are then discounted at the effective interest rate. More than likely, the present value of the expected cash flows will be less than the carrying value and the difference is reflected as a charge in the Profit & Loss account. The new rules have tightened up the calculation procedure, with the result that the calculation is less subjective (though there is still a small element of subjectivity since the probability of default must be estimated).

In addition to individual impairment, entities are allowed to review a portfolio of loans (that do not qualify for individual impairment) for collective impairment. This might be used, for instance, where a bank knows that because say house prices have fallen, a number of loans will default but they cannot identify which individual loans will default. Here, an entity is allowed to make collective impairment and, in broad terms, the standard setters allow a lot of flexibility. Since the calculation is very subjective, different financial institutions will more than likely calculate the same provision in different ways, which makes comparison difficult. The standard setters therefore believe that analysts can make more meaningful comparisons between financial institutions if more disclosure on the methodology is disclosed. A similar approach applies for both insurance entities that must disclose their calculation methodology for 'embedded value' and of course pension deficits that are calculated using assumptions and judgements. The requirements in IFRS 7 therefore follow the general trend that if there is any subjectivity in the calculations, greater disclosure is necessary.

Other areas of disclosure covered by IFRS 7 include information on hedge accounting. In broad terms, the definition of hedging as used by accountants is quite different from the term 'hedge' in the general sense. Accountants will basically only recognise a hedging relationship between the underlying and the derivative if it falls under one of three definitions: fair value hedge, cash flow hedge and hedge of a net investment. Fair value hedge accounting allows the entity to adjust the underlying value by the change in the derivative (we assume here that the entire derivative qualifies for hedge accounting). As discussed in earlier chapters, the fair value of assets and liabilities in the balance sheet will be distorted if fair value hedge accounting is used. Therefore, entities must disclose the extent to which the carrying value on the balance sheet of an asset or liability is affected by a fair value hedge adjustment.

IFRS 7 also contains details on fair value and how it is calculated. In some cases the financial instrument concerned is very liquid and not complex. Market prices for these instruments are normally easy to obtain. For the more complex instruments, a pricing model is used. These pricing models can be quite inaccurate and dangerous. This was certainly the case in 2007, when regulators became worried about the assumptions and methodology used to price complex structured products in an illiquid market. Optimistic assumptions mean high valuations and therefore high bonuses. The accounting standard setters recognise therefore that the profit and loss on these structured products can be misleading. Some of these problems may come to light if the valuation methodology is disclosed. Again, the same principle applies – where the valuation is subjective, disclose more. IFRS 7 specifically requires details of the methods and assumptions used to determine fair value. Disclosure requirements include assumptions about prepayment rates (for securitisations), details on estimated future credit losses and the discount rates used to determine present value, etc. Shareholders of banks are particularly interested in whether the pricing of financial instruments is determined independently (i.e. through observed prices in a liquid market) or non-independently (i.e. where the entity itself makes its own assumptions and then uses these, along with a model, to obtain the fair value of financial instruments).

Nature and extent of risks arising from financial instruments

What is surprising about the second part of IFRS 7 is that very little, if any, mention is made of VaR – despite the fact that it is used widely by banks to control risks. There is the risk, therefore, that standard setters are imposing an additional set of rules on financial entities and these rules are not consistent with best practices in risk management. It is quite clear that standard setters have taken on the responsibility of disclosing to the shareholders the risks of using complex financial instruments. This is perhaps a worrying trend, since accountants and auditors are often not trained in the complexities of risk management. The result is that accountants disclose information that appears to comply with the accounting standards but do not in fact show the real risks that the entity faces. Furthermore, there is a difference in methodology between IFRS 7 and IAS 39. IFRS 7, as we shall see, requires an entity to disclose information about its exposure – i.e. how much of an entity's assets are exposed to changes in interest rates, foreign exchange or equity price movements, etc. IAS 39, on the other hand, is more concerned with cash flow exposure and the hedging of certain assets and liabilities. As pointed out earlier, because of the different emphasis, the definition of hedging in accounting terms is more restrictive and a lot different from the definition of hedging as used by treasurers and risk managers. The result is that readers of financial statements are often unable to link the disclosure notes to the Profit & Loss account and the balance sheet, and therefore have to rely on the auditor to ensure that all is well and that risks are disclosed properly. Unfortunately, in a world where corporate governance activists are encouraging greater transparency, the accounting standards are still a bit behind.

The IFRS 7 requirements are broken down between qualitative disclosures and quantitative disclosures. For all financial instruments, IFRS 7.32 requires details of the exposures to risk and how they arise, the policies for managing the risks and changes in policy where relevant. For corporates, for instance, the main types of financial risks that they face include interest rate risk (because they usually borrow money) and, where they import and export, foreign exchange risks. Banks, of course, face the same types of risk but their risk is much more sophisticated and perhaps more difficult to measure. A corporate may decide to hedge the interest rate risk (i.e. hedge against the risk of a rise in interest rates) using perhaps interest rate swaps and may also hedge the foreign exposure arising from imports and exports. Foreign exchange risks are usually hedged using forward foreign currency contracts and in some cases options. Sometimes, of course, companies do not bother to hedge exposures. Large companies like BP, for instance, have exposures to a wide range of foreign exchange rates and since multinationals often borrow in different countries, they are exposed to different yield curves. Since they are already well diversified, taking out hedges on all exposures would be pointless, complex and costly and so they tend to leave the exposures as they are, only hedging against very severe changes. Other companies, like property development companies, are perhaps very heavily exposed to interest rate changes since they tend to borrow heavily. These entities do need to hedge. The standard setters cannot force a company to adopt a particular hedging policy, they simply require – through IFRS 7 – that the shareholder is aware of the hedging policy that the company adopts. In theory, a shareholder should be able to see the impact on the accounting profit and loss if, say, interest rates were to change or if foreign exchange rates were to move one way or the other. In practice, the notes surrounding risk disclosure are large in volume but not very effective at communicating the risks. This was certainly true of credit risk with financial entities in 2007.

The quantitative disclosures of IFRS 7 are contained in IFRS 7.34 and IFRS 7.35. Summary quantitative data about exposures to risk, as contained in internal reports to management, is all that is required for market risk. Paragraph 35 simply states that if the quantitative data disclosed is unrepresentative, an entity shall provide further information that is representative. Obviously, these guidelines are very vague and so it is possible, given the complexities of financial risk, that an entity will comply with the rules of IFRS 7 without disclosing too many useful details. In simple terms, it is often difficult to prove that an auditor or accountant has failed to comply with IFRS 7 even if they hide the risks because of its very loose guidelines. Throughout 2007, there is evidence that many financial institutions suffered huge losses in the credit markets and were therefore very risky, although this was not highlighted adequately in their annual reports.

Paragraphs IFRS 7.34 and 7.35 appear to deal with market risk while IFRS7.36–38 deal with credit risk. These paragraphs state that entities are required to disclose the maximum exposure to credit risk and the reporting date, along with details of collateral held and information about the credit quality of the financial assets. Where loans are restructured or renegotiated, the value of these loans – as they appear on the balance sheet – must too be disclosed. Obviously, entities will seek to obtain collateral as protection against bad debts. Details of collateral held must be shown as well.

11.7 CONCLUSION

The decision by the accounting profession to use a 'mixed model' creates a lot of uncertainty and confusion. The uncertainty arises because some entities show certain assets at cost while other entities may show the same assets at market value. While the mixed model continues to exist, artificial volatility in the Profit & Loss account will always exist in some shape or form. The standard setters have attempted to deal with this artificial volatility through the use of fair value and cash flow hedging. However, the requirements to qualify for hedge accounting under these two headings are too restrictive, and so banks end up using derivatives to reduce certain interest rate exposures only to find that the accounting profession regards such hedges as speculative derivatives and so the accounting treatment creates artificial volatility rather than, as the banks had hoped, reducing the volatility of the P&L. This unusual position has created a conflict between the EU and the IASB, and is one of the 'carve-outs' that is, at the time of writing, still unresolved. There is a risk that the accounting profession continues to impose on banks, rules for hedging risk which are very much at variance with normal risk measurement and control practices, namely VaR and Basel 2. The IASB rules are designed to reflect the fact that the mixed model operates, while VaR and Basel 2 focus on the economics of the transaction and therefore use fair value all the time, since it is impossible to do a meaningful sensitivity or risk measurement analysis if the value of the asset or liability is based on cost rather than market value.

In this confusing environment, IFRS 7 has a relatively tough job since it must somehow reconcile best practice in risk management with the more complicated hedging strategies as permitted by IAS 39. The risk is that the IFRS 7 objectives are a pipe dream in the current environment. Financial institutions will therefore continue to meet the requirements of IFRS 7 through complicated and detailed disclosures. However, these disclosures may not reveal the true risks and so end up giving the shareholder a very false sense of security.

Accounting for Insurance

12.1 INTRODUCTION

Prior to the IFRS issuing a specific standard to deal with insurance, there was concern about the lack of consistency amongst insurance companies on accounting practices. Investment analysts were also worried about the 'cherry-picking' opportunities that insurance companies might be tempted to use. For instance, there was the fear that insurance companies could trade credit derivatives, classify them as insurance products and hence keep them off the balance sheet. Therefore, it would be relatively easy for such a company to hide losses and manipulate the Profit & Loss account by cherry-picking the profit-making derivatives and cashing them in while keeping the loss-making derivatives hidden off-balance sheet. A more fundamental problem, however, was that some insurance companies disguised loans as insurance contracts and therefore artificially inflated their Profit & Loss account by entering into loans and treating cash received on loans as insurance compensation. The result was that many insurance companies borrowed money but increased the Profit & Loss account with the cash received, rather than recognising the liability for the loan granted. This problem was unearthed by the former US Attorney General and until very recently, Governor of New York Mr Eliot Spitzer and resulted in a number of investigations with very revealing consequences. Insurance companies also gave away generous guarantees to certain customers but never recognised the liability associated with such contracts.

The solution to these problems is to make sure that derivatives are treated as derivatives in accordance with IAS 39, *Accounting for Financial Instruments* even by insurance companies and similarly, to make sure that loans are treated like loans even if the words 'insurance' or 'reinsurance' are used to describe products. For a period of time, insurance companies were exempt from the requirements of IAS 39, but that exemption was withdrawn following the appearance of a special accounting standard on insurance, known as IFRS 4. Also, it is helpful if the accounting standards can at least nail down the various accounting policies that insurance companies use, which will facilitate comparison. The IASB attempted to achieve these objectives through IFRS 4. Recognising the complexity of the task, they split the project into Phase One and Phase Two. Phase One narrowed down, but did not specify in detail, the accounting policies that the insurance companies could adopt. Phase Two will take things further by encouraging insurance companies to bring on to the balance sheet more assets and liabilities at market value (thus reducing cherry-picking opportunities). Given the very complex nature of the insurance industry, the deadline for the more complicated Phase Two was postponed and is now expected at the end of 2009. Phase One, however, is currently in force through IFRS 4. In essence, IFRS 4 states that financial contracts (even if they are called insurance contracts) must fall under IAS 39, as must loans (again even if they are referred to as reinsurance contracts). IFRS 4 therefore exempts only pure insurance contracts or at least insurance contracts with significant insurance risk. If this exemption didn't apply, then

IAS 39, *Financial Instruments: Recognition and Measurement* most probably would apply. Therefore, derivatives would be shown on the balance sheet at market value, thus reducing cherry-picking opportunities. Also, reinsurance contracts – which are sometimes loans under a different name – would have to appear as a liability on the balance sheet. Therefore, the risk that loans are understated or profits are overstated is substantially reduced. As usual, however, although the designers of IFRS 4 had good intentions and recognised the problems, they have suffered criticism from practitioners on the grounds that the standard is confusing, difficult to implement and the delays to Phase Two leave them with a lot of guesswork and uncertainty.

Insurance products (including life assurance products) have features which are similar to derivatives. Consider a simple case where an individual takes out basic car insurance. In return for an annual premium, the individual is protected from the decline in the value of his car as well as external damages. Like a derivative, the exposure is greater than the premium paid, and the contract's value is derived from the value of the underlying asset (the value of the car after an accident). Also, there is net settlement in that the insurer will only compensate the individual for the difference between the value of the car after the crash and its value beforehand. Therefore, should the instrument – which has the same features as a put option – be treated as a derivative and marked-to-market? The answer in practice is not always clear but in this case, because of IFRS 4, it is definitely 'no' – simply because the payout is contingent on a non-market event occurring. In this case the insurance event is a car accident and the payout will only occur if the insurance event occurs. Unlike ordinary put options, insurance contracts do not give people the ability to speculate. They generally tend to enter into such contracts to reduce the adverse exposure of a car accident – similar to hedging in its traditional sense. The same cannot be said for credit insurance products such as credit default swaps; hedge funds and other entities use these for speculative purposes. These products are now dealt with under IAS 39, which means that losses, where they occur, must be recognised immediately.

IFRS 4 makes a distinction between products which contain 'significant' insurance exposure and those that don't. In practice, entities have a lot more flexibility in how they account for insurance products but not so for pure investment products. In broad terms, all investment products fall under IAS 39 and, as experts on IAS 39 will confirm, the accounting rules – though strict – are not straightforward. In some cases, investment products held for a long period of time or held to maturity may be accounted for on a cost basis. Other IAS 39 investment instruments are accounted for by showing the market value in the balance sheet. However, one important difference between IFRS 4 and IAS 39 is that IAS 39 does not allow entities to recognise up-front marketing or transaction costs. Therefore, if an instrument is classified as an investment product and incurs a transaction or up-front marketing cost, this cost must be released to the Profit & Loss account immediately and not released over the life of the product. The same treatment is not applied to insurance contracts. Instead, accountants in the insurance industry have more flexibility and can allocate the cost evenly over the life of the insurance product and not all up-front.

12.2 SIGNIFICANCE OF INSURANCE RISK

Some insurance companies struggle to determine if a product which combines insurance risk with market risk has 'significant' insurance risk. Unhelpfully, the IASB has a principle of not defining too closely some of the definitions they use throughout the accounting standards.

Their, perhaps understandable, justification for doing so is that two similar products that are marginally on different sides of a defined dividing line might have very different accounting treatments. Also, creative accountants might design or purchase products that just touched the limits and then use the accounting standard to justify what might be an inappropriate but favourable accounting treatment. The IASB has therefore used a 'principle-based' approach but kept the dividing lines vague. The only guidance the accounting standards give is contained in IFRS 4.B23, i.e. the insured event should have a sufficient probability of occurrence and a sufficient magnitude of effect.

Case study: mismatching

The Finance Director of Irish Life & Permanent (ILP) has criticised IFRS 4 on the grounds that practitioners are not allowed to match revenues with costs correctly, leading to artificial volatility in the Profit & Loss account.[1] IFRS 4 permits entities like ILP to use an accounting process known as embedded value – a methodology for calculating profits used in the insurance industry (to be discussed below) for insurance products but not for investment products. In practice, however, insurance companies do report disclosure notes to investors where they use the embedded value methodology for both insurance and investment products. The IFRS restriction means that up-front marketing costs need not be released to the Profit & Loss account. Instead, they can be deferred to future periods – in line with the recognition of future profits. Most accountants will recognise this as the matching concept. However, if the same contract is classified as an investment, the up-front marketing costs must flow through the Profit & Loss account. This means that growing companies are forced to show an accounting loss each time they generate new business, when in reality they have made an economic profit. As the Finance Director put it 'so, if Embedded Value accounting is appropriate for insurance contracts, I can't see why it is not appropriate for investment contracts. It is an inconsistency which is hard to accept but one which we are going to have to live with'. There is the obvious perverse risk that directors of insurance companies, whose bonuses are based on accounting profits, may encourage employees not to sell insurance contracts as it will, in the short term, have an adverse impact on their bonuses.

Whilst the inconsistency is an irritation in this case, there is some logic behind it. The standard setters treat investment contracts very strictly and therefore differently from insurance contracts. In the case of investment products and financial instruments in general, many traders buy them to take positions (speculate) and there is a risk that the lax accounting treatment may allow such traders to simultaneously incur losses and hide them. Capitalising transaction costs, of course, could also enable traders to hide losses, particularly for structured products. As stated before, however, insurance contracts are not normally bought with speculation in mind and therefore the standards (in particular IFRS 4) allow more flexibility on the capitalisation of up-front costs.

Example: embedded value vs. accounting calculation

In this subsection, we comment on an example produced by ILP for its shareholders in July 2005.[2] See Table 12.1.

---

[1] Slide 30 – Irish Life & Permanent PLC, EEV & IFRS Update, 21 July 2005.
[2] Slide 21 – Irish Life & Permanent PLC, Analysts & Investors Briefing, November 2005.

Table 12.1 Single premium product

Single premium	£10,000
Tenor	3
Front end fee	5%
Management fee	2%
Maintenance charge	£20
Fixed acquisition costs	7%
Variable acquisition costs	3%

An insurance company sells an investment product whereby the customer pays £10,000 for an insurance/investment product. This product is expected to last for three years and the insurance company is entitled to a front end fee of 5% plus a 2% management fee over the next three years. The insurance company is expected to incur a maintenance/management cost of £20 in year 2 and £20 in year 3.

The expected cash flows for the product over the next three years are illustrated in Table 12.2.

Table 12.2 Cash flows – investment product

Cash flow	1	2	3	TOTAL
Front end fee	£500			£500
Management fee	£200	£200	£200	£600
Maintenance	£–	−£20	−£20	−£40
Fixed acquisition	−£700			−£700
Variable acquisition costs	−£300			−£300
				£–
	−£300	£180	£180	£60

The total expected profit for the insurance company is £60. The insurance company earns/receives a front ended fee and management fee of £1100 but must pay £1040 in various costs. There are two ways to account for this product, both of which will recognise a cumulative profit of £60 for the three years. The embedded value approach is probably the most appropriate way as it allows the entity to recognise the profit evenly over the three years. The IAS 39 approach will force the entity to show a large loss in the first year and then high profits in years 2 and 3. In effect, the IAS 39 approach prevents the entity from splitting the fixed acquisition cost over the life of the asset – it must be put through the P&L immediately.

As Table 12.3 shows, the net cash inflows for the contract are £180 for year 1 and £180 for year 2 and the cash outlay is £300 at the start of year 1. Obviously, the present values of the cash inflows are less than £360. They come to £330. The result is that the entity can only recognise £30 of the £60 profit up-front, the remainder (£20 and £10) is recognised in future years. This contrasts with the IFRS approach in Table 12.4, where the entity is required to record heavy losses initially and higher losses later on.

As Table 12.4 reveals, both methods recognise profits of £60 over the life of the contract. The embedded value approach spreads this out evenly, whereas IFRS requires the entity to calculate a loss up-front (−£433) and higher profits later on.

Table 12.3   Embedded value methodology

Interest	6%				
Discount factors	1.0000	0.9434	0.8900		
Present value	−£300	£170	£160		£30
	Opening balance	Credit to P&L	Cash flow	Closing balance	
	£−	£30	£300	£330	
	£330	£20	−£180	£170	
	£170	£10	−£180	−£0	
		£60	−£60		

Table 12.4   IFRS profit calculation

Recognised profit	1	2	3	
Front end fee	£167	£167	£167	
Management fee	£200	£200	£200	
Maintenance cost		−£20	−£20	
Fixed acquisition	−£700			
Variable acquisition	−£100	−£100	−£100	
	−£433	£247	£247	
IFRS	−£433	£247	£247	£60
Embedded value	£30	£20	£10	£60

A second criticism of IFRS 4 is that the term 'significant' is not defined. Practitioners will end up trying to guess the intention of the standard with certain products that have a marginal amount of insurance features. Consider the case of an individual who pays a premium to an insurance company. The premium is used to fund an investment on behalf of the individual. However, if the individual dies, he is guaranteed a return of all the premiums he has paid over the life of the contract. If the investment turns negative, the value of the guarantee is quite high but if the investment turns positive, the guarantee of a return of all premiums becomes worthless. In the former case the product should be treated as an insurance contract because any payment is contingent on death. However, if the investment performs well it becomes an investment contract, since the guarantee on death is worth nothing. IAS 39 applies to the investment contract and IFRS 4 applies to the insurance company. Needless to say, many insurance companies will treat such products as insurance because of the more favourable treatment under IFRS 4.

In May 2004 a number of Chief Financial Officers developed a new basis for embedded value reporting for insurance companies. This new method was designed to replace an existing mechanism known as 'Achieved Profits Reporting'. The net result was that insurance companies disclosed their accounting treatment in more meaningful detail and more importantly, were more consistent – thus facilitating comparison between insurance entities.

12.3   IFRS VS. EMBEDDED VALUE REPORTING

Most insurers report their Profit & Loss account under the requirements of IFRS 4, though they will readily admit that the insurance accounting standard paints a misleading picture. To overcome this weakness, many insurance companies present supplementary information which shows the true picture. Generally, regulators are against using disclosure accounting as it may encourage accountants to produce misleading accounting profit figures and then rely on disclosures to reveal additional information which the shareholder never gets round to reading. Enron used this tactic and caused a lot of damage as they simultaneously concealed losses in the calculation of their Profit & Loss account yet revealed the true picture in their disclosure notes. The Chief Executive of Pearson, that owns the *Financial Times*, criticised the financial journalists in that newspaper for failing to spot the scandal earlier. In other words, she expressed concern that both financial journalists and analysts either ignored or failed to read important disclosure notes on Enron's statements. Thus, the risk of an Enron-type crisis erupting in the insurance world is probably very high and will possibly remain so until IFRS 4 is improved.

Lloyds TSB, like many other insurance entities, uses supplementary reporting 'in line with industry best practice' for reporting insurance activities. The supplementary report includes not only insurance contracts but also certain non-insurance contracts such as investment management funds. In a note concerning their 2005 accounts, they point out that the difference between IFRS earnings and EEV earnings relates principally to 'the earlier timing of profit recognition'. The European Embedded Value (EEV) approach also takes into account investment contracts which would not be included under IFRS.

EEV methodology

EEV can be defined as the present value of shareholders' interests in the earnings distributable from assets allocated to certain types of insurance business after sufficient allowance is made for risks. Generally, the EEV methodology applies to what is referred to as 'covered business'. This includes life assurance, investment contracts, pensions and annuity business, etc.

There are three components to embedded value:

1. Free surplus of assets allocated to the covered business.
2. The opportunity cost of required capital.
3. The present value of future shareholder cash flows from in-force business less an appropriate deduction for opportunity costs such as interest and the market value of options and guarantees.

There is an important difference between IFRS and EEV. For certain investment products, the EEC methodology allows an insurance company to recognise future investment fees up-front. Obviously, the up-front profits are discounted to reflect the time value of money. The IFRS (presumably applying the prudence concept) broadly states that investment fees can only be recognised over the life of the contract. The matching concept is of course violated, because any expenses incurred in getting the business (third-party commission) must be recognised as an expense in the Profit & Loss account immediately, whereas the gains are delayed over the investment product's life.

The free surplus is the difference between the value of the assets less the value of the liabilities less supporting capital. An assurance company might, for instance, have assets of

£1 billion and liabilities (to policyholders) of £700,000,000 and the supervisors might require that the assurance company retains capital of £150,000,000 to cover the risk that the assets might fall in value and the liabilities might rise in value simultaneously – placing the solvency of the assurance company into question. The regulators may therefore insist that the assurance company locks £150,000,000 into the business to protect the policyholders.

In the above example, the required capital is £150,000,000. However, this money is locked in by the regulators and therefore prevents the shareholders from getting a return. The missed returns, or 'opportunity cost of capital', represent a reduction in profits for the shareholders and therefore this opportunity cost is calculated and causes a reduction in EEV. For example, suppose the assurance company above had the view that the capital would have to stay tied up for five years at a time when interest rates are 5%, then the present value of £150,000,000 is £117,528,924. Therefore, the opportunity cost of capital would be £32,471,075 and the embedded value would fall by this amount (Table 12.5).

Table 12.5   Opportunity cost value of in-force business

Term	5
Yield	5%
Capital	£150,000,000
Discount factor	0.78353
Present value	£117,528,925
Opportunity cost	£32,471,075

When valuing businesses of any description, the normal practice is to estimate the future cash flows and then discount those cash flows by reference to a yield. As with calculating the projected cash flows, the yield calculation is subjective. The objective, however, is to identify the risks and make sure that the investor is compensated for these risks. The greater the risk, the higher the yield. Since calculating the embedded value of an assurance firm is similar to valuing a business, the same rules apply. An important exception, however, is that goodwill is ignored under the embedded value calculation. When valuing a business, goodwill is very important as it reflects the entity's ability to generate new business. Some experts believe that in the absence of goodwill, the embedded value approach is very conservative. A second advantage of excluding goodwill is that subjectivity is removed. As accountants strictly forbid increases in goodwill going through the Profit & Loss account, the embedded value approach closely resembles the general principles of accounting and to that extent, the IASB permits companies to use embedded value methodology for pure insurance contracts but not for investment products (which should fall under IAS 39). Removing goodwill from the calculations, however, only reduces as opposed to eliminates subjectivity. Most of the subjectivity centres around the choice of the Risk Discount Rate (RDR). The starting point is the base risk-free rate. This is usually the yield offered on government bonds (the assumption is that government bonds are completely risk-free). An allowance is then made for investment risk. This is the difference between the expected return on an equity portfolio vs. a portfolio of government bonds. Since equity is more volatile, it is more risky and investors expect a better return for this class of investment. Assurance companies therefore use a higher discount rate for equity than for government bonds.

Case study: Lloyds

In the year to 31 December 2005, Lloyds TSB Group reported IFRS accounts of £123m. The supplementary valuation under EEV principles was an increase of £131m to £254m for the same period. The difference is largely due to the value of in-force life assurance contracts (VIF). In addition, the embedded value on the balance sheet is different under IFRS than under the supplementary reported EEV principles. This is principally due to the fact that IFRS only allows embedded value methodology for pure insurance contracts whereas the EEV principles include investments as well as insurance contracts. Also, of course, since EEV allows for earlier profit recognition on VIF contracts, it follows that the value on the balance sheet must, in most cases, be greater than under IFRS reporting.

12.4   FINITE INSURANCE AND UNBUNDLING

Finite insurance is an important area of 'financial engineering' that allows insurance companies to simultaneously tailor their risk profile and increase capacity for new business. However, it is complex in nature and as with all complex products, they not only have an operational risk feature but can be exploited to achieve a desired accounting result. With complexity there is the prospect that the arrangers (or sellers of finite products) can introduce 'sweeteners' that make their finite products more saleable. Sweeteners, however, come at a cost. The arranger must suffer if the client benefits. Therefore, the sweeteners are designed in such a way that both the arranger benefits (through high fees) and the client benefits (through a higher accounting profit as opposed to economic profit). It is the shareholder of the client who suffers from the added complexity, but because of the weak accounting rules, he is unaware that he is suffering, or at least has to wait a few years before he discovers that he has suffered.

IFRS 4 has attempted to put a stop to this. The intention of IFRS 4 is to stop entities from treating loans as insurance. Suppose an entity borrows money through a finite insurance arrangement from a reinsurer. If the loan is called a loan then when the principal is paid over the client receives the cash but must recognise a liability in its balance sheet. If, however, the loan is called an insurance product the cash paid is treated as insurance compensation and therefore goes through the Profit & Loss account as opposed to being treated as a liability. For readers familiar with debits and credits, the credit part of the journal entry is the Profit & Loss account for insurance compensation and a liability if a loan.

Paragraph 10 of IFRS 4 requires the entity to unbundle loans and treat them separately from insurance contracts. An example will illustrate how this operates. An insurance company wants to pass on the risk of some of its insurance contracts to a reinsurer. Under the agreement, the insured company pays a premium of 20 every year for the next five years. If a loss is incurred, the reinsurer pays the insured the full compensation as with normal insurance contracts. However, there is included in the contract an 'experience adjustment'. In short, if 90% of any losses are not covered by premiums received, the insured compensates the reinsurer for the difference. Furthermore, if there are no claims, the insured company receives a refund of 90% of the premiums paid. This type of contract is difficult to deal with under IFRS 4 because, although the insured company is transferring the risk to the reinsurance company, under the experience adjustment, the insured is actually clawing back some of the risk. IFRS

4 would nevertheless recognise this as an insurance contract because it transfers a significant insurance risk to the reinsurer (see page 499 of IASB 2005). Nevertheless, the contract can be broken down between a pure loan and a contract with an insurance element, and IFRS 4 as discussed above requires such an unbundling.

Unbundling procedure

In this example we discuss the guidance given by the IASB on how to unbundle an insurance contract from a loan/deposit. Occasionally, insurance companies want to reduce their risk by insuring themselves with a reinsurance company. In order to unbundle the loan from the insurance contract, we firstly need to identify the non-insurance cash flows and more importantly, the yield of the borrower. In this case it is the reinsurance company that is the borrower, since it will receive cash up-front which it will repay later on. The arrangement between the reinsurer and the insurer is that the insurer is refunded 90% of the premium if no claim is made. Also, if a claim is made, the reinsurer pays to the insurer £90 – being 90% of the expected premium. So there is no reinsurance risk with that part and therefore, according to IFRS 4, it is a pure insurance contract. In this example, the agreement is that the insurance company pays to the reinsurer £20 at the start of each year for the next five years. In deciding the yield, the normal practice is to identify the appropriate Libor rate based on the length of the loan and also the credit spread to reflect the risk of the borrower. As the borrower in this case is a reinsurance company, it will more than likely have the same credit spread as a bank (i.e. very small) and so, for simplicity, we will assume that the yield is 5% (the Libor rate at the time of writing). Therefore, the cash flows from the insurer's perspective are summarised as in Table 12.6.

Table 12.6 Cash flows

0	−£20
1	−£20
2	−£20
3	−£20
4	−£20
5	£90
Effective rate	5%

The next step is to identify the present value of the loan. Table 12.7 illustrates an intuitive way of calculating the present value (there is of course an easier way). What can be seen is that the present cash flows of the payments exceed the present value of receipts. The difference of £26.04 is (in theory) because the insurer is paying an extra amount for insurance protection.

Next, we reconfigure the table so that the present value of the cash inflows equals the present value of the cash outflows, by adjusting the premium payments (Table 12.8). We will refer to them as loan installments since that is what they really are.

Table 12.7   Effective interest calculation

	Opening balance	Premium Interest Loan component Deposit interest	£20 0.05 90 Cash flows	Closing balance
0	£0.00	£0.00	−£20.00	−£20.00
1	−£20.00	−£1.00	−£20.00	−£41.00
2	−£41.00	−£2.05	−£20.00	−£63.05
3	−£63.05	−£3.15	−£20.00	−£86.20
4	−£86.20	−£4.31	−£20.00	−£110.51
5	−£110.51	−£5.53	£90.00	−£26.04
		−£16.04	−£10.00	

Table 12.8   Interest calculation with adjusted premiums

	Opening balance	Premium Interest Loan component Deposit interest	15.51213 5% 90 Cash flows	Closing balance
0	£−	£−	−£15.51	−£15.51
1	−£15.51	−£0.78	−£15.51	−£31.80
2	−£31.80	−£1.59	−£15.51	−£48.90
3	−£48.90	−£2.45	−£15.51	−£66.86
4	−£66.86	−£3.34	−£15.51	−£85.71
5	−£85.71	−£4.29	£90.00	£−
		−£12.44	£12.44	−£0.00

The breakeven loan installment is £15.51 and the remaining £4.91 represents the insurance element. The calculation of £15.51 is illustrated in Table 12.8. The journal entries are therefore:

Debit Loans & Receivables (balance sheet)	£15.51
Debit insurance expense (Profit & Loss account)	£4.49
Credit cash	£20

IFRS 4 therefore forces the insured company to treat the majority of the premium paid as a deposit account. From the reinsurance company's perspective, it can only take £4.49 through the Profit & Loss account and not the full £20, which might have been possible in the pre-IFRS 4 days.

12.5   OTHER ASPECTS OF IFRS 4

IAS 8

IAS 8 sets out the procedure for developing an accounting policy if it is not specifically catered for in the accounting standards. Obviously, where an area is not covered by the accounting standards, management judgement is required. IAS 8, *Accounting Policies, Changes in Accounting Estimates and Errors* requires management, in such circumstances, to refer to standards that deal with 'similar related issues'. Where no such guidance is given, management may refer to the IASB Framework for the Presentation of Financial Statements. In addition, management may refer to standards issued by other accounting standard setters (such as the American accounting standards board). IFRS 4 over-rides the requirements of IAS 8; it exempts insurance entities from such requirements in situations where the IFRS standards do not have a guideline for a proposed accounting policy in relation to insurance or reinsurance. In effect this means that insurers do not have to change existing accounting policies for insurance contracts. The IASB presumably viewed this flexibility as necessary because, if they forced insurance companies to change for Phase One and then forced further changes for Phase Two, they would suffer a lot of criticism from insurance practitioners. It must be said, however, that leaving insurance companies in limbo over certain policies and delaying the introduction of Phase Two has left many insurance practitioners very annoyed. From an analyst's perspective the accounting policies chosen by insurance companies still vary a lot. This hardly facilitates comparison between insurance companies. There are currently some 'grandfathering provisions', which effectively reduce the quality of the standards. Grandfathering provisions are used a lot by the regulators, but used reluctantly. In effect they say 'adopting certain practices is not permitted by IFRS but if you have adopted these practices in the past, you can continue to do so until further notice'.

Specifically, an insurance company is required to carry out a 'liability adequacy test' regularly to make sure that the actual expected liabilities do not exceed the liabilities as disclosed on the balance sheet. If there was an excess, the profits of the insurance company would of course be understated. So, while the insurance accounting rules are still a bit vague, there are some specific practices that insurance companies are not allowed to engage in unless they have already adopted them under their existing accounting policies. Namely, the entity cannot:

- Measure insurance liabilities on an undiscounted basis – as this overstates liabilities.
- Measure contractual rights to future investment management fees at an amount that exceeds their fair value by comparison to related fees for other similar services.
- Use different non-uniform accounting policies for different firms.
- Measure an insurance contract with excessive prudence.

12.6 PHASE TWO EMBEDDED VALUE

The IASB produced a discussion paper[3] to illustrate how embedded value is to be incorporated in the accounting standards. This is discussed below.

Suppose an entity enters into an insurance contract on 1 January with details as in Table 12.9. It receives a premium of £1000 and the expected future payout is £950. The expected return on any cash invested is 11% and, given the risks, the discount rate or opportunity cost of capital is 12%.

Table 12.10 shows the expected profit. The premium is £1000 but the expected payout is only £950, giving a profit of £50. The return on the investment is 11% and the total sum

---

[3] Preliminary Views on Insurance Contracts, May 2007 (Example 6, Embedded Value, page 45, part 2), International Accounting Standards Board.

Table 12.9   Embedded value details

Expected return	11%
Opportunity cost of capital	12%
Shareholders' funds	£100
Sum invested	£1000
Expected future payout	£950

Table 12.10   Expected profit on contract

Future gain	
Excess over expected loss	£50
Return on investment	£121
	£171
Opening embedded value start	£100
Embedded value end (future value)	£271
Embedded value end (present value)	£242
Profit for period	£142

invested is £1000 + £100 of shareholders' funds. The expected return is therefore £121, giving a total profit of £171. The expected embedded value at the end of the year is therefore the shareholders' funds at the start (£100) plus the gain made during the year (£171). This equals £271. As the embedded value is measured in present value terms, it must be discounted at 12% to obtain the embedded value at the start of the year: $£271/(1 + 12\%) = £242$. This gives a 'day 1' profit of $£242 - £100 = £142$.

An alternative calculation is as follows. The gain on the contract is the premium as before minus the expected loss, i.e. £50. The customer pays a premium of £1000 which is invested at 11%, adding an extra £110 to the profit. The value of the total profit is £160. Under the embedded value rules, this is discounted to present value $£160/(1 + 12\%) = £143$. The regulators require that shareholders' funds be tied up in the entity. The shareholder demands a return on capital of 12%, while the £100 invested only receives an investment return of 11%. The present value of £111 is $£111/(1 + 12\%) = £99$. Therefore, the opportunity cost of capital (i.e. the opportunity cost of tying up shareholders' funds) is $£100 - £99 = £1$. If we subtract £1 from £143 we end up with the profit for the period, £142 as before.

Table 12.11 shows how the balance sheet will look for embedded value accounting.

We start off with an opening balance sheet of £100. As soon as the premium is received, the asset (£1000 cash) and the expected liability (£950) are brought on to the balance sheet. The expected return of £121 is also shown, and therefore the expected profit at the end of the year (£171) is calculated. As pointed out earlier, embedded value principles require that the expected future cash flows are shown on the balance sheet at present value. The future embedded value of £271 is brought to the present value $£271/(1 + 12\%) = £242$. Therefore, we must reduce the profit and the embedded value (asset) on the balance sheet by £29. Finally, in the illustration produced by the IASB, the regulator requires the insurer to measure the liability at £1040 instead of £950 (which is the expected cash outflow). The difference is buried in the embedded value asset. Both accountants and non-accountants may find this last adjustment confusing. When regulators are calculating liabilities they will normally follow the prudent principle of requiring insurance companies to hold more money to cover the variation

Table 12.11 Balance sheet

Opening embedded value	01-Jan-08 Opening balance sheet	31-Dec-08 Future balance sheet	01-Dec-2008 Present balance sheet	01-Dec-2008 IFRS interpretation
Assets				
Cash	£100	£1100	£1100	£1100
Embedded value (asset)		£121	£92	£182
Liabilities				
Expected payments		−£950	−£950	−£1040
	£100	£271	£242	£242
Shareholders' funds				
Ordinary shares	£100	£100	£100	£100
Profit		£171	£142	£142
	£100	£271	£242	£242

in expected value. However, in accounting terms, the economic liability is the expected future cash outflows and should perhaps therefore be measured at £950 rather than £1040, which is a little confusing. Obviously, the entity needs to lock in more than £950 – perhaps by transferring £90 from the Revenue Reserve to a Capital Reserve, thus reducing the amount of money that shareholders can extract by way of distribution.

Phase Two encourages the measurement of insurance liabilities on the balance sheet using three building blocks:

- An explicit market estimate of future cash flows.
- A discount rate based on market interest rates to bring future cash flows to present value.
- An estimate of a margin that another party would require to take on the risk.

Regulators in the banking world require that banks keep data on past default experience so that they can estimate future credit spreads with more precision. Likewise, the insurance regulator will require insurance companies to develop data storage and modelling systems so that they can estimate expected losses and volatility surrounding those losses. These will be used by auditors to determine if the expected loss calculations are based on solid foundations. Presumably, in the absence of data, insurance companies will be prevented from recognising 'day 1' profits, particularly if the insurance company makes its own assumptions.

Another key feature in Phase Two is that the IASB favour a Current Exit Value (CEV) approach. This means that if, say, an insurance company agrees a premium of £1000 with a customer but can reinsure for £900, then the CEV is £900 and the insurance company must recognise a liability for this amount, giving a total profit of £100. Obviously, this accounting system would work well in a very liquid market but in the absence of such liquidity, the CEV would of course be difficult to ascertain.

APPENDIX: THE COLLAPSE OF AIG

In 2006 the American regulators, the SEC, took action against the American International Group (AIG). The SEC alleged that for a six-year period from 2000 to 2005, AIG materially falsified its financial statements 'through a variety of sham transactions and entities whose purpose was to paint a falsely rosy picture of AIG's financial results to analysts and investors'.[4] Not only did AIG hide losses, they also concealed the substantial risks that they were taking on. They insured banks against losses from toxic investments such as complex securitisations. In September 2008, the government was forced to bail out AIG since there was a risk that if AIG collapsed, so too would a number of counterparties – bringing systemic risk to the world financial system. AIG, a Delaware corporation, is a holding company that, through its subsidiaries, is engaged in a broad range of insurance and insurance-related activities in the United States and abroad. In 2008 it got into difficulty and risked a downgrading from the rating agencies, which would almost certainly have resulted in liquidity problems and possibly bankruptcy. Recognising its highly probable failure as a threat to the financial system, the American government stepped in with a controversial bail-out package under which it acquired 80% control.

Originally, AIG was a huge multinational insurance group with a reputation for solid underwriting and risk management. Problems began to emerge when AIG 'diversified' into the world of derivatives, insuring credit risk through securitisations that it possibly did not understand. According to John Gapper of the *Financial Times*:[5]

> Of course, [AIG] thought it understood [complex derivatives]. In presentations to investors this year, it emphasised how thoroughly its AIG Financial Products arm assessed the risks of insuring CDOs. It ran all the data and decided that, in the worst case it risked losing $2.4 billion. Well $24 billion of write-downs later – a mere 10 times its maximum estimate – the company has burned through its equity and spread financial chaos.

What was interesting about AIG was that it potentially misled its own shareholders with incorrect accounting information and then sold products, which were possibly used by other financial institutions to mislead their shareholders by getting round regulatory requirements so that these institutions could book artificial profits and keep risk off their balance sheet and outside the regulatory regime. In many cases, these financial institutions were able to use a type of gain-on-sale accounting, i.e. buy a complex derivative instrument that paid a high yield (to compensate for the huge risks) and then pay a derisory premium to AIG so that they could argue that the risks and rewards of ownership had moved to AIG and so book artificial profits up-front. This arrangement seems to contravene IAS 18, *Revenue Recognition* and SAB 101. In effect what is happening is that an entity is insuring credit risk over a long period (say five years) and taking the five-year premium up-front to the Profit & Loss account as opposed to matching the premium with the risk and recognising it over the life of the structured product. In theory, the risk was passed on to AIG but in reality, AIG took on so much risk that the transfer of risk was to some extent artificial in nature.

AIG devised a number of schemes to conceal the amount of risk it was taking on. For instance, it classified straightforward loans as reinsurance contracts. This reclassification, now controlled by IFRS 4, *Accounting for Insurance*, was often used by insurance companies to borrow money and conceal their liabilities and losses. The result was that when the loan was drawn down, instead of recognising a liability, the entity indirectly credited the proceeds to

---

[4] SEC vs. AIG 2006.

[5] John Gapper, 'This greed was beyond irresponsible', *Financial Times*, 17 September 2008.

its Profit & Loss account by treating the payment as proceeds of an insurance contract. AIG appear to have done the reverse, i.e. treating a deposit as a reinsurance contract. A counterparty Gen Re entered into an agreement with AIG whereby the former would pay over to AIG $500m. The agreement stated that the payment was a premium to cover future potential losses. In reality, however, there was a separate side agreement which covered AIG against any losses. In other words, no insurance risk was transferred to AIG. Today, IFRS 4 addresses this issue by restricting the use of insurance accounting to genuine insurance contracts where there is an insurable event such as fire, theft or accident. Insuring market risks such as interest rate exposure, foreign exchange exposure, equity exposure and certain types of credit exposure is no longer classified as an insurance event. Therefore, such contracts must now be classified under IAS 39 as loans/deposits or derivatives. Had AIG applied the equivalent of IFRS 4 correctly, they would have had difficulty disguising the liability and loss created from these artificial transactions. Cash transfers on insurance contracts end up going through the Profit & Loss account (or at least through reserves) according to IFRS 4. Cash received and paid for loans and deposits, by contrast, generally does not go through the Profit & Loss account (apart from interest payments) in accordance with IAS 39.

As the SEC observed:[6]

[The Gen Re transactions] were done to accomplish a desired accounting result and did not entail sufficient qualifying risk transfer. As a result, AIG has determined that the transaction[s] should not have been recorded as insurance. In its restatement, AIG recharacterized the Gen Re transactions as a deposit[/loan] instead of as insurance.

Gen Re was the counterparty to the transaction.

The SEC stated:[7]

The sole purpose of these transactions was to make it appear as though Gen Re was purchasing reinsurance from AIG so that AIG could record loss reserves associated with the reinsurance contracts. Had this been real reinsurance involving a real transfer of risk, AIG would have been entitled to record reserves in the amount of the loss that was probable and reasonably estimable under generally accepted accounting principles ('GAAP'). Under Statement of Financial Accounting Standards ('FAS') No. 113, a reinsurer may record a loss reserve pertaining to a reinsurance contract only when the reinsurer is assuming significant insurance risk (underwriting and timing risk) and it is reasonably possible that the reinsurer may realize a significant loss for the transaction.

Another technique that AIG used to conceal trading losses was to convert losses on insurance contracts into capital losses. The analyst might conclude (incorrectly in this case) that capital losses are once-off and therefore have no bearing on future profits whereas trading profits/losses are a better indicator of future trends and as such are treated more seriously when analysing the health of a financial institution. AIG effectively transferred a loss-making insurance company to an offshore sheet company called Capco. Since Capco acquired the

[6] SEC vs. AIG 2006, page 8.
[7] SEC vs. AIG 2006, page 10.

losses as well as the contracts, the investment by AIG in Capco showed a loss which AIG described as an investment/capital loss instead of a trading loss.

The now all-too-familiar off-balance sheet structure was also used by AIG to conceal losses. In the words of the SEC:[8]

> In 1991, AIG established Union Excess, an offshore reinsurer, to which it ultimately ceded approximately 50 reinsurance contracts for its own benefit. Although AIG controlled Union Excess, it improperly failed to consolidate Union Excess's financial results with its own. AIG also took steps to conceal its control over Union Excess from its auditors and regulators.

The result of non-consolidation was that AIG was in a position to hide losses and liabilities. AIG was effectively able to borrow through the offshore insurer and keep the debts off-balance sheet. AIG could also sell, to an offshore vehicle, assets at above market value and recognise artificial profits. Under the consolidation rules which AIG should have adopted, such inter-company profits must generally be cancelled in the inter-company accounts. AIG restated its accounts and noted:[9]

> Union Excess is now included in AIG's consolidated financial statements. The facts and circumstances surrounding SICO's involvement with Union Excess were not properly reflected in AIG's books and records, were not known to all relevant AIG financial reporting personnel and, AIG now believes, were not known to AIG's independent auditors. For example, a significant portion of the ownership interests of Union Excess shareholders are protected against loss under financial arrangements with SICO. Additionally, from its formation in 1991, Union Excess has reinsured risks emanating primarily or solely from AIG subsidiaries, both directly and indirectly.

---

[8] http://www.sec.gov/litigation/complaints/comp19560.pdf, page 20.
[9] http://ir.aigcorporate.com/phoenix.zhtml?c=76115&p=irol-newsArticle&ID=703645&highlight=

13
Conclusion

In 2008 Warren Buffet wrote to his shareholders 'You may recall a 2003 Silicon Valley bumper sticker that implored, "Please, God, Just One More Bubble."' According to Buffett,[1] that wish came true. A bubble did erupt in the American housing market, prompted to a large extent by the willingness of financial institutions to lend money. According to Buffett, 'lenders shovelled out money, confident that house price appreciation would cure all problems'. With house prices falling Buffet continued, 'a huge amount of financial folly is being exposed. You only learn who has been swimming naked when the tide goes out – and what we are witnessing at some of our large financial institutions is an ugly sight'.

The question that many shareholders are puzzled over is firstly why the financial institutions were motivated to behave in the way they did. Shareholders will be particularly puzzled as to the risks that the banks took on. Banking isn't a new industry, they have had generations to perfect and measure credit risk. Also, banking, with its huge salaries and bonuses, has the ability to attract the best talent, and they clearly have done so, paying doctorates and quant specialists vast sums of money not only to come up with innovative and complex financial instruments, but also to devise sophisticated risk measurement systems. JPMorgan spent huge amounts of money developing systems to measure market risk, credit risk and, more recently, operational risk. Some of the best minds in the financial world, including Nobel prize winners, have also addressed the problems of measuring and controlling liquidity risk. Also, the Basel committee on banking supervision has spent vast sums of money on developing a system to ensure that banks measure their risks and finance themselves according to their risk profile. For high-risk banks, therefore, equity finance must dominate while low-risk banks can rely more on borrowings.

Similarly, the shareholder – reassured by major changes in the accounting standards – will ask questions. In particular, since the collapse of Enron, shareholders will want to know why the ugly world of 'off-balance sheet' has not been addressed. Through various accounting standards, the rules of consolidation are tightened up. This means that entities cannot conceal the extent to which they are borrowing money and neither can they mislead the shareholder by creating artificial profits when subsidiaries trade with each other. Perhaps what is more frustrating for the shareholder was the record bonuses that traders and bank directors received at a time when, months later, banks had to announce huge losses – not small financial institutions, that might not have the resources to impose controls, but large financial institutions who should have known better.

Bankers have responded to the recent credit crises by admitting that they have made mistakes but have not been slow to emphasise that they have suffered, perhaps reassuring people that an automatic corrective mechanism is in place. However, it is important to emphasise that those who made the mistakes and encouraged banks to take risks have received bonuses

---

[1] http://www.berkshirehathaway.com/letters2007ltr.pdf

for their troubles – and the likelihood is that few of those bonuses will be returned now that losses are discovered. It is also important to recognise that those with voting power over shares are not necessarily the beneficial owners of the shares. Therefore, there is a risk that those with the power to appoint directors and dismiss them, approve strategic plans, etc. may find it more profitable to encourage and take risks rather than act in the interests of the shareholder. The result is that there is unfortunate evidence that the financial sector is not learning enough from past mistakes. Hedge funds continue to operate on a highly leveraged basis despite lessons from the Long Term Capital Management fiasco many years ago. SocGen could probably have studied the fall of Barings more carefully. The accounting profession may be at fault in allowing financial institutions to exploit the benefits of 'off-balance sheet' activities, despite the lessons from Enron, and indeed despite the fact that the off-balance sheet issue is at least 20 years old. Finally, banks are continuing to lend money without too much regard for the credit risks that they are taking on.

A problem with regulation, Sarbanes–Oxley and the accounting standards is that they may falsely reassure the shareholder that all is well. As Paul Amery[2] points out:

> Here are some financial scandals in the UK from the last 20 years: BCCI, Barings, pensions misselling, endowment mortgages, the internet bubble, Equitable Life, split capital investment trusts, Northern Rock. What do they have in common? All have occurred since the introduction of compulsory regulation of investment business in the UK under the Financial Services Act of 1986.

Some of these scandals have exposed accounting weaknesses. The accountants at Barings, for instance, were unaware of the huge losses Barings was making with financial instruments. The internet bubble also challenged accountants, since they were forced to recognise revenue prematurely from internet companies. The accounting profession also did not disclose to the shareholder the huge transfer of wealth that was taking place through the use of stock options and the inflated profits that those stock options allowed the entities to report. Equitable Life was able to offer guarantees to customers as a selling ploy, and of course it did lead to sales of financial products, but they failed to recognise the liabilities associated with these guarantees on their balance sheet, resulting in huge undisclosed losses. IAS 39, along with IFRS 4, has since dealt with this accounting loophole. Northern Rock and another scandal involving split capital funds are examples of entities that took huge financial risks. There is a question mark over the extent to which accountants should report on risks and whether the auditors of Northern Rock and the various 'split capital funds' should have alerted shareholders to the potential risks. Some argue, with some legitimacy, that it is the accountants' role to report the profits and not the risks. However, in IFRS 7 the following quote appears in paragraph IN2 (which discusses the reasons for IFRS 7):

> The International Accounting Standards Board believes that users of financial statements need information about the entity's exposure to risks and how those risks are managed. Such information can influence a user's assessment of the financial position and financial performance of an entity or of the amount, timing and uncertainty of its future cash flows.

---

[2] Paul Amery, 'Too heavy financial regulation has created danger', *Financial Times*, 12 March 2008.

Greater transparency regarding those risks allow users to make more informed judgements about risks and return.

It is probably fair to say that this idea is a lot more difficult to implement in practice than it sounds. Accountants face two obstacles. Firstly, their masters (i.e. those who decide their audit fees) may be motivated to take on huge amounts of risk and simultaneously conceal what they are doing. Secondly, where there is complexity there is a risk that accountants will simply fill the annual report with risk information but not disclose the important risks. To put this more bluntly, the accountant can avoid going to court for failing to apply the accounting standards if he gives the appearance that he is attempting to comply.

Northern Rock was probably the incident that regulators will remember quite well. When the bank got into trouble, the regulators had difficulty in deciding who was in charge. Mervyn King, the Bank of England Governor, attempted to avoid rescuing banks that were badly managed but he was then forced to do a quick U-turn. Alistair Darling was forced into a situation where the bulk of credit risk was passed from Northern Rock on to the taxpayer, and the light regulatory regime of the Financial Services Authority was also questioned.

A response to all of these incidents is to impose more regulation. Yet, there is a risk that too much regulation will cause financial institutions to act in a manner that complies with the regulation but does not necessarily look after the interests of shareholders or depositors. It simply introduces layers of bureaucracy and allows traders to expose their financial institutions to risks that cannot be picked up or measured by the regulator. More importantly, weak regulation will give investors a false sense of security that all is well when in fact it is not.

Unfortunately, the same illness affects the setting of accounting standards. Like the regulators, there is a danger that the accounting profession tends to be reactionary rather than proactive. Enron is a good case in point. The antics of Enron and their auditors allowed Enron to hide losses and to create artificial profits (or at least hide losses) by transferring assets at inflated values between entities controlled by Enron. Yet this is exactly what is happening today. Banks can borrow money through off-balance sheet vehicles and only bring them on to the balance sheet when they are forced to subsidise the losses of these vehicles. Unfortunately, investors rely on these standards and also rely on the regulators to ensure that profits and risks are reported correctly. Regrettably, there is an abundance of evidence to suggest that their reliance is misplaced in both cases.

It is perhaps also important to realise the extent to which lobby groups are influencing the accounting standards and perhaps the regulations. Arthur Levitt, talking about attempts by lobby groups to control the American accounting standards board, commented:[3]

I smelled a rat. Rather than speed up and improve the standard setting process, I believed this cabal was looking to place it in the corporate equivalent of leg irons.

Investors might take comfort from the accounting profession's eagerness to promote good quality accounting standards. Levitt, however, has a stark warning for such investors.

---

[3] Arthur Levitt, *Take on the Street*, Pantheon Books, New York, 2002, p. 112.

Commenting on the introduction of FAS 133, the standard designed to reveal the extent to which companies were gambling with derivatives, Levitt said:

> The FASB went on to approve a new accounting standard that forced companies to reveal the value of derivatives contracts they held or were exposed to. But, I came away from these back-channel brawls with one overriding impression; accounting firms were passive when it came to standing up for investors' interests. It wasn't surprising that chief financial officers would fight for standards that let them understate expenses and exaggerate profits.

Levitt went on to denounce the accounting profession because they failed to rally to the support of investors, instead switching their loyalties to those who paid their fees, the financial officers they were supposed to supervise. Levitt commented 'I would forever look upon the accounting profession differently after this episode'. Levitt should hardly have been surprised at this breakdown in corporate governance. Accountants have tried successfully over the years to move away from pure auditing, to other more lucrative consulting areas. Occasionally, some auditors boasted that their business strategy was to use auditing as a 'loss leader' in order to get their foot in the door to chase the more lucrative consulting work. Commercially of course that makes sense, but it does impede the integrity and independence of the auditor, something that came to light in the Enron scandal. A cynic might argue that an auditor does not have to worry too much about his reputation, the profession is monopolised by a few firms and unless they do something disastrous like Andersons (the auditors of Enron) they will stay in business. The same is true of the credit rating agencies who, like the accounting profession, enjoy a type of monopoly.

Reading Levitt's comments, one might draw the conclusion that many accountants attempt to maximise fees by siding with the financial director of companies and financial institutions rather than the investor. Since these financial directors enjoy the flexibility of poor accounting standards, it follows that not only have we a disinterested accounting profession, but they are working with standards which are inappropriate for the complex world of financial derivatives. There is also the risk that investors are not represented by those who vote on behalf of shareholders. Many votes are cast by hedge funds and institutional investors. There is the prospect, for instance, that a hedge fund buys insurance protection against the company collapsing. Therefore, it is in the hedge fund's interest to vote in a manner that makes the company more risky. The institutional investor may also have a corporate finance relationship with the company, and may therefore vote to suit the needs of the financial director. It follows, therefore, that there are breakdowns in three levels. The average shareholder is not necessarily aware that the bonus scheme that many directors and chief traders apply is one that motivates them to put shareholders' funds at considerable risk. The accounting professional will not help the investor because he is tempted to do whatever the financial director requires, and those who vote on the shareholders' behalf may have voting power only and not beneficial interest.

Although this may partly explain why major investment banks were able to clock up huge losses, caution is necessary. There are probably many accountants who feel that the previous paragraph is unjust, and with some justification. There are many accountants, probably the vast majority, who see their role as making sure that the accounts show a true and fair value. That may be the case. However, what few accountants will argue against is the view that the more complex financial instruments become, the more difficult it is to portray them accurately on the financial statements. Clearly, after the credit crunch of 2007/08 is contained, regulators and accountants will examine current practices and see how they will improve things. One thing is clear, many will advocate transparency and simplicity. However, there will be a challenge. It will be difficult, for instance, for accounting standard setters to attempt to impose accounting standards on traders and financial directors if those traders see that their bonuses are affected. In particular, regulators and accountants will have difficulty correcting the current status quo. Traders who receive bonuses by exposing shareholders to greater risk are almost guaranteed a bonus, and they are unlikely to give this up easily. Being human, they may realise that poorly designed incentive schemes are the root of many of the evils of today's financial world – however, if they are on the right side of such schemes, correcting them will not feature high in their list of priorities.

There are a few pointers that indicate the way in which regulation and the accounting standards will go in the future:

- Regulators will have to start penalising complexity. If there is evidence that institutions are buying structured products which are complex, illiquid and hard to value, regulators will have to penalise them in terms of requiring that they be financed by shareholders' funds as opposed to borrowings. Doing so means that the risk of another Bear Stearns catastrophe is reduced or eliminated.
- Accountants will have to consider qualifying accounts (i.e. expressing their concerns in an audit letter to investors). Accountants have often relaxed on the assumption that although they don't understand the complexities of complex products, they feel that they can audit them on the grounds that they are receiving independent verification from external consultants like credit rating agencies and independent valuers. Sometimes, however, these external consultants do make mistakes, and do not have the capacity to understand what they are valuing or passing an opinion on.

There is quite a lot that the accounting profession can do to minimise the reputational damage that financial instruments and financial institutions have created during the recent credit crunch. Without action, there is the risk that accountants too will lose their reputation to report on a financial institution's performance. Where financial instruments are complex, auditors should alert investors to the fact that if these instruments have contributed to the profits of an enterprise then that profit is not necessarily reliable. Accountants could also utilse methodologies like Embedded Value (Insurance) and Value at Risk (market risk) to communicate in a meaningful manner the risks of an enterprise so that shareholders can distinguish conservative institutions against those that are in effect speculating.

One important feature of the credit crunch is that banks will have difficulty raising capital in the future unless their annual report is more meaningful and transparent – an opportunity for the accounting profession to make a very positive contribution in resolving this dilemma.

Glossary

Active market	A market where quoted prices are readily available from stock exchanges or pricing services. There must be a willingness to buy and sell on an arm's length basis at these prices.
Available for sale	Non-derivative financial instruments that are not classified as (a) loans and receivables, (b) trading or (c) held-to-maturity.
Beneficial interest	An entity normally has beneficial interest in an asset/liability if its Profit & Loss is exposed to changes in the price or value of the asset/liability.
Cash flow hedge	A derivative which is used to lock in future cash flows which would otherwise be uncertain. This derivative must meet the requirements of IAS 39.88.
Cookie jar reserve accounting	A creative accounting technique whereby an entity hides profits in good years and releases them in bad, in order to either smooth out the Profit & Loss or exploit poorly designed bonus schemes.
Creative accounting	A process whereby accountants manipulate the accounting rules in order to simultaneously comply with them and mislead the shareholders (i.e. keeping some assets and liabilities off-balance sheet).
Credit default swaps	A derivative product principally designed to protect the premium payer against default.
Credit spreads	The extra yield that an investor receives for an investment containing credit risk.
Fair value	The amount for which an asset would be exchanged or a liability extinguished between knowledgeable willing parties in an arm's length transaction.
Fair value hedge	A derivative which protects an entity from changes in the fair value of certain assets or liabilities on the balance sheet – in turn this reduces or eliminates volatility in the Profit & Loss account. This derivative must meet the requirements of IAS 39.88.
Fair value option	An option available to some entities to classify certain assets and liabilities at fair value on the balance sheet with the changes in value going through Profit & Loss.

Hedge of a net investment	A foreign exchange derivative used to hedge the change in value (arising from foreign exchange movements) of a reporting entity's interest in the net assets of that operation.
Held-to-maturity	Non-derivative financial assets with fixed payments and fixed maturity. The entity must have the intention and ability to hold such assets to maturity.
Loans and receivables	Financial assets similar to held-to-maturity (above) but generally not quoted on an active market.
Market risk	The risk that a change in market variables (such as interest rates, foreign exchange rates, equity prices, commodity prices or credit spread) will cause volatility in the Profit & Loss.
Matching concept	A concept in accounting that attempts to release income to the Profit & Loss account when it is earned – as opposed to received.
Minority interest	The proportion of the profit or loss and net assets of a subsidiary attributable to equity interests that are not owned by the parent.
Mixed model	An accounting model that allows entities to show some assets/liabilities at cost on the balance sheet while others are shown at fair value.
Monetary items	Money held and items to be received or paid in money.
Off-balance sheet	A term used by accountants to deal with situations where a company does not reveal on its balance sheet assets that it owns or does not reveal liabilities that it has incurred. The term also refers to instances where an asset's value is not fully reflected on the balance sheet. For instance, an entity might purchase an asset for $10 though its current worth is $1,000. If the entity did not use mark-to-market accounting, the remaining $990 is kept off-balance sheet.
Present value	A future asset or liability discounted to a particular balance sheet date. The assumption is that an asset or liability will continue to earn an expected yield until maturity date.
Provision	A liability where the amount or due date is uncertain.
QSPE	A trust or legal entity that is kept off-balance sheet and therefore does not require consolidation.
Regulatory arbitrage	A means by which banks can reduce the requirement to hold capital against risk, without necessarily reducing risk.
Tier One capital	A measure that regulators use to ensure that a bank is appropriately financed relative to its risk. Tier One capital, in broad terms, includes equity capital (i.e. money that shareholders have invested in the bank).
Tier Two capital	A second measure that banking regulators use to ensure that a bank is appropriately financed relative to its risk. Tier Two capital includes subordinated loans and certain other reserves.

Index

ABN Amro   10, 59, 149–50, 165
Accountancy Age   32
accountants
  consultant ambitions   262
  credit rating agency links   57–8, 263
  fees   261–2
  future prospects   263
  journal entries   214–15
  litigation threats   7
  monopolies   57–8, 262
  qualified accounts   263
  responsibilities   1, 43–8, 140–1, 157, 165–8,
     199–216, 230–41, 260–3
  service limitation proposals   59–60
  shortfalls   48, 55–7, 117–18, 140–1, 165–8, 174–5,
     177–98, 260–3
  true and fair view   217, 220, 262–3
  Value at Risk   235–41
accounting foundations   21–41
accounting manipulation
  Freddie Mac   17–19
  off-balance sheet vehicles   178–98
Accounting Research Board   51 (ARB   51) 51,
     185–6, 187
accounting standards
  see also Financial . . .; International . . .
  artificial volatility   22, 26–8, 67–76, 81–3, 221–41,
     245–7
  bifurcation rules   44, 51–2, 120–1, 139–40, 164–5,
     173–4
  company law   166, 230
  credit derivatives   156–7
  credit risk   119–20, 129, 139–57, 159–75, 237–41
  critique   1–2, 3, 4–6, 15, 21–41, 44–5, 54–7, 59–62,
     65–76, 117–18, 153–7, 164–8, 172–5, 202–16,
     217–41, 244–58, 259–63
  derision   31

embedded derivatives   5, 122–37, 164–5, 245–50,
     253–5
financial crises contributor   21–2, 31–2, 139, 218
future prospects   263
importance perceptions   60
improvement attempts   1, 259–63
insurance   6, 24, 156, 171–2, 193–4, 243–58
loans   15, 21, 24–6, 31, 34–5, 77–115, 146–57
lobbying pressures   1–2, 3, 41, 46, 59–62, 261–2
matching concept   66, 68, 69–70, 185, 245–50
mixed-model approach   4–5, 21–2, 23–41, 65–76,
     217–41
off-balance sheet vehicles   5, 21–3, 177–98,
     221–41, 259–63
post-Enron rules   32–41, 120–1, 139, 187, 219, 248,
     259–62
proactive/reactive approaches   29, 41, 261–2
proprietary trading   202–4
prudence concept   31
reform needs   174–5, 261–3
rogue traders   202–4
securitisation market   159–60, 162, 164–8, 177–98
shareholder protection measures   15, 36–9, 121–2,
     218–19
structured products   119–37, 139–57, 164–75, 263
activism considerations, shareholders   49–50
Adhikari, Ajay   195–6
AIG   255–8
Allied Irish Bank   133, 199, 201–2
American standards
  see also US
  EU standards   5, 177–98
Americredit   184–5
Amery, Paul   260
annual reports   19, 45–6
approvals, loans   142–4, 157
ARB . . . *see* Accounting Research Board . . .

arbitrage opportunities   64, 162, 200–4
  rogue traders   200–4
  securitisation market   162
arrangement fees   22, 36–9, 121
  see also effective interest rates
Arthur Andersen   19, 262
artificial volatility, concepts   22, 26–8, 67–76, 81–3,
  221–41, 245–7
asset treatments
  artificial volatility   22, 26–8, 67–76, 81–3, 221–41,
    245–7
  cherry-picking   6, 18–19, 28, 41, 72–3, 172–3, 221,
    243–4
  classification of assets   18–19, 24–6, 31, 40–1,
    72–6, 93–7, 105–15, 122, 152–3, 164, 172–3,
    191–2, 202, 219–23, 226–9, 236–41
  foreign exchange   104–15
  IAS   39 18–19, 24–6, 31, 67–76, 87–9, 122, 136–7,
    202, 244–57
  impairment requirements   30–1, 33, 53–4
asset-backed commercial papers (ABCPs)   192–4
asset-backed securities   24, 192–4
Association of British Insurers   32
audit committees   32
auditors   2, 6–7, 19, 32, 41, 45–6, 56, 57–60, 139–40,
  165–8, 171–2, 182–4, 192, 199–216, 217–41,
  261–3
  appointments   57–8
  conflicts of interest   2, 6, 46, 140, 160, 202, 262
  consultant ambitions   262
  fees   2, 59–60, 121, 261–2
  risk management systems   32
  service limitation proposals   59–60
  true and fair view   217, 220, 262–3
'Available for Sale' assets classification   18–19, 24–6,
  31, 40–1, 166, 172–3, 220, 236–41
average debt levels   35

the back office   201–4
bad debts   36–8, 53–4, 146–7, 151–6, 159
  see also loan impairments
balance sheets   2–3, 5, 7–8, 9–10, 14–15, 17–18, 21–2,
  23–6, 29, 31, 33, 34, 35, 54–7, 68, 79–115, 126–7,
  153–7, 177–98, 235–41
  see also off . . .
  consolidations   22, 29, 33, 34, 54–7, 177–80,
    185–98
  embedded derivatives   126–7, 245–50, 253–5
  pension accounting   32, 33
  share options   33
Bank of England   167, 261
Bank of Ireland   22
Bankers Trust   52
banking books, concepts   40–1, 219–23, 229
bankruptcy risks, banks   159–60

banks
  see also loans
  approved loans   142–3
  bankruptcy risks   159–60
  Basel 2 requirements   5, 7–8, 15, 35, 44–5, 86,
    119–22, 146–7, 159–60, 162, 166, 203, 217,
    228–41, 259–60
  bonus incentives   1–2, 3–4, 6, 9–10, 11–15, 16–19,
    24, 29, 34–5, 41, 43, 44–5, 63–4, 118–20, 200,
    202–4, 226–9, 259–63
  British Government bailout   63–4, 139–40, 149–50,
    166, 261
  careless behaviour   141–2, 259–63
  credit spirals   217–19, 259–60
  critique   1–2, 6–10, 29, 34, 54–7, 117–18, 120–1,
    139–57, 165–8, 174–5, 199–216, 217–41,
    259–63
  embedded derivatives   128–9, 164–5
  fees   10–11, 119–20, 121, 165, 174–5
  footnotes   177–8
  handouts   1
  hedge fund contrasts   8, 29, 218
  Japanese banking crisis   218–19
  the middle office   201–8
  moral hazard   44–5, 46, 140–1, 146, 159, 161–2,
    167–8
  offshore vehicles   120–1
  risk management failings   1–2, 5, 6–10, 29, 34, 39,
    54–7, 117–18, 120–1, 133, 139–57, 168–9,
    199–216, 223–41, 259–63
  salary levels   46
  shareholders   1–2, 7–8, 34, 36–9, 43–64, 121–2,
    230–41
  sources of finance   232–4
  traders' dilemma   14–15, 16–19, 46–7
  UK Treasury Select Committee attacks   140
  vulture funds   53–4, 56–7
Barclays   63–4, 168–9, 230
Barings Bank   199, 201–2, 207, 210, 216, 260
Barrington, Mike   184–5
Basel 1 requirements   35, 120–1, 162
Basel 2 requirements
  see also risk measurements
  background   5, 7–8, 15, 35, 44–5, 86, 119–22,
    146–7, 159–60, 162, 166, 203, 217, 228–41,
    259–60
  concepts   230–41, 259–60
  credit rating agencies   233
  credit spreads   86, 146–7, 233–5
  critique   44, 119–22, 162, 166
  implementation delays   146
  income distributions   230–1
  internal risk weightings assessments   233–5
  introduction   230
  purposes   231–2, 234–5, 241
  RAROC   119–20, 229

rationale   234–5
regulatory arbitrage   162
volatility   231–4
Bawag   56
BCCI   260
Bear Stearns   7, 44, 46, 160, 263
beneficial interest   23, 45, 49–50, 57
Betancourt, Luis   195–6
bifurcation rules   44, 51–2, 120–1, 139–40, 164–5,
    173–4
Black, Bernard   49
'black box' mentality, credit rating agencies   62–3
Black–Scholes options pricing model   16–17, 30, 137
BNR see Incurred But Not Reported Losses
Bolton, Anthony   35, 143
bonds   8–9, 10–11, 21–2, 31, 39–41, 47–8, 52–3,
    57–61, 77–115, 117–37, 157, 161–2, 171–2, 184,
    186–98, 200, 220–41, 256
  see also credit rating . . .; inverse floaters
  cash flow interest rate swaps   91–7
  CDOs   47–8, 58–9, 157, 171–2, 184, 256
  prices   131–2
  securitisation market   148, 157, 161–2, 168–9,
      171–2, 186–98, 232–41
bonus incentives   1–2, 3–4, 6, 9–10, 11–15, 16–19, 24,
    29, 34–5, 36, 41, 43, 44–7, 63–4, 118–20, 146–7,
    174–5, 200, 202–4, 226–9, 259–63
  bad debts   36
  Barclays   63–4, 168–9, 230
  Black–Scholes options pricing model   16–17
  British Government restrictions   63–4, 149–50, 166
  examples   11–15, 17–19
  financial crises contributor   1–2, 3–4, 14–15, 16–19,
      24, 29, 41, 43, 47, 259–63
  hidden losses   2, 7–8, 9–10, 14–15, 17–18, 23, 24,
      44–6, 48, 54–7, 67–8, 76, 118, 128, 172–5,
      226–9, 259–60
  measuring considerations   16–19
  moral hazard   44–5, 46, 47–8, 159
  proprietary trading   200
  RAROC adjustments   119–20, 229
  risk measurements   6, 11–12, 14–15, 16–19, 43,
      44–5, 118–22, 128–9, 159–60, 174–5, 200,
      202–4, 259–63
  share price alignments   48
  statistics   47–8
  traders' dilemma   11–15, 16–19, 46–7
  Value at Risk   229
  volatility   3, 15, 16–17, 36, 48, 149–50, 200, 202–4,
      226–9
book values see cost model
Boots   144
'breakeven' credit spread   145–6
Brendsel, Leland   17

British Government
  see also UK
  banks   63–4, 139–40, 149–50, 166, 261
  bonus incentives   63–4, 149–50, 166
  credit crunch   63–4, 166
  moral hazard problems   167
bubbles   259–61
Buffett, Warren   7, 10, 17, 48, 259
business combinations see consolidations
Business Week   182–3

Cable, Vince   64
call options   16–17, 22, 48, 137, 200
  Black–Scholes options pricing model   16–17, 137
  proprietary trading   200
Capco   257–8
Carlyle Hedge Fund   218
carry trade   54, 104, 171–2
'carve out' features from IAS 39   1–2, 5, 24–6, 28,
    65–6, 217, 219–41
  see also 'fair value option'
cash flow (CF) hedge qualification
  concepts   69–76, 77–8, 91–115, 208–15, 217–41
  effectiveness   73–4, 112, 115
  foreign currency transactions   100–15
  illustrative examples   77–8, 91–115, 208–15
cash flow interest rate swaps   91–7
CDF see cumulative discount factor
CDOs see Collateralised Debt Obligations
CDS see Credit default Swaps
central banks
  handouts   1
  interest rates   163
CEV see Current Exit Value
CF see cash flow . . .
CFD see Contract for Difference
cherry-picking opportunities   6, 18–19, 28, 41, 72–3,
    172–3, 221, 243–4
chief executive officers
  see also directors
  'retiring' executives   43, 46–8
China   171
Chirac, Jacques   219–20
Citibank   7, 43, 45–7, 140, 164, 177–8, 184, 218
Citigroup   32, 43, 53, 177–8, 184
Citron, Robert   52, 117–19
classification of assets   18–19, 24–6, 31, 40–1, 72–6,
    93–7, 105–15, 122, 152–3, 164, 172–3, 191–2,
    219–23, 226–9, 236–41
classification as debt/equity considerations   15, 34–5,
    122, 189, 191–2
Collateralised Debt Obligations (CDOs)   47–8, 58–9,
    157, 171–2, 184, 256
commercial paper   192–4, 218
commodity risk   117, 129, 141, 164
company law, accounting standards   166, 230

complexity problems   1–2, 3, 5, 7, 9–11, 21–2, 23,
   27–8, 29, 43, 44, 45–6, 48–52, 61–4, 65–76,
   117–37, 139–40, 164–71, 173–4, 203–4, 207–8,
   223–4, 261–3
   attributes   10–11
   bifurcation rules   44, 51–2, 120–1, 139–40, 164–5,
      173–4
   financial crises contributor   3, 5, 7, 29, 31–2, 43,
      48–9, 61–4, 139, 261
   future prospects   263
   liquidity links   166
'conduit'   192
conflicts of interest   2, 6, 9, 10, 45–50, 60–2, 140, 160,
   170–1, 202, 262–3
   auditors   2, 6, 46, 140, 160, 202, 262
   credit rating agencies   2, 6, 10, 45–7, 48–9, 140,
      160, 262
   'independent' valuers   6, 263
   institutional investors   6, 45–6, 60–2, 140, 170–1,
      202, 262–3
   shareholders   49–50, 202
consolidations   22, 29, 32, 33, 34, 54–7, 177–80,
   185–98
   see also goodwill; mergers . . .
   FASB rules   185–9, 195–8
   IAS 27 Consolidation   22, 29, 32, 34, 177
   IFRS rules   185, 189–98
   non-consolidations   55–7, 178–80
   off-balance sheet vehicles   34, 54–7, 177–80
Constant Proportion Debt Obligation (CPDO)   10,
   48–9, 59, 62–4, 165
contagion effect   218
Contract for Difference (CFD)   45, 49–50
convertible bonds   64, 200
'cookie jar' reserves   4, 18–19, 23, 146–7, 152–3
corporate governance   5, 41, 43–64, 144–50, 168–9,
   185–6, 188–9, 260–3
   beneficial ownership   49–50, 57
   complex structured products   48–51
   derivatives   49–51, 168–9
   EU efforts   49, 50
   hedge funds   49–50
   investment entities   60–2
   non-consolidations   54–7, 177–80
   shareholder votes   49–50, 57, 60–1, 144, 185–6,
      188–9, 260, 262–3
   structured products   51–3, 168–9
correlation coefficient   228–34
cost model   6, 18–19, 23–31, 41, 65–76, 172–3,
   217–41, 243–58
   benefits   28, 217
   cherry-picking   6, 18–19, 28, 41, 72–3, 172–3, 221,
      243–4
   concepts   23–31, 65–76, 172–3, 217–41
   general guidelines   26, 31
   impairment treatments   31, 33

insurance   244–58
   mixed-model approach   4–5, 21–2, 23–41, 65–76,
      217–41
'covenant lite' loans   140, 143–4
CPDO see Constant Proportion Debt Obligation
creative accounting   9–10, 17–19, 21–3, 28, 30, 36,
   54–7, 67–76, 102–5, 118, 146–7, 172–3, 180–9,
   243–58
   see also cherry-picking; 'cookie jar' reserves;
      off-balance sheet vehicles
   foreign loans   102–5
   IAS 37 Provisions, Contingent Liabilities and
      Contingent Assets   18, 23, 36, 146–7, 151–3
   insurance products   243–5
credit crunch   1–3, 6–7, 16–19, 24, 31–2, 43, 51, 55,
   58–9, 63–4, 120–1, 139–40, 141, 147–8, 157,
   159–60, 174–5, 217–18, 235, 259–60, 262–3
   see also financial crises
   contagion effect   218
   contributing factors   2–3, 16–19, 24, 31–2, 43, 139,
      217–18, 235, 259–63
   credit rating agencies   147–8
   credit spirals   218–19, 259–60
credit default risk   129, 148–50
Credit default Swaps (CDS)
   see also financial guarantees
   concepts   148–50, 156–7, 163, 173–4, 218, 244
   prepayment risk synthetic securitisations   162–3
credit derivatives   2, 7–11, 63, 141–2, 148–57, 160,
   163, 167–8, 171–2, 173–4, 193–4, 218, 221–41,
   243–58, 262–3
   see also financial guarantees
   accounting rules   156–7
   bank fees   10–11
   concepts   7–10, 63, 141–2, 148–57, 163, 167–8,
      218, 237–41, 243–4
   critique   7–10, 141–2, 148–50, 156–7, 167–8,
      221–41, 243–4, 262–3
   financial crises contributor   156–7, 218
   IAS 39   150, 156–7, 237–8
   insurance   156, 160, 167–8, 171–2, 193–4, 243–58
   loan documentation   9
   prepayment risk synthetic securitisations   162–3
   statistics   8–9
credit migration risk   129
credit rating agencies   2, 6, 10, 45–7, 48–9, 57–9,
   139–57, 160–3, 165–8, 232–41, 262–3
   accountant links   57–8, 263
   appointments   57–8
   Basel 2 requirements   233
   'black box' mentality   62–3
   conflicts of interest   2, 6, 10, 45–7, 48–9, 140, 160,
      262
   CPDOs   10, 48–9, 59, 62–4, 165
   credit crunch   147–8

critique   2, 6, 10, 45–7, 48–9, 57–9, 139–57, 160,
        163, 165–8, 232–3, 262–3
downgrades   237–8, 256
fees   2, 45–6, 52, 160
inverse floaters   52–3, 127–8
litigation threats   61–2, 148
monoline insurance companies   147–8, 171–2,
        193–4
monopolies   57–8, 148, 262
regulatory powers   233
reputations   57–8, 148
responsibilities   165–8
structured products   51–3, 139–57, 160–2, 163,
        165–8
'super-senior' investment products   148, 168–9
UK Treasury Select Committee attacks   140
credit risk   2, 5, 6, 7–10, 51–3, 63, 83–91, 114–15,
        117, 119–20, 129–30, 139–57, 159–75, 190,
        207–8, 221, 237–41, 261
    accounting standards   119–20, 129, 139–57,
        159–75, 237–41
    CDS   148–50, 156–7, 173–4
    concepts   129, 139–57, 159–75, 207–8, 237–41, 261
    credit derivatives   2, 7–11, 63, 141–2, 148–57, 160,
        163, 167–8, 171–2, 173–4, 193–4, 218, 221–41,
        243–58, 262–3
    financial guarantees   141, 156, 167–8
    IFRS 7 disclosures   238–41, 260–1
    loans   142–56
    RAROC adjustments   119–20, 229
    structured products   51–3, 117, 129–30, 139–57,
        159–75, 190, 237–41
    types   129
credit spirals   217–19, 259–60
credit spreads   37–8, 77, 81–97, 144–6, 212–15,
        224–6, 233–5, 237–41
    Basel 2 requirements   86, 146–7
    'breakeven' credit spread   145–6
    concepts   81–97, 144–6, 224–6, 233–5, 237–41
    definition   81, 86
    examples   86–91, 144–6, 234–5, 237–8
    FASB treatment   87–91
    IAS 39 treatment   87–9, 237–8
    incorrect calculations   86
    swaps   81–91
Credit Suisse   169–71
CTW   32
cumulative discount factor (CDF), valuations of swaps
        82–3
Current Exit Value (CEV)   255

Darling, Alistair   261
data-capture failings, rogue traders   201–4
Davies, Paul J.   54
Davis, Paul   178, 194
DB Zwirn hedge fund   6

debt
    see also liability . . .; loans
    average debt levels   35
    bad debts   36–8, 53–4, 146–7, 151–6, 159
    IAS 32 Debt vs. Equity Classification   15, 34–5,
        122, 189, 191–2
    off-balance sheet vehicles   35
'Debtors/Creditors' control accounts   204
Deferred Profit & Loss accounts   72–6
deposit criterion, property clubs   143, 157
derivatives   1–2, 5, 7–10, 13–15, 18–19, 23, 27–8, 29,
        39–40, 49–53, 65–76, 79–115, 121–37, 149–57,
        167–8, 203–16, 221–41, 262–3
    see also credit . . .; forward contracts; futures; hedge
        accounting; options; structured products; swaps
    artificial volatility   22, 26–8, 67–76, 81–3, 221–41,
        245–7
    concepts   13–15, 39–40, 49–53, 65–76, 121–37,
        149–57, 262–3
    corporate governance   49–51, 168–9
    critique   7–10, 18–19, 29, 39–40, 49–53, 65–76,
        117–18, 121–2, 149–50, 165–8, 203–4, 221–41,
        262–3
    definition   129–30
    embedded derivatives   5, 122–37, 245–50, 253–5
    FAS 133   18–19, 59–60, 78–115, 122–6, 128–9, 262
    forms   13–15
    fundamentals   129–30
    IAS 39   1–2, 5, 23, 27–8, 39–40, 65–76, 122, 150,
        156–7, 237–8, 244–57
    loss-making derivatives   30
    market value (mark-to-market) accounting   39–40,
        172–3
    Profit & Loss accounts   39–40, 67–115, 126–7,
        164–9, 245–50, 253–5
    settlement   129–30
    types   130–7
    volatility   39–40, 48, 65–6, 69–76, 81–3, 200, 227–9
    'weapons of mass destruction'   7, 10, 168
Deutsche Bank   50, 61, 127
directors
    see also chief executive officers
    auditors   57–8
    responsibilities   32, 43–64, 202–4, 262–3
    'retiring' chief executives   43, 46–8
disclosures   5, 9, 11, 15, 23, 43, 44, 50, 119, 122,
        126–7, 140–1, 169–71, 178, 190–2, 202–4,
        227–41, 260–3
    see also transparency shortfalls
    accounting   235–41
    credit disclosures   238–41
    critique   178, 235–41, 260–3
    IFRS 7 Financial Instruments: Disclosures   5, 9, 11,
        15, 23, 43, 44, 122, 128–9, 141, 142, 190–2,
        227–41, 260–1

discount factors
  valuations of forwards   101–15, 133–4
  valuations of swaps   80–91, 124–6, 213–15
diversification issues
  hedge funds   8
  structured products   147–8, 159–60, 163
  Value at Risk   227–9
dividends, shareholders   63–4, 230–1
documentation requirements
  headings   114–15
  hedge accounting   100, 114–15
  swaps   59–60
dot.coms   23, 53–4
double-counting   196–8
downgrades, credit rating agencies   237–8,
    256
Dynergy   23, 181–2

Earnings Per Share (EPS)   3–4
EBF see European Banking Federation
Eden, James   64
EEV see European Embedded Value
effective interest rates   22, 36–9, 57, 156, 171–2,
    251–2
  see also arrangement fees
Elan   182–4
embedded derivatives
  see also structured products
  banks   128–9, 164–5
  concepts   5, 122–37, 164–5, 245–50, 253–5
  definition   129
  illustration of the problem   122–6
  new accounting treatment   126–8
  old accounting method   126–7
embedded value process, insurance   245–50, 253–5
endowment mortgages   260
Enron   7, 22, 23, 31–2, 34, 41, 55, 56, 120–1, 139,
    183, 187, 219, 248, 259–62
EPS see Earnings Per Share
Equitable Life   260
equity
  concepts   34–5, 122
  IAS 32 Debt vs. Equity Classification   15, 34–5,
    122, 189, 191–2
  risk   117, 129, 141, 164
Equity Reserve account   26, 40, 72–6, 93–8, 105–15,
    153, 166, 172–3, 210–15, 220–2
Ernst & Young   59
Eurex   199
European Banking Federation (EBF)   223, 226
European Embedded Value (EEV)   248–50
European Union (EU)   1–2, 5, 27–8, 65–6, 177–98,
    199, 217, 219–23
  American standards   5, 177–98
  IAS 39 pressures   1–2, 27–8, 65–6, 217, 219–23,
    241

Sociéte Générale (SocGen)   5, 39, 199–203, 207,
    210, 216, 260
'external' shareholders   188–9

fair value hedge qualification
  concepts   69–76, 77–115, 208–15, 217–41
  illustrative examples   77–115, 208–15
  options   114
'fair value option' (FVO)
  see also 'carve out' features from IAS 39; market
    valuations
  background   5, 6, 24–6, 40, 44, 49, 54, 67–76, 169,
    197–8, 217, 226–41
  concepts   226–7, 237–41
  corporate governance   49, 50
Fannie Mae   3–4, 17
FAS 125 Accounting for Transfer of Assets and
    Extinguishment of Liabilities   19
FAS 133 Accounting for Financial Instruments and
    Hedging   7, 18–19, 59–60, 78–115, 122–6,
    128–9, 262
  critique   18, 59–60, 128–9, 262
  Freddie Mac   18–19
FAS 140   34
FASB see Financial Accounting Standards Board
the Federal Reserve Board   1, 46, 166–7
fees
  accountants   261–2
  auditors   2, 59–60, 121, 261–2
  banks   10–11, 119–20, 121, 165, 174–5
  credit rating agencies   2, 45–6, 52, 160
  insurance companies   244–7
  investment funds   11–15, 46–7, 119, 121
fictitious provisions see 'cookie jar' reserves
Fidelity   143
Financial Accounting Standards Board (FASB)
  see also FAS . . .; SFAS . . .
  consolidation rules   185–9, 195–8
  credit spreads   87–91
  foreign currency transactions   100–15
  hedge accounting rules   66–7, 77–115
  interest rate swaps   87–91
  lobbying pressures   3, 53–4, 60, 261–2
  off-balance sheet vehicles   185–9, 195–8
  QSPEs   177, 179–80, 186–9, 195–6
  revenue recognition   53–4
  SAB 101   23, 54, 256–7
  Statement no 138   89–91
financial crises   1–3, 16–19, 24, 31–2, 43, 51, 55–7,
    58–9, 63–4, 120–1, 139–40, 141, 147–8, 156–7,
    159–60, 174–5, 217–18, 235, 259–60
  see also credit crunch
  contributing factors   2–3, 16–19, 24, 31–2, 43, 139,
    217–18, 235, 259–63
  credit spirals   218–19, 259–60

financial engineering, critique   7, 117–18, 159–60, 165–8, 259–63
financial guarantees   141, 156, 167–8
  see also credit derivatives
financial instruments
  see also derivatives
  complexity problems   1–2, 3, 5, 7, 9–11, 21–2, 23, 27–8, 43, 45–6, 48–51, 61–4, 65–76, 117–37, 139–40, 164–71, 203–4, 207–8, 223–4, 261
  misuse concerns   8–10
  nature and extent of risks   239–41
  valuations   1, 4–6, 9–10, 18, 19, 21–2, 23–31, 65–76, 128–9, 165–6, 221–41
  Value at Risk   239–41
Financial Services Act 1986   260
Financial Services Authority   175, 261
Financial Times (FT)   24, 35, 46, 47, 53, 54, 57, 63–4, 128, 142–4, 147, 149, 156–7, 160, 165, 167–9, 177–8, 183–4, 193–4, 199–200, 203, 207, 218–19, 248, 256
finite insurance   250–2
'First to Default' bonds   173–4
fixed rates, interest rate swaps   65–6, 77–115, 133–7, 207–15, 222–3
floating bonds   40–1
floating rates, interest rate swaps   65–6, 77–115, 133–7, 207–15, 222–3
Flottl, Walter   56
footnotes, banks   177–8
Ford Motor Company   195–6
foreign currency forwards   30, 65–6, 69–76, 100–15
  accounting treatments   108–12
  concepts   69–76, 100–15
  interest rate changes   102
  time value   108–15
  transaction costs   100–15
  valuations   101–15
  value change reasons   108
foreign exchange   5, 30, 65–6, 69–76, 100–15, 208–15
  accounting treatment   108–12
  concepts   100–15
  creative accounting   102–5
  examples   100–2
  IAS 21 The Effects of Changes in Foreign Exchange Rates   102–15
  risk   51, 117, 129–30, 141, 164
foreign loans, borrowing expenses   102–5
forward contracts   30, 65, 66–76, 100–15, 121–2, 130–7, 205–15
  see also derivatives
  examples   74–6, 100–15, 132–7
  futures contrasts   132–3
  hedge accounting   66–76, 100–15
  interest rate changes   102, 133–7
  pre-IAS 39 accounting   67–8
  time value   108–15
  valuations   101–15
  value change reasons   108
Forward Rate Agreements (FRAs)   74–6
Freddie Mac   17–19
FT see Financial Times
FTSE   129
fund managers see investment funds
future prospects   263
futures   49–50, 65, 121, 130–7, 204–16
  concepts   130–2, 204–16
  examples   130–2, 204–15
  forwards contrasts   132–3
  initial margin   130–2, 204–16
  interest rate changes   131–2
  margins   130–2, 204–16
  valuations   131–2
  variation margin   130–2, 204–16
FVO see 'fair value option'

Gapper, John   47, 256
Garland, Michael   32
gearing   12–15, 122, 231
  see also debt . . .; loans
Gen Re   257
German banks   192
Gibson Greetings   52
glossary   265–6
goodwill   22, 23–4, 29–31, 32, 33, 55–7, 64, 249–50
  see also consolidations; reputations
  accounting abuses   29–30, 33, 55–7
  impairment requirements   30–1, 33
  valuations   23–4, 29–30, 33, 55–7, 249–50
Goodwin, Fred   149–50
Greek pension funds scandal   52–3, 127–8
Guardian   56, 173, 180–1
Gulf funds   171

hedge accounting   1–2, 5–6, 8, 16–19, 23, 27–8, 29, 39–41, 65–76, 77–115, 130–7, 208–15, 217–41
  artificial volatility   26–8, 67–76, 81–3, 221–41
  cash flow hedge qualification   69–76, 77–8, 91–115, 208–15, 217–41
  cash flow interest rate swaps   91–4
  concepts   1–2, 5–6, 8, 16–19, 23, 27–8, 29, 39–41, 65–76, 77–115, 130–1, 133–7, 217–18
  credit spreads   81–97, 224–6
  critique   1–2, 5–6, 8, 16–19, 23, 27–8, 29, 65–76, 217–18
  documentation requirements   100, 114–15
  effectiveness   73–4, 112, 115
  fair value hedge qualification   69–76, 77–115, 208–15, 217–41
  FASB rules example   66–7, 77–115
  foreign exchange hedge   100–15
  forward contracts   66–76, 100–15
  FRA example   74–6

hedge accounting (*Continued*)
   IAS   39 1–2, 5, 23, 27–8, 32, 39–41, 65–76, 87–9,
      136–7
   illustrative examples   77–115, 208–15
   interest rate swaps   65–6, 77–115, 208–15
   matching concept   66, 68, 69–70, 185
   net investments in foreign operations hedging
      qualification   69–76
   options   112–14
   permissions   40–1, 65–6, 69–76, 81–97, 108, 112,
      114–15, 130–1, 208–15, 226–9
   pre-IAS 39 accounting   67–8
   rules   40–1, 65–6, 69–76
   swaps   65–6, 77–115, 133–7, 208–15
   swaptions   112–14
   Value at Risk   224–6
hedge funds   6, 8, 9–10, 16–19, 29, 49–50, 53–4,
   56–7, 72–3, 132–7, 139–57, 167–8, 172–3, 191–2,
   200–15, 218–23, 224–6, 244, 260
   bank contrasts   8, 20, 218
   cherry-picking   6, 18–19, 29, 72–3, 172–3, 221
   corporate governance   49–50
   diversification needs   8
   regulation shortfalls   8, 49–50
   relative value trading   200–4
   vulture funds   53–4, 56–7
'Held to Maturity' assets classification   18–19, 24–6,
   31, 40–1, 153, 164, 220, 236–41
Hewlett-Packard   61
hidden losses
   off-balance sheet vehicles   2, 7–8, 9–10, 14–15,
      17–18, 21–2, 23–4, 29, 31–2, 44–6, 48, 54–7,
      65–6, 67–8, 76, 118, 128, 153, 172–5, 180–5,
      218–19, 226–9, 244, 255–8, 259–60
   rogue traders   200–4, 216
HSBC   127, 177–8, 230
Hu, Henry T.C.   49
Hughes, Jennifer   156–7

IAS *see* International Accounting Standard . . .
IASB *see* International Accounting Standards Board
IFRS . . . *see* International Financial Reporting
   Standard . . .
IIF *see* Institute of International Finance
illiquid nature, structured products   51–2, 117–18,
   120–1, 164–6, 207–9, 217–18, 224, 263
ILP *see* Irish Life & Permanent
IMF *see* International Monetary Fund
impairment requirements
   asset treatments   30–1, 33, 53–4
   loan impairments   32, 36, 38, 53–4, 147, 151–6
implied volatility   169
incentives *see* bonus incentives
Incurred But Not Reported Losses (IBNR)   147
independent financial advisors   142–3, 157, 263
'independent' valuers, conflicts of interest   6, 263

inefficient nature
   loans   157
   structured products   51, 157
initial margin, futures   130–2, 204–16
Institute of Chartered Accountants in England and
   Wales   173
Institute of International Finance (IIF)   62
institutional investors   2, 6, 41, 45–6, 49–50, 60–2,
   140, 144, 170–1, 202, 262–3
   conflicts of interest   6, 45–6, 60–2, 140, 170–1, 202,
      262–3
   voting powers   2, 41, 45–6, 49–50, 60–1, 144, 260,
      262–3
insurance
   see also life assurance companies
   accounting   6, 24, 156, 171–2, 193–4, 243–58
   AIG collapse   255–8
   artificial volatility   245–7
   cherry-picking opportunities   243–4
   credit derivatives   156, 160, 167–8, 171–2, 193–4,
      243–58
   critique   1–2, 6, 9–10, 117, 147–8, 160, 171–2,
      193–4, 243–58
   EEV   248–50
   embedded value process   245–50, 253–5
   fees   244–7
   finite insurance   250–2
   IAS 8   252–3
   IAS 39   243–57
   IASB   243–5, 251–5
   IFRS 4   156, 243–58, 260
   Lloyds TSB case study   248, 250
   loans   243–4, 250–1, 255–8
   mismatching case study   245–50
   negative carry trade   54, 171–2, 193–4
   off-balance sheet vehicles   6, 160, 171–2, 193–4,
      243–58
   Phase Two embedded value   243, 253–5
   regulations   156, 243–58
   reinsurance contracts   244, 250–2, 256–8
   significance of risk   244–7
   unbundled loans   250–2
   up-front costs   244–7
Interest Margin Hedging (IMH)   223
interest rate futures   204–15
interest rate risk   51, 117, 129–30, 141, 164
interest rate swaps   19, 27, 56, 59–60, 65–6, 77–115,
   123–6, 133–7, 189–90, 208–15, 221–41
   see also swaps
   cash flow interest rate swaps   91–7
   credit spreads   81–97
   FASB treatment   87–91
   hedge accounting   65–6, 77–115, 133–7, 208–15
   IAS 39 treatment   87–9, 136–7
   interest rate changes   94–7
   long accounting treatment method   87–91, 94–100

short-cut accounting treatment method   87–91, 93–100

shortcut valuation procedures   82–3

two accounting treatments   87–9

unwind of the discount   94–7

valuations   80–3, 124–6, 133–7

value change reasons   94–7

interest rates   10, 19, 22, 26–8, 37–8, 48–9, 52–3, 56, 59–60, 62–3, 65–6, 76, 77–115, 122–6, 129, 131–7, 145–6, 161–2, 164, 171–2, 189–90, 204–15, 222–5, 234–8

central banks   163

credit spreads   37–8, 77, 81–97, 144–6, 233–5, 237–41

effective interest rates   22, 36–9, 57, 156, 171–2, 251–2

foreign currency forwards   102

forward contracts   102, 133–7

futures   131–2

inverse floaters   52–3, 127–8

Libor   10, 37–8, 48–9, 62–3, 76, 78–91, 102–3, 122–6, 129, 133–7, 145–6, 161–2, 164, 171–2, 189–90, 204–5, 209–10, 214–15, 222–5, 234–8

unexpected changes   94–7

internal risk weightings assessments, Basel 2 requirements   233–5

International Accounting Standard, IAS 8 *Accounting Policies, Change in Accounting Estimates and Errors*   253

International Accounting Standard, IAS 18 *Revenue Recognition*   23, 43, 53–4, 171–2, 189, 193–4, 235, 256–7

International Accounting Standard, IAS 19 *Pension Accounting*   32, 33, 118

International Accounting Standard, IAS 21 *The Effects of Changes in Foreign Exchange Rates*   102–15

International Accounting Standard, IAS 27 *Consolidation*   22, 29, 32, 34, 177

International Accounting Standard, IAS 32 *Debt vs. Equity Classification*   15, 34–5, 122, 189, 191–2

International Accounting Standard, IAS 37 *Provisions, Contingent Liabilities and Contingent Assets*   18, 23, 36, 146–7, 151–6

International Accounting Standard, IAS 39 *Financial Instruments: Recognition and Measurement*

asset treatments   18–19, 24–6, 31, 67–76, 87–9, 122, 202

background   1–2, 5, 7, 11, 15, 22–3, 27–41, 44, 51–2, 65–76, 87–9, 102–4, 122, 128–9, 136–7, 140–1, 151–3, 189, 191, 195–8, 202, 209–15, 243–4, 260

bank fees   11

Beneficial Interest   23, 57

bifurcation rules   44, 51–2, 120–1, 139–40, 164–5

'carve out' features   1–2, 5, 24–6, 28, 65–6, 217, 219–41

Classification of Assets   24–6, 32, 40–1, 73–4, 152–3, 164, 172–3, 226–9, 237–41

credit derivatives   150, 156–7, 237–8

critique   68, 122, 128–9, 153–7, 195–8

double-counting   196–8

Effective Interest Rates   22, 36–9

embedded derivatives   122, 128–37

EU pressures   1–2, 5, 27–8, 65–6, 217, 219–23, 241

foreign exchange   102–15

hedge accounting   1–2, 5, 23, 27–8, 32, 39–41, 65–76, 87–9, 136–7

Hedge and Derivative Accounting   1–2, 5, 23, 27–8, 32, 39–41

insurance   243–57

interest rate swaps   87–9, 136–7

Loan Impairment   32, 36, 147, 153–6

loans   32, 36, 147, 151–6

two versions   5, 28, 217, 219–41

International Accounting Standards Board (IASB)

background   1–2, 5, 22–3, 27–8, 65–6, 178, 195–8, 217–41, 243–5, 251–5

EU pressures   1–2, 5, 27–8, 65–6, 217, 219–23, 241

improvements   22–3, 178

insurance   243–5, 251–5

off-balance sheet vehicles   189–98, 243–5

International Financial Reporting Standard, IFRS 2 *Share-Based Payments (employee benefits)*   16–17, 22, 32–3, 45, 60, 192

International Financial Reporting Standard, IFRS 3 *Goodwill (Business Combinations)*   22, 29, 32, 33, 55–7, 64, 76, 189–98

International Financial Reporting Standard, IFRS 4 *Accounting for Insurance*   156, 243–58, 260

International Financial Reporting Standard, IFRS 7 *Financial Instruments: Disclosures*   5, 9, 11, 15, 23, 43, 44, 122, 128–9, 141, 142, 190–2, 227–41, 260–1

concepts   235–41, 260–1

qualitative/quantitative disclosures   240–1

International Financial Reporting Standards

financial crisis contributor   31–2

post-Enron rules   32–41, 187, 219, 248, 259–62

International Monetary Fund (IMF)   140, 156

International Swaps Dealers Association (ISDA)   8, 59–60

Internet bubble   260

intrinsic value of options   112–14

inventory valuations   66–70

inverse floaters   5, 48, 52–3, 127–8

see also structured products

investment banks   32, 53–4, 56–7, 157

see also banks

investment entities, corporate governance   60–2

investment funds   11–15, 46–7, 117–18, 119, 121,
    245–7
  gearing   12–15, 122
  management fees   11–15, 119, 121, 245–7
  performance fees   11–15, 46–7, 119, 121
  traders' dilemma   11–15, 46–7
investment trusts   2, 9–10, 41, 49–50, 260, 262–3
investors
  see also shareholders
  voting powers   2, 41, 45–6, 49–50, 57, 60–1, 144,
    185–6, 188–9, 260, 262–3
IR swaps see interest rate swaps
Irish Life & Permanent (ILP)   245–7
ISDA see International Swaps Dealers Association

Jackson, Tony   24
Japanese banking crisis   218–19
joint ventures   182–4
journal entries, accountants   214–15
JPMorgan   52–3, 127–8, 259
Jubb, Guy   50

Kerviel, Jerome   199–203, 207, 210, 216
King, Mervyn   261
King Pharmaceuticals   50
KKR   144
KPMG   56, 182–3, 186–7

Latin American crises   219
Leeson, Nick   199, 201–2, 207, 210, 216
lessons learned   61–2, 127–8, 259–63
leveraged buyouts (LBOs)   57, 231
Levitt, Arthur   4, 18, 56, 59–61, 261–2
LGD see loss given default
liability treatments   15, 22, 26–8, 30, 34–5, 67–76,
    81–3, 104–15, 122, 189, 191–2, 202, 221–41,
    245–7
  artificial volatility   22, 26–8, 67–76, 81–3, 221–41,
    245–7
  foreign exchange   104–15
  loss-making derivatives   30
Libor   10, 37–8, 48–9, 62–3, 76, 78–91, 102–3, 122–6,
    129, 133–7, 145–6, 161–2, 164, 171–2, 189–90,
    204–5, 209–10, 214–15, 222–5, 234–8
life assurance companies   6, 243–58
  see also insurance
linear derivatives, concepts   13–15
liquidity crisis see credit crunch
liquidity risk   6, 119–20, 174, 190, 207–9, 217–18,
    224, 229, 259–60
  control efforts   259–60
  RAROC adjustments   119–20, 229
litigation threats
  accountants   7, 61–2
  credit rating agencies   61–2, 148
Lloyds TSB   248, 250

loan impairments   32, 36, 38, 53–4, 147, 151–6
  see also bad debts
loans   5, 6, 9, 14–15, 21, 22, 24–6, 29, 31, 32, 34–5,
    36–9, 40–1, 45–6, 53–4, 77–115, 140–57, 159–75,
    186–98, 213–15, 217–41, 243–4, 250–2,
    255–8
  see also banks; debt . . .
  accounting standards   15, 21, 24–6, 31, 34–5,
    77–115, 146–57
  approvals   142–4, 157
  bad debts   36–8, 53–4, 146–7, 151–6, 159
  'cherry-picked' loans   6, 29, 72–3, 172–3, 221,
    243–4
  'covenant lite' loans   140, 143–4
  credit derivative documentation   9
  credit risk   142–56
  credit spreads   37–8, 77, 81–97, 144–6, 233–5
  effective interest rates   22, 36–9, 57, 156, 171–2,
    251–2
  foreign loans   102–5
  IAS   39 32, 36, 147, 151–6
  inefficient nature   157
  insurance   243–4, 250–1, 255–8
  LGD   144–6, 233–4
  moral hazard   44–5, 46, 140–1, 146, 159, 161–2,
    167–8
  PD   144–7, 154–5, 234–5, 238–41
  poor credit controls   142–4
  pre-IAS 39 accounting   151–3
  rules   151–6, 228–41
  securitisation market   5, 142–4, 157, 159–75,
    186–98
  self-certified earnings   157
  SPVs   29, 152–3, 161–2, 178–98
  sub-prime loans   14–15, 24, 43, 57, 141–4, 159–60,
    162, 166–7, 174–5, 178, 184–5, 192, 218, 235,
    259–60
  term sheets   36–9
  unbundled loans   250–2
  vulture funds   53–4, 56–7
'Loans & Receivables' assets classification   24–6, 31,
    40–1, 219–20, 236–41
lobbying pressures, accounting standards   1–2, 3, 41,
    46, 59–62, 261–2
long accounting treatment method, interest rate swaps
    87–91, 94–100
Long Term Capital Management (LTCM)   164–8, 191,
    200, 260
loss given default (LGD)   144–6, 233–4
loss-making derivatives   30
losses
  moral hazard   44–5, 46, 140–1, 146, 159, 161–2,
    167–8
  profit smoothing   4, 17–18, 36, 67–8, 146–7
LTCM see Long Term Capital Management

McCreevy, Charlie   49–50, 199
Mackintosh, James   53
management fees, investment funds   11–15, 119, 121,
    245–7
margins, futures   130–2, 204–16
mark-to-market accounting *see* market value . . .
market risk   2, 5, 51–3, 114–15, 117–37, 139–40, 164,
    190, 227, 229, 244–7
    RAROC adjustments   119–20, 229
    structured products   117–37, 139–40, 190
market valuations   4–6, 10, 18, 19, 21–2, 23–31,
    39–40, 44, 65–76, 128–9, 165–6, 169, 172–3,
    197–8, 217–41, 262–3
    see also 'fair value option'
    concepts   23–31, 39–40, 44, 165–6, 169, 172–3,
        217–41
    critique   5–6, 10, 18, 19, 21–2, 23–31, 65–76,
        165–6, 169, 172–3, 217–41, 262–3
    general guidelines   26, 31
    mixed-model approach   4–5, 21–2, 23–31, 65–76,
        217–41
market value (mark-to-market) accounting   29, 30–1,
    39–40, 128–9, 172–3, 217–41
    benefits   29, 39–40, 217
    concepts   29, 30–1, 39–40, 172–3, 217–41
    derivatives   39–40, 172–3
marking-to-model accounting, concepts   30
matching concept   66, 68, 69–70, 185, 245–50
materiality concept   4
mergers & acquisitions   30, 33–4, 45
    see also consolidations; goodwill
Merrill Lynch   7, 32, 46, 47, 148
the middle office   201–8
misuse concerns, financial instruments   8–10
mixed-model approach   4–5, 21–2, 23–41, 65–76,
    217–41
    see also cost . . .; market value . . .
monetary assets/liabilities, concepts   104–5
monoline insurance companies   54, 147–8, 160,
    171–2, 193–4
monopolies
    accountants   57–8, 262
    credit rating agencies   57–8, 148, 262
Montagnon, Peter   32
Moody's   58, 160, 165
moral hazard   44–5, 46, 47–8, 140–1, 146, 159, 161–2,
    167–8
Morgan Stanley   32, 127
mutual funds   60–1
Mylan Laboratories   50

negative carry trade   54, 171–2, 193–4
net investments in foreign operations hedging
    qualification   69–76
Nigeria   118
non-consolidations   54–7, 178–80

Northern Rock   17, 44, 46, 159–60, 166–7, 191–2,
    202, 260–1
Norwegian structured products crisis   53, 128

off-balance sheet vehicles   1, 2, 5–8, 9–10, 14–15,
    17–18, 21–2, 23–4, 29, 31–2, 34–5, 44–5, 48,
    51–2, 120–1, 142–4, 152–3, 157, 159–75, 177–98,
    221–41, 259–63
    see also Structured Investment Vehicles
    accounting standards   5, 21–3, 177–98, 221–41,
        259–63
    American/European accounting differences   5,
        177–98
    Americredit   184–5
    Bawag   56
    case studies   180–5
    concepts   177–98, 221–41
    consolidations   34, 54–7, 177–80, 185–98
    debt   35
    definition   173
    double-counting   196–8
    Dynergy   23, 181–2
    Elan   182–4
    Enron   56, 120–1, 139, 183, 187, 219, 248, 259–62
    examples   55–7
    FASB rules   185–9, 195–8
    financial crises contributor   2–3, 5, 17–18, 21–2, 24,
        31–2, 173, 221–41, 259–63
    forward contracts   67–76
    hidden losses   2, 7–8, 9–10, 14–15, 17–18, 21–2,
        23–4, 29, 31–2, 44–6, 48, 54–7, 65–6, 67–8, 76,
        118, 128, 153, 172–5, 180–5, 218–19, 226–9,
        244, 255–8, 259–60
    historical background   56, 180–1
    IASB   189–98, 243–5
    IFRS rules   185, 189–98
    insurance products   6, 160, 171–2, 193–4, 243–58
    loans   152–3
    manipulations   178–98
    SEC experiences   179–85
    securitisation market   5, 142–4, 157, 159–75,
        186–98, 232–41, 256–8
    synthetic leases   186–9
    take or pay contracts   186–9
    transparency shortfalls   1, 5, 54–7, 168–9, 174–5
    US GAAP   181–2, 195–6
Office of Federal Housing Enterprise Oversight
    (OFHEO)   17–19
offshore vehicles   120–1, 257–8
OFHEO *see* Office of Federal Housing Enterprise
    Oversight
O'Neill, Stan   46, 47
operational risk   6, 29, 51–2, 119–20, 174, 207–8, 224,
    229
    complex derivatives   207–8, 224
    RAROC adjustments   119–20, 229

opportunity cost of capital   249–50, 253–5
options   3, 15, 16–19, 22, 30, 32–3, 47–9, 76, 112–14,
      124–6, 130–7, 169, 200, 244
      see also call . . .; put . . .
      Black–Scholes options pricing model   16–17, 30,
            137
      hedge accounting   112–14
      intrinsic value   112–14
      valuations   16–17, 30, 137, 169
      volatility effects   16–19, 48, 200
Orange County, California   51–3, 59, 117–19, 127
Ormond Quay   192
over the counter market (OTC)   209–15
overview of book   4–6

Pacific Gas & Electric   59
'park the trade' activities, rogue traders   201–2
Partnoy, Frank   52, 57–9, 148, 207
PD *see* probability of default
Pearson   248
pension accounting   32, 33
pension funds   8, 32, 33, 46–7, 49–50, 52–3, 117–18,
      127–8, 142–3, 157, 260
      Greek pension funds scandal   52–3, 127–8
      regulations   8, 32, 33, 46–7, 49–50, 117–18, 127–8
perfect hedges   27–8, 70–1
performance fees, investment funds   11–15, 46–7, 119,
      121
permissions, hedge accounting   40–1, 65–6, 69–76,
      81–97, 108, 112, 114–15, 130–1, 208–15, 226–9
perpetual equity   35
Perry Corp   50
Pillar 3   requirement   15, 121–2
      see also Basel . . .
precipice bonds   128–9
preference shares   35, 63–4
prepayment risks, securitisation market   162–3
present values   80–115, 124–6, 134–7, 197–215,
      251–5
presentation considerations   15, 34–5, 122, 189, 191–2
Prince, Chuck   43, 47, 178
private equity   231
proactive/reactive approaches, accounting standards
      29, 41, 261–2
probability of default (PD)   144–7, 154–5, 234–5,
      238–41
Procter & Gamble   126
Profit & Loss accounts   3, 16–19, 21–2, 24–8, 33, 37,
      39–41, 53–4, 67–115, 120–9, 151–7, 164–9,
      172–3, 177–98, 206–15, 219–23, 226–9, 236–41,
      245–52, 253–5
      classification of assets   40–1, 72–6, 93–7, 105–15,
            122, 152–3, 164, 172–3, 191–2, 219–23, 226–9,
            236–41
      derivatives   39–40, 67–115, 126–7, 164–9, 245–50,
            253–5

effective interest rates   22, 36–9, 57, 156, 171–2
embedded derivatives   126–7, 245–50, 253–5
hedge accounting   67–76, 79–115
loans   151–7
margin payments   206–15
options   112–14
pension accounting   33
revenue recognition   6, 11, 23, 38–9, 43, 46, 53–4,
      66, 171–2, 189, 193–4, 235, 256–7, 260–1
share options   3, 16–17, 22, 33, 45, 64
profit smoothing   4, 17–18, 36, 67–8, 146–7
profits
      income distributions   230–1
      moral hazard   44–5, 46, 47–8, 140–1, 146, 159,
            161–2, 167–8
      retained profits   67–76, 178–98, 208–15
      revenue recognition   6, 11, 23, 38–9, 43, 53–4, 66,
            171–2, 189, 193–4, 235, 256–7, 260–1
      valuation manipulations   19, 28, 67–8
property clubs, deposit criterion   143, 157
proprietary trading   200–16
      see also 'shorting the market'
provisions   4, 18–19, 23, 146–7, 151–6
      see also bad debts
prudence concept   31
put options   137, 244

Qatar Investment Authority   169–71
QSPEs *see* Qualifying Special Purpose Entities
qualified accounts, future prospects   263
Qualifying Special Purpose Entities (QSPEs)   177,
      179–80, 186–9, 195–6
qualitative/quantitative IFRS   7 disclosures   240–1

Raines, Franklin   3–4
Rajan, Raghuram   47
RAROC *see* Risk Adjusted Return on Capital
reconciliation procedures
      concepts   199–216
      illustrative example   208–15
regulations   8, 15, 21–41, 44–6, 49–50, 51–2, 53–7,
      67–76, 81–3, 117–22, 139–40, 151–7, 159–60,
      162, 164–8, 173–5, 199–216, 218–41, 245–7,
      260–3
      see also Basel . . .
      arbitrage opportunities   162
      artificial volatility   22, 26–8, 67–76, 81–3, 221–41,
            245–7
      bifurcation rules   44, 51–2, 120–1, 139–40, 164–5,
            173–4
      breaches   53–7, 174–5
      credit derivatives   156–7
      embedded derivatives   5, 122–37, 164–5, 245–50,
            253–5
      future prospects   263
      hedge accounting   40–1, 65–6, 69–76

insurance   156, 243–58
loans   151–6, 228–41
the middle office   201–4
mixed-model approach   4–5, 21–2, 23–41, 65–76,
    217–41
pension funds   8, 32, 33, 46–7, 49–50, 117–18,
    127–8
reform needs   174–5, 261–3
rogue traders   199–216
securitisation market   159–60, 162, 164–8, 177–98,
    232–41
Value at Risk   5, 121, 140, 164, 201–2, 207, 217,
    223–41
regulators, responsibilities   166–8
reinsurance contracts   244, 250–2, 256–8
    see also insurance
relative value trading   200–4
reputations   10, 30, 57–8, 148, 166–7
    see also goodwill
responsibilities
    accountants   1, 43–8, 140–1, 157, 165–8, 199–216,
        230–41, 260–3
    credit rating agencies   165–8
    directors   32, 43–64, 202–4, 262–3
    regulators   166–8
retained profits   67–76, 178–98, 208–15
'retiring' executives   43, 46–8
returns on capital, concepts   118–20, 229, 254–5
revenue recognition   6, 11, 23, 38–9, 43, 46, 53–4, 66,
    171–2, 189, 193–4, 235, 256–7, 260–1
    concepts   23, 43, 53–4, 66, 171–2, 189, 193–4, 235,
        256–7
    negative carry trade   54, 171–2, 193–4
rewards
    see also profit . . .; return . . .
    risk   10–15, 45–8, 119–21
risk, rewards   10–15, 45–8, 119–21
Risk Adjusted Return on Capital (RAROC), concepts
    118–20, 229
risk management   1–2, 5, 6–10, 29, 32, 34, 39, 54–7,
    114–15, 117–18, 120–1, 133, 139–57, 168–9,
    199–216, 217–41, 259–63
    audits   32
    documentation requirements   114–15
    failings   1–2, 5, 6–10, 29, 34, 39, 54–7, 117–18,
        120–1, 133, 139–57, 168–9, 199–216, 223–41,
        259–63
    the middle office   201–8
    rogue traders   5, 39, 133, 199–216
risk measurements   2, 3–4, 5–6, 7–8, 11–12, 14–15,
    16–19, 32, 43, 44–5, 46–7, 118–22, 128–9,
    139–57, 159–60, 174–5, 199–216, 217, 223–41,
    244–58, 259–63
    see also Basel 2 . . .; Value at Risk

bonus incentives   6, 11–12, 14–15, 16–19, 43, 44–5,
    118–22, 128–9, 159–60, 174–5, 200, 202–4,
    259–63
data-capture failings   201–4
difficulties   6, 11, 16, 46–7, 140–1
financial crises contributor   2, 3–4, 14–15, 16–19,
    32, 139–41, 159, 235, 259–60
IFRS 7   5, 9, 11, 15, 23, 43, 44, 122, 128–9, 141,
    142, 190–2, 227–41, 260–1
insurance   244–58
the middle office   201–8
RAROC   118–20, 229
risk transfers, credit derivatives   7–8, 141–2, 159,
    167–8
risk-free rates   16–17
Riskmetrics   229
rogue traders   5, 39, 133, 199–216
    accounting standards   202–4
    arbitrage opportunities   200–4
    the back office   201–4
    background   199–216
    common denominators   200, 216
    data-capture failings   201–4
    hidden losses   200–4, 216
    'instincts'   201
    the middle office   201–8
    'park the trade' activities   201–2
    proprietary trading   200–16
    reconciliation procedures   199–216
    relative value trading   200–4
    'shorting the market'   131, 200–16
    'star' traders   200, 202–4
    trading styles   200–1
Ross Capital   56
Royal Bank of Scotland (RBS)   149–50
Rubicon   50
rules *see* regulations
Rusnik, John   133, 199, 201–2

SAB 101   23, 54, 256–7
Sachsen LB   192
salary levels   46
sales, revenue recognition   6, 11, 23, 38–9, 43, 46,
    53–4, 66, 171–2, 189, 193–4, 235, 256–7, 260–1
Salomon Brothers   48
Sarbanes–Oxley Act   7, 260
SEC *see* Securities and Exchange Commission
Securities and Exchange Commission (SEC)   4, 6, 18,
    51–3, 59–61, 179–85, 255–8
securitisation market   2, 5, 8, 45–6, 140, 142–4, 157,
    159–75, 177–98, 218, 232–41, 256–8
    accounting standards   159–60, 162, 164–8, 177–98
    arbitrage opportunities   162
    benefits   159–60
    bonds   148, 157, 161–2, 168–9, 171–2, 186–98,
        232–41

securitisation market (*Continued*)
  concepts   157, 159–75, 186–9, 195–8, 232–41,
    256–8
  critique   157, 159–60, 165–8, 186–9, 195–8, 256–8
  diagrammatic examples   161, 163
  examples   157, 160–2
  negative publicity   157, 159–75
  overview   160–2
  prepayment risks   162–3
  processes   157, 160–3, 167–8
  regulations   159–60, 162, 164–8, 177–98, 232–41
  subordinated interests   196–8
  'super-senior' investment products   148, 168–9
  synthetic structures   162–3
  US GAAP   181–2, 195–6, 257
self-certified earnings, loan applications   157
self-correcting mechanisms   45
settlement, derivatives   129–30
SFAS 107   19
SFAS 125 *Accounting for Transfer and Servicing of
    Financial Assets and Extinguishment of Liabilities*
    187
SFAS 133   19
SFAS 140 *Accounting for Transfer and Servicing of
    Financial Assets and Extinguishment of Liabilities*
    177, 179–95
SFAS 157   174–5
share incentive schemes   16–17
share lending   49–50
share options   3, 15, 16–17, 22, 32–3, 45, 60, 64, 76,
    260–1
  balance sheets   33
  Profit & Loss accounts   3, 16–17, 22, 33, 45, 64
share price alignments, bonus incentives   48
shareholders   1–2, 5, 6, 7, 15, 34, 36–9, 41, 43–64,
    121–2, 140, 144, 170–1, 185–6, 188–9, 202,
    218–19, 230–41, 245–50, 259–63
  see also corporate governance; investors
  activism considerations   49–50
  AGMs   57–8
  banks   1–2, 7–8, 34, 36–9, 43–64, 121–2, 230–41
  Barclays   63–4, 168–9, 230
  conflicts of interest   49–50, 202
  dividends   63–4, 230–1
  EU efforts   49, 50
  'external' shareholders   188–9
  institutional investors   2, 6, 41, 45–6, 49–50, 60–2,
    140, 144, 170–1, 202, 262–3
  opportunity cost of capital   249–50, 253–5
  protection measures   15, 36–9, 121–2, 218–19
  small/large contrasts   45–6
  voting powers   2, 41, 45–6, 49–50, 57, 60–1, 144,
    185–6, 188–9, 260, 262–3
short-cut accounting treatment method, interest rate
    swaps   87–91, 93–100
short-cut swap valuation procedures   82–3

'shorting the market'   131, 200–16
  see also proprietary trading
SIVs *see* Structured Investment Vehicles
Smith, Terry   44–5, 56, 102, 173
Sociéte Générale (SocGen)   5, 39, 199–203, 207, 210,
    216, 260
Sorensen, Arne   53
Soroosh, Jalal   186–8
Soros, George   45
sources of finance, banks   232–4
Special Purpose Entities (SPEs)   29, 152–3, 161–3,
    177, 178–98
Special Purpose Vehicles (SPVs)   29, 152–3, 161–3,
    177, 178–98
  see also off-balance sheet vehicles; securitisation...
speculators   17–19, 23, 65–6, 69
SPEs *see* Special Purpose Entities
Spitzer, Eliot   60–1, 243
split capital funds scandal, UK   61, 128–9, 260
SPVs *see* Special Purpose Vehicles
standard deviations   227–9
  see also volatility
Standard Life Investments   50
'star' traders   200, 202–4
structured credit products   2, 7–10, 63, 139–98,
    221–41, 263
  see also credit derivatives; securitisation...
  accounting methods   172–4
  complexity problems   139–40, 164–71, 173–4
  SFAS 157 valuations   174–5
Structured Investment Vehicles (SIVs)   22, 34, 35, 48,
    51–2, 173–4, 177–8, 189–92
  see also off-balance sheet vehicles
structured products
  see also credit derivatives; derivatives; embedded
    derivatives; inverse floaters; securitisation...
  accounting methods   172–3
  accounting standards   119–37, 139–57, 164–75, 263
  bifurcation rules   44, 51–2, 120–1, 139–40, 164–5,
    173–4
  concepts   5–6, 43, 50–3, 117–37, 139–57, 159–75,
    263
  corporate governance   51–3, 168–9
  credit rating agencies   51–3, 139–57, 160–3, 165–8
  credit risk   51–3, 117, 129–30, 139–57, 159–75,
    190, 237–41
  diversification issues   147–8, 159–60, 163
  future prospects   263
  illiquid nature   51–2, 117–18, 120–1, 164–6, 207–9,
    217–18, 224, 263
  illustration of the problem   122–6
  inefficient nature   51, 157
  market risk   117–37, 139–40, 190
  Norwegian structured products crisis   53, 128
  Orange County   51–3, 59, 117–19, 127

sub-prime loans   14–15, 24, 43, 57, 141–4, 159–60,
    162, 166–7, 174–5, 178, 184–5, 192, 218, 235,
    259–60
  see also financial crises
subjective valuations   23–4, 29, 137, 146, 172–3,
    217–41
subordinated interests   196–8
'super-senior' investment products   148, 168–9
swaps   19, 27, 56, 59–60, 65–6, 77–115, 123–7,
    133–7, 189–90, 207–15, 221–41
  see also interest rate swaps
  cash flow interest rate swaps   91–7
  CDS   148–50, 156–7, 163, 173–4
  credit spreads   81–97
  documentation requirements   59–60
  FASB treatment   87–91
  Freddie Mac   19
  hedge accounting   65–6, 77–115, 133–7, 208–15
  IAS 39 treatment   87–9, 136–7
  interest rate changes   94–7
  long accounting treatment method   87–91, 94–100
  short-cut valuation procedures   82–3
  unwind of the discount   94–7
  valuations   80–3, 124–6, 133–7, 213–15
  value change reasons   94–7
swaptions
  Freddie Mac   19
  hedge accounting   112–14
synthetic leases, off-balance sheet transactions   186–9
synthetic structures, securitisation market   162–3

TAF *see* Term Auction Facility
take or pay contracts, off-balance sheet transactions
    186–9
takeovers *see* mergers & acquisitions
Tavakoli, Janet   167–8
taxpayers   46
Term Auction Facility (TAF)   167
term sheets, loans   36–9
Terra Securities   53, 128
Tet, Gillian   53
tier-one capital   228–9
time value changes in swaps *see* unwind of the discount
traders' dilemma
  banks   14–15, 16–19, 46–7
  concepts   11–15, 16–19, 46–7
  measuring considerations   16–19, 46–7
'Trading' assets classification   18–19, 24–6, 31, 40–1,
    152–3
trading books, concepts   40–1, 219–23
trading styles, rogue traders   200–1
transaction costs, foreign currency forwards   100–15
transparency shortfalls   1, 4–5, 9–10, 45–6, 54–7,
    168–9, 174–5, 201, 260–1, 263
  see also complexity . . .; disclosures
treasurers of corporates, traders' dilemma   14–15

Trichet, Jean-Claude   8
true and fair view   217, 220, 262–3
Tucker, Paul   143
Tweedie, David   178

UBS   7, 45–6, 56, 148
UK
  see also British Government
  bailout efforts   63–4, 139–40, 149–50, 166, 261
  Bank of England   167, 261
  Barings Bank   199, 201–2, 207, 210, 216, 260
  BCCI   260
  Equitable Life   260
  Northern Rock   17, 44, 46, 159–60, 166–7, 191–2,
    202, 260–1
  pensions misselling scandal   260
  scandals   260
  shareholder votes   50, 185–6
  split capital funds scandal   61, 128–9, 260
  Takeover Panel   50
  Treasury Select Committee   140
unbundled loans, insurance   250–2
underlying assets, artificial volatility   22, 26–8, 67–76,
    81–3, 221–41, 245–7
undiversified VaR   228–9
  see also Value at Risk
Union Excess   258
unwind of the discount, swap value changes   94–7
US
  see also Financial Accounting Standards Board
  EU standards   5, 177–98
  the Federal Reserve Board   1, 46, 166–7
  GAAP   181–2, 195–6, 257
  SEC   4, 6, 18, 51–3, 59–61, 179–85, 255–8

valuations   1, 4–6, 9–10, 16–17, 18, 19, 21–2, 23–31,
    39–40, 44, 65–76, 128–9, 137, 165–6, 169, 172–5,
    197–8, 213–15, 217–41, 262–3
  see also cost model; market . . .
  artificial volatility   22, 26–8, 67–76, 81–3, 221–41,
    245–7
  critique   5–6, 10, 18, 19, 21–2, 23–31, 65–76,
    165–6, 169, 172–3, 217–41, 262–3
  financial crises contributor   24, 31–2, 218
  foreign currency forwards   101–15
  forward contracts   101–15
  futures   131–2
  general guidelines   26, 31
  goodwill   23–4, 29–30, 33, 55–7, 249–50
  implied volatility uses   169
  mixed-model approach   4–5, 21–2, 23–31, 65–76,
    217–41
  options   16–17, 30, 137, 169
  profit level manipulations   19, 28, 67–8
  SFAS 157 valuations   174–5
  short-cut swap valuation procedures   82–3

valuations (*Continued*)
   subjective valuations　23–4, 29, 137, 172–3, 217–41
   swaps　80–3, 124–6, 133–7, 213–15
   transparency shortfalls　1, 4–5, 168–9, 174–5
Value at Risk (VaR)
   see also risk measurements
   accounting　235–41
   background　5, 121, 140, 164, 201–2, 207, 217, 223–41
   definition　224–6, 227
   financial instruments　239–41
   hedging principles　224–6
   illustrative examples　227–9
   undiversified VaR　228–9
   users　229
   volatility　226–9
   zero coupon bonds　224–6
value of in-force life assurance contracts (VIF) 249–50
Variable Interest Entities (VIEs)　177, 186–98
variation margin, futures　130–2, 204–16
Varley, John　64, 169
VIEs *see* Variable Interest Entities
volatility　3, 15, 16–19, 22, 26–8, 36, 39–40, 48, 65–6, 67–76, 81–3, 149–50, 200, 202–4, 221–41, 245–7

artificial volatility　22, 26–8, 67–76, 81–3, 221–41, 245–7
Basel　2 requirements　231–4
bonus incentives　3, 15, 16–17, 36, 48, 149–50, 200, 202–4, 226–9
derivatives　39–40, 48, 65–6, 69–76, 81–3, 200, 227–9
   option values　16–19, 48, 200
   Value at Risk　226–9
Volcker, Paul　1
voting powers of investors　2, 41, 45–6, 49–50, 57, 60–1, 144, 185–6, 188–9, 260, 262–3
vulture funds　53–4, 56–7

Wachovia Bank　32
warrants　64
'weapons of mass destruction', derivatives　7, 10, 168
weighting matrix, Value at Risk　229
Weninger, Gunter　56
WorldCom　7, 23

Xerox　23

yield curves　133–7

zero coupon bonds, Value at Risk　224–6

Index compiled by Terry Halliday